A HISTORY OF BANGLADESH

Bangladesh did not exist as an independent state until 1971. Willem van Schendel's state-of-the-art history navigates the extraordinary twists and turns that created modern Bangladesh through ecological disaster, colonialism, partition, a war of independence and cultural renewal. In this revised and updated edition, Van Schendel offers a fascinating and highly readable account of life in Bangladesh over the last two millennia. Based on the latest academic research and covering the numerous historical developments of the 2010s, he provides an eloquent introduction to a fascinating country and its resilient and inventive people. A perfect survey for travellers, expats, students and scholars alike.

WILLEM VAN SCHENDEL served as Professor of Modern Asian History at the University of Amsterdam.

T0381687

A HISTORY
OF
BANGLADESH

SECOND EDITION

WILLEM VAN SCHENDEL

University of Amsterdam

CAMBRIDGE
UNIVERSITY PRESS

University Printing House, Cambridge CB2 8BS, United Kingdom

One Liberty Plaza, 20th Floor, New York, NY 10006, USA

477 Williamstown Road, Port Melbourne, VIC 3207, Australia

314–321, 3rd Floor, Plot 3, Splendor Forum, Jasola District Centre,
New Delhi – 110025, India

79 Anson Road, #06–04/06, Singapore 079906

Cambridge University Press is part of the University of Cambridge.

It furthers the University's mission by disseminating knowledge in the pursuit of
education, learning and research at the highest international levels of excellence.

www.cambridge.org
Information on this title: www.cambridge.org/9781108473699
DOI: 10.1017/9781108684644

First edition © Cambridge University Press 2009
Second edition © Willem van Schendel 2020

First published 2009
3rd printing 2015
Second edition 2020

A catalogue record for this publication is available from the British Library.

Library of Congress Cataloging-in-Publication Data
NAMES: Schendel, Willem van, author.
TITLE: A history of Bangladesh / Willem van Schendel, University of Amsterdam.
DESCRIPTION: Second edition. | Cambridge, United Kingdom ; New York : Cambridge
University Press, 2020. | Includes bibliographical references and index.
IDENTIFIERS: LCCN 2020009196 | ISBN 9781108473699 (hardback) |
ISBN 9781108684644 (ebook)
SUBJECTS: LCSH: Bangladesh – History.
CLASSIFICATION: LCC DS394.5 .S34 2020 | DDC 954.92–dc23
LC record available at https://lccn.loc.gov/2020009196

ISBN 978-1-108-47369-9 Hardback
ISBN 978-1-108-46246-4 Paperback

Contents

v

Plates[*]

---

[*] Unless otherwise indicated, photographs are from the collection of the author. Every effort has been made to secure necessary permissions to reproduce copyright material in this work, though in some cases it has proved impossible to trace copyright holders. If any omissions are brought to our notice, we will be happy to include appropriate acknowledgements on reprinting.

Maps and Figures

Maps

Bangladesh District Maps

Figures

Preface to Second Edition

The first edition of this book was published in 2009. Since then, three developments have prompted this thoroughly revised and updated second edition. First, there is a growing awareness of the global significance of events in Bangladesh. Examples are environmental degradation and climate change, Islamic identity politics, exploited labour in the export-oriented garments industry and precipitous urbanisation. Pressing global issues take shape – and sometimes originate – in Bangladesh, and there is an urgent need to understand them in both their worldwide and local historical contexts. This can help in the wider search for ways to 'de-Europeanise' concepts of modernity and global agency.

Second, the 2010s brought turbulent change to Bangladesh. There was vigorous cultural innovation – including new gender movements and novel interpretations of spirituality. Unprecedented political confrontations erupted over the dispensation of justice and the resurgence of authoritarianism. And economic growth showed remarkable acceleration amid severe inequalities and deep concerns about its environmental costs. All these changes need to be explained by unravelling their historical origins.

And third, there has been an extraordinary blossoming of new scholarship on Bangladesh. This necessitates a reassessment of how we understand the country's past and present. For example, we now know more about the deep history of human settlement in the region; how ecology shaped state formation and local Islam; the histories of international trade and the Bengali diaspora; identity politics that connect the Partition of 1947, the war of 1971 and current political turmoil; histories of sexuality; and the transmutation of Bangladesh's worldwide linkages. Incorporating scholarly insights from many recent studies has been an important endeavour in shaping this new edition.

This is a book that aims at providing an outline of the history of Bangladesh. Its format does not allow for detailed discussion, but I have made every effort to point you to key literature that will introduce the most prominent current debates. Needless to say, many other excellent contributions simply could not be included in what has already become a voluminous bibliography.

Acknowledgements

It is impossible to do justice to all those, in Bangladesh and beyond, who have influenced the writing of this book and guided me over many years. Perhaps the best way to thank them all – friends, colleagues and acquaintances – is by thanking just one of them. Md. Moyenuddin of Goborgari village in Rangpur district acted as my mentor when, as a student, I first tried to make sense of Bangladeshi society. His lessons have always stayed with me and I owe him an enormous debt of gratitude.

For their direct contributions to this book – in the form of advice, comments, support, permissions and hospitality – I am most grateful to Rahnuma Ahmed, Shahidul Alam, Md. Abdullah Al-Faruque, Kamran Ali, Jenneke Arens, Sanjib Baruah, Boys of Bangladesh, Ratnabali Chatterjee, Shib Shankar Chatterjee, Sadek Reza Chowdhury, Anima Das, Meghna Guhathakurta, Mehedi Haque, Dory Heilijgers, Lotte Hoek, Iftekhar Iqbal, Sadequl Islam, Naveen Kishore, Shahriar Kabir, Ruby Lal, Muntassir Mamoon, Nayanika Mookherjee, Munira Moshed Munni, Tahdina Nazneen Nipa, Gyanendra Pandey, Md. Mahbubar Rahman, Tapas Rudra, Ahmed Saleem, Samita Sen, Gautam Sengupta, Dina Mahnaz Siddiqi, Tony Stewart, Malini Sur, Syed Rashad Imam Tanmoy, Marcel van der Linden, Laura van Schendel, Tobias van Schendel and two anonymous readers.

I owe very special thanks to Sirajul Islam, Nienke Klompmaker and David Ludden, who read the entire manuscript with critical scrutiny and gave detailed and immensely helpful feedback. Needless to say, they bear no responsibility for the final product.

The International Institute of Social History and the Amsterdam School of Social Science Research generously contributed towards travel and research expenses in Bangladesh, India, Pakistan and the United Kingdom. I would like to thank the Netherlands Organisation of

Scientific Research (NWO) for supporting the final stage of writing with a replacement subsidy and my colleagues Marjoleine Cornelissen, Mario Rutten, Rosanne Rutten, Sharika Thiranagama, Sanderien Verstappen and Sikko Visscher for making it possible for me to utilise this subsidy.

Finally, I am grateful to Marigold Acland for commissioning this book, and to Lucy Rhymer for initiating the second edition.

Timeline

c. 40,000 BCE	Earliest stone tools found in western hills.
Pre-1,500 BCE	Cultivation of irrigated rice and domestication of animals. Fossilwood industries.
Fifth century BCE	Urban centres, long-distance maritime trade, first sizeable states.
	Indo-European languages and Sanskritic culture begin to spread from the west. Regions and peoples of Bengal identified as Rarh, Pundra, Varendri, Gaur, Vanga, Samatata and Harikela.
Third century BCE	Mahasthan Brahmi inscription.
c. 640 CE	Chinese pilgrim Xuanzang ('Hiuen Tsiang') describes eastern Bengal.
Eighth–twelfth centuries	First Muslim influence in coastal areas.
Ninth century	Construction of Paharpur in northwestern Bangladesh.
Tenth century	Bengali language develops; earliest surviving poems known as *Charyapada*.
Twelfth century	Lakhnauti-Gaur is capital of Sena state.
Thirteenth century	Islam reaches Bengal delta via the land route. Muhammad Bakhtiyar establishes a Muslim-ruled state, the first of many dominated by non-Bengalis, including Turks, North Indians, Afghans, Arakanese and Ethiopians.
1346	Ibn Battutah visits Shah Jalal in Sylhet.

Sixteenth century	Rice from the Bengal delta exported to many destinations, from the Moluccas in eastern Indonesia to the Maldives and to Goa in western India.
	Large textile industry, cotton and silk exports.
1520s	First Europeans (Portuguese) settle in the Bengal delta.
1580s	Portuguese open the first European trading post in Dhaka (Dutch follow in 1650s, English in 1660s, French in 1680s).
Sixteenth–seventeenth centuries	Rise of Islam as a popular religion in the Bengal delta.
1610	Mughal empire captures Dhaka, now renamed Jahangirnagar. It becomes the capital of Bengal.
1612	Mughal rule over much of the Bengal delta.
1650s	Bengali translator-poet Alaol active at the Arakan court.
1666	Portuguese and Arakanese relinquish Chittagong to the Mughals.
1690	Kolkata (Calcutta) established by the British.
c. 1713	Bengal becomes an independent polity under Murshid Quli Khan. The capital is moved to Murshidabad.
1757	Battle of Polashi (Plassey); after further clashes, notably the battle at Baksar (Buxar) in 1764, the British East India Company establishes itself as *de facto* ruler of Bengal.
1757–1911	Kolkata is the capital of Bengal and British India.
1760s–90s	Fakir–Sannyasi resistance.
1769–70	Great Famine, which may have carried off one-third of Bengal's population.
1774	Birth of mystic Baul poet Lalon Shah (Lalon Fakir, Lalon Shai).
1782–7	Earthquake and floods force the Brahmaputra river into a new channel and lead to food scarcities.
1790	New system of land taxation ('permanent settlement') introduced. Codified in 1793, it will persist until the 1950s.

1830s	English replaces Persian as the state language.
1830–60s	Rural revolts inspired by Islamic 'purification' movements.
1840	Dhaka's population reaches its lowest point, 50,000.
1850s	Railways spread through Bengal.
1857	Revolt ('the Mutiny') has little impact on the Bengal delta.
1858	East India Company abolished and British crown assumes direct control.
1860	British annex the last part of Bengal, the Chittagong Hill Tracts.
1897	Earthquake with a magnitude of 8.7 hits Bengal and Assam.
c. 1900	Water hyacinth begins to spread in Bengal's waterways.
1901	Territory of future Bangladesh has 30 million inhabitants.
1905–11	Separate province of Eastern Bengal and Assam. Dhaka is its capital. Swadeshi movement. Muslim and Hindu become political categories.
1905	Rokeya Sakhawat Hossain writes *Sultana's Dream*.
1906	All-India Muslim League founded in Dhaka.
1910	Varendra Research Museum established in Rajshahi.
1921	University of Dhaka established.
1940	Muslim League adopts Pakistan (or Lahore) Resolution: demand for independent states for Indian Muslims.
1943–4	Great Bengal Famine causes about 3.5 million deaths.
1946	Muslim–Hindu riots in Noakhali, Kolkata and Bihar.
1946	Elections return the Muslim League as the largest party.
1946–7	Tebhaga movement.

1947	14 August: British rule ends and British India is partitioned. The Bengal delta becomes part of the new state of Pakistan under the name 'East Bengal'. Dhaka is the provincial capital.
1947–8	About 800,000 migrants arrive in East Pakistan from India; about 1,000,000 migrants leave East Pakistan for India. Cross-border migration will continue for years.
1948–56	(Bengali) language movement in protest against imposition of Urdu as official language of Pakistan.
1949	Awami Muslim League (renamed Awami League in 1955) founded by Maulana Bhashani.
1950	East Bengal State Acquisition and Tenancy Act eliminates the superior rights that zamindars (landlords/tax-collectors) had enjoyed under the permanent settlement.
1950	Muslim–Hindu riots in East Pakistan and West Bengal (India).
1951	Territory of future Bangladesh has 44 million inhabitants.
1952	21 February (*Ekushe*): killing of 'language martyrs'; first Shohid Minar (Martyrs' Memorial) erected.
1952	Passport and visa system introduced.
1953	V-AID community development programme initiated.
1954	Provincial elections in East Pakistan. Muslim League defeated. Sheikh Mujibur Rahman becomes junior cabinet member.
1954–62	Four new universities established in Rajshahi, Mymensingh, Chittagong and Dhaka.
1955	Adamjee Jute Mill goes into production in Narayanganj.
1955	Pakistan Academy for Rural Development established in Comilla.
1955	First direct passenger air connections between East and West Pakistan.
1955	Bangla Academy and Bulbul Academy for Fine Arts established in Dhaka.

1955	The first commercially useful gas field discovered in Haripur (Sylhet).
1956	'East Bengal' renamed 'East Pakistan'.
1957	Maulana Bhashani and others establish the National Awami Party (NAP).
1958	Army coup. Military regime in Pakistan headed by Ayub Khan (1958–69).
1960	World Bank's Aid-to-Pakistan consortium.
1961	Kaptai hydroelectric project completed. Lake Kaptai forms in the Chittagong Hill Tracts, forcing the 'Great Exodus' of displaced people.
1963	Chhayanot celebrates Bengali New Year publicly for the first time.
1965	India–Pakistan War. Train connections with India not resumed afterwards.
1966	Awami League launches Six-Point Programme.
1968–9	Popular uprising against Ayub Khan. The military replace him with Yahya Khan (1969–71).
1970	Cyclone kills 350,000–500,000 people in the Bengal delta.
1970	First national general elections in Pakistan. Awami League wins majority.
1971	25 March: beginning of Bangladesh Liberation War.
1971	16 December: end of war. East Pakistan becomes independent state of Bangladesh.
1972	Sheikh Mujibur Rahman heads Awami League government.
1972	Bangladesh declares itself a people's republic and introduces a constitution asserting that 'nationalism, socialism, democracy and secularism' are its guiding principles.
1972	First issue of weekly *Bichitra* (1972–97).
1972	Establishment of the JSS (United People's Party) and Shanti Bahini in the Chittagong Hill Tracts.
1973	Bangladesh's first general elections. Constitution and parliamentary system.
1974	Bangladesh has 71 million inhabitants.

1974	Famine causes excess mortality of some 1.5 million.
1975	January: constitutional coup and autocratic rule by Sheikh Mujibur Rahman.
1975	August: army coup. Sheikh Mujibur Rahman and family killed in Dhaka.
1975	November: two more army coups. Military regime headed by Ziaur Rahman (1975–81).
1975–97	Chittagong Hill Tracts war.
1975	National Museum opened.
c. 1975–90	Green Revolution technology begins to push up agricultural yields.
1976	Death of Maulana Bhashani (c. 1880– 1976).
1978	Leaders of the Jamaat-e-Islami allowed to return from exile in Pakistan and resume political activities.
1980s	Ready-made clothing industry takes off.
1981	Ziaur Rahman assassinated in Chittagong.
1982	General H. M. Ershad takes over as dictator (1982–90).
1982	National Monument for the Martyrs in Savar is completed.
1983	Bangladesh parliament buildings are completed.
1985	National Archives and National Library opened.
1988	Major floods cover 60 per cent of Bangladesh for fifteen to twenty days.
1988	Bangladesh Hindu Buddhist Christian Unity Council formed.
1990	Popular uprising. Ershad forced out of power. Return to parliamentary democracy.
1991	General elections won by Bangladesh Nationalist Party (BNP). Khaleda Zia becomes prime minister (1991–6).
1991	Cyclone kills 140,000 people in southeastern Bangladesh.
1992	Nirmul Committee stages Gono Adalot (people's court).
1993	Fatwa against Taslima Nasrin.
1993	Groundwater arsenic poisoning discovered.

1996	General elections won by Awami League. Sheikh Hasina becomes prime minister (1996–2001).
1996	Liberation War Museum opened.
1996	Kolpona Chakma disappears.
1996	Thirty-year agreement with India over division of Ganges waters.
1997	December: peace agreement with JSS in Chittagong Hill Tracts.
1998	Major floods cover 60 per cent of Bangladesh for sixty-five days.
1998	Jamuna Bridge opened.
2000s	Four-fifths of the population survives on less than US$2 a day and one-third on less than US$1 a day.
2000	Bangladesh produces a surplus of food grains for the first time in its modern history.
2001	General elections won by Bangladesh Nationalist Party (BNP). Khaleda Zia becomes prime minister (2001–6).
2001	Bangladesh Indigenous People's Forum formed.
2006	Nobel Prize for Grameen Bank and Muhammad Yunus.
2006	Protests against Phulbari coal-mining.
2006	Ready-made garments make up three-quarters of Bangladesh's exports.
2007	General elections postponed and military-backed interim government installed.
2007	Cyclone hits southwestern coast, killing thousands and devastating the Sundarbans wetlands.
2008	Postponed general elections won by the Awami League. Sheikh Hasina becomes prime minister (2009–14).
2009	Bangladesh Rifles mutiny.
2010	Five former army officers executed for assassinating Sheikh Mujibur Rahman.
2011	Bangladesh co-hosts Cricket World Cup.
2013	War Crimes Tribunal and Shahbag movement.
2013	Rana Plaza garments factory collapses.
2013	Bangladesh recognises third gender.

2014	General elections won by Awami League. Sheikh Hasina remains as prime minister (2014–18).
2015	Land Boundary Agreement with India.
2016	Jihadist attack on Dhaka café.
2016	Bangladesh cancels deep-sea port agreement with China.
2017	Hundreds of thousands of Rohingya refugees arrive from Myanmar (Burma).
2018	Government launches 'Bangladesh Delta Plan 2100'.
2018	General elections won by Awami League.
2019	Sheikh Hasina remains as prime minister (2019–).

Introduction

This is a book about the amazing twists and turns that have produced contemporary Bangladeshi society. It is intended for general readers and for students who are beginning to study the subject. Those who are familiar with the story will find my account highly selective. My aim has been to present an overview and to help readers get a sense of how Bangladesh came to be what it is today.

How to write a history of Bangladesh? At first glance, the country does not seem to have much of a history. In 1930 not even the boldest visionary could have imagined it, and by 1950 it was merely a gleam in the eyes of a few activists. Only in the 1970s did Bangladesh emerge as a state and a nation. There was nothing preordained about this emergence – in fact, it took most people by surprise.

Even so, you cannot make sense of contemporary Bangladesh unless you understand its history long before those last few decades. How have long-term processes shaped the society that we know as Bangladesh today? It is a complicated and spectacular tale even if you follow only a few main threads, as I have done. I have greatly compressed the story. To give you an idea: each page of this book stands for about a million people who have historically lived in what is now Bangladesh. This is, by any standard, a huge society folded into a small area. More people live here than in Russia or Japan. Bangladesh is the eighth most populous country on earth.

I have chosen to distinguish three types of historical process that still play a principal role in Bangladesh. Part I looks at very long-term ones. It explains how, over millennia, forces of nature, geographical conditions, and the interplay of local and larger events have shaped Bangladeshi society. I speak of the 'Bengal delta' to describe the region that roughly coincides with modern Bangladesh, and I argue that it developed a very distinct regional identity quite early on. Part II describes how, over the last few centuries, these age-old trends encountered middle-range ones, especially foreign rule and its lasting effects. Parts III to V conclude the book, and they examine the most recent developments. These chapters explain what happened in the Bengal delta over the last several decades as it first became part of Pakistan (1947–71) and then independent Bangladesh.

Bangladesh is a country in which history is palpably present. It is keenly debated and extensively researched. As a result, there is a huge historical literature. I have not even tried to summarise this body of knowledge because it would have led to information overload. Instead, I refer to selected readings that will provide a more nuanced and detailed understanding of the themes that I only touch on in passing. Wherever possible I have opted for publications in English, assuming that these will be the most easily accessible to the majority of readers. This book has also been informed by the vast and hugely important historical literature in Bangladesh's national language, Bengali, but I refer to it only sparingly. The notes and the bibliography show my debt to the many specialist researchers on whose shoulders I stand. Anyone writing on Bangladesh has to make decisions about names and transliterations. For two reasons it is not easy to render Bengali words in English. First, there are many sounds in Bengali that do not exist in English and that linguists mark with various dots and dashes. In this book I have used a simple version of local words, roughly as they are pronounced in Bangladesh, followed by a standard transliteration that goes back to the Sanskrit language, an early precursor of Bengali. Thus the word for the Bengali language is pronounced 'bangla' but its transliteration is *bāṃlā*. A glossary at the end of the book provides the different versions.

A second reason why it is difficult to write Bengali words correctly in English is that many have several forms. Often one is the historically familiar form and another is the more correct one. This is especially true for place names. Thus we have Polashi/Plassey, Borishal/Barisal and Sylhet/Shilet. In the absence of any consistent or official guideline, the choice is often a personal one. In two cases there has been an official change, however. The capital city of Bangladesh, which used to be written as 'Dacca' in English-language texts, took its more correct form of Dhaka (*Ḍhākā*) in the 1980s. Similarly, 'Calcutta' became Kolkata (*Kalkātā*) in 2001. Rather than confuse the reader with changing names, I use Dhaka and Kolkata throughout.

PART I

The Long View

Part I Aerial view of the Sundarbans wetlands.

CHAPTER I

A Land of Water and Silt

Imagine yourself high in the air over the Himalayas. Look down and you see a forbidding landscape of snow-capped mountains and harsh vegetation. But now look to the southeast and discover an immense floodplain stretching between the mountains and the sea. That shimmering green expanse is Bangladesh.

You may well wonder why a book about Bangladesh should begin with the Himalayas. There is a good reason: without the Himalayas, Bangladesh would not exist. In a sense, Bangladesh *is* the Himalayas, flattened out. Every spring the mountain snow melts and the icy water sweeps along particles of soil, forming into rivers that rush to the sea. As these rivers reach the lowlands, they slow down and deposit those particles, building up a delta. This age-old process has created the territory that we now know as Bangladesh – a territory that pushes back the sea a little further with every annual deposit of new silt.[1]

The delta is huge because almost all water running off the Himalayas, the highest mountain range on earth, has to pass through it (Map 1.1). On the southern side numerous rivulets and rivers run together to form the mighty Ganges that flows eastwards through India for hundreds of kilometres before it enters western Bangladesh, where it is also known as the Padma.[2] On the northern side of the Himalayas an equally majestic river, the Brahmaputra (or Tsangpo), forms in Tibet. It too flows east, past the capital, Lhasa, and then makes a sharp turn, breaking through the mountains into the far northeastern corner of India. It then flows west until it enters northern Bangladesh, where it is known as the Jamuna. It joins the Ganges in central Bangladesh and together they empty into the sea. Both rivers are truly gigantic: the Ganges is up to 8 km wide and the Brahmaputra spreads to the improbable width of 18 km.

This is the big picture. When you look closely you will notice that many more rivers criss-cross Bangladesh. A third giant is the Meghna, which enters Bangladesh from the east, and over fifty other rivers flow from India across the border into Bangladesh. They join, split and join again in a crazy pattern of channels, marshes and lakes (Plate 1.1). In historical times there has been a tendency for the water to be discharged through more easterly channels and for the western reaches of the delta (now in India) to become drier. Together these many rivers have deposited very thick layers of fertile silt that now form the largest river delta on earth. Not all the silt ends up in Bangladesh, though. Every year, over a billion metric tons are delivered to the Indian Ocean, building up the world's largest underwater delta, the Bengal Fan, which has a maximum thickness of more than 16 km and extends over 3,000 km south on the ocean floor, well beyond Sri Lanka.[3]

Surrounded by higher land and hills to the east, north and west, the Bengal delta acts as the narrow end of a funnel through which an area more than ten times its size annually discharges a mind-boggling 650,000,000,000 m³ of water. And almost all this silt-laden water flows through the delta between May and October, when the rivers are in spate.

These huge forces have shaped the natural environment of Bangladesh, and they continue to exert an enormous influence on human life today. But majestic rivers are not the only source of water. There are two other forms in which water has always played a vital role in Bangladesh: rain and seawater. Each year in June, as the rivers are swelling rapidly, the skies over

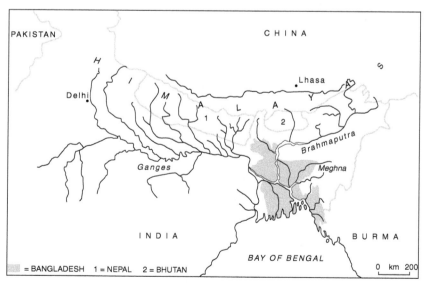

Map 1.1 The catchment area of the Bengal delta.

Bangladesh begin to change. In winter they are blue and hardly any rain falls, but in late May or early June, as temperatures shoot up, immense clouds form in the south. As they float in from the sea they release torrential downpours that continue off and on until late September. The wet monsoon has arrived, and in this part of tropical Asia it is truly spectacular. Not only may rains continue for days on end, turning the soft soil into a knee-deep muddy slush, but the sheer amount of water being discharged over Bangladesh is impressive. It is rain that has made Cherrapunji a household word among meteorologists the world over. This little village just across the border between northeastern Bangladesh and India claims to be the world's wettest place. Here the monsoon clouds hit the hills of Meghalaya in a downpour that continues for months. Annually a staggering 11 m of rain falls here; the maximum rainfall ever recorded during a 24-hour period was over 1 m.

Seawater is a third companion of life in Bangladesh. During the dry season (October to May), saline water from the Bay of Bengal penetrates watercourses up to 100 km inland and the lower delta becomes brackish. In addition, the lower delta is very flat: its elevations are less than 3 m above sea level. As a result, it is subject to tidal bores from tropical cyclones that make landfall here about once a year. These are particularly hard on the

Plate 1.1 'Knee-deep in water, whatever you do' (*hore-dore hatu jol*). An aerial view of central Bangladesh in the dry season.

many islands and silt flats that fringe the coast of Bangladesh. Some protection is provided by the Sundarbans, a mangrove forest that used to cover the coastal delta but has been shrinking since the eighteenth century as a result of human activity. This largest mangrove forest in the world is not impervious to the power of tropical storms, however. In 2007 it took a direct hit when a cyclone raged over it, destroying much vegetation.

These three forms of water – river, rain and sea – give Bangladesh a natural Janus face. In winter, the rivers shrink in their beds, the skies are quietly blue, and saline water gently trickles in. Nature appears to be benign and nurturing. In summer, however, nature is out of control and Bangladesh turns into an amphibious land. Rivers widen, rains pour down and storms at sea may hamper the discharge of all this water. The result is flooding.[4]

Summer floods are a way of life. About 20 per cent of the country is inundated every summer, mainly as a result of rainfall. Rivers may cause floods as well. Usually the big rivers reach their peak flows at different times, but if they peak together, they will breach their banks and inundate the floodplain. It is in this way that rivers forge new courses in what is known as an active delta. As a river flows through its channel for many years, it becomes shallower because of silt deposits. It slows down and may even get choked. On both sides silt banks may build up to keep it flowing through the same course even though its bed may be raised to the level of the surrounding floodplain, or even above it. But when an exceptionally large amount of water pushes its way through, the banks are eroded and the river will breach them, seeking a new, lower channel. The old channel may survive as an oxbow lake or it may be covered in vegetation. The Bangladesh landscape is dotted with such reminders of wandering rivers. Although most floods are caused by rainfall and inundation in deltaic rivers, they may also result from flash floods after heavy rain in the hills, pushing their way through the delta, or by tidal storm surges.[5]

This combination of rainfall, river inundation, flash floods and storm surges has made it impossible to control summer flooding in Bangladesh. Even today, the timing, location and extent of flooding are very difficult to predict, let alone control, and floods vary considerably from year to year. Every few years big floods occur and occasionally, during extreme floods, over 70 per cent of the country is covered by water.

From the viewpoint of human life, flooding has had both positive and negative effects. Annual floods constantly replenish some of the most fertile soils on earth. Rich silt has always allowed luxuriant natural vegetation and it made early and successful agriculture possible.[6] But the uncontrolled nature of floods, and the certainty of severe inundation every ten years or so, have played havoc with human life as well. It is not the amount of water that determines the harmful effects of flooding, however. As we shall see, human life in Bangladesh has long been adapted to cope with regular inundation. What makes some floods more harmful than others is the force with which the water pushes through (damaging life and goods) and the number of days it stays on the land (killing the crops). Thus a flash flood or storm surge can be very destructive, even though the amount of water or the area affected is not very large. In 1991 a cyclone hit the southeastern coast of Bangladesh at Chittagong. Huge waves travelling inland through water channels and across islands had a devastating effect. Despite early warnings and the evacuation of 3 million people, up to 70 per cent of the population in coastal villages was wiped out. According to official estimates, nearly 140,000 Bangladeshis perished. Casualties had been far worse in 1970, before a national system of cyclone warning had been developed. A cyclone made landfall at the Noakhali coast, and its storm surge is thought to have killed at least 325,000 people.[7]

In contrast to these very destructive cyclone floods, a rain or river flood can spread over a much larger area and yet do little harm if it lasts only a few days. In fact, such a flood is typically followed by a bumper harvest. But long-term inundation does pose a serious problem: the floods of 1988, which covered 60 per cent of Bangladesh for fifteen to twenty days, caused enormous damage to crops, property, fish stocks and other resources, in addition to claiming human lives. Ten years later another flood again inundated 60 per cent of the country and, because this time it lasted for sixty-five days, its effects were even more damaging.[8]

Living in this environment means living on a perennially moving frontier between land and water, and it is this moving frontier that dominates the *longue durée* of Bangladesh history. Despite regular setbacks, humans have been extraordinarily successful in using the resources of this hazardous, water-soaked deltaic environment. Today, with over 1,200 people per km², Bangladesh is one of the most densely populated countries in the world. Such pressure on the land ensures that the ancient environmental frontier remains of everyday significance. Encounters at the water's edge have become more crucial over time as Bangladeshis are forced to push the margins of their sodden environment as never before, settling on low-lying land, coastal areas and islands exposed to storms and floods. In this way, some Bangladeshis are forced continually to put themselves dangerously in water's way (Plate 1.2).

Plate 1.2 'Be prepared for floods! Save your life and possessions by seeking a high shelter.' Educational poster, 1990s.

Floodplains dominate life in Bangladesh – they cover about 80 per cent of the country – but not all of Bangladesh is flat. On the eastern fringes some steep hills surrounding the delta have been included in the national territory and they provide an altogether different terrain. These hills (in the Chittagong Hill Tracts and Sylhet) point to geological processes occurring far below the smooth surface of Bangladesh. Here tectonic plates collide: both the Himalayas and the Bangladesh hills (and beyond these the mountains of Myanmar (Burma) and northeastern India) are fold belts resulting from these collisions. The faults running underneath Bangladesh also push up or draw down parts of the delta, creating slightly uplifted terraces that look like islands in the floodplain (notably the Barind in the northwest and Modhupur in central Bangladesh) and depressions (*hāor* or *bil*)* that turn into immense seasonal lakes. Tectonic movement is also tilting the entire delta, forcing rivers towards the east. The unstable geological structures underlying Bangladesh generate frequent earthquakes, most of them light but some strong enough to cause widespread destruction.

In Bangladesh the natural environment has never been a mere backdrop against which human history unfolded. On the contrary, time and again natural forces have acted as protagonists in that history, upsetting social arrangements and toppling rulers. For example, in the 1780s an earthquake and floods forced the Brahmaputra river into a new channel, wiping out villages in its course and causing trade centres along its old channel to collapse. More recently, in 1970, the mishandling of cyclone damage robbed the government of its legitimacy and precipitated a war of independence.[9] And floods in 1988 cost Bangladesh more than that year's entire national development budget.

Managing the natural environment has been a central concern for all societies and states that have occupied the Bengal delta. The people of Bangladesh have never been able to lull themselves into a false belief that they controlled nature. They live in an environment where land and water meet and where the boundaries between these elements are in constant flux. As a result, settlement patterns have always been flexible and often transient. Bangladeshi villages have been described as elusive.[10] They are not clustered around a central square, protected by defensive walls or united in the maintenance of joint irrigation works. Instead they consist of scattered homesteads and small hamlets known as para (*pāṛā*), perched on slightly elevated plots that become islands when moderate floods occur.

---

* Bengali terms are explained and transliterated in the Glossary at the end of this book.

Few rural dwellings are built to last, and traditional irrigation requires hardly any joint organisation because it is largely rain-fed. As the lie of the land changes in the active delta, villagers are often forced to relocate and rebuild their houses. Thus nature's changing topography acts as a social and economic resource, and the mobile and fragmented nature of settlement has shaped rural politics. Bangladeshi villages are not tightly organised communities under a single village head. Instead, they are dominated by continually shifting alliances of family and hamlet leaders. States seeking to control the rural population have always had to find ways of dealing with this flexible pattern of power sharing adapted to life on the frontier of land and water.

Predictions for the future point towards a renewed need for flexibility. It is expected that deforestation, soil erosion and melting glaciers in the Himalayas will lead to more silt and water in the rivers during the peak season. Experts on climate change are convinced that Bangladesh will be one of the countries most severely affected by rising sea levels resulting from global warming. But available evidence does not support popular assumptions that global warming has already seriously enhanced Bangladesh's current susceptibility to floods, tropical cyclones and drought.[11] On the other hand, in a world increasingly concerned about water scarcities, Bangladesh's abundance of fresh water could be turned into a critical resource. It is clear that Bangladesh will continue to balance precariously on the frontier between land and three forms of water: river, rain and sea.

CHAPTER 2

Jungle, Fields, Cities and States

For hundreds of thousands of years, the fertile Bengal delta was covered by dense rainforests and wetlands, an environment of high biodiversity. Much of it survived well into historical times. In the last few centuries, however, what had been one of the richest wildlife areas of the world went into sharp decline.[1] Many species of plants and animals disappeared from Bangladesh – among the larger animals: rhinoceros, wild buffalo, banteng, nilgai, various species of deer, wolf, marsh crocodile, pink-headed duck and peafowl. Others, such as elephant, tiger and leopard, became very rare (see box 'Spotting a shishu').[2]

Spotting a shishu

If you are lucky you may have a rare encounter in Bangladesh. As your boat glides through the muddy water of one of the country's myriad rivers, a slick body suddenly shoots up from the depths, breaking the water for a moment. You will just have time to notice a narrow snout, a curved grey back and a broad tail – and it is gone again below the murky surface. Congratulations: you have met your first shishu.

What is a shishu? It is a freshwater dolphin that is indigenous in the Ganges and Brahmaputra river systems. The creature is known officially as the Ganges River dolphin (*Platanista gangetica gangetica*; Plate 2.1) and in Bangladesh as shishu or shushuk (*śiśu, śuśuk*). A powerful swimmer up to 2.5 metres in length, it eats fish and shrimps. It forages by swimming on one side, its flipper trailing the riverbed and its long snout stirring the muddy bottom. Shishu have very poor eyesight. They navigate by emitting sounds and mapping their environment by the echoes that travel back through the water.

Dolphins used to be abundant. In 1781 a famous biologist of Bengal, William Roxburgh, reported that they 'are found in great numbers in the Ganges [and] seem to delight most in the slow-moving labyrinth of rivers and creeks which intersect the delta of that river to the south and east of Calcutta'. Over the years, their numbers have dwindled. Today there may only be several thousand left (including those found in India and Nepal) and their survival is

---

PLATE 28.

THE SOOSOO OF THE GANGES

Plate 2.1 An early portrait of the shishu.

now threatened. Dams and embankments separate breeding populations and impede seasonal migration. Dredging and river development degrade their habitat, and water pollution shortens their lives. Many shishu drown when they get entangled in fishing nets – being mammals they need to come to the water surface to breathe air. Protection methods are only slowly being put in place.

    The decline of the Bengalian rainforest was directly related to the success of one of its denizens: human beings. People have been roaming the forests and rivers of Bangladesh, making use of their rich resources, from very early times. However, few early remains have been found, and experts cannot be certain when humans first made their appearance. There is recent evidence that they first reached this region from the west more than 40,000 years ago, and that this corridor between the Himalayas and the Bay of Bengal acted as the main thoroughfare for the peopling of eastern Asia and the Americas. Many subsequent waves of migration – both from west to east and from east to west – are thought to have shaped the complex genetic makeup of contemporary Bangladeshis.[3]

    The basis for claims about prehistoric humans in Bengal is still restricted. On the one hand, there is the environment of the floodplains with their frequent inundations and a humid tropical climate, both particularly unkind to material remains of human settlement not made of the sturdiest material. Since stone does not occur naturally in the Bengal delta, early humans are likely to have relied on materials such as wood, bamboo and mud, which have not survived.[4] On the other hand, the prehistoric record of Bangladesh is also limited because archaeologists of South Asia have long treated the region with indifference, training their sights on other parts of the Indian subcontinent. And those archaeologists who did work on the Bengal delta were, until recently, mainly interested in more recent times.

The prehistoric discoveries that have been made so far are mostly from higher terrain surrounding the floodplains. Today the eastern hills of Bangladesh and the western plateaux (now in West Bengal, India) give the best clues to the early inhabitants of the region. Here stone, pebbles and petrified wood (fossilwood) were available. Fossilwood industries producing hand axes, blades and scrapers have been found in Lalmai (a small range of hills in Comilla district), Sitakund (Chittagong district) and Chaklapunji (Sylhet district) (Map 2.1). Archaeologists have linked these with similar tools from West Bengal, Bihar and Orissa (India) and the Irrawaddy delta Myanmar (Burma). The makers of these early tools may have survived by hunting animals and gathering plants. In Jaintiapur in northeastern Bangladesh huge stones (menhirs and dolmens) were erected, some of them thought to be prehistoric; such stones have been found in larger numbers in the adjoining hills of India.[5]

Cultivation of plants and domestication of animals occurred before 1500 BCE.[6] The earliest evidence of settled agricultural communities comes from western Bengal. Here sites have yielded stone and bone tools, pottery with geometric designs, iron agricultural implements, domesticated rice and the bones of domesticated animals such as goats, cattle and buffaloes. On the basis of these findings it seems likely that the subsistence base for people living on the poorer plateau soils was a combination of agriculture, animal husbandry and hunting, but that those living on the more fertile alluvial soils of the delta depended heavily on agriculture and fishing. In this zone a crucial shift occurred when agriculture evolved from shifting cultivation and dependence on collected wild rice to the domestication of rice on permanent irrigated fields. This type of agriculture was possible only after social systems emerged that could mobilise labour to create field systems. Agriculture became so productive that populations expanded, settlements grew and various crafts flourished. Ever since, rice has shaped the history of Bangladesh. The assured production of irrigated rice became

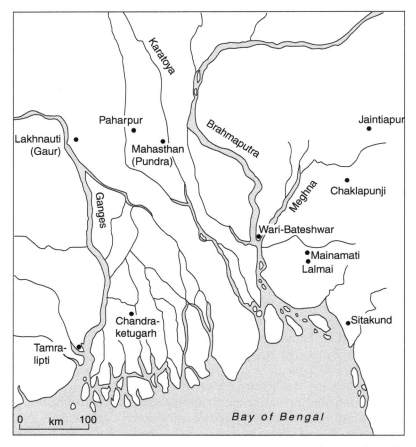

Map 2.1 Ancient sites. River courses are approximate. Note that the main channels
of the Ganges and Brahmaputra differ from their current channels.

the foundation for all societies and states in the delta down to the present.
Producing rice became the inhabitants' main occupation and rice was their
staple food. The miracle of sustained rice cultivation over millennia is
perhaps the greatest feat of Bangladesh history.

Originally a swamp plant, rice is extremely well suited to the ecology of
Bangladesh. New evidence suggests that this region may actually be where
humans first domesticated rice.[7] Today rice is known as dhan (*dhān* =
paddy) when on the field or unhusked, chaul (*cāul* or *cāl*) when husked and
bhat (*bhāt*) when boiled. There are many different words to describe rice in

other forms: parboiled, flattened, ground or puffed. Generations of cultivators selected and adapted rice to suit their needs, especially with regard to
resistance to disease, growing season and taste. In this way, they developed
thousands of varieties (cultivars) to suit a multitude of local agro-ecological
conditions.[8] In the deltaic environment special cultivars were developed for
different levels of flooding. Perhaps the most unusual is 'floating rice'
(*jalidhān*), grown on low-lying land. With the onset of flooding, these
plants elongate with astonishing rapidity until their stems reach a length of
5–6 m. This allows them to survive by floating in very deep water.

Early on a pattern of land use developed in which the highest delta lands
were reserved for homesteads and orchards (mango, jackfruit, coconut and
betel nut). Slightly lower grounds were used to grow rice seedlings and
vegetables, and middling and low lands took rice. On middling lands there
were usually two rice crops: spring rice (aush; *āuś*; March to August),
followed by autumn rice (amon; *āman*; June to December). On low
lands with annual flooding the main crop was autumn rice followed by
winter rice (boro; *boro*; February to April). The countryside became dotted
with clumps of homesteads built around man-made ponds (pukur; *pukur*)
that were used for drinking-water, washing and fish-breeding. Over time,
cropping patterns would change as new crops arrived from other parts of
the world (such as potatoes, tomatoes, chillies and tobacco from the
Americas) and as some crops became commercially important (indigo,
sugarcane, jute and tea).

THE EMERGENCE OF URBAN LIFE

The success of rice-based deltaic agriculture provided the basis for sedentary lifestyles, which, by about the fifth century BCE, led to urban centres,
long-distance maritime trade and Bengal's first sizeable states. At Wari-
Bateshwar (Narsingdi) in eastern Bangladesh archaeologists have begun to
excavate an important port city that traded with Southeast Asia and the
Roman world. So far, they have discovered a fortified citadel, silver punch-
marked coins, bronzes, glass beads, a goddess figure decorated with numerous eyes, amulets, iron and pottery artefacts, and a road made of potsherds
and crushed bricks. These discoveries indicate that Wari-Bateshwar was
a major administrative centre on the banks of the Brahmaputra river
(which has since moved far away) and that it boasted iron-smelting as
well as semi-precious-stone bead industries.[9] There is abundant evidence
here of the use of clay, a locally available material. In an environment with
very little stone, walls were made of clay or bricks and the art of pottery was

important. Artists and artisans in Bangladesh have used clay ever since to express their imagination, most significantly in the form of terracotta (burnt clay).[10] It is the terracotta work of early artists that provides us with the liveliest information about everyday life in Bangladesh down the ages (Plate 2.2).

By the third century BCE complex urban centres were well established in the Bengal floodplains, for example Tamralipti (now Tamluk) in the southwest, Mahasthan in the north and Mainamati in the east. The earliest written record in Bangladesh is an inscription on a piece of stone that was discovered at Mahasthan in the district of Bogra. It shows that this city (then known as Pudanagala or Pundranagara) was an important urban

Plate 2.2 Harvesting. Fragment of a terracotta plaque, Chandraketugarh, c. first century BCE.[11]

Plate 2.3 The Mahasthan Brahmi Inscription, third century BCE.

centre when the Maurya empire dominated northern India. It has been suggested that Mahasthan may have been a provincial capital of that empire. The inscription is in Prakrit, a language from which, by the tenth century CE, the Bengali language would develop, and it appears to be an order to fill up a storehouse with rice, oil, trees and coins against any emergency caused by water, fire or a devastation of the crops by parrots. The text is in the Brahmi script and hence this important discovery is known as the Mahasthan Brahmi Inscription (see Plate 2.3).[12]

Mahasthan (or Mahasthangarh) was inhabited before this period and has been continuously inhabited ever since. So far eighteen building levels have been discovered in this large site enclosed by 6 m-high rampart walls.[13]

Early terracotta plaques demonstrate the use of clay as a sophisticated expression of urban culture. The best known are magnificent plaques from an area in the southwestern delta that archaeologists refer to as Chandraketugarh, now just across Bangladesh's western border with India (Plate 2.4).[14] These plaques show deities and power holders, copulating couples, scenes of nature and impressions of everyday life.

Who were the inhabitants of these early villages and towns of the Bengal delta? The various communities of cultivators, fishing and craft persons, religious specialists, traders and rulers certainly were not Bengalis in the modern sense. Place names in Bangladesh, as well as words in various dialects of the Bengali language, suggest that most people spoke languages belonging to entirely different language families: Tibeto-Burman (or Trans-Himalayan), Austro-Asiatic and Dravidian.[15] Bengali belongs to the Indo-European

Plate 2.4 'Royal family.' Terracotta plaque, Chandraketugarh, c. first century BCE.

language family, to which several other languages spoken in Bangladesh today (Chakma, Bishnupriya-Manipuri and Urdu) also belong. Indo-European languages were relative latecomers in the region. They began to spread only from about the fourth century BCE, possibly as languages of rule. Speakers of these languages referred to the languages that they encountered in Bengal as vile (*āsura*).[16] Some common sounds in modern Bengali are thought to derive from these local languages – notably 'retroflex' sounds, formed by the upturned tongue touching the hard palate, which in transliteration appear with a dot underneath. Local languages are also viewed as the source of many modern Bengali words relating to water, land, nature, agriculture, fishing, settlement and numerals. Examples are homestead (*bhiṭā*), village (*paṭṭi*), mud-made (*kãcā*), plough (*lãṅgal, hāl*), fishing net (*jāl*), forest (*jaṅgal*), siltbank (*car*), low land (*bil*), high land (*ḍãṅgā*), open land (*kholā*), waterhole (*ḍobā*), 1½ (*der̥*), 2½ (*ār̥ãi*) and 20 (*kur̥i*). Today these older language families are still represented in Bangladesh but in terms of numbers of speakers they have been dwarfed by Bengali. Among the many Tibeto-Burman languages are Garo (Abeng), Koch, Kok Borok, Arakanese (Rakhain), Mro (Mru), Mizo, Hyow and Marma; among the Austro-Asiatic languages are Khasi, Santali and Mundari; and the Dravidian languages are represented by Kurux (Oraon) and Sauria Paharia.

The linguistic history of Bangladesh explains why archaeologists have long avoided the prehistoric period. Our understanding of South Asian archaeology is intimately related to the extensive early literature in Indo-European languages, notably Sanskrit and Prakrit. Writers in these languages were from more western parts of the Ganges valley and they had little knowledge of the area now covered by Bangladesh. In the most ancient epics the Bengal delta appears as a distant land of barbarians, beyond the pale of Sanskritic culture, and anyone returning from there had to undergo expiatory rites. Over time writers in Sanskrit revised their opinion somewhat. As their centres of cultural production shifted eastwards from the upper to the middle Ganges delta, they became more knowledgeable about western Bengal, which they still saw as inhabited by rude peoples but nevertheless an important area for conquest, plunder and tribute. Eastern Bengal would remain largely unknown to them for much longer. Getting to know this region was a slow process. By the seventh century – perhaps a thousand years after they had reached the western edge of the delta – they described Sylhet in eastern Bengal as 'outside the pale of human habitation, where there is no distinction between natural and artificial, infested with wild animals and poisonous reptiles, and covered with forest out-growths'.[17] In fact, Sanskritic learning may not have begun to spread widely in Bengal until towards the end of the eleventh century.[18]

To Sanskrit writers, Bengal was not a clearly defined region. They had a range of designations for areas and groups in what we now know as Bengal, and these vary between texts. Today scholars are often not quite sure where these areas and groups were located. Rarh (*Rāṛha*) is a term for a region in western Bengal and Pundra (*Puṇḍra*), Varendri (*Varendri*) and Gaura (*Gauṛa*) for regions in northern Bengal. Vanga (*Vaṅga*) is thought to have been located in central Bengal, and Samatata (*Samataṭa*) and Harikela (*Harikela*) in eastern Bengal. Sanskrit texts also speak of Pundra, Vanga and Rarh as peoples who occupied areas now probably in Bangladesh.[19]

The rich literature in Sanskrit has focused scholarly attention on the regions that were best known to writers in that language. Bengal was clearly not one of these regions, and since there are no written records of Bengal before the arrival of speakers of Indo-European languages, archaeologists of early South Asia have tended to neglect Bengal. Archaeologists of Bengal, on the other hand, have often been motivated by a desire to show that Bengal was not an uncivilised place. For this reason they have concentrated on monumental relics of proven 'high culture' at later times.

But to understand early Bangladesh we need more than the 'Sanskritic gaze' or a self-congratulatory search for past glory. From the fifth century BCE, when Sanskritic culture first reached the Bengal delta from the west, Bangladesh has been a frontier zone where Sanskritic and non-Sanskritic worldviews met, clashed and intermingled. This interaction has been the very stuff of Bangladesh history, and to tell the story from only one side of the divide is to diminish it. The frontier was cultural as much as it was territorial, influencing the identities of communities and individuals all over the Bengal delta. Since Sanskritic culture first made itself felt here, it moved slowly eastwards during the first millennium CE, being altered in the process by numerous non-Sanskritic elements. And the frontier never disappeared. Even today the clash between Sanskritic and non-Sanskritic can be observed in Bangladesh's culture, and even territorially in eastern Bangladesh.

New approaches to archaeology can be very important in filling in this picture of Bangladesh as a meeting ground of non-Sanskritic and Sanskritic worldviews over millennia. Fortunately, these new approaches are now being introduced in Bangladesh for the first time. Scientific excavations with detailed attention to archaeological strata and to everyday life in the early Bengal delta are already showing that there is still a world to discover here.[20]

THE RISE AND FALL OF STATES

The Bengal delta's productive agriculture made it possible for socially stratified and economically diversified societies to develop from early times. As we have seen, the archaeological record indicates that urban centres came up as early as the fifth century BCE. During the following centuries large towns would develop along major rivers rather than on the exposed seacoast. The fortunes of these towns were linked to the whims of the deltaic rivers: whenever a river moved course and the port silted up, the town would decline. An early victim was Tamralipti, one of India's largest ports and possibly 'the chief trade emporium of the wide area between China and Alexandria' (Map 2.1).[21] Famous for a thousand years, its fortunes reversed in the eighth century CE as the delta expanded southwards and its port silted up. Today it is a land-bound district town known as Tamluk.

The case of Lakhnauti-Gaur also demonstrates the vicissitudes of riverside urbanisation. It is not known when this busy port in the northwestern delta at the junction of three channels of the Ganges was established, but it clearly went through many cycles of development and decay (Map 2.1). In the twelfth century CE it was the capital of the Sena dynasty and the Moroccan traveller Ibn Battutah visited it 150 years later. In the fifteenth century it was one of the largest cities of South Asia. In 1521 a Portuguese visitor found that the streets were broad and straight and yet so thronged with traffic and people that it was difficult to move. The houses were one-storeyed and had courtyards and gardens. Many had walls and floors covered with ornamental blue and gold tiles that may have been Chinese imports. The city is thought to have had a population of 200,000 (although one estimate at the time put it at 1.2 million).

Like all riverside cities in the history of Bangladesh, Gaur felt the power of the river to give prosperity or to take it away. During its heyday (early 1200s to 1575), Gaur was settled and abandoned several times, depending on the Ganges moving westwards and back again. When the river moved away, it was not only an economic disaster (even though feeder canals were made, ships could no longer reach the port), but also a health disaster, as swamps formed and malaria and other fevers broke out. In 1575 a severe epidemic sounded the death knell for Gaur: the river had moved away once more and this time a combination of political instability and problems in trade with Southeast Asia sealed its fate. Today, the river flows about 15 km from Gaur's ruins, which stretch over an area 30 km by 6 km and include monumental gates, fortifications, palaces, mosques, bridges, causeways, canals, loading platforms and underground sewers (Plate 2.5).[22] Part of the ruins lie in Bangladesh and part across the border in India.

The rise and fall of Gaur was just one episode in the delta's long history of flexible urbanisation. Like the rivers and villages of deltaic Bengal, centres of urban power and commerce have always been remarkably mobile and so have their inhabitants and the trade routes they served. The same holds for the political organisations and states ruling the delta.

The early history of state formation in the Bengal delta can be described as a continual emergence and decline of local and regional polities that only occasionally became integrated into large realms. It is often unclear how

Plate 2.5 Ruins of the northern gateway to the fort of Gaur, constructed around 1425 CE.

firm such integration was, how it affected local power holders and what it meant for the population at large.[23] Many scholars suggest that the Maurya (c. 324–187 BCE) and Gupta (c. 320–570 CE) spheres of influence covered most of the delta. The evidence is fragmentary, however, and it would appear that the western delta (now West Bengal (India) and western Bangladesh) was more often part of large states than the eastern delta. This pattern of states in the Indian heartland extending their influence eastwards was only occasionally reversed when a regional state in Bengal expanded to the west. This may have happened in the seventh century CE, when Sasanka, the ruler of the north Bengal state of Gaur (*Gauṛa*), ventured into northern India, and the Pala rulers repeated it with more success in the eighth and ninth centuries. The eastern delta and the southern region of Chittagong saw a succession of local states and episodic integration into states whose centres of power lay in Tripura, to the east, and Arakan, to the south.

Most of the time, however, Bengal polities appear to have been relatively small and transient, a situation that an early source aptly describes as 'fish-

Plate 2.6 The ruins of Paharpur in northwestern Bangladesh.

eat-fish' (*mātsyanyāyam*). In such periods of political fragmentation, 'every Ksatriya, grandee, Brahman and merchant was a king in his own house . . . and there was no king ruling over the country'.[24]

The actual power of the rulers over the agricultural population is difficult to assess. According to Sheena Panja, the impressive monuments that rulers such as the Pala dynasty constructed in the floodplains were actually signs of weakness. These towering brick constructions (for example Paharpur, c. 800 CE, see Plate 2.6) were attempts to inscribe the permanence of their authority in the shifting landscape of the floodplain, but the local population, whose lives were attuned to impermanence, probably set little store by them.[25]

Fragmented though the archaeological record for the Bengal delta still is, it shows a pattern that runs through the entire history of the region: the delta's socio-economic and political development rarely conformed to an all-South-Asia or even a north-Indian model. Although there were all kinds of economic and political links between the delta and surrounding areas, the region followed its own course, and attempts to integrate it into larger political entities were often unsuccessful.

CHAPTER 3

A Region of Multiple Frontiers

The history of Bangladesh is a history of frontiers. From the earliest times the Bengal delta has been a meeting ground of opposites, and it is these encounters, clashes and accommodations that have given Bangladesh its distinct character. In this chapter I expand on Richard Eaton's idea of thinking about Bangladesh history as predicated upon a series of moving frontiers.[1]

We have already encountered *the land–water frontier* – moving primarily from north to south – and *the Sanskritic frontier* – moving from west to east. Both are ancient and both are still very much part of contemporary Bangladesh. In this chapter we encounter four more frontiers, all of them historically moving in an easterly direction.

THE AGRARIAN FRONTIER

This frontier divides cultivators of irrigated fields from shifting cultivators and the forest. In the delta, embanked fields irrigated by monsoon rain-water and worked by ploughs appeared at least 2,500 years ago. Since then this form of crop production has been expanding gradually across the lowlands at the expense of an older system of hoe cultivation on temporary plots. Today the latter system is still found in Bangladesh, but it is restricted to hill terrain where irrigated fields cannot be maintained.[2]

The spread of irrigated agriculture was slow and uneven because establishing it requires much labour. Cultivators had to clear the forest, level the ground and construct field embankments and irrigation channels. Even more labour was needed to keep irrigated agriculture running. If successful, however, it was capable of permanently supporting dense populations. The urban centres of early Bangladesh could develop only after irrigated agriculture had established itself and had begun producing sufficient food not only for the cultivators themselves but also for emerging classes of non-cultivating consumers. Cultivators rarely depended completely on agrarian production – their livelihoods were also based on fishing, hunting and artisanal production.

The eastward march of the agrarian frontier went hand in hand with the gradual destruction of the luxuriant Bengalian rainforest. The earliest states encouraged this to expand their tax base as well as their ideological control over land. Copperplates found all over Bangladesh document how early rulers gave out land grants to religious specialists on the understanding that, to quote a tenth-century inscription, the 'inhabitants and cultivators, obedient to command, must meet the payments of the correct dues'.[3] Centuries later, the Mughal state would apply the same logic with more vigour, resulting in Islam emerging as an ideology of taming the forest.

In the early nineteenth century large patches of the Bengalian rainforest still survived. A French adventurer, who visited the ruined city of Gaur in 1812, described the richness of the natural environment. In a matter of hours after entering the jungle his party met with (and shot some) wild buffalo, rhinoceros, tigers, elephants, hyenas and black bears, as well as several species of birds.

The entire surrounding country is a dreadful wilderness that travellers fear to enter. There have been several attempts to penetrate the forests that cover Gaur these days, but they have met with little success. Europeans contemplating this trip have been dissuaded by the stories of exertions and dangers told by the fearless ones who have visited. I say 'Europeans' because Gaur is a cursed place for Hindus and Muslims. In their imagination it is terrorised by evil spirits such as *dives*, *guls*, and *affrits* ... After we had crossed some rough terrain and passed through huge bushes, we found that the bamboo forest in front of us was so dense that we could hardly see objects ten feet away. Our elephants made a horrific noise as they pushed aside bamboos more than forty feet high and as thick as your wrist and snapped them like reeds.[4]

In the mid-nineteenth century, however, the assault on the Bengalian rainforest accelerated. In central and southern Bengal population densities were increasing, and it was mostly small-holding peasants who expanded cultivation in this region. In more sparsely populated northern Bengal, however, the story was different. Here the British colonial state, hungry for income and following the example of its precursors, gave large tracts of forest to wealthy men in order for them to clear these for plough agriculture and thereby contribute revenue to the colonial exchequer. The arduous task of actually clearing the jungle was carried out by labourers, among them Santals, Oraons and Mundas from the hill country to the west. Some were seasonal, while others settled down, hoping to get possession of some land of their own.[5]

By the late nineteenth century this process had converted most forests into farmland. The disappearance of the forests precipitated an agrarian crisis. Bangladesh's agrarian system had been based on an expansionary dynamic; the moving frontier was necessary to support a gradually growing population. With the disappearance of the forest, delta agriculture ran into a brick wall. Bangladeshi cultivators, unable to reclaim new fields, sought to combat looming stagnation by means of two strategies. The first was a process known as 'agrarian involution'.[6] They used more labour to intensify cultivation and increase production, they raised two or three crops on the same field during the year and they introduced more market crops. A second strategy was self-rescue by migration. Cultivators from the delta sought to keep the frontier moving by bringing into cultivation areas that were previously thought to be too dangerous (such as islands in the big rivers or out in the Bay of Bengal) or too far away. It is from this period that settlers began to move in considerable numbers into regions beyond the eastern boundaries of the Bengal delta, especially Assam and Tripura (now in India) and Arakan (or Rakhine, now in Myanmar (Burma)). In this way they introduced a new element into the history of Bangladesh. Moving into regions occupied by other ethnic groups, they initiated a political dynamic that took on ethnic overtones. In the twentieth century, in Assam, Tripura and Arakan alike, popular movements and state regimes would turn against Bangladeshi immigrants.

THE STATE FRONTIER

A second frontier in the Bengal delta was that between states and other forms of rule. We have seen that states first emerged in the south and west and gradually spread to cover most of the delta. But this form of territorial organisation was not the only one. Other forms of rule prevailed in parts of the delta and in the hills surrounding it, including small-scale and often unstable alliances of village leaders. For much of the delta's history, it was such alliances that dominated the scene, occasionally punctuated by the emergence of large states. Sometimes such large states were able to incorporate small statelets and chiefdoms, but they were unable to 'climb the hills'.[7] The state frontier did not close until well after the establishment of the British colonial state, largely as a result of the colonial armed forces fighting their way into the hills and annexing them.

The last part of Bangladesh to come under state rule was the mountainous region in the southeast, invaded by the British in 1860 and dubbed the Chittagong Hill Tracts. Today the forms of state rule here continue to differ from those in the plains. In a sense, the frontier still lives on in the administrative arrangements of the Chittagong Hill Tracts, where the Bangladesh state continues to uphold regional regulations and political forms originating in the colonial period. Among these are vestiges of indirect rule (the office of three Chiefs or Rajas), a regional system of taxation, and land rights and forms of representation (for example a 'Regional Council' and a Ministry of Chittagong Hill Tracts Affairs) that differ from the rest of Bangladesh.[8]

THE RELIGIOUS FRONTIER

A third frontier was the one separating inhabitants with different religious visions. The early history of religious identities in Bangladesh is still poorly understood. Archaeologists have unearthed many images of female and male figures that they interpret as representations of powerful goddesses and gods, but we know little about the community religions that gave these images meaning. The picture becomes clearer when, over 2,000 years ago, deities came to exhibit iconographical characteristics that place them within broader religious traditions found in other parts of South and Southeast Asia. In the Bengal delta, these traditions – now known as Buddhism, Jainism and Hinduism – appear to have coexisted for centuries as part of the eastward expansion of Sanskritic culture.[9] Early Chinese pilgrims described cities in Bangladesh as places of religious learning. For example, Xuanzang – also known as Hiuen Tsiang – visited Samatata in eastern Bangladesh around 640 CE. In his words:

The land is low and is rich. The capital is about eight km round. It is regularly cultivated, and is rich in crops, and the flowers and fruits grow everywhere. The climate is soft and the habits of the people agreeable. The men are hardy by nature, small of stature, and of black complexion; they are fond of learning ... There are thirty or so monasteries with about two thousand priests. They are all of the Theravada Buddhist [*Sthavira*] school. There are some hundred Brahmanical [*Deva*] temples ... The naked ascetics called Jains [*Nirgrantha*] are most numerous.[10]

Although religious specialists such as Xuanzang clearly distinguished between traditions, we do not know to what extent ordinary believers in Bangladesh understood these religious forms as separate or as an amalgamated whole. Neither do we know how these forms interacted with pre-existing religions or to what extent they spread beyond urban centres. It is clear, however, that very gradually many local deities became incorporated into the Sanskritic religions, giving these a particular regional flavour. One distinct regional feature is the persisting popularity of powerful female deities: Monosha (*manasā*), who protects worshippers against snakebites; Chondi (*caṇḍī*), the goddess of forest life and hunting; Shitola (*śītalā*), who guards against smallpox; and the fierce and vengeful Kali (*kālī*).[11]

Evidence of the overlapping of various frontiers – Sanskritic, agrarian, state and religious – is provided by early Bengali literature. Narrative poems in honour of deities (mongolkabbo; *maṅgalkābya*) describe a struggle between adherents of different gods that took place around 1300–1500 CE. The main god of the early farming people was known as Shiva (*śib*):

a benevolent, kindly deity, who shares only a name with that majestic being who churned the ocean and drank down its tide of poison. To his people, he is *gosāi*, the owner of the herd, and *prabhu*, master, simple terms for the simple deity of men who lived by the soil. His emblem is the plough, not the trident.[12]

His adherents struggled with those of two goddesses. One of these, Monosha, may have started out as a domestic goddess associated with women, herdsmen and fisherfolk.[13] Another, Chondi, was associated with hunters and the forest. Both are thought to have been indigenous pre-Sanskritic deities linked with non-plough cultivation. Neither was associated with professional priests. And yet their worship gradually became very popular among Bengali-speaking wet-rice producers who were coming under the influence of a state-supported religion today known as Brahmanical Hinduism.[14] In this way, these deities crossed not only the Sanskritic frontier but also the agrarian, state and religious frontiers.

It was in this complex world of multiple and transforming religious identities that a new creed, Islam, entered in two separate waves. It first reached coastal Bangladesh as a by-product of seaborne trade between the eighth and twelfth centuries. By this time, Arab and Persian travellers and traders were Muslims. Many of them settled along the southeastern coast, where Arab sources mention a port city, Samandar, possibly an early name for contemporary Chittagong.[15] In the thirteenth century Islam also reached Bangladesh by the land route, this time as the religion of powerful invaders. This is how Eaton describes the event:

Sometime in 1243–44, residents of Lakhnauti, a city in northwestern Bengal, told a visiting historian of the dramatic events that had taken place there forty years earlier. At that time, the visitor was informed, a band of several hundred Turkish cavalry had ridden swiftly down the Gangetic Plain in the direction of the Bengal delta. Led by a daring officer named Muhammad Bakhtiyar, the men overran venerable Buddhist monasteries in neighboring Bihar before turning their attention to the northwestern portion of the delta, then ruled by a mild and generous Hindu monarch. Disguising themselves as horse dealers, Bakhtiyar and his men slipped into the royal city of Nudiya [probably in what is now Rajshahi district]. Once inside, they rode straight to the king's palace, where they confronted the guards with brandished weapons. Utterly overwhelmed, for he had just sat town to dine, the Hindu monarch hastily departed through the back door and fled with many of his retainers to the forest hinterland of eastern Bengal, abandoning his capital altogether.[16]

The arrival of these newcomers turned out to be momentous because it marked the beginning of an era in which Islam was the creed of those who ruled most of Bengal (and, indeed, most of the Indian subcontinent). This era lasted some five centuries and is usually referred to as the Sultanate period (up to the sixteenth century),[17] followed by the Mughal period; it ended only when the British conquered Bengal in the mid-eighteenth century. What made the establishment of Muslim rule in Bengal particularly significant was that it initiated a process that did not occur in other parts of India: in Bengal, the majority of the population gradually adopted Islam as their religion (see box 'Shah Jalal the saint'). At the time no one could have imagined that this would one day have a fateful effect on state formation. Without a majority of Muslims in the population of Bengal, there would never have been a twenty-first-century state named Bangladesh.

Shah Jalal the saint

It must have been a memorable visit back in 1346 CE, when two adventurers from the Mediterranean met in the Bengal delta. The host was Turkish. He had settled in a remote corner of the delta some thirty years previously. The visitor was from Morocco. He had been travelling around Asia for over twenty years and found his way to Bengal after having been shipwrecked in the Indian Ocean on his way to China. The host, Shah Jalal, was already famous, and his guest, Ibn Battutah, was destined for fame through his account of his travels.

Shah Jalal had arrived overland from his native Konya (Turkey)[18] in Sylhet (northeast Bangladesh), when the army of a neighbouring principality conquered this region. He may have fought in the army, but that is not what made him legendary. Soon after he settled in Sylhet stories about his unusual spiritual powers and miraculous acts began to circulate. Shah Jalal was a highly successful Muslim preacher.

To find a Turkish missionary in fourteenth-century Bengal is not as exceptional as it may appear. Shah Jalal was a Sufi, a member of the Islamic sect that seeks to establish a direct relationship with Allah through meditation, asceticism and preaching. Sufis were active in spreading Islam all over South Asia. The first had arrived in Bengal some 150 years before Shah Jalal, and Sufi preachers would continue to trickle into the region for centuries. Most came from Central Asia, Arabia, Iran and Turkey.

Plate 3.1 Shah Jalal's shrine in Sylhet.

It was Shah Jalal's reputation as a powerful Sufi saint that prompted Ibn Battutah to take the long boat trip up the rivers of Bengal. Ibn Battutah describes the old man as tall, lean and with a thin beard. After three days in Sylhet, Ibn Battutah travelled to nearby Habiganj – now an insignificant country town but then, according to this eyewitness, 'one of the biggest and most beautiful cities' – and from there to Sonargaon (near Dhaka), a fifteen-day trip down the 'Blue River', possibly the Meghna. Ibn Battutah was impressed by the abundance of rice in Bengal.[19]

Shah Jalal died the following year, and his tomb became a place where followers would gather to pray for his blessing (Plate 3.1). Although turning the grave of a spiritual guide into an object of veneration is frowned upon in more orthodox, scriptural interpretations of Islam, it is encouraged in Sufism and remains exceedingly popular in the Bengal delta. Shah Jalal's shrine is one of the largest and most venerated. It draws thousands of devotees, not only from all over Bangladesh but also from other parts of South Asia.

How could Islam emerge as the majority religion in this region far from the Middle East and surrounded on all sides by areas where Islam never had such an impact? How did it become the majority faith among the rural population, whereas elsewhere in South Asia it was chiefly an urban creed? What did conversion to Islam actually mean? And why was Islam far more successful in eastern Bengal than in western Bengal? Eaton, who has examined these questions in detail, suggests that the answers lie in the fact that eastern Bengal was a zone where the agrarian, state and religious frontiers moved together during a crucial period in the region's history.

In the seventeenth century, when the Mughal state ruled most of what is now Bangladesh, the agrarian frontier began to move decisively into the eastern delta. State officials rode the crest of an ecological change: the Ganges shifted its channel to the east (the current Padma) as the Bengal Basin slowly tilted eastwards, a movement that is still continuing. As a result, the agrarian potential of the eastern delta increased. Keen to augment their tax base, Mughal officials encouraged the clearing of forests and the establishment of wet-rice plough cultivation. To this end they issued permits and grants to enterprising colonists who undertook to reclaim land in the eastern delta and pay taxes in return for land rights. Colonists needed to mobilise labour and this gave the edge to 'charismatic pioneers', men with a reputation for religious power and piety. They would enlist followers to build a shrine, a requirement under the state grant, and settle them around it. The shrine-orientated organisation (commonly known as shomaz (*samáj*) among Muslims) provided social order. The newly established community – usually made up largely of immigrants from western and northern Bengal, now less fertile than before – would clear the forest and create rice fields. The local population of shifting cultivators and fisherfolk would either join them or choose to move deeper into the forest or swamps, placing themselves out of reach of the state but maintaining trade relations with the sedentary rice growers.

It is essential to understand that Islam spread in the Bengal delta because people interacted with Muslim mystics, and not because conquerors forced them to convert. Muslim rulers in Bengal had never had an interest in promoting Islam or converting Bengalis to the faith. The Mughal state was no exception: many charismatic pioneers who received state patronage were Hindus. The majority, however, were Muslims, quite a few of them known as spiritual guides (*pir*). Thus, Eaton suggests, in the eastern delta – inhabited by 'communities lightly touched, if touched at all, by Hindu civilization' – Islam came to be associated with state-recognised control of reclaimed land, the expansion of wet-rice cultivation and literacy.[20] The agrarian, religious and state frontiers fused as Islam evolved into an ideology of taming the forest and promoting settled agriculture. In a process of creative adaptation and translation, the religious traditions of eastern Bengal and the rituals associated with the new village mosques and shrines began to coalesce, creating a completely new blend of Bengali and Islamic worldviews.[21] Islam's success in the Bengal delta was predicated upon its domestication. Islamic superhuman beings were first added to the existing pantheon, then they were identified with powerful local deities, and ultimately they rose to such prominence that they succeeded in appropriating Bengali culture – or in being appropriated by it. In short, 'when figures like Adam, Eve, and Abraham became identified with central leitmotifs of Bengali history and civilization, Islam had become established as profoundly and authentically Bengali.'[22] It was a religion in which the traditions of Sufi mysticism, devotion to spiritual guides and worship at their shrines was of crucial significance – and these traditions are still manifest in Bangladesh today.

Importantly, Islamic Bengali identity remained strongly rooted in the eastern deltaic milieu. In a sense, it is a lowland identity that points west, to the Sanskritic and Islamic heartlands. It never managed to climb the hills or enter the forest. The people living in the hills and mountains surrounding the Bengal delta never adopted either Bengali or Islamic identities.[23] Some parts of these hills are now included in Bangladesh, notably the Chittagong Hill Tracts. When you enter these hills from the plains, you realise immediately that you have crossed a cultural frontier. In the hills architecture, food, gender relations and many other elements point east, towards Southeast Asia. The religions are diverse: community religions among the Mro, Khumi and Khyeng; local forms of Buddhism among the Marma, Chakma, Taungchangya and Chak (Sak); local forms of Hinduism among the Tripura and Riang/Brong; and, from the beginning of the twentieth century, various forms of Christianity among the Bawm, Pangkhua, Khyeng, Mro and Lushai. None of these groups identify themselves as Bengalis. With the exception of the Chakma language, none of the languages they speak are related to Bengali.[24]

Similarly, the Islamic Bengali identity did not succeed in areas of the delta that remained forest-clad until recent times. Here many non-Islamic, non-Bengali identities persisted, for example Garo (Abeng) in the central delta; Khasi, Garo and Hajong in the northeast; Santal, Oraon, Koch, Malo and many others in the northwest; and Rakhain (Rakhine, Arakanese) on the southern and southeastern coasts.[25] When the present borders of Bangladesh were drawn, all these very different groups of people came to be placed in a single category: that of ethnic minorities facing the dominant ethnic identity in the country, Islamic Bengali.

THE LANGUAGE FRONTIER

The state/agricultural/religious frontier was also linked to language change. Today the country is often equated with the Bengali (or Bangla; *bāṃlā*) language – 'Bangladesh' means 'country of Bengalis' – and this reflects the political significance that the Bengali language assumed in the second half of the twentieth century. But historically the emergence of Bengali as the region's dominant language was a slow process. In terms of language the history of Bangladesh is clearly one of multilingualism. For centuries other languages, now often seen as marginal or 'hill' languages, were widely spoken in the plains: Garo (Abeng) in central Bangladesh (Dhaka and Mymensingh), Khasi in the northeast (Sylhet), Arakanese in the south (Patuakhali and Chittagong) and Koch in the north (Rangpur and Dinajpur).

The language we now recognise as Bengali evolved from regional forms of Prakrit, whose speakers had first arrived in Bengal in the last few centuries BCE. The use of these languages gradually spread eastwards and it is thought that by 500 CE they were fairly widely spoken in the delta. The first writings in Bengali appear by 1000 CE, so Bangladesh's national language is usually assumed to have originated more than ten centuries ago. Its subsequent history is well known because it was the language of elites who produced a particularly abundant and varied written literature.[26] Nevertheless a translator's lament of over half a century ago remains largely true today: 'The literary tradition is unbroken, from the ninth or tenth century Buddhist esoteric texts . . . to the present. It is somewhat surprising that little is known in the West about a literature so old and so rich.'[27]

The spread of Bengali as a dominant language of the region took centuries. This was not only because of the existence of other vibrant linguistic communities, however. Equally important was the fact that Bengali was not always the language of rule, ritual or trade. Over the centuries state power in the Bengal delta has been held by a truly remarkable array of non-Bengalis, including Afghans, Turks, North Indians, Arakanese and Ethiopians. These elites would conduct their business in Turkish, Persian and Hindustani rather than in Bengali. The dominant ritual languages of the region were Sanskrit, Pali and Arabic. And Arabic, Portuguese and English were important languages of maritime trade. Thus there was a remarkable linguistic diversity, and many residents of Bangladesh must have been multilingual. The emergence of Bengali as a lingua franca and then as a mother tongue was very uneven. For example, in southeastern Bangladesh, Arakanese retained its position as the link language until the turn of the nineteenth century, and many communities never accepted Bengali as their mother tongue.[28] Even today, over forty other languages are spoken in Bangladesh – some written in their own scripts.[29] And among certain communities in Bangladesh (for example Mro), not everybody speaks or understands Bengali.

As new speakers adopted Bengali, the language developed distinct dialects by which Bangladeshis today easily recognise each other's regional roots. In four cases these dialects are incomprehensible to speakers of standard Bengali and they should be considered as separate languages. The first is Sylheti (Siloti, *silăṭi*), spoken by about 10 million people in northeastern Bangladesh and across the border in adjacent districts of Assam (India) – as well as by a large community of Sylheti settlers in the United Kingdom. The second is Chittagonian (Chatgaiya Buli; *cãtgãiyā buli*), spoken by some 10 million people in southeastern Bangladesh. The third is Chakma (Changma; *cāngmă*), spoken by several hundreds of thousands in the Chittagong Hill Tracts as well as in Mizoram, Tripura and Arunachal Pradesh (India). The Chakmas are known to have previously spoken a Tibeto-Burman language; they developed their current language in the eighteenth century. Chakma is related to Chittagonian in structure, but it has a very distinct vocabulary and pronunciation. And the fourth is Rohingya, the language spoken by (mostly) Muslim inhabitants of northern Arakan (Rakhine state, Myanmar (Burma)). This language is also related to Chittagonian and features elements of the Arakanese and Burmese languages. It has become important in Bangladesh after successive waves of refugees from Myanmar (Burma) started spilling over the border from the 1970s onwards. Today, several hundreds of thousands of them live both inside and outside refugee camps in Bangladesh. Speakers of each of these languages, except Chittagonian, have developed their own scripts to distinguish the written form of their language from Bengali (which is written in Eastern Nagari script).[30]

MULTIPLE IDENTITIES

The long-term interplay of these different frontiers has given contemporary Bangladesh culture a particularly multilayered structure. Very often surface meanings hide inner understandings that are quite different and can be diametrically opposed. It is essential to understand this complexity when analysing Bangladesh culture. Let me give two examples.

First, gender relations in contemporary Bangladesh are routinely described in terms of stark power differences between men and women. There is much evidence to support the view that many women live very choice-restricted lives, but this is not the entire story. The common representation of Bangladeshi women as powerless victims of patriarchy fails to acknowledge that they have access to cultural traditions with which to challenge prevailing gender roles. We have seen that powerful goddesses have featured in the Bengal delta's religions from the earliest times and that several of them remain part of the cultural repertoire. More importantly, the region's literature has produced a number of female characters who are far from downtrodden:

These heroines don armor to fight *dacoits* [robbers], slay raging rhinos (and naturally cut off their horns in wonderfully Freudian fashion), harness flying horses to rescue their lovers, transform ignorant men into billy goats to serve as breeding stock for their passions . . . and generally instruct the kings and princes of the world in the ways of statecraft.[31]

Such women who take charge – Behula and Lalmon are famous examples in Bangladesh – provide popular cultural resources that challenge current gender relations and contradict dominant practices of patriarchal control.[32] Significantly, old Bengali poetic forms included 'anti-husband tirades' (poti-ninda; *pati-nindā*) in which wives complained about the physical and social shortcomings of their husbands. Here are two fragments:

> Although my husband is living, I have become a widow.
> He eats four *pana* of opium (daily), there is no strength in his body.
> He sold all my arm bangles.

How can I speak of my husband? My head hangs in shame.
My husband is big and fat. He has a great pot-belly.
Hearing of the joys of others, my heart burns in grief.
Not once ever is there a kiss or embrace.
When he wants to kiss my face and begins by bending down,
or wants to hold me tight, his belly shoves me away.[33]

Apart from these female literary characters, we will see in the following chapters that there have been many influential women in the delta's history – especially in politics, education, advocacy and the arts. Anyone analysing changing gender relations in Bangladesh needs to go beyond the stereotypes and assess the power of such role models.

My second example concerns the religious frontier, which is usually presented as a clear contrast between monotheistic Islam and polytheistic Hinduism. The domestication of Islam to the pre-existing worldviews of the inhabitants of the Bengal delta makes such a simple juxtaposition untenable.[34] For many Bangladeshis who consider themselves Muslims the distinction is far less straightforward. They combine a belief in the god of scriptural Islam, Allah, with a belief in other superhuman protectors. For example, inhabitants of southern Bangladesh fear to enter the Sundarban marshlands without praying to Bonbibi (*ban(a)bibi*), a benevolent 'Muslim' forest goddess, who, like her male counterpart Gazi Pir (*gāji pīr*; Plate 3.2), can protect them from tigers and crocodiles. Travellers on large rivers in eastern Bangladesh invoke the deity Bodor (or Badr; *badar*) to ensure a safe journey. Bodor's Islamic identity is emphasised by sometimes referring to him as Bodor Pir (*badar pīr*), suggesting that he is seen as the deified form of some legendary pir or Islamic spiritual guide. Some spiritual guides lived many centuries ago (for example Shah Jalal, mentioned earlier in this chapter). Others lived much more recently, or are still alive. Their connection with Sufism is no longer an important marker for their followers. Pirs are usually male, but female counterparts (*pīrani*) also exist.[35]

In this way Bangladeshi Muslims have pragmatically incorporated worship of many deities, some in animal or bird form, into their religious practices.[36] Many of these are worshipped by Hindus and Muslims alike. Bonbibi and Bodor are joined by a host of other popular gods – such as Panch Pir (*pãch pīr*; Plate 3.3), Shotto Pir/Shotto Narain (*satya pīr/nārāyan*); the jungle deity Badshah (*bādsāh*) and the cholera goddess Olabibi/Oladebi (*ōlābibi/devi*) – who continue to cross the religious frontier.[37]

What is true of deities is true of a range of other rituals and practices; followers of Islam and Hinduism in Bangladesh share many of them. One

Plate 3.2 Scene from the legend of Gazi Pir, showing the spiritual guide riding
a tiger. Scroll painting, early 1800s.

example is religious architecture, which developed a distinctive 'Bengal style'
based on the curving eaves of the village hut (Plate 3.3) and a lack of towers and
minarets.[38] In medical and veterinary practices, local spiritual traditions and
supernatural beings (for example Manik Pir (*mānik pīr*), who can restore life
and protect human and animal health) continue to be evident.[39] Shared
performances and festivals are another common tradition that is very much
alive.[40] A boy who grew up in the small town of Kishorganj around 1907 later
had vivid memories of 'the great fair of the Swing Festival of Krishna, held on
the southern outskirts of the town' (Plate 3.4 shows a similar festival):

Plate 3.3 Female pilgrims laying flowers at the shrine of Panch Pir (Five Saints),
Mograpara (Narayanganj district, central Bangladesh).

It was held annually during September and October. To it came not only all the
local traders, all the craftsmen of eastern Mymensingh, but also big merchants
from Dacca and Narayanganj ... The very first row to our left on entering the
fair was formed by the stalls of book-binders. Whenever we went to the fair we
found them busy. All the year's new purchases of the Koran and all the year's
worn and damaged copies of the Koran were brought here for binding and
rebinding and silver-tooling ... The fair, though held on account of a Hindu
festival, drew Hindu and Mussalman alike ... [Another occasion] was the Id
festival of the Mussalmans, which, although Hindu boys ourselves, we looked
forward to with the keenest expectation ... What we waited for ... was the
march of the common folk to the field of prayer, the passage of the elephant
procession of the Muslim zamindar [landlord] family, a senior member of which
acted as the leader of the prayers, and the return of the ordinary people as well as
of the elephants.[41]

This sharing of religious practices is of particular significance in view of
the fact that dominant understandings of contemporary Bangladesh hardly
acknowledge its importance. In analysing Bangladesh society and history,
writers overwhelmingly privilege 'Muslim' and 'Hindu' as mutually exclusive, oppositional and monolithic terms. It is crucial to recognise that this
dichotomy is a modern construct that has its roots in oppositional politics
that developed in the late British-colonial period. Neither 'Hindu' nor

Plate 3.4 Elephants lined up during the Janmashthami festival, celebrating the birth of the god Krishna, in Dhaka, c. 1905.

'Muslim' were ever monolithic terms in Bengal; there were, and continue to be, sharp divisions and struggles within each of these religious identities in terms of class, sect, jurisprudence, doctrine, heterodoxy, caste and region. Recurrent attempts at bipolar categorisation have always met with strong cultural resistance in Bangladesh, not only with regard to social stereotyping but also at the most basic religious level. '[F]or many Bengalis religion is not always about sectarian exclusion, but about the celebration of life. Bangladeshis have for centuries moved effortlessly through a plural world where the stark divisions that characterize the contemporary political use of Islam, Buddhism, and Hinduism do not adhere.'[42]

Insistence on spiritual unity rather than opposition is perhaps most vocally expressed in the devotional songs of a community known as the Baul (*bāul*), who refer to themselves as followers of the path of unorthodoxy (*bartamān-panthī*).[43] They form a small community, but their music is remarkably popular in Bangladesh. An annual festival is held in Kushtia, the home district of one of the most famous Baul composers, Lalon Fokir or Lalon Shai (*lālan phakir/sāi*), who was born in 1774. His songs (*lālan-gīti*) are an established genre of contemporary Bengali popular music (Plate 3.5). Another eighteenth-century composer, Modon Baul (*madan bāul*), expressed the sense of a Bengali religious unity underneath the separation forged by Islam and Hinduism as follows:

Plate 3.5 Performing a devotional song at Lalon Fokir's shrine, Kumarkhali (Kushtia district), 2006.

The path that leads to you is cluttered with temples and mosques.
O Lord! I have heard your call but I cannot proceed:
Hindu and Muslim teachers block my way.
There are many locks to your door: the Puranas, the Koran, and recitations.
Alas Lord! What a terrible torment this is, cries Modon in despair.[44]

Although the Baul themselves are a marginal group in Bangladeshi society, the broad appeal of their poetry shows how the devotional traditions on which they draw (notably Tantric, Vaisnava and Sufi) continue to reverberate with Bangladeshis of various religious persuasions today.

A REGIONAL CULTURE

Gradually, diverse and often opposing cultural strains produced a recognisable regional culture in the eastern Bengal delta. Partly fostered by the various states that rose and fell over time, partly resulting from life in deltaic agrarian communities and the integrating effect of moving frontiers, it came to cluster around two main identities. Unlike the surrounding populations, most inhabitants of the active delta came to define themselves as both Muslims and Bengalis. To be sure, this process was never homogeneous and there was continual transformation of what it meant to be a Muslim Bengali or a Bengali Muslim. There were considerable differences in the meaning of these identities, partly spatial and partly temporal. For example, Islamic identities in eastern Bangladesh tended more towards the puritanical than in western and northern Bangladesh. Inclusion in Bengali identity came late for large communities in the northwest who would identify themselves as, for example, Rajbongshi until well into the nineteenth century, and who are currently reasserting that identity.[45] Even today, there are many people in Bangladesh who subscribe to only one of the two identities or to neither. Thus, there are many millions of Bengalis in Bangladesh who are not Muslims but who identify themselves as Bengali Hindus, Christians or Buddhists. There are also Muslims who do not identify themselves as Bengalis, for example several groups of Urdu-speaking Muslims. And there are numerous groups who identify themselves as neither Bengali nor Muslim, for example Chakma, Santal, Manipuri and Garo (Mandi).

Nonetheless, a crucial hyphenation of Bengali and Muslim did occur in the region and it became the leitmotiv of the delta's modern history. A perpetual creative reworking of what it meant to be a Bengali Muslim or a Muslim Bengali energised cultural expression, political mobilisation and social organisation. The inherent instability of this identity proved highly productive of a sense of regional belonging: nowhere but in what is now Bangladesh did Bengaliness and Islam become domesticated as they merged. As we shall see, it was successive ruling elites' failure to gauge the centrality of this merged identity among the majority of the population that would actually increase its salience. During the nineteenth and twentieth centuries various emancipation movements insisted upon it. Their struggles with state elites contributed to a tortuous course of state formation and the emergence of the state that we know as Bangladesh.

CHAPTER 4

The Delta as a Crossroads

The Bengal delta has always had a remarkably mobile population. This has often led to tensions between the territorial rights of sedentary people and the rights of mobile others. These tensions revealed themselves in multiple moving frontiers and a dynamic economy that was open to both the immense expanse of the Indian Ocean and an enormous hinterland. For as far back as we can reconstruct, the Bengal delta was integrated into networks of long-distance trade, pilgrimage, political alliance, cultural exchange and travel. It served as a gateway to the wider world for people and goods from the landlocked Ganges plains in the west, from Tibet and Nepal in the north and from the Brahmaputra valley and China in the east. Conversely, traders, Buddhist pilgrims, political emissaries and adventurers who wanted to visit these regions had to pass through Bengal. It was in the coastal waterways of Bengal that Southeast Asians, North Indians, Sri Lankans, Chinese, Arabs, Central Asians, Persians, Ethiopians and Tibetans met from very early times. The geographical reach of this traffic hub was enormous, as can be illustrated by Ibn Battutah's visit in 1346 CE. When this Moroccan traveller left the Maldive Islands south of India, he followed the trade routes via Sri Lanka to the Bengal delta. After spending some time there, he decided to leave and boarded a Chinese junk bound for Java.[1]

The inhabitants of the Bengal delta played host to many visitors, but they themselves were also important actors in long-distance trade, travel and maritime warfare.[2] Seaborne trade, wealth and boats were closely associated. Tellingly, the earliest coins from ancient cities such as Chandraketugarh and Wari-Bateshwar were stamped with pictures of boats.[3] In an early legend we find the description of a trading fleet from Bengal headed by the merchant Chando (*cāndo*), who sets out on a voyage to Sri Lanka with a fleet of seven to fourteen ships led by his flagship, *Honeybee*.[4]

In the delta, water transport was far more important than transport over land. Bengal was a country of boats and waterways. Early inscriptions frequently defined land boundaries with reference to river ports and landing places for boats (*ghāṭ*), important functionaries were entrusted with security and tolls along the river Ganges, and the main cities were always built on the banks of navigable rivers.[5] Boats are also a recurring theme in the earliest surviving poems in Bengali, the tenth-century Charyapada (*caryāpada*).[6] These poems refer to an old occupation in the delta: ferrying people across its many streams. 'Row on, Domni, row on', one poet urges a woman, and it is clear that customers paid in cowries (kori; *kaṛi*; small shells) to be ferried across.[7]

This reference to cowrie shells illustrates the openness of the delta's economy and its early use of currency. Cowries were not found locally; they had to be imported from the Maldive Islands, some 2,000 km away. This trade had ancient roots: the third-century BCE Mahasthan Brahmi Inscription (Plate 2.3) mentions payment in *gaṇḍakas*, a term probably referring to cowries. In the far northeastern delta (northern Sylhet), cowrie shells were the only currency up to the nineteenth century, and cowries continued to circulate as small change in parts of rural Bangladesh until the end of that century.[8]

In the floodplains, however, metallic currencies appeared very early on, indicating the prominent role that successive states played here in commercial activities. Metal relics of old trade routes have been found, for example locally made punch-marked coins dating to about 300 BCE as well as imported coins from the Maurya empire, the Kushan empire, the Parthians and Sri Lanka. Ancient connections with Greece are attested by a silver drachma (coin) of about 300 BCE, found near Dhaka,[9] and this is how the Bengal coast is described in a Greek text of the first century CE:

sailing with the ocean to the right and the shore remaining beyond to the left, Ganges comes into view, and near it the very last land toward the east, Chryse. There is a river near it called the Ganges, and it rises and falls in the same way as the Nile. On its bank is a market-town which has the same name as the river, Ganges. [*] Through this place are brought malabathrum [cassia†] and Gangetic spikenard [‡] and pearls, and muslins of the finest sorts, which are called Gangetic. It is said that there are gold-mines near these places, and there is a gold coin which is called

---

* Usually identified with Chandraketugarh (see Chapter 2). Schoff (1912).

† Cassia, a plant with leaves whose taste is reminiscent of cinnamon, was sought after in ancient Greece and Rome to flavour wine, to use in cooking and for its oil. It is still commonly used in Bangladeshi cuisine, where it is known as tezpata (*tejpātā*). Van Schendel (2015a).

‡ Spikenard (or nard, or muskroot) is a plant that grows in the Himalayan region. Its roots contain an intensely aromatic essential oil that was used as perfume and incense in ancient Egypt, West Asia (it found mention in the Bible) and Rome. Quoted in Eaton (2009), 200.

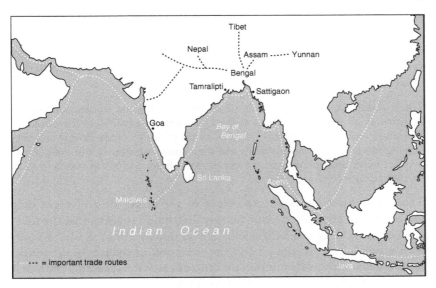

Map 4.1 Trade routes passing through the Bengal delta.

caltis. And just opposite this river there is an island in the ocean, the last part of the inhabited world toward the east, under the rising sun itself; it is called Chryse;[$] and it has the best tortoise-shell of all the places on the Erythraean Sea [Indian Ocean].[10]

The route described here was one of two major ones that coastal vessels could use safely. From the Bengal delta it steered west, following the coast of India to Sri Lanka, and from there to the Maldives, western India, eastern Africa, Arabia and the Mediterranean. A succession of port cities in the western delta controlled this trade – the earliest and best known was Tamralipti (Map 4.1). The other maritime route went east, following the coasts of Arakan and Burma and then on to Southeast and East Asia.

For many centuries, the delta acted as the only link between this maritime network and the river-borne network connecting northeastern India to the Himalayas and southwestern China. The crucial entrepôt was the town of Chittagong, located just east of the active delta and therefore the region's only stable seaport.[11] It served as a hub for the trans-shipment

---

[$] The island of Chryse may refer to any of the islands in the Bay of Bengal. Today sea turtles still nest on several of these, for example Narikel Jinjira (St. Martin's Island) in southeastern Bangladesh. Historians have sometimes assumed that Chryse referred to Arakan or Burma. R. Chakravarti (2003), 184.

of goods from faraway places and different ecological zones, but also for the riches of the delta itself. The eastern delta was so productive that by the sixteenth century it had become the world's major exporter of rice. After spending the spring of 1607 in Chittagong, the Frenchman François Pyrard observed,

There is such a quantity of rice that, besides supplying the whole country, it is exported to all parts of India, as well to Goa and Malabar, as to Sumatra, the Moluccas, and all the islands of Sunda, to all of which lands Bengal is a very nursing mother, who supplies them and their entire subsistence and food. Thus, one sees arrive there [Chittagong] every day an infinite number of vessels from all parts of India for these provisions.[12]

There were other ports of importance in the delta, most of them long forgotten. For example, a tenth-century inscription suggests that the town of Savar, now in central Bangladesh, derives its name from its role as a port with warehousing facilities.[13] And the river port of Sylhet, in the northeastern delta, was another important centre of activity, especially because it was a pivotal distribution point for cowrie currency from the lowlands to the southwestern Silk Road, which stretched into China and Tibet.[14]

Over time the trade goods carried back and forth along these routes changed. The most ancient maritime exports from Bengal appear to have been cassia and spikenard (from the Himalayas), aloe wood and rhinoceros horn (from Assam), silk fabrics, yarn and floss (overland from China), war horses (from north India) and – from the delta region itself – river pearls and cotton fabrics, especially finely woven muslin cloth. Agricultural products, notably paddy, betel nut and betel leaf, may also have been exported in ancient times. By the fourteenth century, Bangladesh paddy was exported to the Maldives in exchange for cowries, and sixteenth-century sources show that rice from the delta fed people in a swathe of land extending across much of southern Asia.[15] At this time, other important exports from the delta were fine and coarse cotton cloth, sugar, clarified butter, oil, and silk yarn and fabrics. Most of the trade with Southeast Asia, Sri Lanka and the Maldives was in the hands of merchants and officials from Bengal. These included Muslims, Hindus and Armenians.[16]

Early maritime imports were cowries and silver, as well as conch shells (to make bangles). Both cowries (from the Maldives) and silver (from mines in Yunnan (China) and northeastern Myanmar (Burma)) were crucial for the economy as they formed the foundation of the monetary system. Silver coins were known as tonka (*ṭaṅkā*). In 1971, when Bangladesh became independent, its leaders chose to name the national currency Taka (*ṭākā*), after this pre-colonial precursor.[17] Imports were for use in the delta, as well as for trading to the hinterland together with merchandise from Bengal, which included textiles, elephants and slaves, especially eunuchs.[18] In the fifteenth century there were direct contacts by sea between Bengal and China. Envoys and traders from Bengal visited the Chinese imperial court, offering gifts to the emperor that the Chinese interpreted as tribute. It is documented that twice these presents included something truly astonishing: an African giraffe.[19] Chinese traders arrived in Bengal and brought gold, silver, porcelain, satin and silks, and Burmese merchants were said to bring only 'silver and gold, and no other merchandise' to Bengal.[20] With these precious metals they bought what Bengal had to offer them: primarily rice and textiles, but also cane sugar, dried and salted meat and fish, preserved vegetables and candied fruits.[21]

By then, Bengal's export manufactures had a venerable history and a high reputation throughout the Old World. According to North Indian, Greek and Roman sources, the region had traded fine cotton and silk textiles across Asia, both overland and by sea, as early as the third to first centuries BCE. Bengal's textile industry was based on cotton cultivation and silkworm rearing in different parts of the region. The textile industry was scattered throughout the rural areas because water routes made it cheap to transport the finished product from weaving villages to the urban markets where it was sold for export.[22] Some of the largest centres of cotton manufacture were located around Dhaka. In 1586, a European visitor judged the fine cotton fabrics made in Sonargaon, near Dhaka, to be the best in the whole of India.[23] These luxury cotton and silk textiles – which were relatively cheap because of Bengal's abundant and highly skilled labour – were traded to elite markets overseas, as well as overland to South and Central Asia.

The delta's wealth attracted foreign traders and, conversely, Bengali traders settled in centres of commerce abroad, for example in northern Sumatra.[24] The cities of Bengal were cosmopolitan places where goods and money changed hands and where ideas from all over the known world intermingled. After 1500, however, an important change took place: the known world expanded considerably because newcomers from the far northwest began to appear on the scene. Following long-established routes around Africa, Portuguese traders entered the maritime trade networks of the Indian Ocean. By the 1520s they were beginning to settle in Bengal, notably in Gaur (then the capital of Bengal), Chittagong and the island of Sandvip, places that appear on a Portuguese map, the earliest surviving one that we have of the delta (Plate 4.1).[25] These Portuguese newcomers became

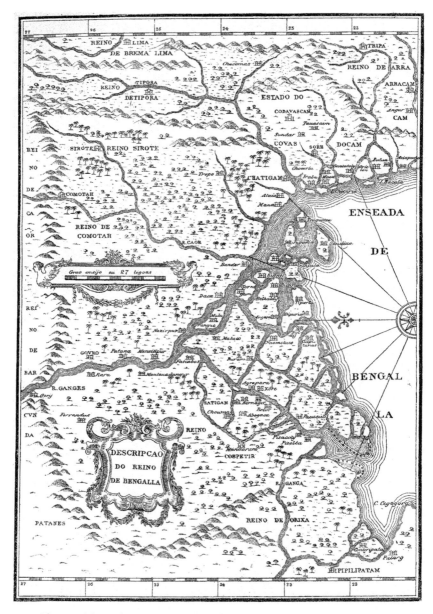

Plate 4.1 The earliest European map of the Bengal delta, by João-Baptista de Lavanha, c. 1550. It shows localities that were important to the Portuguese, such as Chittagong (Chatigam), the island of Sandvip (Sundiva), Dhaka (Daca) and Gaur (Govro). In this map the north is shown on the left-hand side.

known dismissively as Firingi (*phiriṅgi*; Franks). They were a motley and uncoordinated crowd comprising state-sponsored and private merchants as well as adventurers and pirates. They were interested in tapping into Asian trade flows but also in establishing power bases. To this end they engaged in slave trading, hired themselves out as freebooters to various kings and became involved in political struggles in the region. They established control over Chittagong in southeastern Bengal and built a custom house there in 1537. Chittagong was then Bengal's major port and an important centre of shipbuilding, using timber from the nearby hills. The town had long been a bone of contention between kings in Arakan, Tripura and Bengal.[26] Thirty years after the Portuguese took over Chittagong – which they called 'the Great Port' – a visitor counted eighteen Portuguese ships anchored there.

The Portuguese turned out to be the first of a long list of traders from different parts of Europe who were attracted by the opportunities of the Bengal delta. The rulers of the region generally welcomed them because trade augmented their revenue from customs duties, because the traders imported precious metals on which the monetary system increasingly depended, and because their trade contributed to an expansion in real income and output in the Bengal economy.[27] European trading posts began to appear along the major rivers. Most of these were in the western delta, but there were important settlements in what is now Bangladesh as well. Dhaka saw the Portuguese establish a textile trading post in the 1580s, the Dutch (who referred to prolific Bengal as 'the fat meadow') followed in the 1650s, the English in the 1660s and the French in the 1680s (Plate 4.2). There were many smaller settlements ('factories'). Some of these buildings can still be seen, for example the Dutch silk factory at Sardah on the Padma (now the Bangladesh Police Academy) and another one in Rajshahi city. Goods from Bengal (notably raw silk, textiles, opium and saltpetre) became essential to the Europeans in both intra-Asian trade and the export trade to Europe. By the 1660s almost half of the cargo that the Dutch sent to Japan consisted of goods from Bengal, and by the early 1700s about two-fifths of the total Dutch exports from Asia to Europe were procured in Bengal.[28] What the Europeans brought to Bengal was overwhelmingly precious metals – gold from Japan, Sumatra and Timor, silver from Japan, Burma and Persia, and silver coins from Mexico and Spain – but also copper, tin and a variety of spices such as pepper, cloves, nutmeg and cinnamon.

Goods from Bengal supported new lifestyles in Europe and began to educate Europeans about this part of the world. That education also

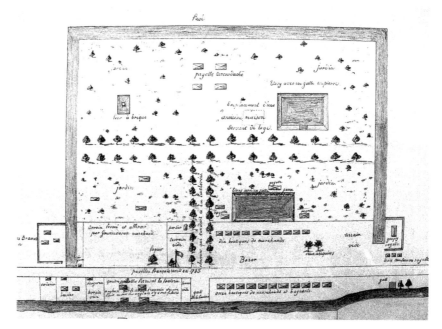

Plate 4.2 The French trading post in Dhaka, 1780s.[29]

included the marvels of Bengal's natural wealth. Perhaps the most famous of these was Clara, a rhinoceros born in northeastern Bangladesh or Assam in 1738 (Plate 4.3). She arrived in Europe in 1741 and made her owner a small fortune as he showed her around Europe's royal courts and to crowds who paid to see her. At the time very few Europeans had ever seen a rhino, and many doubted the animal's very existence. As a result, Clara became a celebrity.[30]

The inhabitants of the delta observed the European traders carefully and, whenever possible, used them to their own advantage. Sometimes the newcomers appeared as dangerous and predatory (the old Bengali term for the Dutch, *olandāj*, also means 'pirate') and sometimes as convenient partners in trade. Between the sixteenth and eighteenth centuries Europeans became more prominent in the Indian Ocean trade and their relationship with local traders varied from cooperation to conflict. Individual South Asian, Armenian and European traders collaborated in financing voyages to and from various Asian ports, and occasionally South Asian traders would charter a European ship and crew for freighting

Plate 4.3 Clara the rhinoceros. This engraving was made when she was on show in Mannheim (Germany) in 1747.

goods.[31] On the whole, however, the relationship was one of conflict because of European attempts to regulate shipping on the high seas by means of a passport system. The newcomers tried to deny South Asian traders the right to trade freely in Asian waters and sought to enforce monopolies in particular commodities and branches of Asian trade. Introduced by the Portuguese, this passport system was taken over by the Dutch and English. Today, bands of pirates, operating off the coast of Bangladesh and in the mouth of the river Meghna, use a remarkably similar system of passports for vessels passing through waters that they control.[32]

Despite these attempts at regulation, 'the distorting effect of this system on the operations of the Indian maritime merchants was quite small and confined to specific and limited time periods and branches of trade'.[33] Indian maritime trade on some routes, for example Southeast Asia, did decline from the late seventeenth century but this was not related to European competition or interference; rather, it was a result of political and economic changes in South Asia. At the same time trade from Bengal to other destinations, such as the Maldives, increased. The bulk of trade from the Bengal delta remained in the hands of local merchants, who had lower overhead costs and a more intimate understanding of the Asian markets and banking systems.[34] In other words, the Europeans' impact on the pre-colonial economy should not be exaggerated. Very likely European trade formed a net addition to the region's growing maritime trade. Bengal had a highly diversified society, and market exchange and cash transactions existed at various levels well before the upsurge in maritime trade.[35] Trade and manufacture formed a much smaller sector of the economy than agriculture, and the European trade companies were involved in only certain branches of maritime trade. They were mere 'minor partners' even in silk, the commodity they prized most highly. They were unable to control the silk market, unlike South Asian merchants who based their supremacy on exports of silk by both sea and land routes.[36]

The impact of European activities in the Bengal delta was not merely economic and political. When sailors from a shipwrecked Dutch vessel were washed ashore in Noakhali (eastern Bangladesh) in 1661, they found that fishermen and villagers spoke to them in Portuguese.[37] There were also Portuguese-speaking Africans who served as soldiers in various armies in the Bengal delta at the time.[38] The Portuguese had many small settlements in the districts of Borishal (Barisal), Patuakhali, Noakhali, Chittagong and Dhaka in which missionaries actively promoted Christianity and not without some success.[39] Here inhabitants were developing Christian identities at the same time as Islamic identities were taking shape in other parts of the delta.

In short, openness was an essential feature of the delta, adding a constant stream of goods to the economy and acting as a boon to local export industries. The Bengal delta was like a giant beehive, constantly humming with the mobility of its inhabitants as they were liaising between the sea, the plains and the mountains. They were not land-bound: their mobility took them well beyond the delta itself. For example, they participated in overseas trade in various roles: as merchants, as sailors and as producers of export products such as rice, textiles and ships. Last but not least, the openness of the delta also exposed the population to a constant stream of external cultural influences and new ideas.

Colonial Encounters

Part II Statue of poet Michael Madhusudan Dutt (1824–73) in Shagordari (Jessore district).

CHAPTER 5

From the Mughal Empire to the British Empire

On a fine June day in 1757, thousands of men were fighting in a mango orchard close to the border of present-day Bangladesh. This battle became famous as a turning-point in the history of South Asia. It took place in the small village of Polashi ('Plassey'; *palāsi*), and the encounter established the British East India Company as the new territorial overlord over Bengal. Within a century this trading conglomerate would capture practically all of South Asia. Historians have often described the Battle of Polashi as the beginning of British colonial rule in South Asia, a rule that would last until 1947.

In many ways Polashi is a useful marker of change. It ended a style of government that the Mughal state had introduced some 150 years previously. British rule introduced new ideas, arrangements and coercions that would shake Bengal's society profoundly. But these changes did not occur all at once, nor were they clustered tightly around the year 1757.

In Indian nationalist history writing, Polashi is often used as a marker of South Asian ignominy, when foreigners took control of the state and a colonial system of exploitation took effect. According to this narrative, it took an anti-colonial struggle to remove this blot on the national escutcheon: the colonial state was dismantled and sovereign power returned to indigenous rulers in 1947. From the perspective of Bangladesh history, however, this representation of Polashi is less helpful.

First, in the delta foreign rule long preceded the British conquest. Here the Mughal empire, centred in far-off Delhi, had taken control in 1612 after many battles with local opponents. The delta became one of the Mughals' conquered dependencies, a source of large amounts of tax and loot. In other words, before the British rose to power in Bengal, its inhabitants had long been accustomed to a mulcting administration dominated by foreign officials.

Second, Bangladesh historians emphasise that colonial rule did not come to an end when the British retreated in 1947: those who ruled the delta as part of the post-1947 state of Pakistan should also be considered as foreign colonialists. The Pakistan state was dominated by West Pakistani interests to such an extent that it led to a war of secession that created Bangladesh in 1971. The post-1971 state elite in Bangladesh were doubtless indigenous but according to many observers hardly sovereign, having been largely dependent for their survival on donations and direction from abroad.

What ended at the Battle of Polashi, then, was not indigenous rule in the Bengal delta but the *ancien régime* of the Mughal state. By this time, the power of the central Mughal state had weakened in Bengal but regional rulers had retained the structures and institutions of Mughal rule. Polashi marks the beginning of European colonial rule in Bangladesh. European colonialism ceased in 1947 but it was followed by Pakistani colonial rule (1947–71), and one way of describing the period since 1971 is as a period of neo-colonial domination.

THE MUGHALS IN BENGAL

When the first European adventurers arrived in the Bengal delta, they were bystanders who witnessed a turbulent process of state fragmentation. They saw how the delta was entering one of its periods of chaotic warfare as the Mughal state made many unsuccessful attempts to expand from its heartland in northern India into the riverine region of Bengal.[1] In 1538 the regional Husain Shahi state collapsed, and for a brief moment the Mughal emperor Humayun held its capital, Gaur. Soon, however, his army was defeated and he had to retreat to the west. Then followed a period in which numerous local chiefs and landholders (collectively known as the Baro Bhuiya (*bāra bhũiyã*), or 'twelve chiefs') controlled smaller parts of the delta. These were mostly Afghan and Bengali Hindu grandees, some from old ruling families and others new power grabbers. They formed anti-Mughal groupings and resisted renewed Mughal attempts to annex Bengal. The Mughals intensified their forays after they won an important battle in 1576, but it took their armies and flotillas another forty years to overcome intense resistance in the central and southern delta, a region they referred to as Bhati. Finally, in 1610, the Mughal governor fought his way east to Dhaka, which he fortified and renamed Jahangirnagar after the Mughal emperor Jahangir (Map 5.1).[2] He made it the capital of Bengal, mainly because it was best positioned to suppress resistance in the delta and to check the growing power of the Portuguese and Arakanese in the southeast. By 1612 he had subdued the local chiefs and reduced them to landholders acknowledging Mughal suzerainty. The Mughal state now covered the territory of Bangladesh, with the exception of the southeastern region of Chittagong (held by the Arakanese and Portuguese until 1666) and the Chittagong Hills (independent chiefdoms until 1860).[3]

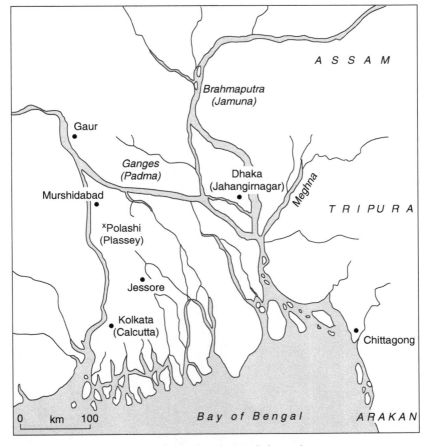

Map 5.1 Bengal in the Mughal period.

Thus began Mughal rule in the delta. In Bengal the structure of government was less uniform than in the Mughal heartland in north and central India. Rather than introducing a relatively integrated political system, the new rulers imposed a layer of centralised authority over quite disparate forms of local control. As a result, outside the urban areas local lords of varying grandeur were in charge of law and order. In many parts of the delta these lords – known to the Mughal state as zamindars (*jamindār* or *jamidār*) – remained semi-independent. They constituted 'a secular aristocracy – separated from the masses of the population by their military and political power and an appropriate life-style. It was an aristocracy open to the successful adventurer.'[4] They coexisted with appointed imperial officials who were from outside Bengal and who did not settle in Bengal. The main task of these officials was to ensure a steady flow of tax revenues to the imperial court in Delhi. To the people of the Bengal delta, this was the new dispensation's most important activity. The top revenue official in charge of the province of Bengal was the diwan (*deoyān*), appointed by the Mughal emperor himself.

Whenever the Mughals conquered an area in the delta, they set up several outposts with a garrison (*thānā*) to enforce the peace. Once this was achieved, the area was incorporated into the territorial system of Mughal administration in which a province (*subā*) consisted of a number of regions (*sarkār*), each comprising several subdivisions (*parganā*). The smallest territorial unit was the 'revenue village' or mouza (*maujā*), on which tax assessments were fixed. Three of these old terms are still in daily use in

Plate 5.1 Arakanese raiders selling slaves from the Bengal delta to Dutch traders at Pipli (now in India) in the 1660s (detail).[5]

Bangladesh: shorkar (*sarkār*) now means the government, thana (*thānā*) a police station or a county, and mouza (*maujā*) retains its old meaning of revenue village. Today many family names in Bangladesh – for example Sarkar, Khan, Choudhuri and Talukdar – are derived from titles that refer to positions in the Mughal landholding aristocracy.

The Mughal conquest brought Bengal devastation and brutality. Recurring military campaigns by both imperial forces and local rebels relied on scorched-earth tactics, killing, plunder and rape, for example, during the Mughal campaign to subdue the town of Jessore.[6] After the establishment of 'varying degrees of Mughal authority' in different parts of Bengal, more peaceful circumstances came about, but rebellions continued to occur and border regions were home to competing sovereignties.[7] In addition, Arakanese and Portuguese invaders marauded the coastal areas. According to one contemporary writer, Shihabuddin Talish, they took away no less than 42,000 slaves from various Bengal districts to Chittagong between 1621 and 1624 (Plate 5.1; see box 'Alaol, the translator-poet').[8]

Alaol, the translator-poet

The early seventeenth century was definitely not a safe time to travel the coastal waters of Bengal. One boy who learned this lesson the hard way was Alaol (*Ālāol*). He was born in Jalalpur village (Faridpur district) in 1607, the son of an official serving a local ruler. One day, when he and his father were travelling by boat to Chittagong, Portuguese and Arakanese pirates intercepted them. The attack left Alaol wounded and his father dead. The pirates took Alaol away and he ended up in Arakan, where he was put to work as a bodyguard or cavalry soldier.

Alaol was no ordinary slave, however. He was well educated and knew Bengali, Persian, Sanskrit and Hindi. Training in music was also part of his upbringing. These skills allowed him to leave menial work behind him: he was given a job as a music teacher and began to be known as a poet and songwriter. Soon Magan Thakur, an important poet-courtier at Arakan's royal court, took him under his wing and Alaol's career flourished.

The Arakan court was a cosmopolitan place. Its power was rapidly expanding and slave raids on coastal Bengal were an important strategy for acquiring much-needed skilled labour. In addition, the court attracted numerous mercenaries, notably Christians and Muslims, to man its naval forces. As a result, the court became a cultural and religious melting pot. It upheld the royal traditions of the Buddhist courts of Southeast Asia, but it also embraced the aristocratic traditions of the Muslim courts of Bengal. These circumstances guaranteed that Alaol's skills were appreciated.

Alaol wrote a treatise on music and composed songs in one of Arakan's court languages, Bengali, and then set to work to translate literary works into Bengali. Around 1650 he translated and adapted *Padmavati*, a romantic poem, originally in Hindi, about the doomed love of a Delhi sultan for a Sri Lankan princess. Later he specialised in translations of Persian romantic tales. Written in a courtly and elegant style and embellished with his own songs, his works gave Bengali poetry and music a new direction.[9]

To Mughal officials the Bengal delta remained throughout 'a "hell full of bread," a place of exile for incompetent officers and, in the declining days of the grand empire, a milch cow to suckle the famished army and administration of the whole subcontinent'.[10] On the other hand, however, the Mughal conquest eventually brought political unification to the delta, a more regulated system of surplus extraction and a relaxation of the constant fighting. More peaceful conditions led to an expansion of agricultural cultivation and to more agrarian and industrial prosperity (see box 'Poor and rich'). Bengal's political centre of gravity shifted east to the Dhaka region, which flourished and attracted traders as never before.

Poor and rich

There were great differences in wealth among the residents of the Bengal delta. The poor dressed in loincloths and saris made of coarse cotton or jute. They lived on a diet of rice, salt, vegetables and lentils, supplemented with some fish and milk. If they ate meat at all, it was likely to be chicken, mongoose, lizard, duck or porcupine (Plates 5.2 and 5.3).[11]

The rich wore elaborate clothes of fine cotton or silk, shoes, golden ornaments and precious stones. Their refined food included many varieties of fish, fowl, meat and vegetables, as well as milk-based sweets (Plates 5.4 and 5.5).

The Mughal government actively encouraged European trade, mainly because it yielded the imperial exchequer a handsome income from duties. At the same time the Mughal elite consumed a large array of goods from the Bengal delta. In addition to rice, textiles, sugar and salt, the delta sent to the Mughal court fragrant aloe wood and timber from Mymensingh, Sylhet and Chittagong; elephants and buffaloes from Jessore, Khulna, Borishal (Barisal) and Chittagong; eunuchs from Rangpur and Sylhet; betel nut and long pepper from Rajshahi and Bogra; horses from Rangpur and Bhutan; lac from the Sundarbans; and talking birds from various Bengal forests.[12]

Plate 5.2 A fish seller.

Plate 5.3 A fisherman.

Plate 5.4 A woman of distinction.

Plate 5.5 A man of distinction.[13]

THE FADING OF THE MUGHALS

After 1700 the influence of the Mughal imperial court over Bengal declined rapidly. A new diwan by the name of Murshid Quli Khan presided over a peaceful transition to independence from Delhi and his successors would style themselves nawabs (*nabāb*), or independent princes. He moved the provincial capital from Dhaka to Murshidabad and reformed revenue collection. By 1713 the posting of officials from Delhi stopped as the Mughal empire descended into disorder. Although Bengal was nominally still a province, it became independent under the nawabs, who were a non-Bengali dynasty. The last nawab of Bengal, Sirajuddaula, attempted to block unauthorised trade from the region. This led to repeated confrontations with British traders and his ultimate defeat at Polashi in 1757.[14] After further clashes, notably the Battle of Baksar (Buxar) in 1764, the British controlled not only the Bengal delta but also large swathes of land in the Ganges valley to the west.

Now a European trading corporation, the British East India Company, came to rule one of the most prosperous regions of Asia. Formally the Company became the diwan of Bengal (including Bihar and Orissa), but in reality it was wholly free from Mughal interference. It was a highly lucrative position. The Company could now marginalise European and Asian competitors in Bengal, exert much greater control over the producers of vital trade goods, and benefit from Bengal's well-organised system of land taxation. For the British the victory at Polashi marked not just the fact that it gained commercial, military and administrative control of an area much larger than Britain and with five times its population; it meant the beginning of empire. They used Bengal's riches to conquer the rest of India and other parts of Asia. For the people of Bengal the British victory at Polashi meant not just the emergence of yet another foreign overlord. It meant the beginning of European domination, new forms of capitalist exploitation, a racially ordered society and profound cultural change.

CHAPTER 6

British Legacies

European rule brought the people of Bengal economic upheaval, a social shake-up and a cultural kick in the teeth. The British were unlike the Mughals – they wanted more than just to extract Bengal's riches. It was their ambition to transform Bengal's economy to make it yield them much more income. To this end they combined experiences from Britain and Ireland with South Asian practices, subjecting the population of Bengal to an endless series of social, administrative and economic experiments.

Some of these turned out to be successful, others were downright disastrous. The early introduction of a system of increased tax collection proved to be calamitous in the uncertain natural conditions of Bengal. It was applied rigidly despite a depletion of people's incomes as a result of drought and then floods in 1769–70. Together with unchecked profiteering in the food-grain markets, this led to intense suffering and an epic famine which is still remembered as the 'Great Famine of 1176' (*chhiyāttarer manbantar*).[*] It is thought that one third of Bengal's population, or a staggering 10 million people, perished. This is how a nineteenth-century researcher described the famine:

All through the stifling summer of 1770 the people went on dying. The husbandmen sold their cattle; they sold their implements of agriculture; they devoured their seed-grain; they sold their sons and daughters, till at length no buyer of children could be found; they ate the leaves of trees and the grass of the field; and in June, 1770, the Resident at the Durbar affirmed that the living were feeding on the dead. Day and night a torrent of famished and disease-stricken wretches poured into the great cities. At an early period of the year pestilence had broken out. In March we find small-pox at Moorshedabad [Murshidabad] ... The streets were blocked up with promiscuous heaps of the dying and dead. Interment could not do its work quick enough; even the dogs and jackals, the public scavengers of the

---

[*] The Bengali calendar differs from the Common Era calendar (CE) in its starting point. It has solar years and each year begins in mid-April. Thus the year 2000 CE equals the year 1406/7 BE (Bengali Era) and the Great Famine of 1176 refers to the year 1769/70. For details, see Van Schendel (2001a).

East, became unable to accomplish their revolting work, and the multitude of mangled and festering corpses at length threatened the existence of the citizens . . . In 1770, the rainy season brought relief, and before the end of September the province reaped an abundant harvest. But the relief came too late to avert depopulation. Starving and shelterless crowds crawled despairingly from one deserted village to another in a vain search for food, or a resting-place in which to hide themselves from the rain. The epidemics incident to the season were thus spread over the whole country; and, until the close of the year, disease continued so prevalent as to form a subject of communication from the government in Bengal to the Court of Directors [in London]. Millions of famished wretches died in the struggle to live through the few intervening weeks that separated them from the harvest, their last gaze being probably fixed on the densely-covered fields that would ripen only a little too late for them.[1]

This unconscionable debacle forced the British overlords to find more sustainable ways of exploiting the resources of their new colony. They developed a plethora of policies that shaped a new colonial society. Historians of Bengal, who have concentrated their studies mostly on the British colonial period, have provided us with a richly textured and enormously detailed understanding of the complex social, economic and cultural permutations of Bengal under British rule between 1757 and 1947.[2] Here we highlight only a few major effects of special significance for the emergence of post-colonial Bangladesh.

A STATE SHAPED BY UNRULY NATURE

It was not easy to embed colonial governance in the water-soaked active delta. Ecological conditions and the extreme monsoon climate made this a landscape in continual flux. Like all rulers before and after them, the British had to deal with constantly moving land–water frontiers, impermanent rural settlements and the seasonality of communications. The unpredictability of nature, combined with heightened state ambitions, required flexible forms of administration.

But how to go about it? Early-colonial officials 'operated with two competing narratives – one coloured by their experiences of the devastating natural disasters and the other by their own ambition to establish an ordered agrarian landscape'.[3] This dilemma played out in many ways, for example, in the location of district towns, the nodes of state governance in the countryside. The British had serious apprehensions about health, natural hazards and the presumed delicacy of the European body – and these were as important as, and sometimes trumped, issues of central location with regard to tax collection and political and military control. District towns 'were invariably located on easily drainable and elevated land'. Even so, new worries about Europeans' health could lead to such towns being dismantled, as in the case of the district town of Backergunj in southern Bengal – it was relocated to Borishal (Barisal) town in 1801.[4]

Early-colonial officials were pulled between trying to constrain a rapid territorial advance – which could turn out to be reckless and expensive – and pushing ahead in search of more profit and revenue. As a result, the territorial expansion under the British East India Company – a mercantile corporation more interested in profits than in territorial control – proceeded haphazardly and in a much less resolute manner than many later observers assumed. This was not the story of an all-powerful juggernaut – a colonial state bullying a helpless colonised society into submission. It was the story of a budding state apparatus being at the mercy of natural and social forces and gingerly feeling its way forward.

The British had great difficulty devising bureaucratic, technical and legal tools to cope with the delta ecology. Their attempts to survey the territory and establish stable relationships with their colonial subjects were often defeated by nature's volatility. It was essential to survey the labyrinthine network of delta rivers and embankments, but this was an uphill task.[5] From year to year rivers wandered and submerged cultivated fields, threatening tax income and prompting cultivators to move to a new house and reclaim forests. Carefully drawn maps of the territory became obsolete within years. General rules turned out not to be applicable because local conditions varied enormously and were changing all the time. And local understandings of rights in land, produce, water and forests were difficult to codify in a flexible way. State officials were constantly struggling to make sense of the capricious natural environment – their actions were always shaped by climate and landscape. Numerous endlessly 'touring' officials embodied the day-to-day fluidity of governance. All over provincial Bengal, resthouses and temporary residences were constructed for these travellers, and the circuit houses, postal bungalows (*dāk bāṃlā*) and forest lodges that they frequented are still in official use today.

The early-colonial bureaucratic and legal solutions that the British devised to cope would cast a shadow of centuries: their after-effects are still noticeable in Bangladesh today, a new state faced with the same natural volatility. Among the most momentous solutions was a novel system of land rights and taxation that came to be known as the 'permanent settlement'.

THE PERMANENT SETTLEMENT

The permanent settlement was a system of land rights and taxation that enabled the British to distance their administration from the vagaries of nature and climate in the Bengal delta.[6] Introduced in 1790 and codified in 1793, it was important because it was more than merely a tax system. It formed the nucleus of the colonial system of control; other parts of the administration such as the executive, the judiciary and the police were geared to the desired working of the permanent settlement.[7] It survived with modifications into the 1950s and moulded social and economic relations in the delta to such an extent that contemporary Bangladesh society cannot be understood without reference to it.

The permanent settlement was a deal that the British East India Company struck with the tax-collecting rural gentry, the zamindars. The British (who arrogated the ultimate property rights of all land in Bengal) changed the role of the zamindars, who had previously been hereditary revenue farmers. They now became *de facto* landowners and the peasants became their tenants. The British fixed the tax demand in perpetuity and pledged that they would not enhance the rate in future. In return, the zamindars were bound to pay their taxes to the state, collected from their tenants, with clockwork punctuality on pain of their land being auctioned off. Such auctions happened quite regularly, ruining old landed families and making zamindari status attainable for moneyed social climbers.

The permanent settlement harnessed zamindari dominance of local society to the colonial regime, and zamindars became the mainstay of colonial control and extraction.[8] At the same time their power was circumscribed by the threat of expropriation in case of arrears in tax payments to the state. The British rulers had created an effective human buffer – the zamindars – between themselves and the capriciousness of the Bengal delta's environment and climate.

The administrative category of zamindar concealed an immense social spectrum. In some regions zamindars were opulent titled princes with enormous estates. Take the Rajshahi Raj family: it held sway over an estate of 13,000 km² and lived in a palace in Nator that is today owned by the Bangladesh state and in use as its Northern People's Mansion (*uttarā gaṇabhaban*). In other regions (for example Chittagong) zamindari holdings were typically much smaller, and sometimes tiny. Moreover, inheritance rules were partible, so over time zamindari rights came to be shared by many descendants; it was not at all uncommon to come across individuals who owned a mere one-sixty-fourth share in an estate. Yet all of them were subject to the same rules, forged to provide the British rulers with an assured tax income from millions of peasants without the inconvenience of having to bother with its risky collection.

The expectation behind the permanent settlement was that, over time, zamindars would become improving landlords who would invest in agricultural development. Fixed government taxes, rising produce prices and new land under the plough would leave more and more wealth in the zamindars' hands. By reinvesting in agriculture, they would boost the delta's economy. This did not happen, however, partly because zamindars lacked government support for agricultural development, improvement of infrastructure, technological innovation and marketing, and partly because there were easier ways to grow rich.

Popular strategies included squeezing the peasantry by (illegally) increasing rents and forcing tenants to pay contributions to events in the zamindar's family such as marriages, festivals, pilgrimages and funerals. The zamindars could enforce these illegal payments despite the fact that the permanent settlement had stripped them of their pre-British policing powers. In an attempt to discipline rural society, the British had set up a salaried police force answerable to state officials, but the zamindars were able to retain power over village policemen and they also hired bands of armed retainers to control their tenants. The state judicial system rarely reached down below the district level; and when it did, it had to find ways to accommodate landlords and village elders and their local ways of dispensing justice. These local ways outlived the British colonial period and the demise of the zamindars: in Bangladesh informal village dispute management by means of public gatherings (mojlish; *majlis*) easily survived into the twenty-first century.

As their incomes grew, zamindars began to distance themselves from agriculture and tax-collecting. They turned themselves into rentiers and shifted their responsibilities to intermediaries. Bengal's peasants produced so much wealth that these intermediaries were often able to follow the zamindars' example by appointing their own intermediaries. In this way, a multitiered system of leisured tenure-holders developed, all living off the wealth of the land. This system, known as sub-infeudation or pottonidari (*pattanidāri*), was most developed in what is now southern Bangladesh. For example, in the district of Borishal (Barisal) you had to cut through five to seven layers of intermediate tenures to get to the tiller of the soil.[9] In this way, the permanent settlement encouraged the development of a very hierarchical social structure dominated by an extensive leisured class.

There was another reason why the permanent settlement was a system with momentous consequences: it denied the peasantry any property rights in land. Previously there had been complex and locally variable bundles of property rights vested in both peasant producers and land-lords. Now these rights were granted only to the landlords who could freely sell, mortgage or gift their land. In the eyes of the law, cultivators became mere tenants with a right to work the land – if they paid their rent regularly – but they could transfer this 'occupancy right' only by inheri-tance, not by sale. Not all tenants acquired occupancy rights, and over time a growing proportion of cultivators were no more than tenants-at-will whom the landlord could eject at any time. In this way colonial rural Bengal came to be dominated by zamindari landowners whose land was tilled by tenants with occupancy rights – in which case they were known as *rāiyat* – or without such rights.

The zamindari gentry benefited enormously from the colonial state's patronage. Many of them grew very rich indeed, acquired the lifestyle of aristocrats and built palatial mansions on their estates (Plate 6.1). Some also developed new cultural sensibilities (see box 'First-rate art in a country town').

Plate 6.1 Remains of a zamindari mansion in central Bangladesh (*Baliati rājbāri* (palace), Manikganj district).[10]

First-rate art in a country town

In contemporary Bangladesh the zamindari landlords are remembered mainly as a bossy and parasitic gentry. Their grandiose lifestyle was based on the exploitation of peasant labour, and it is true that most of them gave little in return. There were exceptions, however: landlords who set up rural schools, libraries and clinics, improved the infrastructure of their estates, donated water supply systems or provided their tenants with support in times of scarcity.

Plate 6.2 Twenty-four enlightened ascetics are depicted on this stone sculpture from Dinajpur district. A votive object linked to the Jain religion, it dates from the ninth century. The Varendra Museum received it as a donation in 1933.

One priceless inheritance of zamindari initiative is the Varendra Research Museum in Rajshahi, a town in western Bangladesh. It is Bangladesh's oldest museum, established in 1910 by a group of aristocratic history buffs who wanted to promote the study of North Bengal. They gave their museum the ancient name for this region – the term also survives in 'Barind', the modern name for much of northern Bangladesh. The initiators of the Varendra Museum undertook numerous trips around the region to gather objects of antiquarian value, and they even sponsored and organised archaeological digs. Soon the museum was filling up with an outstanding collection from different historical periods.

After its main benefactors died, or fled to India in 1947, the museum went through a long period of serious neglect. Luckily, its collections survived this dark interlude and have now regained much of their former glory. Today the museum is best known for its spectacular sculptures of Hindu, Jain and Buddhist deities from the ninth to the twelfth centuries, its stone inscriptions, coins and terracottas, and a large collection of ancient palm-leaf manuscripts (Plate 6.2).[11]

At the same time the composition of the zamindari elite changed. Whereas Muslims had dominated during the reclamation of the eastern delta in the Mughal period, the British period saw an advance of Hindu landlords. Although neither Muslim zamindars nor Hindu tenants were rare by any means, in many parts of the eastern delta religious and class identities began to merge, with Hindu zamindars at the apex of a local society consisting largely of Muslim cultivators. In the western delta Hindu zamindars dominated as well but here the majority of the cultivators were also Hindus. This regional difference had no political ramifications in the early period of British rule, but it would become a highly salient political question towards its end.

CROPS FOR FAR-FLUNG MARKETS

A second major change during the British era was the introduction of large-scale export-oriented cash cropping. Earlier, Bengal's agriculture had been considerably commercialised, producing cotton, rice, sugar cane, mulberry, betel nut, opium and many other crops for various markets. These crops had been processed in Bengal's industries (for example cotton and silk textile manufacture) and often exported. In other words, commercial crop production was nothing new and cultivators had long been involved in market transactions, both as producers and as consumers.[12] What set the

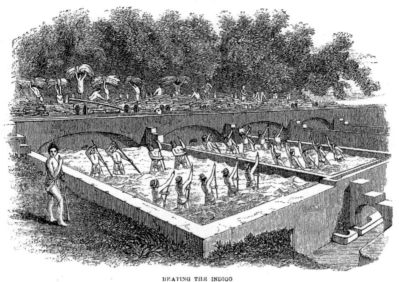

BEATING THE INDIGO

Plate 6.3 Producing indigo – a blue dyestuff derived from a field crop – for export to Europe.

British period apart, however, was the organisation of cash cropping, the scale of its production and a succession of new crops that began to be produced for overseas markets. European and South Asian capital was invested in the large-scale production of 'commodities of empire' – opium, indigo, tea, silk and jute – and the construction of railways to expedite exports. Some of these crops were grown under systems of coerced labour, others on plantations – capitalist agricultural enterprises run by Europeans – and yet others by indebted smallholders (Plate 6.3).

Cash cropping was important because it forged new ties between Bengal's rural economy and European and Asian markets. British imperial expansion, in South Asia as well as elsewhere in the continent, was buttressed by the wealth generated in Bengal, and at the same time cash cropping had a number of fundamental effects on the delta's society. It led to the beginnings of a developmentalist state (which would expand greatly after decolonisation)[13] and a new regional specialisation of the Bengal economy: sugar, indigo and silk were concentrated in western Bangladesh; eastern Bangladesh became the heartland of jute production; and tobacco was widespread in the north. Particular forms of social organisation and land control were associated with these crops.[14] In eastern Bangladesh peasant smallholders were faced with dwindling holdings resulting from population growth and partible inheritance. Unable to feed their families with subsistence crops alone, they were forced into market production. The regional economy became highly monetised as foreign funds flowed in to finance agrarian exports – mainly jute – and credit-dependent peasant producers were fully exposed to international market uncertainties.[15] By contrast, in northern and western Bangladesh rural elites were major providers of agrarian credit, often in the form of rice loans to sharecroppers, and this shielded the primary producers from the direct effects of market forces.[16]

Both regional systems were affected by the world economic crisis of the 1930s. Eastern Bangladesh was particularly hard hit because the market for jute collapsed, credit dried up and it was impossible to return to the subsistence agriculture of the nineteenth century for lack of sufficient land. The result was widespread immiseration.[17] Old relations of social and political control broke down, giving way to increasingly violent conflicts between peasants and the regional elite made up of moneylenders, traders and landlords. In northern and western Bangladesh, the crisis initially intensified sharecroppers' and labourers' dependence on the grain-lending elite, but when land and crop prices recovered a decade later, sharecroppers began to demand better conditions, culminating in widespread agitations in the closing years of British rule.

NEW INSTITUTIONS OF RULE

Mughal rule had brought important administrative innovations to the Bengal delta. British rule introduced further major changes, some of which were to have long-lasting effects. The permanent settlement, discussed earlier in this chapter, was just one example of new ideas about law and rights that were translated into novel judicial institutions. Another was personal law, which was codified separately for followers of different religions. By treating certain classical religious writings as canonical legal texts, British intervention created four unified systems of personal law that deviated from, and dismissed, local customs and practices. Thus Muslims, Hindus, Buddhists and Christians in Bengal came to live under discrete systems of personal law that survive, with small adaptations, in Bangladesh today.[18]

A further example was the language of rule and education. By the 1830s the British dropped Persian – the Mughal language of rule – as the state's official language. English-language schools and colleges trained a small proportion of the Bengali elite to prepare them for employment at the lower and middle levels of the colonial system. Two modern universities were set up in Kolkata (1857) and Dhaka (1921) and quickly established excellent academic reputations. Bengalis learned to see 'the West' and the wider world through British eyes and the filter of English-language texts, and this would be a lasting imprint. Long after decolonisation, Britain remained a cultural and moral yardstick and a resource for interpreting the world, until this position was gradually taken over by another former British colony, the United States, around the turn of the twenty-first century.

Education in the Bengali language also expanded under British rule. There was a long pre-colonial history of village education in public localities and private houses, usually funded by villagers themselves. Children learned to read and write in locally useful languages (Bengali for most; Persian, Arabic, Sanskrit, Pali, Chakma or Marma for some), as well as arithmetic, agricultural and commercial practice, and moral principles.[19] During the British period, Christian missionaries and, later, the government supported Bengali-language primary schools in towns and some villages, and a select group of children became literate. The vast majority of children did not go to school, however, because the curriculum was of little or no relevance to their working lives. They remained illiterate and received informal education from their families and local religious specialists.

This mixed English/Bengali educational system, introduced by the British, existed side by side with remnants of indigenous forms of religious education, and this arrangement still characterises contemporary education in Bangladesh: formal English-language schools coexist with Bengali-language ones, and religious education is imparted separately, primarily in Islamic schools known as moktobs (*maktab*; Plate 6.4) and madrashas (*mādrāsā*). It is only in recent years that some linguistic minorities in Bangladesh have been allowed to teach their primary-school-age children in their mother tongues.[20]

Education also took place outside formal education, for example regarding hygiene and health. Scientific medical ideas were not necessarily appropriate to the realities of medical practice in Bengal. As one European observer warned in 1855: 'The greatest danger which appears to beset the Native Medical Student is that of becoming too exclusively *English* in his lore and in his practice.'[21] Even so, Bengali-language texts began to spread new ideas about hygiene and health to many. British-era

Plate 6.4 Children studying at a moktob on Bangladesh's southernmost edge,
St. Martin's Island, 2003.

demographic growth is thought to have owed much to the fact that
people learned more about hygiene, and that medical practitioners had
access to better medicines and new health institutions – clinics and
hospitals.[22]

As communications improved across the Bengal delta – roads,
bridges and railways made transport less dependent on waterways –
the movement of goods and people accelerated. But there was
a downside: the railways are thought to have had a disastrous effect
on the delta's ecology. Their high embankments blocked waterways,
created stagnant water bodies (which became breeding grounds for
malaria), increased flooding and contributed to the agrarian stagnation
of the late-colonial period.[23] In other words, they were an early example of what became a familiar occurrence in what is now Bangladesh:
technocratic 'development' interventions that fail to factor in their
ecological price tag.

Technological advances such as the telegraph, telephone and radio made
it easier to spread information, and the span of state control increased as
the police and army became better funded and organised. The state

remained firmly authoritarian, but political pressure compelled the British to experiment cautiously with restricted forms of popular representation in the closing decades of their rule.

These institutional innovations proved to be long-lived: despite turbulent state formation since British times, they remain clearly visible in Bangladesh's judicial, educational, health, engineering, military and political institutions today, as well as in the condescending treatment citizens often receive from bureaucrats. Even today, Bangladeshi citizens regularly have to use the tactics of colonial subjects – such as obsequious behaviour, handing over bribes, and offering petitions written in flowery and deferential style – to move state officials and politicians to lend them their ear.

SUFISM AND ITS OTHERS

British rule forced the inhabitants of the Bengal delta to reconsider many aspects of their worldviews. Their confrontation with a European culture, a racialised social order, a proselytising religion and Orientalist attitudes (which degraded local cultures as exotic and less advanced) had a great impact on their self-esteem. The new situation required a cultural response. It set in train a judicious recombination of social resources that would continue throughout the British era and helped shape the culture of contemporary Bangladesh.

To understand Bangladesh today it is especially important to look at how this response produced a new confrontation within Islam. In Chapter 3 we have seen that, in this region, Islam was not a religion of the sword or trade. It was not imposed from above but grew very gradually as an ideology of taming the forest and promoting settled agriculture. It became the religion of those who reclaimed the delta. Its cultural roots were twofold. Sufi mystics (pir; *pīr*) had been trickling into the region for centuries, and they had made Islamic ideas and practices accessible to the delta cultivators. Little by little these ideas and practices merged with locally existing religious ideas and worldviews, and finally came to dominate them. By the time the British conquered the delta, most inhabitants thought of themselves as Muslims. Theirs was a faith of rich diversity that converged on worship, devotion and spiritual union with Allah – core elements of Sufi understandings of the Quran and Hadith.[24]

Muslim religious life revolved around spiritual guides, shrines and mosques. Village mosques were used for daily prayer and contemplation but the thousands of tomb-shrines that dotted the delta served another purpose. Known as mazar (*mājār*) or dorga (*dargā*), these saintly buildings embodied the spiritual and miraculous power of departed Sufi mystics who continued to act as conduits between the devotee, the Prophet and Allah. Shrines and other commemorative objects such as amulets and food – and even animals such as pigeons, fishes, crocodiles, turtles and monkeys – were considered to be full of the saint's charisma and blessing, and therefore they attracted pilgrims and supplicants eager to partake of the sanctified power (see box 'Reptilian blessings').[25] The ritual high point was the annual commemoration of the saint's death, known as urs (*urs, orch*), when thousands gathered to recall the saint's miracles in songs, dance and prayers.

Reptilian blessings

Coming upon a huge man-made pond in southwestern Bangladesh, you may wonder why a throng of people are gathered at its edge, staring intently at its tranquil water. A man calls out two names – Kalapahar and Dholapahar – and something stirs. As people start muttering, an old bearded man in skullcap flings a chicken into the pond. It turns out that these people are communing with a portly crocodile.

It was shortly after 1400 CE that an enterprising pioneer appeared in the Sundarban forest. His name was Khan Jahan Ali, an ethnic Uzbek or Turk. He was a classic charismatic colonist, keen to turn the forest into cultivable fields and able to achieve this by mobilising labour based on his reputation for religious power and piety. He reclaimed a large tract of land over which he ruled, and his followers constructed settlements, mosques and roads, and they dug truly enormous ponds. The one we are looking at covers a surface of some 60 hectares (or 150 acres). In it Khan Jahan Ali is thought to have kept crocodiles that he named Kalapahar and Dholapahar.

Khan Jahan Ali became famous as a Sufi mystic, and when he died in 1459 he was buried in the shrine that he had built on the bank of the pond. This burial place marking the frontier between land and water became a very prominent centre of Islamic devotion, and today, almost 600 years later, it is still a magnet for believers. Every day hundreds come to visit and pray, to circumambulate and touch the tomb, to donate money and buy souvenirs, and, most importantly, to receive the saint's blessing. His spiritual power is everywhere, mediated through the building and various objects, as well as through the sacred crocodiles in the pond. Devotees know that feeding them a chicken or a goat will bring good fortune and the fulfilment of their desires.

Plate 6.5 A sacred crocodile waiting for a ritual offering at Khan Jahan Ali's tomb, Bagerhat district, 2006.

During British rule this faith began to come under attack from groups who considered themselves to be more orthodox and who strove to 'purify' Islamic practices. They claimed to have a better, more doctrinaire interpretation of Islamic texts than Sufis had, and they were hostile to mystics and their role as spiritual guides. Most importantly, they rejected the notion that Islam could have multiple, equivalent, local forms and sought to impose a single, universal ritual format. They wanted to 'restore' the faith to what they thought of as its pristine piety, and they fought against what they considered its degeneration and un-Islamic elements.

The first wave of this rectifying campaign came in the 1820s and 1830s and was led by preachers who had spent long years in Mecca. They returned home with ideas derived from Arabian Wahhabism and the teachings of Shah Wali Allah of Delhi. These had produced puritanical movements whose more militant strands were keen to establish a muscular and politically resilient Islam. Among the best-known proponents in Bengal were Haji Shariatullah, who initiated the Faraizi movement, and Titu Mir, who headed the Tariqah-i-Muhammadiyah movement.[26] Both these religious purification movements would end up violently confronting the zamindars and the colonial state. The tension they articulated between two streams of Islam in colonial Bengal – Sufi-inspired, locally embedded spirituality and reformist puritanism[27] – would wax and wane over the generations and flare up with each new attempt at 'purifying' Bengali Islam. The most recent wave took off around the turn of the twenty-first century and is currently ongoing in Bangladesh.

THE EMERGENCE OF OPPOSITIONAL RELIGIOUS CATEGORIES

As we have seen, the long-term interplay of different frontiers has given contemporary Bangladesh culture a particularly multilayered structure. These layers have always been in motion. It is no exaggeration to say that some of the identity shifts that occurred during British rule were fateful because they are still highly relevant in Bangladesh today. Foremost among these was the creation of two new political categories – 'Hindu' and 'Muslim' – which emerged at the turn of the twentieth century. These must be understood as new categories: they had only a superficial resemblance to previous meanings of these terms. Various forms of Islam and Hinduism had, of course, been important markers of worldview and social position in Bengal for centuries, but there was no overarching sense of a single 'Muslim community' or 'Hindu community'. The people adhering to each of these worldviews distinguished themselves from co-religionists in many ways – by class, sect, jurisprudence, gender and residence – and these identities were often more meaningful to them. In addition, the religious landscape of the Bengal delta was far more intricate. There were many who identified neither with 'Hinduism' nor with 'Islam' but with other faiths. Some of these are well known – for example, Buddhism and Christianity – but others less so. Among the local religions that came into existence during the British period are, for example, Matua and Trinath.[28]

It was under British rule that, for the first time, specific versions of Hindu and Muslim identity became politically acute. This resulted from a combination of factors that were not restricted to Bengal but concerned all of British India. First, British attempts to 'read' the colonised leaned heavily on categorisation by creed. They canonised religious identities in legal practice (for example personal law) and in the population censuses, which sought to order society by grouping people according to faith, sect and caste, as well as by 'race', 'tribe' and language. Second, British occupation fired various reformist movements. Some of these stressed the need for Muslims to unite against the foreign rulers and to emancipate themselves vis-à-vis Hindus. Others were concerned with the proper education of women of different faith communities or the emancipation of groups of low-caste Bengalis.[29] Third, such ideas gathered strength as communications across the delta became easier with improved infrastructure and the dissemination of thought in print.

Things came to a head in 1905, when the British decided to divide Bengal into an eastern and a western half (see Chapter 8). At this point community identities irrevocably crystallised around the religious, pitching 'Muslim' against 'Hindu', and oppositional 'communal' politics was born. Ever since, politics and religious identity have been inextricably intertwined in Bengal.

THE RISE OF KOLKATA

A final major change during the British period was the emergence of Calcutta (now Kolkata) as the new centre of political power and cultural renewal. The city, established by the British in 1690, became the capital of colonial Bengal and, as British power expanded, also the capital of all of colonial India. This is where the government of India resided from 1757 to 1931. Up to the mid-nineteenth century this government was headed by successive governors-general who were appointed by the directors of the British East India Company. From 1858 the British monarch appointed the head of the government of India, now styled the Viceroy of India. Kolkata was the nerve centre of the colonial administration, and it developed rapidly. Ambitious Bengalis of all kinds soon flocked to the city. Among them were the scions of wealthy families with landed estates, often in the eastern delta, who set the cultural tone. Many soon acquired an English education and took up professions or positions in the colonial state. Historians later labelled this group, in which upper-caste Hindus predominated, the 'bhodrolok' (*bhadralok*; gentlefolk).[30] These people distinguished themselves from the vast majority of Bengalis, whom they referred to as 'chhotolok' (*choṭalok*), a pejorative term that can be translated as 'lowly people' or 'the little man'. The bhodrolok became pre-eminent cultural brokers between ordinary Bengalis and the British overlords, not just in Kolkata but also in the provincial towns and zamindari mansions of the East Bengal countryside.[31] Throughout Bengal, many sought to emulate the distinct and refined Kolkata-orientated bhodrolok lifestyle, but in eastern Bengal, where it was closely associated with (absentee) landlordism, elitism and casteism, this lifestyle was also deeply resented. Here, in market towns and small cities, a distinct mofussil (*maphasval*; countryside)

intelligentsia was taking shape. In post-colonial eastern Bengal the ideas,
lifestyle and politics of the 'little man' would turn into crucial cultural
resources.

Colonial Kolkata was more than Bengal's prime administrative and
cultural city. It also emerged as its commercial and economic hub.
Valuable cash crops such as opium (for the Chinese market) and indigo
and tea (for the European market) were trans-shipped in its port, and
sailors from eastern Bengal boarded seagoing vessels here. Jute from the
fields of eastern Bengal was processed in Kolkata's many jute factories
before being exported worldwide. From the 1850s a network of railway lines
began to radiate from Kolkata to speed up the transport of goods from the
hinterland. In the early-colonial period, many industrial centres in eastern
Bengal had stagnated or decayed. The most dramatic example was Dhaka,
which, until the early eighteenth century, had been the capital of Bengal
and, until the British takeover, a major textile-exporting city. By 1800,
however, British commercial policies and the rise of Kolkata had led to
a sharp decline.[32] Dhaka's exports of fine textiles had halved and would
soon disappear; its population had shrunk to about 200,000 and would
dwindle to about 50,000 in the 1840s, Dhaka's lowest point (Plate 6.6).[33]

Plate 6.6 A view of Dhaka in 1823 ('The Great Kuttra', by Charles D'Oyly).

After that Dhaka began to recover gradually, mainly as a result of the jute trade and administrative expansion, but it did not recover the population level of 1800 until the 1930s and did not regain its industrial prowess until the 1970s.

After victory on the battlefield of Polashi in 1757, the British East India Company had proceeded to turn Bengal into the hub of its expanding colony of British India. A century later all of South Asia was ruled from Kolkata (now the second city of the British empire). The East India Company was no longer in charge: the British Crown had nationalised the colony and taken over direct control of India after the Indian Rebellion of 1857, in which Bengal had not been a hotspot. The Indian Ocean was now a 'British sea' because it was surrounded by territories under British jurisdiction. The Bengal delta became tightly integrated into the world economy, but under political and economic conditions that its residents could not control. A few of them benefited enormously from colonial patronage, but for many without close links to the colonial overlords it was a period of hardship.

CHAPTER 7

A Closing Agrarian Frontier

When the British annexed eastern Bengal in 1757, it was a largely rural society. When they left 190 years later, it was still overwhelmingly rural – 96 per cent of all people lived in the countryside. In the meantime, however, much had changed. After the depopulation of the late eighteenth century, the more fertile eastern and southern districts supported denser populations than the western and northern ones. Towns and cities shrank as industries disappeared. Bengal's ruralisation did not stop until the mid-nineteenth century, after which towns began to grow again, but slowly.

By 1901 the territory that was to become Bangladesh had 30 million inhabitants, but only 2.5 per cent (0.7 million) of them lived in towns and cities. Although by 1947 there were 42 million inhabitants, the four largest cities were small – Dhaka had about 250,000 inhabitants, Chittagong 200,000, Khulna 60,000 and Rajshahi 40,000 – and the urban population represented only 4 per cent of the total. In other words, at the end of British colonial rule, almost everyone in eastern Bengal earned their living in the countryside and would think of themselves as 'gramer lok' (*grāmer lok*): village people. Most of them were engaged in agriculture.

During the colonial period the agrarian economy underwent important change.[1] As eastern Bengal's industrial exports declined, its agrarian exports expanded. Driven by extensive capital investments, export crops – such as indigo and later jute – transformed the agrarian economy. Small market towns (gonj; *gañj*) developed along rivers and railway lines, connecting rural producers to global markets. Under the 'permanent settlement', agrarian production increased by means of a steady expansion of cultivated area rather than improved technology or higher productivity. Landlords were happy to appropriate agrarian surpluses to sustain their comfortable lifestyle, but they did not invest in agriculture. Cultivators, who often had to support several layers of landlords, were unable to introduce new technology such as improved seeds, commercial fertilisers, irrigation or better implements. The result was a 'horizontal' expansion: agrarian production grew because cultivators brought more and more land under the plough.

The state and the peasants saw eye to eye on this: the state welcomed horizontal expansion (or land grab) because it saw the transformation of 'wastelands' into settled rice fields as a productive use of the delta environment. Peasant reclamation did not cost the state anything and it augmented state income from land taxation. It also helped lessen the ecological uncertainties that the state faced in governing the waterlogged landscape, and in bringing the unruly residents of the shifting alluvial lands, watery mangroves, forested lands and wandering rivers under control.[2]

By the end of the nineteenth century, however, a period of relative prosperity came to an end as the population grew (leading to rural crowding and fragmentation of agricultural holdings) and the extension of cultivation reached its natural limits. Much of the last remaining forest had been reclaimed – sometimes by specialised groups such as immigrant Santals and Oraons in northwestern Bangladesh – as had coastal and river islands, and much of the Sundarban mangrove swamp in the south.

SELF-RESCUE BY OUT-MIGRATION

Bengal's cultivators were now fast running out of land and sliding into debt. They countered this crisis by various means: pushing up agrarian output by multiple cropping (planting two or three crops on the same plot during the year), intensifying cultivation (applying more labour to increase yields) and reducing post-harvest crop losses. They also curtailed their consumption and diversified their sources of income, often seasonally, by taking to wage labour, fishing and petty trade. Many migrated from the densely populated parts of eastern Bangladesh to western and northern Bangladesh, where they could still find land to cultivate or work as labourers (see Map 7.1 and box 'Nozir the migrant'). They began to move beyond the delta region as well – to Arakan, Assam and Tripura. This was the beginning of a long-term trend, continuing today, in which tens of millions of Bangladeshis left their homeland in search of a better life.[3]

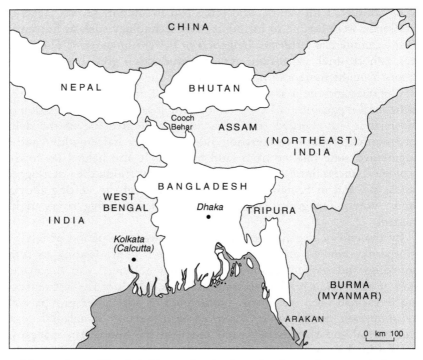

Map 7.1 Areas of Bangladeshi out-migration from the nineteenth century: Arakan, Assam and Tripura. The map shows today's state borders.

Nozir the migrant

In the late 1940s a not uncommon disaster struck the village of Chor Mozlishpur in Noakhali, a district in southeastern Bangladesh. The nearby river changed its course and submerged many fields, destroying the livelihood of numerous cultivators. What to do? There was no local employment to be had, so the affected households decided to look for work elsewhere. First the men left. They wandered north to Mymensingh and Assam and from there into Rangpur, working as day-labourers and religious teachers. They formed a very loose-knit party, sometimes travelling together, more often alone, but catching up with one another via messages sent through fellow migrants. One group decided to stay in Assam, because, as one of them put it later, 'the people there are not as clever as we are; there's a lot of money to be earned from them'. Another group favoured Rangpur in northern Bangladesh because they thought the climate was healthier than that of Assam, while the local people were, in their opinion, equally slow-witted. A third group moved on to the neighbouring district of Dinajpur.

The small group in Rangpur worked as day-labourers in several villages. One of them was Nozir, then about thirty-five years old. He found a large plot of uncultivated land in a village called Goborgari, inhabited by Hindus. The local landlord was willing to give the plot in tenure to anyone who was willing to pay the land tax. Nozir decided to take the risk, and he and his teenage son began the arduous job of clearing away the shrubs and trees in their free time. When they finally succeeded, they planted garlic on the newly reclaimed field and soon reaped a fair harvest. With the money thus earned they set out to Noakhali, some 450 km away, to gather their family. As Nozir remembered thirty years later:

'At that time I had two sons and four daughters. Their mother was young and healthy then. We built a shack on the cleared land. The local people here just looked on. They needed us, for labour was not easily had in those days, and they liked to have labourers right at their doorstep. That first year was very tough, with all those mouths to feed, but we made it somehow. Then I asked my wife's brother to join us. He was very religious and could start a proper mosque here. He took a plot in tenure, found work as a religious teacher in another village, and soon was building his own hut. From then on the nephews and cousins started arriving.'

Relations between the newcomers and the original inhabitants of Goborgari were strained. Nozir's policy was to recruit as many relatives and near-relatives as possible to settle around him in order to ensure both safety and respect. He was highly successful: by the 1970s Noakhali immigrants made up almost half of the village and Nozir had become their esteemed patriarch (Plate 7.1).[4]

Plate 7.1 Nozir (first row, far right) amidst his sons, nephews and cousins during Id prayers in Goborgari village, 1975.

CAUSES OF POPULATION GROWTH

In addition to emigration, Bengal's cultivators intensified another important strategy: high fertility. Unlike some other peasantries, they did not
practise fertility control on a large scale: the age of marriage for women was
extremely low, the proportion of unmarried adults was negligible, contra-
ception was uncommon, and adoption was not used extensively to 'redis-
tribute' children. In the nineteenth century high reproduction was an
effective way to counter both high mortality and landlord demands: it
ensured a regular expansion of the household's labour supply, which made
it possible to cultivate more land and do so more intensely, thereby
increasing household income. Bengal's population was growing at the
moderate rate of about 1 per cent a year. In the long run, however, the
very success of this strategy became its undoing. What had been developed
as a means of staving off poverty gradually turned into a factor that
increased it. As the safety-valve of the open agrarian frontier closed,
cultivators continued to reproduce at a high rate because there were no
better alternatives and because high fertility provided short-term gains,
especially additional household labour.[5]

From the mid-nineteenth century the population began to grow, and
the rate of growth began to accelerate.[6] In 1872 the first population census
revealed that 23 million people were living in the territory that is now
Bangladesh, a figure that doubled in the mid-twentieth century and has
multiplied more than sevenfold today.

Nowadays Bangladesh is a truly huge society crammed into a very small
area. Roughly the size of Wisconsin or Greece, Bangladesh now has a larger
population than Russia or Japan. It is the eighth most populous country on
earth. Bangladesh is also one of the most densely populated countries on
earth: with a total area of 144,000 km^2 (and a land area of 133,000 km^2) it
has 1,265 persons per km^2, compared to 59 for the world, 149 for Asia and
464 for India.[7] For Bangladeshis this has meant making do with tremen-
dously diminished access to space and resources. Today each Bangladeshi
has less than a quarter of the space that his or her forebears enjoyed
a hundred years ago; by 2050 (when, according to predictions, there will
be over 200 million Bangladeshis) it is likely to be one tenth (Figure 7.1).

Rural crowding became a problem because agricultural productivity did
not increase to keep up with it. On the contrary, from the turn of the
twentieth century per capita output declined. As rural prosperity diminished, life became less secure for many and poverty increased noticeably.

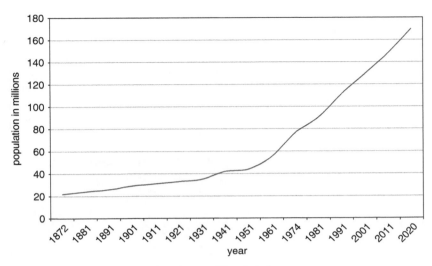

Figure 7.1 Population of Bangladesh, 1872–2020.

There were also environmental changes that made life more difficult (see box 'An unwanted import').

An unwanted import

In April 1939 all over the Bengal delta people could be seen pulling up clumps of bright green plants with beautiful lilac flowers from rivers, canals and ponds. The government had launched 'Water Hyacinth Week', a concerted effort to eradicate the floating aquatic weed.

Water hyacinth, a native of Brazil, had begun its worldwide expansion in the late nineteenth century. It may have been a Scottish jute merchant from Narayanganj who imported it from Australia to Bengal as an ornamental botanic curiosity around 1900. It spread with extraordinary rapidity, using its 'bladder-like leaf stalk and sail-like leaves' to travel with the wind, even against the stream, and propagating with incredible speed. It had found a perfect environment in the moist, warm climate of Bengal. Soon it choked up the waterways and rice fields of the delta and it moved up the Brahmaputra river into Assam. By the 1920s it was considered an environmental, economic and health disaster of the first order. Rice and fish cultivation became difficult in many places, inland navigation was hampered, and the weed was accused of causing cholera and other diseases.

How to deal with it? Was it a pest or an opportunity? Could it be used fruitfully in any way or should it be destroyed? Some thought the plant's ash could be used as a fertiliser, its fibres could be put to some commercial purpose or the plants could be pressed into solid building blocks. Others considered eradication to be the only solution. The latter group won the battle and in 1936 the Water Hyacinth Act was passed to eradicate the unwanted import from the Bengal delta. The plant proved a truly formidable adversary, however. It easily survived chemical sprays, popular mobilisation during Water Hyacinth Week and the efforts of successive post-colonial states. Today it is totally domesticated in Bangladesh, floating quietly and persistently on practically all water bodies – as beautiful, useless and unmanageable as ever (Plate 7.2).[8]

Plate 7.2 Water hyacinth on a canal in Nator (western Bangladesh).

The emergence of commercial crops provided some relief, however. The very fertile deltaic fields of eastern Bengal were particularly suited for the cultivation of jute, an indigenous seasonal crop that yields a fibre used for gunny bags, rope, industrial packaging and canvas. From the mid-nineteenth century eastern Bengal became the world's prime production centre for this fibre, with a truly global reach. From the fields it moved by boat and train to factories in Kolkata and Scotland. There it was turned into hundreds of millions of sacks for anything from Brazilian coffee and Ghanaian cocoa to Thai rice and Russian oats. Other uses were as diverse as sandbags for twentieth-century warfare, carpet backing and garden twine.

Jute was grown by smallholders all over the delta, particularly in the districts of Dhaka, Mymensingh and Rangpur.[9]

Sugar cane was another significant cash crop. Rice, produced by millions of households for their own consumption, was also of increasing commercial value; by the end of the colonial period about two-fifths of it was marketed. All these crops required huge labour inputs on a seasonal basis. During the months of peak demand labour migrants would come from other parts of the delta and from 'upcountry' (Uttar Pradesh and Bihar in India) to help bring in the harvest.[10] Plantation crops, a feature of colonial agriculture all over the world, were not important in the Bengal delta, with the exception of tea, grown in the hills of Sylhet and Chittagong. Indigo was also produced in large-scale agricultural establishments, but these did not take the form of true plantations.[11] Tea plantations were set up in the 1850s and they have been in production ever since (today there are about 160 tea plantations in Bangladesh, including new ones in the far northwest of the country). Labourers for these plantations did not come from the surrounding areas. Instead they were recruited from central and southern India and are still a clearly distinguishable group.[12]

By the end of British rule, the age-old agrarian frontier had closed, and further agrarian expansion was no longer possible in the delta. The closure of the frontier had been spurred on by new developments during colonial rule. The zamindari system of taxation, landlord parasitism and peasant indigence had blocked a transformation of agricultural production methods. Commercial cropping was based largely on the labour of smallholders working with simple technology who incurred debts to keep going from one harvest to the next. And a general strategy of high reproduction had resulted in an expanding population trying to make a living from an increasingly crowded land. Rural living standards had been low at the beginning of British rule; they were lower still at its end.

THE FAMINE OF 1943

The general insecurity of life was demonstrated in a grisly manner in the closing moments of British rule. In 1943–4, during the Second World War, a severe famine hit Bengal. It caused the death of about 3.5 million people, mostly in rural eastern Bengal.[13] It was a man-made disaster in that it was not a scarcity of food that caused so many to die but a collapse of the grain-marketing system.

The background was complicated. The wartime advance of Japanese forces obliterated the British strongholds in Hong Kong and Singapore and, in May 1942, forced the British to retreat from Myanmar (Burma). About

300,000 refugees arrived in Bengal. By June the Japanese army and the anti-British Indian National Army were closing in on northeast India, and the British expected them to attack Bengal in late 1942. In the delta, the authorities drove some 150,000 people off their lands to make room for hastily constructed military airfields and army camps. Some of the wartime airfields (which were located in Comilla, Feni, Chittagong, Chakaria, Cox's Bazar, Tejgaon, Kurmitola, Sylhet, Jessore, Rajshahi and Lalmonirhat) would later be turned into civilian airports.

The Japanese army never made it to Bengal, but Japanese planes repeatedly bombed Chittagong and Kolkata, and the British, who had now lost naval control of the Bay of Bengal, panicked and were planning to evacuate. Their panic was spotted in a humorous folk poem of the time:

> Do re mi fa so la ti do,
> The Japanese have dropped bombs,
> There are cobras in the bombs
> The British shout 'bap-re-bap!' [= an expression of fear and surprise][14]

As a precaution against a Japanese invasion, the British proceeded to destroy over 60,000 country boats capable of carrying ten or more people in the coastal districts. This boat denial scheme 'deprived hundreds of thousands of peasants of their livings. Fishermen could no longer reach their fishing-grounds, cultivators of island-paddies and sandbars had to abandon their crops, and potters could no longer carry their goods in bulk to markets.'[15] On top of this, in October 1942 a cyclone hit the western Bengal districts of Medinipur and 24-Parganas (now in India), killing 14,000 people and devastating the ripening rice crop.

These developments prompted 'a subordination of local needs, including subsistence, to official and military priorities'. The government became obsessed by an anxiety to feed Kolkata and 'tried to force and then to inveigle primary producers to bring their rice forward'. Government agents with unlimited sums were sent out to buy up paddy and rice quickly and at a fixed maximum price, cutting out local traders and leaving cultivators cautious about making sales at all. The grain-marketing system broke down and 'millions of market-dependent consumers in rural areas, unprotected like their fellows in the capital, paid extraordinary prices for very limited amounts of rice in the market places'. Millions could not pay and therefore died of starvation. In parts of the districts of Faridpur, Comilla and Chittagong one out of ten inhabitants perished, and on the large island of Bhola one out of seven.[16] Distress migration into towns often did not save the starving, and thousands of dead bodies were strewn across streets, parks and squares. The

Great Famine of '50' (the Bengali year 1350, or 1943/4 CE; *pañcāser manbantar*) became etched into the collective consciousness as a major traumatic experience. Its notoriety was kept alive not least by the 'famine sketches' of Zainul Abedin, a young artist from Mymensingh who would go on to become one of Bangladesh's most celebrated painters (Plate 7.3).[17]

Plate 7.3 *Famine*. Drawing by Zainul Abedin.

The famine of 1943 turned out to be the first of three enormous shocks that Bengal society would have to endure within one generation. The famine was followed by Partition in 1947, at the very end of British rule, and the Bangladesh Liberation War in 1971. These two further upheavals also resulted from the cultural and political transformations that had taken shape in the colonial period.

CHAPTER 8

Colonial Conflicts

It would be a mistake to think that the people of the Bengal delta took colonial rule lying down. Establishing British authority was not simply a question of defeating former rulers at Polashi and controlling zamindars. It took the British East India Company decades to insert itself into the societies of the eastern Bengal delta and to rule effectively.[1] An authoritarian state based on an alliance with rural grandees was bound to call forth opposition, and, indeed, rebellion was a frequent companion of colonial rule. Right at the outset British rule was challenged severely and unexpectedly by thousands of armed religious mendicants who were enraged by an ill-advised government policy of banning the collection of alms. The revolt turned against tax collectors and armed forces. Known as the Fakir–Sannyasi resistance – fakir and sannyasi being the terms for Muslim and Hindu religious men, respectively – it combined guerrilla tactics and mass battles in which thousands participated. These rebels engaged the British all over Bengal and Bihar from the early 1760s to the 1790s.[2] Resentment against the encroaching colonial state also found expression in various local revolts – for example in Chittagong, Rangpur and Mymensingh[3] – and these movements took the form of protecting community rights.

By the middle of the nineteenth century, however, British rule was no longer threatened in the Bengal delta.[4] When the large Indian Rebellion of 1857 – known to the British as 'the Sepoy Mutiny' and to some nationalist historians as 'the First War of Independence' – brought the near-collapse of British rule in many parts of northern and central India, the Bengal delta remained aloof. Certainly, there was a soldier rebellion in Chittagong and trepidation among the British in Dhaka, but because neither the landlords and the middle classes nor the peasantry supported the revolt, it fizzled out after some skirmishes. In the Bengal delta disaffection now focused on the effects of commercial agriculture and cultivators' legal rights. Resistance typically pitted cultivators and a rising middle class, on the one hand, against zamindars, European entrepreneurs and the colonial state, on the other.

Several movements turned against the forced cultivation of indigo and successfully ended the hated indigo industry in the Bengal delta. The leaders of these movements were Islamic preachers who had been on extended pilgrimages to Mecca and who, upon their return, had started campaigns to 'purify' the religious practices of Bengali Muslims (see Chapter 6). Soon, however, they turned into champions of peasant class interests. The result was armed resistance against zamindars, planters and British rule. Titu Mir (1782–1831) spent five years in Mecca and then became the leader of the Tariqah-i-Muhammadiyah revolt in Bengal. Haji Shariatullah (1781–1840), who was in Mecca for nineteen years, returned to lead the Faraizi revolt. His son and successor Dudu Miah (1819–62) also spent five years in Mecca before leading peasants into the 'Blue Mutiny' (1859–62) that wiped out indigo in Bengal.[5] Not all peasant revolts were religiously inspired, however. The Pabna revolt (1873) emphasised the class angle more exclusively. It was linked to the success of another cash crop, jute, and the emergence of a new rural middle class that began to assert itself against the zamindars.

The late nineteenth century saw the beginnings of a political connection between some members of the bhodrolok gentry and peasant activists. This is how an annoyed landlord from western Bengal described it at the time:

They are for the most part east Bengal men, joined by some English-returned natives, who also hail from that part of the country. Many of them have seen something or read still more of the doings of Irish agitators ... They go to the ryots [tenants], pretend to be their friends, sow seeds of dissension between them and the Zamindars, and thus set class against class.[6]

This political connection between peasant activism and upper-class contestation became an important model for many twentieth-century movements in the Bengal delta. Hopes for an end to economic exploitation and dreams of self-determination merged in a plethora of anti-colonial, nationalist and communist agitations. Many of these were linked to organisations at the all-India level. The British responded with a mix of violent repression and concessions. Concessions included somewhat loosening the government's alliance with the zamindars, giving more rights to cultivators and allowing more bhodrolok representation and participation in policy-making. But ultimately it was a question of too little, too late. The last decades of colonial rule were very turbulent as nationalists staged non-cooperation and civil disobedience campaigns and demanded that the

British quit India, while communist-inspired tenant movements struggled against agrarian oppression.

DIVISION IN 1905

In the Bengal delta, the shape of things to come was prefigured by an administrative change. In 1905 the British divided the huge province of Bengal into a western part ('Bengal') and an eastern part ('Eastern Bengal and Assam') (Map 8.1). The official explanation was that this change would lighten the growing administrative burden on Kolkata (which acted as the capital of Bengal as well as of all of British India) and provide a much-needed economic stimulus to the economy of the eastern delta. But the political

--- = border between *Eastern Bengal* & *Assam* and *Bengal* (1905–11)
--- = border between Assam and Eastern Bengal (1905–11)
——— = present border of Bangladesh

Map 8.1 The division of the province of Bengal in 1905.

fallout of this decision turned out to be momentous – it led to a sharp division of minds all over Bengal (and indeed all over India). Many saw the Bengal partition of 1905 as a calculated move to break the anti-colonial movement, which was particularly strong in Bengal, and to 'divide and rule' the Bengali-speaking population.[7]

A very vocal opposition developed, especially among the middle and upper classes in Kolkata. They feared a loss of economic power (tea and jute exports might now go through the port of Chittagong), inconvenience (East Bengal's absentee landlords had settled in Kolkata) and competition (a new court system in East Bengal might exclude Kolkata lawyers, and new newspapers might restrict the circulation of the Kolkata press). What turned this local opposition into a significant force, however, was its national momentum. It galvanised the Indian nationalist movement and gained it popular support. It also demonstrated that conventional moderate forms of protest (press campaigns, petitions, meetings and conferences) did not work. As a result, the protesters developed new strategies. The first became known as the Swadeshi movement (shodeshi; *swadeśi*; own-country).[8] It entailed a boycott of British goods, education and administration and advocated self-help in the form of establishing Indian-owned industries, reviving handloom and craft production, setting up national schools and developing village improvement schemes.

The second strategy – which came to the fore as the limitations of the boycott and self-help programmes became clear to more radical opponents of the division of Bengal – was political assassination. Known as 'Bengal terrorism', this strategy first developed in revolutionary youth groups that took their cue from Russian, Italian and Irish secret societies. They used the public display of violence against high-ranking British individuals and local collaborators as an anti-colonial tool. The campaign proved highly successful, because not only the attacks themselves but also the trials following them were widely publicised.[9] These created revolutionary heroes whom many in Bangladesh still remember as martyrs, especially Khudiram Basu (who was hanged in 1908), 'Mastarda' Surya Sen (who organised an elaborate raid on the Chittagong armoury in 1930 and was hanged in 1934) and Pritilata Waddadar, a young woman from Chittagong who took part in the Chittagong armoury raid and committed suicide at the age of twenty-one when she was surrounded by police in 1932 (Plate 8.1).[10]

The administrative division of Bengal in 1905 ushered in a new period of anti-colonial organising all over South Asia. In Bengal, however, it was also a watershed of another sort: it exposed the weakness of political solidarity between religious communities. After 1905 'Muslims' and 'Hindus' became

Plate 8.1 Pritilata Waddadar.

clear-cut *political* categories, and these categories have figured very prominently in Bengal political life ever since.

A number of factors combined to make this happen. First, in the new
province of Eastern Bengal and Assam, Muslims formed a clear majority of the
population. The new capital was Dhaka and a number of impressive buildings
were constructed to house the administration, for example the Governor's
Residence and Curzon Hall (Plate 8.2). Many educated Muslims hoped to get
jobs in the provincial administration or in Dhaka's growing service sector.
These educated Muslims saw the new province as a career opportunity.

Second, although quite a few Muslims, in both parts of Bengal,
initially joined the protests against the division of their province, their
enthusiasm soon waned because of the cultural politics imposed on these
protests. The bhodrolok gentry took the lead in the anti-division movement, and, as we have seen, this group was dominated by high-caste
Hindus from Kolkata. Their particular socio-religious location set the
tone of the Swadeshi movement: the anti-division movement was fuelled
by a romantic, anti-colonial Bengali nationalism, which was 'inevitably

Plate 8.2 Curzon Hall, constructed as Dhaka's city hall, now part of Dhaka University.

drawn toward a mythic or imagined past – a bygone golden age against which to contrast India's degenerate present. Almost inevitably, this mythic past was imagined as a Hindu past.[11] This attempt to mobilise popular support by linking patriotism with Hindu revivalism backfired. For example, many Muslims objected strongly to the adoption of the song *Bande Mātaram* ('Mother, I Bow to Thee') as the movement's anthem. This song, taken from a novel by Bengali author Bankim Chandra Chattopadhyay (1838–94), was a hymn to the Hindu goddess Durga. Rabindranath Tagore, who set it to music, later remarked: 'Of course Bankim does show Durga to be inseparably united with Bengal in the song, but no Mussulman can be expected patriotically to worship the ten-handed deity as "Swadesh" [the Homeland].'[12]

Plans for national education also underlined the need to revive a glorious Hindu past, revolutionary youth clubs were inspired by Hindu spirituality, and lower-caste Hindus were persuaded to join the boycott by means of traditional caste sanctions.[13] This religious flavour strengthened the movement's hold over millions of Hindus – but it antagonised non-Hindus.

Third, Muslims in Bengal had recently begun to define themselves self-confidently as a community. Since the 1870s the British had treated Muslims as a separate political community and thus encouraged the development of political consciousness on the basis of religious identity.[14] This was not easy, however, because Bengal's Muslims did not see themselves as a distinct community at all. Any notion of unity among various groups of Muslims was prevented by profound differences between them. The principal distinction was socio-cultural. Until the late nineteenth century, the vast majority of Bengali Muslims were 'more a part of the larger Bengali community comprising Hindus, Muslims, Buddhists, and animists than any specific Islamic community'.[15] They subscribed to a popular Islam with deep roots in the region's rural culture. A much smaller but more powerful group of co-religionists was orientated towards an urban, upper-class culture. They thought of themselves as aristocratic and of Arab, Persian or Central Asian descent (ashraf; *āśrāph*). Many of these Bengal ashraf tried to emulate a northern Indian model of Islamic culture – based on Persian and Urdu and orientated towards Delhi, Lahore, Agra and Lucknow – and they considered themselves to be the guardians of authentic Islamic culture in this eastern hinterland. They looked down upon the Islam of local cultivators and artisans, whom they considered to be parochial low-born native converts (ajlaf or atrap; *ājlāph, ātrāp*) whose religious practices, language and lifestyle were uneducated and tainted by non-Islamic influences. In the nineteenth century these self-appointed arbiters of Islamic rectitude undertook various attempts at 'ashraf-ising' Islamic practices in the Bengal countryside (where over 95 per cent of Muslims lived), a civilising offensive that became easier as the means of communication and the rate of literacy increased. As more Bengal Muslims became educated, there was a flowering of various new ideas and literary expression among them (see box 'Rokeya the satirist').

Although many educated Muslims continued to be reluctant to accept lowly peasants steeped in Bengali culture – which they categorised as non-Islamic – as 'true' Muslims, the notion of a common Muslim identity had taken root by the time the British decided to divide Bengal and allowed electoral politics.[16] Thus the idea of a political party representing all Muslims became a possibility, and at a meeting in Dhaka in 1906 a group of ashraf politicians established the All-India Muslim League. This new party emerged to counter the anti-division agitation and the party behind it, the Indian National Congress. Its appeal to the Muslim community – not just in Bengal but all over India – was a harbinger of a new era of political mobilisation on the basis of religious identity. Such politics – in which Hindu and Muslim politicians participated in equal measure[17] – came to be described as 'communal' politics or 'communalism'.

Finally, tensions between Hindus and Muslims in Bengal were intensified by economic grievances. In eastern Bengal the tenants (overwhelmingly Muslims) began to assert their economic rights *vis-à-vis* the landlords and moneylenders (mostly Hindus). An emerging 'agrarian Islamic' discourse – more emancipatory than anti-Hindu – suggested 'the possibility of a viable, prosperous, ethical, and moral peasant life in a market-entangled agrarian economy'.[18] The rural Muslim middle class of eastern Bengal also had grievances: they were frustrated in their social and political ambitions by the disdainful attitude of Hindu notables, who continued to regard them as far below themselves in terms of prestige and status. In 1906 and 1907, Hindu Swadeshi activists and their Muslim opponents began to use mob violence against each other in several parts of eastern Bengal, notably Mymensingh and Comilla.[19] These 'communal riots' and the sense of insecurity they produced proved to be powerful instruments in strengthening oppositional religious solidarities. They created and nurtured communal stereotypes. Many Hindu bhodrolok now saw rural Muslims not just as inferior but as dangerous anti-Swadeshi hooligans who acted as agents of the British. Among Muslims, on the other hand, Hindus were increasingly depicted as arrogant, wily and insensitive exploiters who sought to rule over Muslims in perpetuity.

Rokeya the satirist

In 1905 a Bengali woman set pen to paper to create Ladyland, a feminist utopia in which clever, scientific-minded women rule a perfect country after their men had almost ruined it through incessant warfare. The narrator is Sultana, an astonished visitor from Bengal, who is shown around by Sister Sara:

> *I met more than a hundred women while walking there, but not a single man.*
> *'Where are the men?' I asked her.*
> *'In their proper places, where they ought to be.'*
> *'Pray let me know what you mean by "their proper places".'*
> *'O, I see my mistake, you cannot know our customs, as you were never here before.*
> *We shut our men indoors.'*
> *'Just as we are kept in the zenana [women's quarters]?'*
> *'Exactly so.'*
> *'How funny,' I burst into a laugh. Sister Sara laughed too.*
> *'But dear Sultana, how unfair it is to shut in the harmless women and let loose the men [...] Why do you allow yourselves to be shut up?'*
> *'Because it cannot be helped as they are stronger than women.'*

'*A lion is stronger than a man, but it does not enable him to dominate the human race. You have neglected the duty you owe to yourselves and you have lost your natural rights by shutting your eyes to your own interests.*'
'*But my dear Sister Sara, if we do everything by ourselves, what will the men do then?*'
'*They should not do anything, excuse me; they are fit for nothing. Only catch them and put them into the zenana.*'

It was Rokeya Sakhawat Hossain (now best known as Begum Rokeya) who created this satirical dream of a society where 'ladies rule over the country and control all social matters, while gentlemen are kept in the Mardanas [men's quarters] to mind babies, to cook and to do all sorts of domestic work'.

Rokeya (1880–1932; Plate 8.3) was born into a well-off Muslim family in Rangpur (northern Bangladesh). In her circles female education was frowned upon because it broke the strict rules of female seclusion. Nevertheless, her elder siblings secretly taught her to read and write Bengali and English. Married at sixteen to a much older high official in Bhagalpur (Bihar), she found in him a

Plate 8.3 Rokeya Sakhawat Hossain.

supporter of her writings on women's emancipation, which soon began to be published in periodicals for the educated elite. Widowed at twenty-nine, she set up schools for girls. Her two roles – that of provocative feminist writer and that of educationist trying to persuade parents to entrust their daughters' education to her – often clashed.

Today Rokeya is widely claimed as one of the pioneers of South Asia's women's movement; her writings are translated and continue to be published in both Bangladesh and India.[20]

In 1911 the British annulled the 1905 division of Bengal and at the same time announced that the imperial capital was to be transferred from Kolkata to Delhi in northern India. It took twenty years to construct a new administrative capital (New Delhi) and its inauguration did not take place until 1931. Nevertheless, from 1911 most of Bengal's politicians lost power as their arena shrank from the national to the regional level. The move of 1911 achieved relatively easily what, according to many, had been the main purpose of the 1905 division: to undermine Bengali politicians' remarkable hold on nationalist politics in India. What the division of Bengal of 1905–11 did not accomplish, however, was a separation of Bengalis on regional terms. If anything, it strengthened a sense of Bengaliness across the region. But what it did effect was the creation of a specific regional political framework in which religious identity began to overrule regional and class identities. Thus, for Muslims and Hindus across Bengal, irrespective of their local and class diversities, the region of Bengal now became the focus of lively – but largely separate and antagonistic – identity politics.

The remaining decades until the end of colonial rule saw a complex struggle between those who resisted this trend towards communal politics and those who promoted it. Among the former were all-India nationalists, all-Bengal nationalists, socialists and communists. Among the latter were Hindu and Muslim chauvinists, as well as those who thought that the economic emancipation of Muslims in Bengal could best be achieved by creating organisations focusing on their interests. The political connection between peasant activism and upper- and middle-class contestation was visible in all successful movements of the period, from communist-inspired strikes and sharecropper revolts to broad support for both nationalist and communalist causes all over the Bengal delta.

Meanwhile representative politics were developing in Bengal. Elections were first introduced in urban municipalities on the basis of a very limited vote in the late nineteenth century. Under popular pressure the system gradually expanded to include the rural areas, provincial and central legislative councils and larger groups of voters.[21] It never extended to universal voting rights, however, and in 1909 Muslim leaders obtained a system under which Muslims could vote separately for reserved seats. This structure of separate electorates was later extended to include designated seats for low-caste Hindus ('scheduled castes', today: *Dalits*) and it endured until the end of colonial rule.

Up to 1920, candidates contested elections independent of party affiliation. Even after the introduction of party-nominated candidates, independents remained important: in elections in 1937 one third of the 250 Bengal seats went to independent candidates. But soon afterwards party politics advanced quickly. A combination of separate electorates and party-nominated candidates ensured that the communal trend became firmly embedded in Bengal's representative politics: the elections of 1946 returned only 3 per cent independents. Now two parties clearly dominated the scene: the All-India Muslim League and the Indian National Congress (Figure 8.1). Electoral politics underlined Bengal's regional specificity: Congress, which won control everywhere else in India (except Punjab), never succeeded in doing so in Bengal.

	1937	1946
Independent candidates	32	3
All-India Muslim League	21	46
Indian National Congress	16	34
Other parties and groups	31	17
Total (N = 250)	100%	100%

Figure 8.1 Results of the Provincial Assembly elections in Bengal, 1937 and 1946 (percentage of seats).

The political ferment of the first decades of the twentieth century began to point to the possibility that British rule might come to an end sooner than previously expected. It also entrenched Hindus and Muslims as political categories more firmly than before. By 1940, however, the political future of the Bengal delta still seemed to be completely open, and nobody could possibly imagine that some thirty years down the road there would be a state called Bangladesh.

CHAPTER 9

Towards Partition

In the 1940s the Bengal delta went through breathtaking change. The Second World War shook the established order as the Japanese advanced and the terrible famine of 1943–4 struck. Soon afterwards the social and political system began to crack. Among the many factors involved, three are of particular importance for the subsequent development of Bangladesh: a rapidly increasing rivalry between the political categories of 'Muslims' and 'Hindus', a countryside overcome by class-based revolts, and the British overlords' decision to extricate themselves from their long-held colony.

HINDU–MUSLIM RIVALRY

In the late 1930s various politicians and intellectuals in India had been toying with the idea of safeguarding the rights of Indian Muslims by means of some sort of territorial division between Muslim-majority zones and the rest. These ideas crystallised in a resolution that the Muslim League adopted in 1940. It stated:

> it is the considered view of this Session of the All India Muslim League that no constitutional plan would be workable in this country or acceptable to the Muslims unless it is designed on the following basic principles, viz., that geographically contiguous units are demarcated into regions ... [and] that the areas in which the Muslims are numerically in a majority as in the North Western and Eastern Zones of (British) India should be grouped to constitute 'independent states' in which the constituent units should be autonomous and sovereign.[1]

This Lahore (or Pakistan) Resolution caught the imagination of many Muslims in British India. As a result, the idea of carving one or more Muslim homelands out of the colony became politically relevant for the first time. It challenged the basic principle underlying the Congress Party's campaign, namely, that all Indians constituted one nation fighting for self-determination. The movement for a Muslim homeland started from the assertion that Muslims were not merely a community within the Indian nation but a separate nation with a right to self-determination. Hence there were two nations in British India, the Muslims and the others. This became known as the 'two-nations theory'.

The idea of a Muslim homeland remained ambiguous, however. Was it going to be one state or several? Was it going to be completely independent or an autonomous part within a federation comprising the entire former colony? Did the omission of the word 'Islam' from the Lahore Resolution indicate that Pakistan was not going to be a state ruled by Islamic laws and institutions? Such issues remained up in the air until the very end of British rule: the imagined homeland encompassed a swathe of different imaginations.[2] The homeland for Indian Muslims came to be referred to as 'Pakistan', an acronym coined in the early 1930s that did not catch on until the 1940s. It stood for a number of regions claimed as parts of the homeland: P stood for Punjab, A for Afghans (Pashtuns), K for Kashmir, S for Sindh and 'tan' for Baluchistan. It made no mention of Bengal. Even so, groups of Muslims in Bengal aspired to the new homeland, and they did so in many different ways. Among them were Kolkata intellectuals who began to speak of 'Purbo [East] Pakistan' and a 'Pak-Bangla' culture, as well as peasant organisers imagining a classless society based on the idea of 'Rabubiyat', which interpreted Islamic teaching as advocating equality between all, irrespective of faith, and the abolition of private ownership.[3] Thus began the end-game of nationalist politics under colonial rule. The two major parties were sharply divided over the future, and their differences were popularly perceived in terms of Muslim/non-Muslim, or Muslim/Hindu, rivalry. From now on, attempts to highlight all-Bengal unity lost out and communal politics would dominate Bengal's (and South Asia's) progress.

RURAL REVOLTS

While urban politicians were battling over the future of the state, Bengal rural society was in upheaval. In the late 1930s there had been several anti-landlord campaigns, and in the aftermath of the famine these grew into sharecropper revolts all over Bengal. The core demand of the largest, the Tebhaga movement (from *tebhāgā*; three shares), was for sharecroppers to be allowed to keep two-thirds of the crop rather than half or less, as was customary.[4] The movement peaked in 1946–7, when in many localities groups of volunteers armed with bamboo clubs took effective control of the rice crop by collectively harvesting it and taking it to the sharecropper's threshing floor rather than

at the paddy field　20·12·46

Plate 9.1 Tebhaga activists with communist flags and bamboo clubs during collective harvesting, Rangpur district, December 1946. Sketch by Somnath Hore.[5]

to that of the landlord (Plate 9.1). They then issued notices to the landlord to come and take his one third of the crop and issue a written receipt. A few landlords gave in but most tried legal tactics or resorted to force.

Since government policy was not clear, local official responses varied. In many places violent confrontations occurred between sharecroppers, landlords' retainers and police. The first agitations had taken place in parts of Bengal where the Peasant Organisation had been actively mobilising. The Peasant Organisation (Krishok Shobha; *kṛṣak sabhā*) was the local chapter of a national communist-led organisation committed to peasant interests. Soon it spread to many other parts, where the same demands were raised. Local struggles differed in tactics, intensity and outcomes. In districts such as Jessore, Dinajpur, Rangpur and Mymensingh the sharecroppers were strong enough to establish 'liberated areas' (*tebhāgā elākā*) for some time before the movement broke down into more localised and limited agitations that in some cases continued until the early 1950s (see box 'Ila the revolutionary'). Meanwhile, other rural confrontations were also taking place. Tenants rose against their landlords in what became known as the Tanka movement in Mymensingh and the Nankar movement in Sylhet.

Ila the revolutionary

In January 1950 a twenty-four-year-old woman found herself being interrogated, tortured and raped by police in the western district of Rajshahi. She was Ila Mitra, a Kolkata-educated bhodromohila (*bhadramahilā*; gentlewoman) whose husband Ramen was a scion of a substantial zamindari (landlord) family of the area. She had just been arrested, together with a group of companions, as they were fleeing westward.

Ila Mitra (1925–2002) was not your average landlord's wife. She and her husband were revolutionary organisers who fitted the Bengal pattern of upper-class rebels trying to make common cause with popular insurgents. In her student days she had become a member of the Women's Self Defence Association and the All-India Communist Party, and after marrying Ramen she joined him in his activities for the Peasant Organisation (Krishok Shobha). In 1946 she visited Noakhali (southeastern Bengal), the scene of Hindu–Muslim killings, and helped in organising a movement to resist Hindu–Muslim violence. Back home she became active in the Tebhaga uprising, which locally came to be known as the Nachol rebellion. When Pakistan and India were partitioned in 1947, the rebellion in Nachol continued. The main reason was that here upper-class communist organisers and insurgent peasants were not driven apart by their religious identities, as was the case in most other parts of the country. In Nachol both peasants and leaders were overwhelmingly non-Muslims. Most of the peasants were Santals and Bengali Hindus, and most communist cadres trying to organise the revolt were Bengali Hindus as well.

Ila rose to prominence around 1948 as the Pakistan government banned the Communist Party – most members of the party in Bengal had opted for East Pakistan rather than India[6] – and the Nachol movement radicalised. Leaving briefly for Kolkata to give birth to her son, she returned to a movement that was turning more violent. By late 1949 most landowners in the region had been forced to accept the movement's demands: two-thirds of the crop to the sharecropper and one third of husked rice as wages to the labourer. By this time the Tebhaga movement had collapsed in most of the country and the authorities had launched operations to defeat it in Nachol as well.[7]

Things came to a head in January 1950, when a mob of enraged villagers armed with bamboo clubs, spears, bows and arrows attacked a police posse of five and killed them. Now the Pakistan army descended on the region, ransacking, raping and setting fire to villages. The Nachol rebellion was crushed and hundreds were killed. Many tried to escape across the border. Ila Mitra was among the unlucky ones who were arrested. Despite being dressed as a Santal peasant woman, she was recognised as she was resting with a group of Santal refugees. All of them were taken in but only Ila Mitra became a *cause célèbre*. Her statement in the Rajshahi court of law in 1951 exposed police and army brutality and added to a general disgruntlement with the Muslim League government among residents of East Pakistan. Serving a life sentence, she benefited from a change of government in 1954. Her very poor health moved the new government to allow her to go to Kolkata for medical treatment (Plate 9.2). She did not return until after Bangladesh had gained independence. Each time she returned, she was given a heroine's welcome.

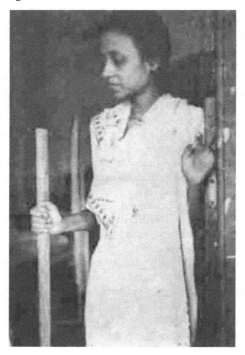

Plate 9.2 Ila Mitra at Dhaka Medical College Hospital, 1954.

These rural confrontations shook the economic framework that had supported colonial rule since the late eighteenth century. There was now widespread talk of abolishing the zamindari system of taxation and legally removing the prerogatives of landlords. It was becoming clear that the end of colonial rule would also mean an economic upheaval in the countryside. This reinforced the differences between Hindu and Muslim identities. Bengal's privileged landowning groups, its assertive bhodrolok intelligentsia and professionals, and its powerful businessmen saw a fundamental challenge to their economic and political dominance. Most members of this elite shared a Hindu identity, and their political leaders decided to boost their power by shifting from nationalism to strategic communalist politics. They began to recruit lower-class and 'scheduled caste' Hindus as well as nominally Hindu groups to their main party, the Bengal chapter of the Indian Congress Party, on a platform that promised to safeguard 'Hindu interests'. They were, however, not always successful in persuading these groups to see the advantages of Hindu unity. 'We worked among the Scheduled (*dalits*) caste people to get their support, but we did not get much response ... The high caste Hindus had kept out the lower caste people for centuries; so these people did not respond to the calls of high caste leaders.'[8] Increasingly, these high-caste leaders came to the conclusion that a partition of Bengal might be preferable to Muslim rule – the province of Bengal had a Muslim majority – and in 1946 they started a campaign to demand a separation of West Bengal (with a Hindu majority) from Muslim-dominated East Bengal.[9]

Among the largely Muslim peasantry, on the other hand, the imminent collapse of the landlord system was a source of hope. East Bengal's peasants realised that the Congress Party had little to offer in this respect. It had shown itself unwilling to champion tenant demands and yet considered itself to be the sole party representing India's national ambitions. It refused to countenance other nationalist parties and ruled out political coalitions that might have attracted peasant support. It was for this reason that the Muslim League, the only regional party with enough clout to take on Congress, emerged as the best alternative in the closing years of colonial rule. Most peasants in East Bengal saw the attainment of an independent 'Pakistan' as their best option to rid themselves of landlord domination and achieve a 'peasant utopia' of cultivator land ownership, egalitarianism and justice.[10] It was for such economic reasons, far more than because of any religious motivation, that they finally threw in their lot with the Muslim League and its claim for an independent Pakistan.

Unlike the Hindu communalists, however, the Muslim League did not strive for a division of Bengal. Certainly, it wanted to create a homeland for Muslims – but its vision of Pakistan included all of Bengal. It was Congress that insisted upon the division of Bengal in order to eliminate the Muslim League from India's post-independence political equation. As the British period drew to a close, it was clear that a division of the spoils had become inevitable – but nobody knew what it would look like, or who would reap the benefits.

BRITISH WITHDRAWAL

Up to the end of the Second World War the British had met nationalist demands with a mixture of repression and concession. They had introduced constitutional reforms – the Government of India Act of 1935 – that brought provincial government departments under the control of elected Indian ministers but retained crucial powers for the British at the all-India level. The Act was intended to safeguard British rule by deflecting the nationalist challenge. In Bengal this worked well: it created a provincial political arena in which communal infighting flourished.

After the Second World War, however, British policy changed rapidly. Events in India (large-scale public protests, mutinies in the armed forces), financial problems (the war had turned Britain from a creditor to a debtor of India), a change of political mood and a new government in Britain spelled the end of the British empire in India. In early 1946 a Cabinet Mission arrived from Britain to discuss the terms of India's independence. It suggested a loose federal structure for the post-colonial period. Immediately, the political temperature shot up. In Bengal the relationship between Hindus and Muslims, already under strain, deteriorated rapidly as thousands of people died in politically instigated communal riots in Kolkata, Noakhali and Comilla, and in neighbouring Bihar. Some Congress Party and Muslim League leaders in Bengal made a last-ditch attempt to avert the looming disaster of partition by proposing that a United Bengal could become an independent country. This initiative received the blessings of some influential national politicians (notably M. K. Gandhi and M. A. Jinnah) but it was shot down by the national Congress Party leadership, who demanded Bengal's partition. Bengal's fate was now sealed: its western half was to join an independent India and its eastern half an independent Pakistan. It would be misleading to see this as the outcome of Pakistani separatism or secession. Rather, the Congress Party leadership's 'aversion to substantial provincial autonomy as well as the prospect of having to concede [to the Muslim League] a substantial share of power at the centre suggests that exclusion, not separatism, might better explain the outcome of 1947'.[11]

By early 1947 the British were very keen to extricate themselves as soon as possible from an increasingly unmanageable state of affairs. In February they announced that they would leave in a year and a half, but in June they changed the date to 15 August 1947. Feverish weeks of politicking and administrative preparation followed amidst increasing political radicalisation and violence. Only six weeks before British rule was to end, two Boundary Commissions (for Punjab and Bengal) were formed to decide where the new borders between Pakistan and India should be drawn. These commissions – both headed by the same chairman, Cyril Radcliffe – were besieged by lobbyists trying to sway the verdict. In the end, neither of the two commissions could come to a unanimous decision and the chairman had to take responsibility for the territorial dismemberment of the colony.

CHAPTER 10

Partition

In the early 1940s, the Bengal famine had played havoc with the delta's social fabric. Now, in 1947, the Partition of India tore that fabric asunder. Without an understanding of Partition and its effects, it is not possible to make sense of contemporary Bangladesh. True, the shock of 1947 is no longer a living memory for the vast majority of Bangladeshis – but it created economic facts, historical myths and political mindsets that continue to haunt society today.

The Partition of India was a geographical solution to a political fiasco. The partitioner's knife cut through three provinces (Bengal, Assam and Punjab) and through innumerable trade routes and family ties. It created two long borders and left the partitioned societies in shambles, ruining millions of lives and upsetting cherished social arrangements. Many of the effects were unintended, unanticipated and long term.

The province of Bengal bore the full brunt: it was divided between the two new states. It is usually assumed that Bengal was cut in two. The reality is far more complicated: it was cut into no fewer than 201 pieces (Map 10.1). Pakistan received the largest part of the province's territory (64 per cent) and the majority of its population (65 per cent). Smaller sections to the west, north and east joined the new Republic of India, and the two states divided 197 tiny enclaves between them (see box 'Lives in limbo').

Pakistan's territory was augmented by the addition of most of Sylhet, a district that had been administered as part of Assam.[1] The combined territory was generally referred to as East Pakistan (although from 1947 to 1955 its official name was East Bengal). It shared a 4,000 km-long border with India. When East Pakistan seceded from Pakistan in 1971 to become Bangladesh there were no changes to its territorial shape. In other words, the geographical unit that we now know as Bangladesh was fashioned in 1947, well before anybody could imagine an independent Bangladesh.

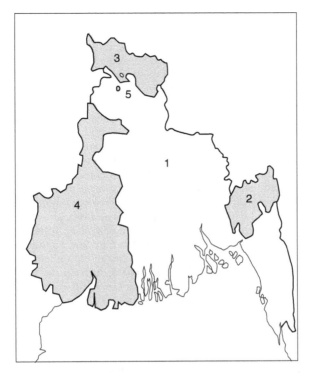

Map 10.1 The 201 parts of partitioned Bengal. 1. East Bengal (sixteen districts of Bengal that joined Pakistan in 1947); 2. The Princely State of Tripura that joined India in 1949; 3. North Bengal (two districts that joined India in 1947, and the Princely State of Cooch Behar that joined India in 1950); 4. West Bengal (twelve districts that joined India in 1947); 5. 197 enclaves.

Lives in limbo

One of the most bizarre outcomes of the Partition of India was the creation of 197 enclaves in North Bengal. For some people in the northern borderland, Partition meant the end of effective citizenship. Although they were in every respect similar to their neighbours, these people happened to be living in villages that were now – for quirky historical reasons going back to the pre-colonial period – distributed to India and Pakistan, even though they were completely surrounded by the territory of the other state. Thus, in a band of some 100 km there were 123 Indian enclaves that lay surrounded by Pakistan and 74 Pakistani enclaves that lay dispersed in Indian territory. To make matters worse, India and Pakistan were not on good terms and refused to let each other's officials cross their territory to reach the enclaves. As a result, state presence in the enclaves came to an end. There was no taxation, but also no police, schools, health services, land registration, banks, postal services or road maintenance. Neither India nor Pakistan was happy with this unanticipated situation and soon talks were underway to exchange the enclaves. It proved impossible to agree, however, and after 1971 the Pakistani enclaves became Bangladeshi ones.

The inhabitants of the enclaves were forced to lead shadowy lives. They had to break numerous laws as they went about their daily business. For example, imagine you were Abdul Bari, a young inhabitant of the Bangladeshi enclave of Nolgram, surrounded by the territory of West Bengal (India) (Plate 10.1) When you visited your uncle or went to market in the next village (there were no markets in the enclaves), you crossed an international border (between Nolgram and India) without a proper passport or a visa, and without permission to take across whatever you bought or sold, or indeed to use Indian currency. You were a non-citizen, an illegal entrant and a smuggler.

Abdul Bari may have been a Bangladeshi citizen but only in the most tenuous sense: he had never had any dealings with Bangladeshi officials (who could not visit the enclave and who were unaware of his existence), and he did not possess any documents to prove his identity. He had been effectively stateless since his (unregistered) birth. His siblings could not go to school or see a doctor without giving a false (Indian) identity. And who would protect him and his possessions against robbers? There were no police in Nolgram and the Indian police could not enter there.

To cope with this absurd life thrust upon them by bureaucratic caprice and political stalemate, enclave people developed their own local institutions, such

Plate 10.1 People and border pillar in Nolgram, a Bangladeshi enclave surrounded by Indian territory.

as enclave citizens' committees, land registration systems or some semblance of public works through corvée labour. These differed from one enclave to the next, but all enclave people shared a sense of pride in their resilience: 'We people of the enclave can cope with anything.'[2]

After almost seven decades of living in limbo, the fate of the people of the enclaves finally turned. Soon after Bangladesh became independent, India and Bangladesh had reached an agreement to exchange the enclaves – but this agreement of 1974 was not ratified and remained a dead letter. It took another forty years before bilateral relations improved sufficiently for the two governments to decide on an exchange, which formally took place in August 2015, and to grant the enclave dwellers citizenship rights over the next few years.[3]

Map 10.2 shows that it was not easy to translate the idea of a homeland for Muslims into a geographical reality. The Boundary Commission allocated considerable non-Muslim-majority areas to Pakistan (for example Khulna in the southwest and the Chittagong Hill Tracts in the southeast) and, conversely, allocated Muslim-majority areas such as Murshidabad to India. The members of the Boundary Commission never explained or justified these anomalies. Historians assume, however, that one reason for Murshidabad – whose population was 57 per cent Muslim – to be awarded to India was an attempt to keep the port of Kolkata linked to the Ganges/Bhagirathi river system serving its hinterland. Similarly, the Chittagong Hill Tracts – whose Muslim population was a mere 4 per cent – went to Pakistan, presumably to keep the port of Chittagong connected with the Karnaphuli river system. Border-making threw up many other anomalies, surprises and ambiguities, and these led immediately to recrimination between India and Pakistan. Over time quite a few points of disagreement were sorted out, but today India and Bangladesh still bicker about territorial issues. These frictions have been showing up in frequent border incidents, often with casualties, all along the partition border.[4]

Some parts of the new international border followed old divisions between lowlands and hills or pre-existing administrative borders between districts – but other stretches of the new border lopped off parts of districts and necessitated their rearrangement.[5] Thus Pakistan received half of Dinajpur and Nadia (renamed Kushtia) and other districts gained territory (for example Rajshahi) or lost it (Jessore, Sylhet). When the dust of Partition settled, East Pakistan had sixteen districts. In

Map 10.2 The Partition border and Muslim (grey) and non-Muslim (white)
majority areas in 1947. 1. Khulna; 2. Chittagong Hill Tracts; 3. Murshidabad.

1969 that number rose to eighteen when two more districts were created:
Tangail was carved out of Mymensingh and Patuakhali out of Borishal
(Barisal) (Map 10.3).

The point of Partition was to create a homeland for Muslims. In Bengal,
Islam had become a mass religion in the Mughal period, when the fertile
eastern delta was brought under the plough. It was no surprise, therefore,
that East Pakistan's centre of gravity was the active eastern delta and that its
population was overwhelmingly rural. Dhaka, the city now chosen to be
the provincial capital, was the very one that the Mughals had built up to

Map 10.3 Districts of East Pakistan, 1947–71.

control the marshes and riverscapes of what they had called 'Bhati' and the British later referred to as 'Lower Bengal'.

For the first time in its history, the Bengal delta was encased in a modern international border, a phenomenon that its inhabitants had no previous experience of whatsoever. The new border encircled most Muslim-majority areas of Bengal and, in that sense, East Pakistan became the homeland of most of Bengal's Muslims. But millions of Bengali Muslims were now in Indian territory and millions of non-Muslims continued to live in East Pakistan. No less than 42 per cent of the total *non*-Muslim population of undivided Bengal found that they had become Pakistani citizens; they made up one fifth of East Pakistan's population. This ensured that the political fiasco that had prompted Partition in the first place – the inability to overcome communalist politics – was set to carry on under the new dispensation.

One of the unintended consequences of Partition was mass migration across the new borders. In Bengal, this took a course that differed from the one in Punjab where a swift, bloody and almost complete exchange of Muslim and non-Muslim inhabitants occurred within a few months. The scenario in Bengal did include vast population exchange, but it was a much slower, longer and complicated process. Hundreds of thousands of people crossed the border in both directions, making Partition not only an exercise in spatial demarcation, but also a horrifying personal and social disaster (see Chapter 13).

The states of India and Pakistan set out to demarcate the border and take control of their sides of the new borderland.[6] Meanwhile, those who lived there realised only gradually what had happened. At first the vivisection of their social world seemed unreal and many thought that Pakistan and India would reunite after some time. As the irreversibility of Partition sank in, however, they had to come to terms with the fact that geography was destiny: they were now assigned the citizenship of one of a pair of distinct – and squabbling – states (see box 'Intaz the fivefold citizen'). A new state, Pakistan, took charge of the territory and the people of eastern Bengal. It built up institutions and set in motion new processes, many of which would survive the demise of Pakistan in 1971.

Intaz the fivefold citizen

Intaz Ali was born in 1947 and he grew up in a Muslim family in Chor Madhobpur, a rural community on the south bank of the Ganges. When he was an infant, Bengal was partitioned and his village became part of the territory of East Pakistan. Intaz became a Pakistani boy. Soon the villagers learned that the new states of India and Pakistan were quarrelling over them. India claimed possession of Intaz's village and of many others on the banks and islands (chor; *car*) of the Ganges (Plate 10.2). There were border skirmishes and conferences, but to no avail. Not being able to resolve the issue themselves, the governments of India and Pakistan decided to go for arbitration. They set up an international tribunal and promised to abide by its decision.

Plate 10.2 On a Ganges river island, near the Indian border.

When Intaz was in primary school, he and his fellow villagers learned that the Bagge Tribunal – named after its Swedish chairman – had awarded their village to India. What did that mean? Were they Indians or Pakistanis? More to the point: should he now go to high school in the nearest town in Pakistan or in India? It was a hard decision to take because nobody knew whether the tribunal's verdict was going to be implemented. It was now unclear to them whether their community was still in Pakistan or had become part of India. In late 1959 Intaz's father could wait no longer. He made up his mind and sent Intaz to a high school on the Indian side. He also changed his son's citizenship to Indian so that he could attend that school. But three years later anti-Muslim disturbances broke out in Intaz's village, and his father sent him across to Pakistan for safety. It was there, in the nearby border town of Rajshahi, that Intaz completed his high school and eventually became a Pakistani citizen again. A few years later, however, East Pakistan broke away from Pakistan to become Bangladesh. Now Intaz made the fourth 'nation-switch' of his twenty-four-year life. A fivefold serial citizen, he had become something of a record holder – from British Indian to Pakistani to Indian to Pakistani to Bangladeshi.

Although Partition had been anticipated with a mix of elation and foreboding, it was the euphoria of attaining independence that dominated the moment itself. In the town of Borishal:

victory gates were erected and musical soirees were organised [and] at 12 midnight [of 14 August 1947] all the steamers, steam launches [and] motor boats anchored in the river Kirtonkhola blared out the birth of the new nation; the riverine town reverberated with sky-rending shouts of 'Quaid-e-Azam zindabad' [Long live the Great Leader (= M. A. Jinnah)], 'Pakistan zindabad' [Long live Pakistan].[7]

Right after Partition, there was a strong sense of hope in East Pakistan. Despite the calamitous territorial dissection that would leave many traumatised, there was a feeling that this was a fresh start offering new opportunities.

CHAPTER II

Population Exchange

Throughout history, mobility has been one of the hallmarks of the inhabitants of the Bengal delta. People moved in and out of the delta, and there was constant relocation within it. As we have seen, the earliest evidence suggests that *Homo sapiens* arrived here from the west, moving on into Southeast and East Asia (Chapter 2). For as far back as we can reconstruct, settlement patterns have been complex and usually transitory, with many villages and towns being abandoned after one or more generations, and sometimes resettled later. In the centuries before British rule two patterns stood out: reclamation of forests in eastern Bengal, often by agrarian pioneers from western Bengal, and migration in many directions that resulted from wandering rivers that swallowed up villages and arable land. The British period saw further reclamation of forests and 'self-rescue' migration but also a new pattern: large-scale settlement beyond the delta. Agrarian settlers moved into Assam and Tripura (today in India) and Arakan (today in Myanmar (Burma)), middle-class Bengalis spread out across India in the service of the British colonial state and as traders, and others settled overseas as traders and fortune seekers. [1] And just before the end of British rule, the famine of 1943–4 led to massive distress migration, particularly into towns.

The Partition of 1947 added a new pattern to this complex picture. It provoked a demographic disruption of the first order. Huge numbers of people were suddenly on the move, both inside each of the new national territories and across their borders. In the Punjab, in the west, population exchange was a massive and swift fratricidal horror. In Bengal it was slower, not quite so violent, but equally massive. Here migration prefiguring Partition had begun in 1946, after riots in Kolkata, Noakhali and Bihar. In August 1947, at the time of Partition, a number of distinct groups began to migrate. Their mobility was not primarily the result of widespread purposeful communal rioting (as it was in far-away Punjab). Some moved to improve their career prospects or out of enthusiasm for the

Pakistan experiment. Others fled a situation that they found intolerable.[2] For example, many well-off Hindus in East Pakistan were confronted with a situation that they had not anticipated. They found that formerly respectful Muslim tenants, employees and neighbours, now freed from fear, expressed an antagonism that could take the form of stark intimidation, hatred and hostility. Unable to cope with this suddenly transformed atmosphere, and feeling unprotected by the Pakistan authorities, many Hindus in East Pakistan saw no option but to leave their property and homeland behind and face an uncertain future in India. Exactly the reverse happened to many Muslims in northern and eastern India.[3] When such traumatised and embittered refugees settled in their new homes across the Partition border, they often added fuel to already inflamed communal relations and helped dislodge families of the other religious community.

Nobody knows the size of these cross-border migrations. As one Bangladeshi poet put it much later in a poem entitled 'Broken Bengal':

> They shook violently the roots of the land
> And people were flung about who knows where,
> None kept account of who perished or survived.
> . . .
> The two parts of the land stretch out their thirsty hands
> Towards each other. And in between the hands
> Stands the man-made filth of religion, barbed wire.[4]

Although these migrations were state-induced, they were completely self-driven. Neither India nor Pakistan had anticipated them, and both made efforts to rein them in. They only became involved in managing migrants once these showed up in the national territory. But only relatively few received state assistance. The vast majority of Partition migrants had to rebuild their lives on their own. The two new states were quite unable even to monitor the incoming migrants and often manipulated the figures for political ends. By early 1948, when the flows reduced, officials guesstimated that about 800,000 people from India had migrated to East Pakistan and about a million people from East Pakistan were now living in India.

After these initial exchanges, however, cross-border migration did not come to an end. It continued in a boom-and-slump pattern over the years, fluctuating in response to political events such as India's 1949 invasion of Hyderabad (a region in the southern subcontinent that was poised to join Pakistan) and widespread communal rioting in both parts of Bengal in 1950. A third upsurge occurred in 1952 just before a passport and visa system was imposed. Up to then travel between India and East Pakistan had been relatively easy, with considerable return migration after each exodus. The remaining years of the 1950s saw little cross-border migration but it shot up again in 1961–5 after riots occurred in both parts of Bengal.

There were many reasons for people to choose whether to migrate or not, and these did not fit the simplistic contrast between Hindu and Muslim. First, many non-Muslims migrated from East Pakistan but far more stayed behind. Unlike West Pakistan, which saw its non-Muslim population dwindle into insignificance after Partition, East Pakistan continued to be home to about 10 million Hindus – one fifth of the population – and half a million Buddhists, Christians and others.[5] And the same is true of West Bengal, where Muslims made up one-fifth of the post-Partition population. Second, it is often assumed that the non-Muslims who stayed in East Pakistan did so because they were unable to make the trek to India. This may have been true for some, but many others saw no point in leaving their ancestral home for an unknown land and an uncertain future. Or they were actually pro-Muslim League, as was the case among groups of Dalits (low-caste Hindus).[6] Historian Ahmed Kamal describes the varying attitudes of upper-caste Hindus. On the one hand, 'the caste Hindu employees of Sylhet hospital plundered the hospital's property and then crossed over to India'; on the other, a left-wing Hindu politician put it this way:

I decided that I would not leave the country. I should stay on in Pakistan. By sharing the happiness and sufferings of the people of Pakistan I would stay on. This country, East Bengal, is my country. Why should I have to leave my country?[7]

Muslims entering East Pakistan came mostly from neighbouring regions: West Bengal, Assam, Tripura and Bihar, but also from Uttar Pradesh in northern India. The Pakistan authorities felt that they had a special duty towards the non-Bengali immigrants, whom they called 'Muhajirs' (or 'Mohajirs' – persons leaving a place to seek sanctuary), a term recalling the migration (hijra; *hijrā*) from Mecca to Medina that the Prophet and his followers had undertaken in 622 CE. About 100,000 Muhajirs are thought to have settled in East Pakistan. Some received state support such as housing and rations, but many others had to fend for themselves. Bengali immigrants (few of whom received any state aid at all) and many locals felt that the state showed partiality towards these non-Bengali newcomers.

Most migrants from East Pakistan ended up in Bengali-speaking regions in India. Many lived in refugee camps for years.[8] Some of those who had left behind property in East Pakistan continued to derive income from tenants and sharecroppers for a long time after Partition. Eventually, however, they lost control of their houses, land and businesses, which the Pakistan state declared to be 'enemy property'.

Although most Partition migrants from East Pakistan moved to West Bengal, others sought refuge in Tripura and Assam. In each of these regions they changed demographic realities and today the political and cultural fallout is still very noticeable – for example strong anti-Bengali sentiments in Tripura and Assam, or the significant cultural distinction in West Bengal between locals (ghoti; *ghaṭi*) and East Bengalis (bangal; *bāṅāl*).

The Indian government resettled groups of low-caste refugees from East Pakistan elsewhere, notably in the far-away Andaman and Nicobar Islands in the Bay of Bengal, where they were expected to clear jungles and start cultivation. The state categorised these forced migrants as Hindus – the majority were of Dalit origin – but their identities did not fit the simplistic Hindu/Muslim classification of Partition politics and much of the scholarly research since then. 'At the time of their forced migration, many of them did not even know about the existence of such a thing as "being Hindu", and even now many active members of the community are keen to identify their religion as a philo-Buddhist, Dalit, anti-Brahmanical movement, rather than anything "Hindu".'[9]

Partition migration has usually been studied one-sidedly – as if the streams leaving and entering East Pakistan were unconnected.[10] Moreover, we know much more about Hindu migration from East Pakistan than about Muslim migration to East Pakistan, partly because of the different political conditions in India and Pakistan. Kolkata became a city of refugees and a centre of East Bengali elite émigré nostalgia. Here the lost homeland in East Pakistan became a glorified memory of harmony and the good life, which lingered on as a wistful longing and was passed on to the younger generation. They grew up with this longing and the hardship of refugeehood as important tropes in family stories, literary writings and movies.[11] By contrast, writings in East Pakistan did not celebrate nostalgia but rather a 'new dawn'.[12] For Muslims from India:

the journey to [East] Pakistan was like travelling to a 'promised land' – an image that later became tarnished as Pakistan entered its most repressive stage under the Ayub regime ... In the oppressive atmosphere of a martial-law regime, whose favourite occupation was 'India-bashing', it was understandably very difficult to write, much less be nostalgic about one's homeland in India. There is a reticence, even now, among Bengali Muslims to talk publicly of their '*desh*' (the term for 'ancestral home' in the Bengali language) if it happens to be in India.[13]

Partition and forced migration became the essence of the master narrative of the nation on both sides of the border because the political elites of Pakistan and India needed legitimation. Many non-elite inhabitants, however, experienced Partition in a different way, as the distinct events that they had lived through: 'when their buffalo had been killed or their field set ablaze or their mosque torn down. It wasn't a grand overarching narrative; it was what had struck an individual family [or] village.'[14]

The fallout of Partition migration is still noticeable in Bangladesh today: divided and trauma-scarred families, people occupying houses and land abandoned by emigrants, ruined palaces, crumbling Hindu temples, and linguistic and religious minorities forever hovering between fight and flight. As the second major shock of the twentieth century, after the catastrophic famine of the 1940s, Partition became associated with a mobility of loss. Bangladeshis have long laid to rest any claims that they had to lost property in India, and they see the Indian nation as distinctly separate. Today there is a strong awareness of a rupture that cannot be undone.

Becoming East Pakistan

Part III Students making a memorial for those who died in the defence of the Bengali language, February 1952.

CHAPTER 12

The Pakistan Experiment

Under its new name – East Pakistan – the Bengal delta now joined a unique experiment in state-making.* There were three reasons why Pakistan was a very special state. First, it was founded upon religious nationalism. Religion was supposed to cement a new national identity, something that had not been tried before – the only other modern example of a religiously based nation-state being Israel, which was founded a year later than Pakistan. Second, Pakistan was a state administering two discrete territories, separated from each other by about 1,500 km of Indian terrain (Map 12.1). West Pakistan was by far the larger of these two wings, but East Pakistan was more densely populated. In fact, most Pakistani citizens lived in East Pakistan: the first population census in 1951 revealed that Pakistan had 78 million inhabitants, of whom 44 million (55 per cent) lived in East Pakistan.

These two factors combined with a third: Pakistan did not become heir to any of the colony's central state institutions. India, on the other hand, inherited the capital New Delhi as well as most of the civil bureaucracy, armed forces and police. The bulk of the colony's resources and industries, and its major port cities of Mumbai (Bombay) and Kolkata, also went to India. By contrast, Pakistan inherited largely raw-material producing regions. Whereas the new rulers of India supplanted the British in the old centre of colonial power, the new rulers of Pakistan had a much harder time to establish themselves. In other words, Pakistan was uniquely experimental: no other post-colonial state combined the loss of its administrative hub, the need to govern two unconnected territories and the ambition to base a national identity on a religious one.

In the eastern 'wing' of the country the situation was especially difficult. In August 1947, 'the new East Pakistan government was hastily housed in a College for Girls [Eden College in Dhaka], with a large number of improvised

---

* Initially the eastern wing of Pakistan was known officially as 'East Bengal'. It became 'East Pakistan' in 1956.

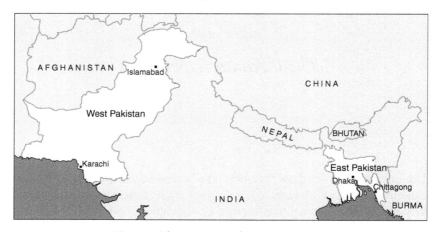

Map 12.1 The two wings of Pakistan, 1947–71.

bamboo sheds added to it for greater accommodation. On partition, East Pakistan received only one member of the former Indian Civil Service [the elitist corps of colonial bureaucrats, the "steel frame" that had kept the colony together] who belonged to that region. Six others were hastily promoted from the Provincial Civil Service.[1] As a result, the civil service of East Pakistan was largely non-local, and decision-making was in the hands of officials with little knowledge of East Pakistan's needs. An official publication described the predicament of the administrators in heroic terms:

For the many directorates there was no accommodation at all and these were sent to outlying districts. One Minister sat in a boat on the Buriganga river, disposing of files and transacting official business. Hundreds of officers chummed together in ramshackle tenements. Even camps were a luxury and bamboo constructions sprang up to provide shelters for officials and staff who were used to comfortable Calcutta flats and rooms.[2]

The General Officer Commanding (East Bengal), who arrived in January 1948, later reminisced:

The provincial government . . . was newly formed and poorly staffed. But worse still, it was politically weak and unstable. There was no army. All we had in East Pakistan at the time of Independence were two infantry battalions [one with three and one with only two companies]. We had very poor accommodation: at Headquarters there was no table, no chair, no stationery . . . we had virtually nothing at all; not even any maps of East Pakistan.[3]

These initial uncertainties and the artificial nature of Pakistan's unity fuelled the desire for a strong, centralised state and a robust national identity. The ruling party, the Muslim League, benefited from the prevailing mood in Pakistan, which was one of exultation. Having attained a sovereign homeland, Muslims could now safeguard their political, religious and cultural rights and they could complete their economic emancipation. But it did not take long for them to realise that the road ahead was anything but smooth: the two elements that most Pakistanis shared – an Islamic identity and a fear of India – proved insufficient to keep them united. Immediately fights broke out over the equitable distribution of resources, both material and symbolic. Only three months after independence a first serious crack in the edifice of Pakistan appeared over the question of the national language. It was the initial portent of enormous tensions over how the new state should be organised and imagined. These strains would gradually spoil the prospect of building a Pakistani nation. Right from the beginning, they took the form of a confrontation between Pakistan's two wings over issues such as language, autonomy, food security and economic policy. In the unfolding drama of Pakistani politics, the Bengal delta would play the role of the disenfranchised sibling clamouring consistently and unsuccessfully for rights withheld. Throughout the twenty-four years of the Pakistan experiment, the country's various rulers shared two nightmares: to be humiliated by India and to see control of the state pass democratically to East Pakistan. The latter fear would be their undoing. It animated an extraordinary political obstinacy that would, in the end, lead them to wage war on the majority of Pakistan's citizens. This strategy blew up in their faces, resulted in their utter humiliation by India and left them no other choice but to separate themselves from East Pakistan and hang on to what was left of their power in the western wing, which they renamed Pakistan.

LANGUAGE

In 1947 the new Pakistani elite faced the difficult task of welding its citizens into a united Pakistani nation. Immediately the question arose of the language in which to conduct Pakistan's state business. The Pakistan Educational Conference of November 1947 proposed Urdu as the national language, a suggestion that was opposed by representatives from East Pakistan. A few months later an East Pakistan member of the Constituent Assembly tabled an amendment to allow the Bengali language to be used in the Assembly alongside Urdu. He was sharply rebutted by the prime minister, Liaquat Ali Khan, who averred:

Pakistan has been created because of the demand of a hundred million Muslims in this subcontinent and the language of a hundred million Muslims is Urdu . . . It is necessary for a nation to have one language and that language can only be Urdu and no other language.[4]

This was a quite extraordinary statement in view of the fact that Pakistanis spoke dozens of languages and that Urdu was spoken by only 3 per cent of them. Bengali was very clearly the principal language of the country: it was spoken by 56 per cent of all Pakistanis.[5] So why was the prime minister so adamant about Urdu?

The language issue stood for a more general cultural and political divide within the fledgling state. Muslim politicians in Bengal had imagined Pakistan differently from their counterparts in northern India. The Bengalis had dreamed of a land free from the economic domination of Hindus, and they imagined a leading role for themselves as representatives of the majority of Pakistan's citizens. Northern Indian Muslim politicians, on the other hand, had pictured themselves as the natural leaders of Pakistan because they considered themselves to be the guardians of the Muslim renaissance movement in South Asia and, therefore, arbiters of the future of all Muslims. They insisted that their vision of Pakistan should rightfully take precedence.

From the beginning, the 'northern Indian' view dominated the institutions of state. There were two regional groups that endorsed it. The first became known as the Muhajirs (= migrants). They were largely members of Urdu-speaking intellectual and trading elites from northern India who moved to Pakistan's cities in their hundreds of thousands and immediately exerted an influence on politics and social life that was way out of proportion to their numbers. What made them unusual immigrants was that many of them expected the local population to adapt to them rather than the other way around. They took hold of almost all higher positions in the administration and the executive power. Most of these immigrants settled in West Pakistan, but over 100,000 Muhajirs made their new homes in East Pakistan. The second regional group was Muslims from Punjab. They were heavily over-represented in the armed forces, manned the state administration and controlled valuable irrigated land. The Punjabis progressively outflanked the Muhajirs to become the hegemonic power in Pakistan. This was symbolised in 1959 by the transfer of the capital from Karachi (Pakistan's prime Muhajir city) to the Punjab garrison town of Rawalpindi and from there to newly constructed Islamabad a decade later (Map 12.1).

The Bengali political elite took exception to the northern Indian view of Pakistan's future. But after Partition, ironically, power in the East Pakistan branch of the Muslim League had shifted away from them. A non-Bengali coterie now ran the provincial party: 'the Muslim League remained mortgaged to *Ahsan Manzil* [the palace of the Urdu-speaking nawabs of Dhaka] for its leadership, to the owner of the daily *Azad* for its publicity, and to the commercial house of the [immigrant] Ispahanis for its finance'.[6] The Muslim League hardly represented the voice of East Pakistan, and only weakly pushed back against the northern Indian view. Predictably, political opposition began to build up immediately.

In their search for legitimacy, Pakistan's new rulers used Islam as the political idiom to justify their actions. This attitude broke with the 500-year tradition of Muslim rulers in Bengal who had never propagated Islam or used it to discipline their Bengali subjects. The West Pakistani political idiom caught the Bengalis in a quandary: their protests were easily dismissed as un- or anti-Islamic. But using Islam was no mere tactical ploy on the part of West Pakistani politicians: for them, it was a civilising mission. There was a widespread perception in West Pakistan that Bengali Muslims were not only socially inferior but also lesser Muslims because they did not adhere to many of the cultural practices that northern Indians considered properly Islamic. The message from West Pakistan was that however passionately Bengalis might think of themselves as Muslims, they fell short of the mark and they could not be fully fledged Pakistanis unless they shed much of their Bengaliness. In this climate the dilemma for politicians from East Pakistan was that they needed constantly to underline their Islamic *bona fides* and at the same time defend a regional religious and cultural interest.

The language issue became the focal point of this conflict because imposing Urdu was part of a mission to 'Islamise' East Pakistan. Many in West Pakistan knew very little about the Bengali language but thought of it as in need of 'purification' from Hindu influences. To them the Bengali script (evolved from Sanskrit), the Sanskritic vocabulary of Bengali and the dominance of Hindus in the Bengali literary pantheon were all irksome (see box 'The Bengali script').[7] The Bengali Muslims' obvious attachment to their language and literature was puzzling and their rejection of Urdu rather suspect.

The Bengali script

South Asia is a subcontinent of many languages but also of many different scripts. Most major languages use their own alphabet. Bengali or Bangla (*bāṃlā*) is no exception. Written from left to right, its elegantly rounded letters hang from a headline (unlike English letters, which stand on a baseline) (Plate 12.1).

The Bengali (or East Nagari) script evolved over centuries from the Brahmi script (see Chapter 2). It has more letters than the English alphabet (eleven vowels, thirty-six consonants and many composite letter forms) and these render sounds that are difficult to reproduce in English writing. Hence transliterations of Bengali have recourse to inconvenient dots and dashes (diacritical marks) to distinguish various sounds, such as *n/ṇ/ṅ, s/ṣ/ś* and *a/ā/ã*.

The visual distinctiveness of written Bengali had always been a matter of pleasure and appreciation for literate Bengalis. After the emergence of Pakistan, however, it took on a new meaning. The language movement made it politically significant. Now it was not just the language itself that grew into a symbol of resistance and cultural pride. Each Bengali letter could be used as a badge in the cultural guerrilla war. As a result, even today, the Bengali script is much more than just a way to write a language. It has become a deeply emotive emblem of cultural distinctiveness and self-respect.

আমার ভাইয়ের রক্তে রাঙানো একুশে ফেব্রুয়ারী
আমি কি ভুলিতে পারি

Plate 12.1 A sample of Bengali writing.
'How can I forget the twenty-first of February, splattered with my brother's blood . . .?'
These are the first lines of a famous song of the 1950s, composed by Abdul Gaffar Chowdhury. They can be transcribed as 'Amar bhaier rokte rangano ekushe February ami ki bhulite pari?' Their formal transliteration is 'Āmār bhāiyer rakte rāṅāno ekuśe phebruyārī āmi ki bhulite pāri?'

When students in East Pakistan came to know about the plan to make Urdu the national language, they held meetings and demonstrations and then formed the first Language Action Committee in December 1947. Things came to a head in March 1948, when general strikes were observed in East Pakistan's towns and the movement's leaders were arrested and injured. Mohammad Ali Jinnah, governor-general of Pakistan at the time, visited Dhaka a few days later. Addressing a large audience, he stated that the Bengali language could be used in East Pakistan:

but let me make it clear to you that the state language of Pakistan is going to be Urdu and no other language. Anyone who tries to mislead you is really the enemy of Pakistan. Without one state language, no nation can remain tied up solidly together and function. Look at the history of other countries. Therefore, so far as the state language is concerned, Pakistan's language shall be Urdu. But as I have said, it will come in time.[8]

This uncompromising attitude led to rapid disillusionment with the Muslim League government among East Pakistani intellectuals, civil servants, politicians and students.[9] This was not just a matter of regional pride, cultural identity and democratic principles but also a reflection of frustrated career ambitions. Urdu-speaking candidates were preferred for jobs in the state bureaucracy; in East Pakistan, this excluded almost all locals (fewer than 1 per cent spoke Urdu as a second language) and favoured northern Indian immigrants.

The language movement, or Bhasha Andolon (*bhāsā āndalan*), gave rise to a new type of politician in East Pakistan: the Bengali-speaking student agitator.[10] Throughout the Pakistan period students at schools, colleges and universities often played a decisive role in turning political grievances into popular resistance and forcing the Pakistan state to change its policies. But in the late 1940s the state elite was undeterred in its civilising mission: in 1949 a government committee proposed that henceforth the Bengali language be written in the Arabic script:

East Pakistan being the major area of the new State, the language of this area should grow according to Muslim ideology . . . Adoption of the Arabic script is the first pre-requisite for the above purpose. It will help a natural flow of Arabic words and phrases . . . Persian and Urdu are the two best illustrations of the importance of the script and its effects on the cultural development of language.[11]

The most critical event of the language movement, and a pivotal moment for the Pakistan experiment, occurred in early 1952. There was a growing sense of deprivation and disappointment in East Pakistan, and a feeling was spreading that a new form of colonial rule had replaced British imperialism. The language movement, which had declined after 1948, reignited when the new prime minister of Pakistan, Khwaja Nazimuddin, came to Dhaka and addressed a large crowd at a central green. When he announced that the people of East Pakistan could decide what would be the provincial language but only Urdu would be Pakistan's state language, there was a very angry reaction. Students responded with the slogan 'We demand Bengali as a national language!' (*rāṣṭrabhāṣā bāṃlā cāi!*). Dhaka University went on strike and a number of organisations called a protest meeting, chaired by Maulana Abdul Hamid Khan Bhashani. Bhashani was a long-term supporter of the idea of Pakistan who had broken with the Muslim League in 1949 to form a new party, the Awami [People's] Muslim League.[12] The meeting sharply denounced the decision to make Urdu the state language and also rejected the government plan to introduce Arabic script for written Bengali. It decided to call a general strike (hortal; *hartāl*) and demonstrations throughout East Pakistan on 21 February 1952.

The government imposed a ban on these demonstrations in Dhaka, and although some organisers hesitated to violate it, many students were determined to persevere. Thousands of boys and girls from schools and colleges all over Dhaka assembled on the campus of Dhaka University together with university students. They then started marching and shouting slogans. As soon as they passed the campus gates armed policemen baton-charged them. The students retaliated by throwing bricks, upon which the police used tear gas and then fired into the crowd. Many were injured, and five people, including a nine-year-old boy, were killed. Over the next few days more demonstrations, killings and arrests occurred, and a memorial was hastily erected on the spot where the first killings had taken place (Plate 12.2).

This memorial was removed by the authorities and recreated several times before it was replaced by a concrete monument, the Martyrs'

Plate 12.2 Students making a memorial for those who died defending the Bengali language, February 1952.

Memorial or Shohid Minar (*śahīd minār*), in 1962 (Plate 12.3).[13] Today
this monument continues to be a focal point of national identity
politics and there are martyrs' memorials in every delta town. The
twenty-first of February (*Ekushe*) became a key national holiday, and
in 1999, following a proposal by the Bangladesh government,
UNESCO created International Mother Language Day, celebrated
annually on 21 February.

The events of 1952 were critically important, and not just because the
Pakistani armed forces had turned murderously violent against fellow
Pakistanis demonstrating for their rights, thus exposing the brutal nature
of the state's leadership. This had happened before, for instance in July
1948, when the army put down a police revolt in Dhaka. What made 1952 a
defining moment was that it marked a sharp psychological rupture.[14] For
many in the Bengal delta, it signified the shattering of the dream of
Pakistan and the beginning of a new political project, still hazy and fully
supported by only a few: the search for a secular alternative to the communal idiom of Pakistan politics and for an autonomy that the delta had
last experienced in pre-Mughal times.[15]

Plate 12.3 Central Martyrs' Memorial or Shohid Minar, Dhaka.

The Pakistan government completely failed to understand the depth of feeling underlying the language movement and the demand for regional autonomy for East Pakistan, first voiced formally during constitutional discussions in 1950. It critically misinterpreted the movement as a conspiracy by 'clever politicians and disruptionists from within the Muslim community and caste Hindus and communists from Calcutta as well as from inside Pakistan'.[16] The Pakistan government would use this conspiracy theory time and again in an attempt to expose any East Pakistani protest as the work of puppets of, or conspirators with, the 'enemies of Pakistan' – among whom Hindus, communists and Indians figured prominently.

ELECTORAL POLITICS

The events of February 1952 turned East Pakistanis categorically against the Muslim League government. This became clear to all in 1954, when East Pakistan held its first provincial elections (the rulers of Pakistan did not dare concede national general elections until 1970, twenty-three years after the state was formed).[17] The elections of 1954 were also the first elections ever in the Bengal delta on the basis of a universal adult franchise. Throughout East Pakistan, the ruling Muslim League was routed and deeply humiliated: out of 309 seats, it won only seven. In a West Pakistan newspaper this debacle was blamed on 'the attitude of businessmen and Government officers from West Pakistan [that] caused certain misunderstanding in the minds of the people of East Pakistan'.[18] The language movement continued until 1956, when the Pakistan Constituent Assembly agreed to accept both Urdu and Bengali as state languages after all and Pakistan finally had a constitution.[19] By that time, however, the struggle for autonomy among East Pakistanis had moved beyond the question of language.

The elections of 1954 were won by an alliance known as the United Front and its style of politics has dominated politics in the Bengal delta ever since. This style is best described as mobilising the street: it depends heavily on drumming up popular support by means of fiery speeches delivered at enormous public rallies, organising protest marches and general strikes, and issuing political manifestos. The United Front was a shaky coalition of parties sharing little more than being against the incumbent Muslim League. The largest of these parties was the Awami Muslim League; it alone bagged about 46 per cent of the seats, replacing the discredited Muslim League as a new political organisation with broad legitimacy. The United Front's election manifesto consisted of twenty-one points. Four of these had to do with language questions; others dealt with autonomy, citizens' rights and economic emancipation.

The economic demands reverberated strongly with the rural electorate. Most people in the eastern delta had imagined Pakistan first and foremost as a peasant utopia that would bring deliverance from Hindu landlords, merchants and moneylenders as well as an end to agrarian stagnation. Prosperity was far more important to them than the division of state power, language issues or religious disputes. They were enthusiastic about the manifesto points demanding that the zamindari system be abolished, agriculture modernised and floods controlled. The middle classes, on the other hand, were attracted to the idea of rationalising pay scales, reforming education and nationalising the jute trade. Economically, the first years of Pakistan had been a struggle. The defeat of the Muslim League was as much a verdict on its failure to bring prosperity as on its political and cultural arrogance.

The mid-1950s were a brief period of rekindled hope for East Pakistan's middle classes. To many it seemed that it might yet be possible to bring the state under the control of the people. In the British period the state had been distant and autocratic, and the early Pakistan state had turned out to be quite similar. Only a minuscule elite from East Pakistan had been allowed to take part in the Pakistan state, always on terms not of their own making. As a result, even the most powerful East Pakistanis never had a sense of owning the post-1947 state. The elections of 1954, however, gave them renewed hope of a real partnership. This hope was soon tempered, however, when the new government was summarily (and undemocratically) dismissed, initiating a four-year period of political confusion and instability.

In 1955 the Awami Muslim League renamed itself Awami League in order to stress its non-communal character. The party carried its reformist and secular message to a wide readership through its daily newspaper *Ittefaq* (Harmony). Events at the apex of the Pakistan state strengthened its appeal. Awami Leaguers walked out of the Constituent Assembly in protest against Pakistan's first constitution, which did not meet the party's long-standing demands. Nevertheless, the constitution came into force in March 1956 and the National Assembly was inaugurated (Plate 12.4). The constitution declared Pakistan an Islamic state and installed a president with extensive powers. In the ensuing political confusion, the Awami League leadership was actually asked to join a new provincial government in East Pakistan and, after much discussion, decided to do so. One of the junior members of the new cabinet was a thirty-six-year-old party organiser by the name of Sheikh Mujibur Rahman. The decision to join the

Plate 12.4 The National Assembly of Pakistan in session, Dhaka, October 1956.

government caused a schism in the party. Its founder and president, Maulana Bhashani, called a conference in Kagmari (Tangail district) in early 1957 to demand political reform towards regional autonomy and a non-aligned foreign policy. He warned that 'if East Bengal were not granted autonomy, the people would ultimately say "Assalamu Alaikum" (good-bye) to Pakistan'. Later that year, Bhashani left the party to form the National Awami Party (NAP), which attracted many left-wing and rural followers because it reaffirmed the need for class struggle, religious tolerance and regional autonomy.[20]

Soon, however, all this political turmoil was of little direct relevance. The entire political class was swept aside when, in October 1958, the Pakistan army staged a *coup d'état*, abrogated the constitution and imposed martial rule. Thus ended Pakistan's first experiment with electoral politics and parliamentary democracy. A dictator now headed the state. He was Ayub Khan, the commander-in-chief of the armed forces.

The coup capped a process in which, during the mid-1950s, Pakistan's bureaucratic and military institutions had gradually risen to a position of dominance over elected institutions. Another way of putting it is that the popular, participatory nation lost out to the non-democratic state apparatus that Pakistan had inherited from British rule. This was reflected not only in the timing of the coup – just months before the first national elections that had been scheduled for early 1959 but were now cancelled – but also in the personality now taking charge of Pakistan's affairs. Unlike the politicians he brushed aside, Ayub Khan had spent his whole life in the service of the colonial state (from military training in Britain in the 1920s to fighting for the British empire in Myanmar (Burma) in the 1940s) and then in that of the Pakistan state (becoming commander-in-chief in the 1950s). Throughout his rule, his main concern would be to strengthen the state and make it impervious to popular forces.

The coup of 1958 was as critical an event as the language movement for understanding contemporary Bangladesh. It provided a crucial model for successive military rulers, who used it after Bangladesh became independent and who would rule the country during most of the final quarter of the twentieth century. Whereas the language movement was a clear manifestation of the popular, participatory nation attempting to influence the state, the coup of 1958 augured in a state that was relatively autonomous from the nation. Rather than depending on links with the structures of economic power and social control within the country, senior civil and military officials came to rely increasingly on their connections with international guarantors. This constellation gave rise to intense misgivings about the legitimacy of their power.[21] Bangladesh was to inherit this state structure designed to favour the military and bureaucratic top brass and in perpetual need of external financial and political support against popular forces within the country.

DICTATORSHIP

The coup of 1958 signalled the determination of Pakistan's elite – its army leaders, top bureaucrats and richest businessmen – to put a stop to what they saw as the politicians' ineptitude and corruption. The defeat of the Muslim League in East Pakistan had left the country without any party that could claim to have nationwide legitimacy. Building a unified Pakistani nation seemed harder than ever. The coup leaders were confident that the army was the only institution in the country that could provide the firm hand that Pakistan needed to put it on the right track. To this end they abolished parliamentary democracy, locked up troublesome politicians, curtailed the judiciary, muzzled the press, suspended citizen's rights and introduced martial law. Now army men took control of the civil service, and the executive branch of the state became all-powerful. Initially the military became involved in economic policy-making as well, but when this led to chaos they decided to exert control from the background, leaving the limelight to the civil service.

For East Pakistan, all this took on a special meaning. Here military rule meant that power was now even more decisively in the hands of non-locals. East Pakistan's elite had wielded power mainly through political mobilisation, not through the army or the bureaucracy. The headquarters of Pakistan's army, air force and navy were all in West Pakistan. The vast majority of the armed forces' personnel were recruited from West Pakistan; a mere 3 per cent of the higher ranks were East Pakistanis. West Pakistanis dominated Pakistan's central administrative apparatus (filling 93 per cent of the higher posts) and even East Pakistan's provincial administration. Even though the new regime inducted more East Pakistanis, particularly in the provincial administration, this did not alter the general impression among East Pakistanis that their province was essentially an internal colony of West Pakistan, or, more precisely, of its dominant province, Punjab. Ayub Khan's personal views of Bengalis were in fact classically colonial. In his autobiography he described Bengalis as having 'all the inhibitions of downtrodden races and [having] not yet found it possible to adjust psychologically to the requirements of the new born freedom. Their popular complexes, exclusiveness, suspicion, and a sort of defensive aggressiveness ... should be recognized and catered for and they be helped so as to feel equal partners and prove an asset.'[22]

True to the tradition of many military dictators, Ayub Khan declared that the coup had been carried out in the defence of democracy. It was aimed 'not against the institutions of democracy, but only against the manner in which these were functioning'. In his view, the prevalent forms of democracy were too complex to be operated successfully by the 'simple and illiterate peoples of Pakistan, and too remote to attract their active participation'.[23] A new system was introduced in 1959, ostensibly to teach the populace democratic ways and to prepare them for eventual full participation in representative government. This system was given the name 'basic democracies'. It was reminiscent of the British colonial system of political tutelage known as 'local self-government', and, like this precursor, it aimed at bringing political processes under bureaucratic control and at localising political issues. Rejecting the parliamentary form of government, banning political parties and restricting urban influence, the basic democracies combined paternalism and full control by state officials with some trappings of electoral representation, but only at the lowest level.

Plate 12.5 The Bangladesh Parliament, originally conceived as Pakistan's National Assembly Building. Designed by Louis Kahn in 1962, it was completed in 1983.

In 1962 an authoritarian constitution was promulgated with a view to perpetuating the regime indefinitely. It breathed an utter distrust of popular power and representative government, gave extraordinary powers to the president (as Ayub Khan now styled himself) and created a feeble national assembly. Islamabad would be the seat of the national government and Dhaka (now designated the 'second capital') would be the principal seat of the national assembly. Soon a complex of prize-winning futuristic buildings materialised on the outskirts of Dhaka to accommodate the assembly. Today these buildings – a statement of 'dictator chic'[24] – house the Bangladesh parliament (Plate 12.5).

The military regime saw itself as stern, fair, constructive, efficient and avuncular. Most East Pakistanis, however, saw it as autocratic, imperialist, violent and geared to perpetuating the vice-regal power of Ayub Khan. The Ayub regime was even less prepared than Pakistan's politicians had been to give concessions to East Pakistan – not surprising in view of the fact that both the civil service and the army were essentially West Pakistani institutions. The regime thought that firm paternalism was the magic solution to the perennial fear of Pakistan's rulers: disruption of national unity if East Pakistan was given its democratic share of power. Instead of the superfluous pyrotechnics of political rivalry and 'narrow-minded provincialism', the regime promised competent economic management, steady growth, a robust state and national harmony. Its mantra was economic development.

CHAPTER 13

Pakistan Falls Apart

For some in the Bengal delta, Pakistan had been a let-down from the word go. Right after Partition an elderly villager approached a local politician and asked him: 'Now that Pakistan has been achieved, should there still be police, courts and kutcheries [zamindar's courts], soldiers and sentries, jails and lockups?' When the politician replied in the affirmative, the man was bewildered: 'Then what kind of Pakistan [have we got]? Change the name please. You will name it Pakistan [the Land of the Pure, and yet] allow sins and corruption to exist.'[1]

Unlike him, many others were very hopeful about the benefits of independence and self-determination. And yet, by the mid-1960s, the Pakistan experiment was in deep trouble. By now East Pakistan's elite had long struggled to get a better deal for themselves at the national centre – but it had gradually dawned on them that this was not going to happen. They came to the conclusion that only a movement for far-reaching regional autonomy could protect their interests.

Between 1962 and 1968 the Ayub regime was personified in the delta by a hostile provincial governor, Abdul Monem Khan, who persecuted and arrested political opponents, tightened control over the media and created an atmosphere of fear. He renewed the attack on the Bengali language – infamously banning songs by Rabindranath Tagore, the most revered poet, from Radio Pakistan – and thereby revived the politics of language. Now, celebrating 21 February or Tagore's birthday, or writing street signs and signboards in Bengali, became popular acts of defiance.[2]

The unpopularity of the regime deepened further in 1965, when Pakistan started a war with India over Kashmir. During the six weeks of the war national sentiments ran high in East Pakistan, but this proved to be the last flicker of the dying flame of national unity. East Pakistanis soon realised that there were hardly any armed forces in the province to defend them, leaving them completely exposed in the event of an Indian invasion. Even though India did not invade, the inhabitants of East Pakistan felt virtually cut off from West Pakistan. Feelings of insecurity, betrayal and anger intensified the desire for autonomy, and this proved to be the making of a charismatic politician who would dominate the scene during the next ten years.

In early 1966 Sheikh Mujibur Rahman of the Awami League captured the mood by presenting a list of demands known as the Six-Point Programme. It was more radical than previous demands for autonomy because it no longer advocated a federal structure for Pakistan. Instead, it demanded a confederation of two separate units. Only defence and foreign affairs would remain as subjects of the all-Pakistan government.

East Pakistan would be in complete control of its own taxation, financial management, earnings from foreign trade, trade agreements with foreign countries and paramilitary forces. It could also have its own currency. To counter any accusations of provincialism, secessionism or anti-Pakistan activity, the Six Points referred emphatically to the Lahore Resolution of 1940, which had called for the creation of Pakistan. Everybody remembered that this resolution had stated that 'the areas in which the Muslims are numerically in a majority as in the North Western and Eastern Zones of (British) India should be grouped to constitute "independent states" in which the constituent units should be autonomous and sovereign'.

The Six Points spawned a militant movement that drew strength from revived linguistic nationalism as well as from economic hardship following the war.[3] For the first time, workers played a very prominent part, and this led to more confrontational tactics. The movement still featured large meetings and student processions ending in clashes with the police, but this time there were also mob attacks on police stations, banks, government buildings and the offices of pro-government newspapers. As the movement developed a mass character, its ways became rougher and the elite codes that had previously framed oppositional politics gave way to more street-wise methods.

Predictably, the government responded with heavy-handed repression and threats. This policy proved to be effective in the short run and the movement abated. It backfired in the longer run, however, because the government turned the leaders of the Awami League into martyrs by arresting them and keeping them imprisoned for over two years. The government built up Sheikh Mujibur Rahman's public image, in particular, when it brought the 'Agartala conspiracy case' to trial in 1968. In this case Mujib and others were accused of a conspiracy to separate East Pakistan from Pakistan with the help of the Indian government, a plan worked out during a secret meeting with Indian officials in the border town of Agartala (India). The regime had thought that this case would demolish Mujib's reputation by exposing him as an enemy of Pakistan and an Indian agent, but the reverse happened; mass agitations in support of the accused forced the authorities to abandon the case midway.[4] At a large public meeting immediately following his release Mujib was given an honorific that would stick: Bongobondhu (*bangabandhu*), or Friend of Bengal.

The resurgence of the Awami League after 1965 was embedded in a broader development in East Pakistan politics: a polarisation of left and right. The Awami League was made up of Bengali nationalists who were socially middle-of-the-road or conservative; their Six Points did not envisage social change. Pitted against them were leftists of various parties who advocated social revolution. The most popular was the National Awami Party, which had recently split into pro-China and pro-USSR factions.[5]

This division became important in 1968–9, when a new wave of unrest swept over Pakistan.[6] Started in West Pakistan with the aim of toppling the Ayub regime, the uprising spread to East Pakistan where it took on Bengali nationalist overtones. An alliance of East Pakistani student organisations took the initiative to form a united front that adopted an eleven-point manifesto. This included the Awami League's Six Points but also social demands to attract leftists: lower taxes on farmers, higher wages for workers and the nationalisation of big industries and banks. The movement radicalised as industrial workers and urban and rural poor pressed for their own demands. The leaders of the established political parties were not in control of the movement and they had a hard time following the popular upsurge. Months of gheraos (*gherão*; a mass tactic to surround employers physically and hold them captive until they accede to workers' demands) and street violence followed. The movement came out victorious when Ayub Khan fell, the governor fled and the autonomists were emboldened to up the ante. Mujib now demanded a dominant position for the eastern wing as well as parliamentary government with full regional autonomy and relocation of the country's capital to East Pakistan.

When Ayub Khan was forced to step down in March 1969, the commander-in-chief of the Pakistan army, General Yahya Khan, took his place. Yahya represented the same military–bureaucratic alliance as his predecessor and he immediately declared martial law with a view to protecting that alliance's position. But Yahya chose a different path from Ayub. He sought

Plate 13.1 Sheikh Mujibur Rahman campaigning by train, 1970.

conciliation rather than confrontation, and he tried to bring the politicians back into the power equation in Pakistan. He announced that political activities were to be allowed from early 1970 and that Pakistan's first general elections for the National Assembly would be held later that year. As president, he retained extensive powers, however, and the military–bureaucratic elite considered these sufficient to guarantee their future hold on the state, whatever the outcome of the elections.

Soon, East Pakistan's politicians were campaigning as never before: East Pakistan had been allotted a majority of seats in the assembly, so if any party managed a landslide victory in East Pakistan it might control the assembly. This is what the Awami League went all out for (Plate 13.1). West Pakistan's politicians were less sanguine about the outcome of the elections, and one of the most prominent, Zulfikar Ali Bhutto, was already considering violent repression. According to Yahya Khan, Bhutto advised him in the summer of 1970 to forget about the elections: 'Yahya the soldier and Bhutto the politician will make a very good team and can together run the country.' When Yahya asked him what he proposed to do about East Pakistan, Bhutto reportedly replied: 'East Pakistan is no problem. We will have to kill some 20,000 people there and all will be well.'[7]

At this point the delta's capricious natural conditions upset the well-laid plans of Pakistan's rulers. The summer of 1970 saw immense floods in East Pakistan, forcing a postponement of the elections to December. Then, in November, a cyclone hit the Bengal delta. This was no run-of-the-mill cyclone but the most devastating one that had ever been registered in the region. According to official figures an unimaginable 500,000 people perished in the gale and tidal surges (other sources suggest at least 325,000). The president, Yahya Khan, visited East Pakistan. 'He flew over the stricken area in a Fokker Friendship aircraft and drank several cans of imported beer during the flight. He was not frightfully impressed by what he saw.'[8] Relief was slow and insufficient, and the Yahya regime's utter incapacity to deal with the disaster stood exposed. Worse, the regime was widely seen as callously indifferent to the fate of the victims, causing extreme anger in East Pakistan. The leftist parties now called for immediate independence from Pakistan and decided to boycott the December elections. This left the Awami League a wide-open field and bagged them an even more massive win than they had dreamed of. When the votes were counted, they had won all but two of the 162 seats allotted to East Pakistan (one of these remaining seats was won by the Chakma Raja (see box 'Tridiv the Raja')) as well as all seven women's seats. This huge success gave the Awami League an absolute majority in Pakistan's 300-seat National Assembly, something that hardly anybody had foreseen. The second largest party in the assembly (with eighty-one seats) was the Pakistan People's Party, headed by Bhutto. This party had not fielded any candidates in East Pakistan and drew its votes entirely from West Pakistan.[9] To everybody's surprise, the Pakistani voters had completely abandoned the national parties and created a polarised National Assembly dominated by two regional parties.

Tridiv the raja

One afternoon in 1953 a festive mood pervaded the hill town of Rangamati. The audience hall of the palace was crowded with dignitaries participating in a ceremony combining Mughal, British and Pakistani elements. The republic of Pakistan was installing a new raja (king, chief) in the Chittagong Hill Tracts. Rifle salutes, an official proclamation and the presentation of a ceremonial sword to a nineteen-year-old boy marked the occasion. This was how Tridiv Roy succeeded his recently deceased father as the Chakma raja. Later that afternoon a boat with a gilded peacock bow glided into view. It carried Tridiv's bride and her party, who were brought up to the palace 'in brocaded palanquins on the shoulders of traditional serfs', accompanied by guards and drummers. That night the bride, Arati Dewan, 'dressed in a gold Benares silk sari and coronet and ornaments', became the new Chakma rani (queen). (Plate 13.2)

Plate 13.2 Newly installed Raja Tridiv Roy with his bride Arati in Rangamati, 1953.

This romantic scene was an important moment in a life that would be buffeted by political developments. Raja Tridiv played many different roles. Educated in elite boarding schools around colonial Bengal and connected to aristocratic families across the region, he was now a chief collecting taxes for the Pakistan state during an annual gathering at his Rangamati palace. He was also the titular head of the Chakma people, a magistrate, a politician and occasionally a member of official delegations abroad. In 1962 he became an environmental refugee as the Kaptai hydroelectric project was completed and a huge lake flooded the central valleys of the Chittagong Hill Tracts. Tridiv's palace was one of thousands of homes that disappeared under water. He built a new mansion on one of the new islands in the lake.

In 1971 Raja Tridiv's life, like that of so many in Pakistan, changed unrecognisably. Elected to the National Assembly in 1970 as one of two independent candidates from East Pakistan (all other members belonging to the Awami League), he did not join the movement for Bangladesh, largely because he thought the regional autonomy of the Chittagong Hill Tracts would be more threatened in an independent Bangladesh than in Pakistan.

When the Bangladesh Liberation War broke out, he sought to stay neutral but ultimately sided with Pakistan, acting as its envoy on a goodwill trip to Sri Lanka and Southeast Asia and serving as a minister in the army-dominated provincial government. At the end of the war, he moved to Pakistan, leaving his family behind in newly formed Bangladesh. The Bangladesh government, regarding him as a traitor, deposed him and recognised his son Devasish as raja. Raja Tridiv became a minister in the post-war Pakistan cabinet and later Pakistan's ambassador to Argentina and other countries. As some of his children joined him, the family spread over several continents. He passed away in Islamabad in 2012.[10]

The Yahya regime was now confronted with an unanticipated situation. Miraculously, the nightmare of East Pakistani control of the state seemed within reach after all. Mujib confidently assumed that he would soon head an all-Awami League government of Pakistan and his party set about preparing a new, more democratic constitution for the country. Both the military–bureaucratic elite and the West Pakistan politicians, however, found this unpalatable. Bhutto demanded a share of power, which Mujib rejected. Bhutto then announced that he would boycott the first session of the National Assembly on 3 March 1971 and threatened members from smaller West Pakistani parties who were planning to travel to Dhaka (where the National Assembly was located) with dire consequences. He also asked Yahya Khan to postpone the session. This is what

Plate 13.3 'Mujib: This Time It Is a Struggle for Independence.'

Yahya did on 1 March, provoking spontaneous demonstrations and clashes between protesters and the armed forces in East Pakistan. It was clear that Pakistan was facing a crisis of legitimacy as never before – and that this time something had to give.

In the chaotic final days of united Pakistan, Mujib came under intense pressure from leftist politicians and activists in East Pakistan to declare independence right away. The military rulers, on the other hand, flew in troops to make sure that Mujib would abstain from such a pronouncement. As East Pakistan reeled under violent battles between demonstrators and armed forces, Mujib tried to steer a strategic middle course by launching a non-violent movement of non-cooperation. It was an instant success, paralysing the East Pakistan administration and putting Mujib in *de facto* control of the province. He declared that East Pakistanis were now engaged in a struggle for independence, but at the same time he continued to seek a solution within the framework of Pakistan. He imagined that he could still be the prime minister of a united Pakistan (Plate 13.3).

In mid-March 1971, Yahya flew to Dhaka, ostensibly in a last-ditch attempt to work out a political solution. He was joined there by Bhutto, but none of the proposed arrangements for the transfer of power met with the approval of all three parties. Yahya was ready to grant the far-reaching autonomy to East Pakistan that the Six-Point Programme demanded and he was willing to accept Mujib as Pakistan's prime

Plate 13.4 'Parade of the *Joy Bangla Bahini* (Victory to Bangladesh Troops).'

minister. Bhutto saw this as a massive betrayal of West Pakistan.[11] As deadlock continued in the conference rooms, political turmoil reached fever pitch on the streets and even more West Pakistani troops were secretly flown in. The Awami League presented a draft proclamation on regional autonomy to Yahya on 23 March, warning that it needed to be issued within forty-eight hours or else East Pakistan would spin out of control. Everybody was now talking about independence, and activists carrying the new flag of 'Bangladesh' could be seen taking arms training (Plate 13.4).

On 25 March, while keeping the Awami League engaged in talks, the Yahya regime decided on a pre-planned military solution to the crisis.[12] That night Yahya stealthily flew back to West Pakistan after ordering the Pakistan army to attack the nuclei of the autonomy movement. As the soldiers started their targeted killings in Dhaka and all over East Pakistan, they ignited the Bangladesh Liberation War. We will take up that story in Chapter 17, but first we will consider the economic and cultural developments that underlay the political estrangement between East and West Pakistan.

CHAPTER 14

East Pakistani Livelihoods

The political collapse of Pakistan had deep roots in economic frustration. In the 1940s, most supporters of Pakistan had been full of hope for the Bengal delta's rapid improvement. They thought that independence was bound to make the region flourish. It would rid itself of the exploitative British colonial system and remove the landlords, merchants and officials who had personified it. Of course, Partition would create initial dislocations that needed to be overcome, but the longer-term prospects were thought to be bright.

After Partition, however, things suddenly looked much more complicated. The Muslim League leadership was ill-prepared to govern, its policies were not geared towards invigorating the Bengal delta economy, and its attempts to construct a national economy turned out to have numerous unanticipated effects. Moreover, population exchange was far more extensive and disruptive than had been expected. The early years of East Pakistan (as the Bengal delta was now known) were characterised by political volatility and economic turmoil.

A RURAL ECONOMY

Throughout the Pakistan period East Pakistan was a massively rural society: more than nine out of ten people lived in the countryside. For most East Pakistanis, life was closely linked to the rhythms of agriculture. A rural household's day would typically begin before dawn. The household tasks were allocated according to gender and age. The wife would light straw and cow-dung cakes in the courtyard hearth to prepare breakfast. Her father-in-law might amble off to attend early-morning prayer at the village mosque. As day broke, she served a breakfast of leftover rice with salt, chillies and some vegetables to her husband, in-laws and children before sweeping the yard and feeding the family animals. Her husband then led the small bullocks along the village path, raised as a causeway above the floodplain, to the field, where he yoked them to the wooden plough. A son took the goats grazing and a daughter went to fetch water from the nearby pond. The wife and her mother-in-law spent their day cooking, cleaning, washing clothes, replastering the woven-bamboo walls of the house, taking care of the smaller children and the household chickens, and tending the vegetable patch. The husband ploughed and had his cooked lunch brought to him in the field. He returned home in the afternoon for a rest and then did odd jobs around the house. The children helped their parents, played or attended the village school. As daylight faded, the husband walked to the next village, where a market was held twice a week (Plate 14.1). He sold a chicken there and returned with

Plate 14.1 A village market.

kerosene oil, fish, cigarettes and the latest gossip. After a late dinner, lit by small oil lamps, the family went to sleep at around 9 p.m.

The social order in the Bengal delta rested on kinship, not surprising in view of life in communities in which family groups worked the land and acted as society's main safety nets. The ideology of kinship was extremely strong and it even embraced people who were not related through blood or marriage. It was (and continues to be) a general rule that strangers quickly establish a fictive kinship bond.[1] Thus a man would call the wife of an acquaintance 'elder sister' (apa, didi; *āpā, didi*) and an elderly shopkeeper 'uncle' (chacha; *cācā*). The kin ideology came with complex rules of respect and deference, codes of mutual obligation and protection, and intense feelings of belonging. This is not to say that there could not be enormous tensions within the large, often multigenerational households that formed the basis of society, but kinship was undisputedly the model of the rural social order.

Agriculture dominated the economy. According to census data, 83 per cent of the East Pakistan labour force worked in agriculture at the beginning of the Pakistan period in 1951, a figure that went up to 85 per cent in 1961, and stood at about 77 per cent when Pakistan collapsed. Agriculture contributed 65 per cent of East Pakistan's gross product in 1951 and 56 per cent by 1970, indicating both technological stagnation in agriculture and a measure of diversification of East Pakistan's economy.[2] In other words, East Pakistan was essentially a rural society that underwent little structural change during the Pakistan period. The average inhabitant lived in a village, derived a livelihood from the growing of crops and the rearing of livestock, could not read or write, and was embedded in rural networks of kinship, marketing, faith and sociability. At the end of the Pakistan period, four out of five East Pakistanis were still illiterate. The state provided few services and it was distant and aloof. State institutions, if available at all, were far less relevant and accessible than local forms of healthcare (Ayurvedic medicine offered by village doctors), justice (village courts), moral guidance (village imams) and social security (rotating saving groups).

ECONOMIC POLICY

After Partition, the governments of both India and Pakistan were concerned with improving living standards and developing more balanced economies. They built on policies and plans initiated during the period of British rule – the developmentalist state long predated Partition but now became more dynamic. Both Pakistan and India prioritised rapid industrialisation, but they chose different policies to achieve this. Pakistan, unlike India, sought to encourage private enterprise to the fullest. Except for a few strategic industries (arms, railways, hydroelectric power), the state's policy was to leave economic development to private entrepreneurs and to support them lavishly with subsidies and facilities. Where did these subsidies go? Pakistan spent much of its budget on security. In fact, it developed what Ayesha Jalal has called a 'political economy of defence', characterised by the maintenance of defence budgets well beyond its resource capacities.[3] Between 1947 and 1970, more than half of Pakistan's central expenditure went to defence. About a third of the remaining budget went to industry and a mere one tenth to agriculture, starving development projects.[4] As a result, army generals and the biggest entrepreneurs formed tight alliances with top bureaucrats. By the late 1960s, according to Pakistani chief economist Mahbub ul Haq, just twenty-two families owned 66 per cent of Pakistan's industrial wealth and controlled 87 per cent of the assets of the banking and insurance industries. This finding suggests an extreme concentration of wealth and power, but it also indicates something else: none of these families were Bengalis.

This concentration of economic power in the country's western wing, combined with political power in the hands of West Pakistanis as well, set the scene for a very imbalanced economic relationship between the two wings. For example, two-thirds of Pakistan's foreign exchange was earned in East Pakistan – mostly through jute exports – but much of it was diverted to West Pakistan.[5] In this way, West Pakistan received considerable resources from East Pakistan to finance its own development. On the other hand, the government spent less than a quarter of its budget in East Pakistan, where the majority of Pakistanis lived.[6] During the 1950s, per capita income rose in West Pakistan but declined in East Pakistan, and education and communications advanced much more rapidly in West Pakistan.[7]

When Pakistan came into being, the eastern wing had been at an economic disadvantage. In the Pakistan period the economic gap between the two wings increased. Although many in East Pakistan blamed this squarely on wilful discrimination in government development policy, there were other factors as well. Government allocations were larger in West Pakistan because most immigrant entrepreneurs settled there and because Pakistan's capital city was in West Pakistan. Foreign investments were lower in East Pakistan on account of the low level of indigenous entrepreneurship and considerable political volatility and labour unrest.[8]

Finally, the industrial and urban bias in Pakistan's development policies did not favour the overwhelmingly agricultural and rural economy of East Pakistan.

Facts of geography exacerbated Pakistan's lopsided economic development. First, Partition had left East Pakistan almost completely surrounded by India, cutting old trade links and transport connections. Partition amputated East Bengal from the regional economy that Assam, East Bengal and West Bengal had formed for centuries. This economic disruption put East Pakistan at a disadvantage to West Pakistan. Second, the distance between the two wings of Pakistan was 1,500 km as the crow flies, but the uncertain and often difficult relations with India made the two wings actually even more remote. The principal means of communication between them was by sea around the mass of the Indian subcontinent, and this added several thousands of kilometres to the effective distance between East and West Pakistan. Air traffic across Indian territory was possible most of the time, especially for passenger services (Plate 14.2), but only 1 per cent of what came to be known as 'inter-wing' trade went by air.

Over time the economic disparities between the wings did not decline. Initially observers of Pakistan described the eastern wing as a region neglected and overlooked by the government. Gradually, however, most came round to the view that the region was not so much neglected as systematically exploited by West Pakistani overlords.[9] As the post-Partition euphoria wore off, East Pakistanis began to see themselves very much in the role of second-class citizens, a feeling captured by cartoonist Ahmed in Plate 14.3.[10]

To some extent Pakistani rule resembled the Mughal annexation of the Bengal delta some 300 years previously. Dhaka had once again become the garrison town from which northern Indian rulers sought to dominate the countryside, agriculture was the mainstay of the delta's economy and the delta's wealth subsidised the centre of power. The West Pakistan elite consumed a large variety of goods from the Bengal delta, officers sent to East Pakistan felt that they had landed a hardship posting and economic improvement occurred mainly for the benefit of a select few in West Pakistan.

In one important way, however, Pakistani rule differed radically from Mughal rule. The Mughals had developed a system of land taxation in the Bengal delta that the British took over and adapted. Their 'permanent settlement' had made the zamindars owners of land and payers of a fixed tax to the government. This system was now dismantled. The East Bengal State Acquisition and Tenancy Act of 1950 eliminated the superior rights of

SUPER CONSTELLATION SERVICE

KARACHI - LAHORE - DACCA

Commencing 4th June, you can fly in Super Constellation comfort between Karachi and Dacca via Lahore.

No passport formalities for Pakistan citizens, travelling by this Non-Stop service between Lahore and Dacca.

From Karachi every **SATURDAY**.

From Dacca every **TUESDAY**

NEW COACH SERVICES

LOWEST FARES EVER
COMMENCE 8TH JUNE

Karachi - Multan - Lahore - Rawalpindi - Peshawar

Two Services to MULTAN *and* LAHORE
One Service to PESHAWAR *via* MULTAN, LAHORE *and* RAWALPINDI

FARES

KARACHI - MULTAN Rs. 84/- KARACHI - LAHORE Rs. 120/- KARACHI - RAWALPINDI Rs. 150/- KARACHI - PESHAWAR Rs. 165/- MULTAN - LAHORE Rs. 36/- MULTAN - RAWALPINDI Rs. 66/- MULTAN - PESHAWAR Rs. 81/- LAHORE - RAWALPINDI Rs. 30/- LAHORE - PESHAWAR Rs. 45/- RAWALPINDI - PESHAWAR Rs. 15/-
(THE ABOVE FARES ARE FOR SINGLE JOURNEY)

For more details contact your travel agent or

PAKISTAN INTERNATIONAL AIRLINES

The Mall, LAHORE.

Flashman's Hotel, RAWALPINDI. Dean's Hotel, PESHAWAR.

Plate 14.2 Pakistan International Airlines announces its first direct flights between East and West Pakistan in 1955, eight years after the birth of Pakistan. Up to then, air travel between the 'wings' was via Indian airports.

AFTER THE HONEYMOON

Plate 14.3 'After the honeymoon.' Cartoon by Ahmed.

zamindars and those of the many intermediaries below them and made all landholders direct tenants under the government. It also imposed a ceiling on landholdings of about 13 hectares per family. The result was a land tax reform and an increase in state tax demand. It was not a land reform, however. By the end of British rule almost 75 per cent of the land had belonged to Hindu landlords, many of whom had been absentees or had migrated to India after Partition. The new legislation caused powerful Muslim families in the rural areas feverishly to reshuffle and invent claims on land as they grabbed the property of zamindars who had left. They portrayed intermediary rights as direct tenancies and circumvented the land ceiling by registering their fields in the name of dependents. The reform did eradicate the old tax-receiving elite, but it actually reinforced the unequal agrarian structure of the delta. It denied sharecroppers any

SUPER CONSTELLATION SERVICE

KARACHI-
LAHORE -
DACCA

Commencing 4th June, you can fly in Super Constellation comfort between Karachi and Dacca via Lahore.

No passport formalities for Pakistan citizens, travelling by this Non-Stop service between Lahore and Dacca.

From Karachi every **SATURDAY**.

From Dacca every **TUESDAY**

NEW COACH SERVICES

LOWEST FARES EVER
COMMENCE *8TH. JUNE*

Karachi - Multan - Lahore - Rawalpindi - Peshawar

Two Services to MULTAN *and* LAHORE
One Service to PESHAWAR *via* MULTAN, LAHORE *and* RAWALPINDI

FARES

KARACHI - MULTAN Rs. 84/- KARACHI - LAHORE Rs. 120/- KARACHI- RAWALPINDI Rs. 150/- KARACHI - PESHAWAR Rs. 165/- MULTAN - LAHORE Rs. 36/- MULTAN - RAWALPINDI Rs. 66/- MULTAN - PESHAWAR Rs. 81/- LAHORE - RAWALPINDI Rs. 30/- LAHORE - PESHAWAR Rs. 45/- RAWALPINDI - PESHAWAR Rs. 15/-
(THE ABOVE FARES ARE FOR SINGLE JOURNEY)

For more details contact your travel agent or

PAKISTAN INTERNATIONAL AIRLINES

The Mall, LAHORE.

Flashman's Hotel, RAWALPINDI.   Dean's Hotel, PESHAWAR.

Plate 14.2 Pakistan International Airlines announces its first direct flights between East and West Pakistan in 1955, eight years after the birth of Pakistan. Up to then, air travel between the 'wings' was via Indian airports.

AFTER THE HONEYMOON

Plate 14.3 'After the honeymoon.' Cartoon by Ahmed.

zamindars and those of the many intermediaries below them and made all landholders direct tenants under the government. It also imposed a ceiling on landholdings of about 13 hectares per family. The result was a land tax reform and an increase in state tax demand. It was not a land reform, however. By the end of British rule almost 75 per cent of the land had belonged to Hindu landlords, many of whom had been absentees or had migrated to India after Partition. The new legislation caused powerful Muslim families in the rural areas feverishly to reshuffle and invent claims on land as they grabbed the property of zamindars who had left. They portrayed intermediary rights as direct tenancies and circumvented the land ceiling by registering their fields in the name of dependents. The reform did eradicate the old tax-receiving elite, but it actually reinforced the unequal agrarian structure of the delta. It denied sharecroppers any rights in land and equated them with wage labourers. It fell far short of the expectations of the smallholders and landless peasants who had looked forward to receiving the excess land previously held by large landholders. Even though entitled to this land under the new law, they did not get it. In this regard the Pakistan experiment was a bitter disappointment to them: the utopia they had imagined never materialised.

For most inhabitants of East Pakistan, land was the main measure of wealth. Around 1960 some 20 per cent of the rural population had no access to land except as wage labourers. The vast majority of landholdings were quite small: over 50 per cent of all farms were smaller than 1 hectare (together accounting for only 16 per cent of the cultivated area) and almost 90 per cent were smaller than 3 hectares.[11] To complicate matters, individual landholdings were usually fragmented into many different small plots – a result of partible inheritance as well as the need to own both low-lying and higher land. State attempts to consolidate these plots met with fierce resistance and had to be abandoned.

With such small landholdings and very little state investment in agriculture, yields were low, technological change sluggish and poverty widespread. Nevertheless, rice yields increased from 900 kg of clean rice per hectare in the early 1950s to 1,100 kg in the late 1960s, an increase that is thought to have been largely the result of an ever more intense application of labour.[12]

Rice was East Pakistan's staple food, but jute was its most important export crop. The fast-growing seasonal jute plant, indigenous in the region, yielded a fibre that was sought after worldwide for making bags, rope, burlap, garden twine, carpets, canvas, tarpaulin and many other industrial products. Its leaves were also used as a vegetable. Both because of its colour and because of its economic importance jute was known in Bengal as the 'golden fibre'. In the late 1940s the Bengal delta had a virtual monopoly in jute production: it supplied 80 per cent of world demand. The Partition of 1947 posed a serious challenge, however: almost all jute was grown in the eastern delta (which now fell to Pakistan) and all but one of the more than 100 processing factories were near Kolkata in West Bengal (which now fell to India). The Pakistan authorities, keen to create a national economy, forbade the export of jute to India. Now East Pakistan's jute growers were branded as smugglers when they sold to India's jute mills, the only buyers of their crop. In East Pakistan a tussle ensued between the state and the jute producers that only abated when new jute mills were established in East Pakistan. The best known of these – and the largest in the world – was the Adamjee Jute Mill, which came into production in 1955 (Plate 14.4). By the

Plate 14.4 A woman labourer sewing jute bags for export in the Adamjee Jute Mill.
Narayanganj, c. 1960.

end of the Pakistan period, there were over seventy jute mills in East
Pakistan. Meanwhile, India had promoted jute cultivation in its own
territory to supply its factories in West Bengal. Thus, Partition resulted
in the breaking up of what had once been a unified jute production and
manufacturing system, replacing it with two competing ones: one in East
Pakistan and the other in West Bengal. By the 1970s, however, world
demand for jute declined as both systems faced strong competition from
synthetic fibres, notably polypropylene.[13]

State attempts to partition the economy in other spheres were less
effective. Most trade between India and Pakistan was prohibited, but it
proved impossible to stop unauthorised cross-border exchange. There
was much evidence of brisk smuggling, and even the most energetic
policies backfired. For example, in 1957–8 Pakistan militarised the East
Pakistan border corridor in a bid to stamp out smuggling. This
'Operation Closed Door' brought terror to the borderland population
but was abandoned because it failed miserably in checking unauthorised
cross-border trade.[14]

Plate 14.5 Bamboo raft on Kaptai Lake, 1964–5.

Industrial development in East Pakistan, largely by state-supported entrepreneurs from West Pakistan, typically took the form of processing local materials in a relatively simple manner. Apart from jute manufacturing, other notable new initiatives included the establishment of sugar mills and a silk factory in the western and northern districts, tea factories in the northeast and a large paper mill in Chandraghona (Chittagong Hill Tracts).[15] The raw material for this paper mill was bamboo, cut from a decommissioned reserved hill forest and floated down the Karnaphuli river in enormous rafts (Plate 14.5). Another industry that developed after Partition was the cotton textile industry. By this time the Bengal delta had long given up producing the cotton that had once made its textiles a household word around Asia and Europe. Now, the raw material had to be imported.

Although the urban population was still a minute proportion of the total population, East Pakistan's major towns were growing fast. The population of Dhaka tripled to about 1 million inhabitants. Most newcomers were rural jobseekers who tried to find a niche in urban industries and services. One service sector that grew steadily was public transport, especially in the form of cycle-rickshaws. These had been introduced in Dhaka in the late 1930s – following two other towns, Mymensingh and

Narayanganj – and by the 1950s they had largely displaced the horse-drawn carriages that had been a common sight before. The first rickshaws were of drab appearance, but in the 1950s colourful decorations were added and these soon blossomed into what became known as urban Bangladesh's signature popular art: 'New rickshaws in Dhaka are a blaze of colour. Every square inch is decorated. Tassles, tinsel and twirly bits hang from all parts. Plastic flowers sprout in the front and sides, and pictures and patterns are painted or pinned all over.'[16] Tens of thousands of rural men found their first work in the city as rickshaw-pullers, just as women found work as domestic workers. Most new settlers lived in working-class neighbourhoods that sprang up beyond the periphery of the colonial city as Dhaka spread and added other neighbourhoods as well: office blocks were built in the Motijheel neighbourhood (Plate 14.6), administration complexes and a new market building in Ramna, factories in Tejgaon and elite housing in Dhanmondi.

By the end of the Pakistan experiment, the Bengal delta had changed a lot. It had become a territorial unit that was quite separate from the

Plate 14.6 New commercial buildings appearing in Dhaka in the 1960s.

Indian territory surrounding it. Political struggles in East Pakistan were for regional autonomy or independent statehood, not for rejoining India. In the twenty-four years since 1947 the population had grown by 60 per cent. Nine out of ten people lived in the countryside. Because most of them were dependent on agriculture, rural crowding was a serious issue, especially since poverty had not decreased. By 1971 there were many more East Pakistanis who lived in poverty than in 1947. Life expectancy at birth had improved somewhat but still stood at below fifty years. In terms of improving the quality of life, the Pakistan experiment had been a disappointment to most citizens.

CHAPTER 15

The Roots of Aid Dependence

Pakistani policy-makers saw themselves as champions of modernisation. They were confident that they knew how to jog the sluggish economy into a high gear and thus bring about 'development'. What they needed was money and a population that would follow their lead.

To be sure, this was nothing new. Agricultural stagnation in the Bengal delta had first become a policy concern in the early twentieth century. The British colonial authorities noticed that a closing agrarian frontier and population growth led to stagnating agrarian output and declining rural incomes. This prompted the first attempts at rural development (or 'rural rehabilitation', as it was then called): experiments with village cooperative societies, debt relief, crop research, agricultural extension and the application of fertilisers. Although most initiatives came from the government, some non-governmental organisations (such as the Salvation Army) were also active. The roots of the developmentalist state and development policy, which became such a central theme in independent Bangladesh, reach back more than a century.[1]

From the birth of Pakistan, the central government saw itself as devoted to development. It assumed an interventionist role, but the funds it released were unimpressive. It also overrated its capacity to transform the economy: 'with few exceptions, projects financed by the centre were among the finest textbook cases of abysmal planning, widespread corruption and gross mismanagement'.[2]

After the coup of 1958 the military regime presented itself as the only force capable of modernising Pakistan. It understood modernisation basically as economic development by centralised and authoritarian means, and it aimed at maximising growth and revenues rather than at participation or social welfare. To this end the bureaucracy was changed from an agency administering the law to an agency in charge of economic engineering. Now young bureaucrats were sent for part of their training to the newly established Pakistan Academy for Rural Development in Comilla, a town east of Dhaka.

In terms of growth, the regime's policies were quite successful: during the Ayub era Pakistan's economy grew by some 5.5 per cent annually.

This was not economic development by state diktat, however, let alone state socialism. Throughout, Pakistan's philosophy of economic development was 'private enterprise leavened with government investment', and the gains of economic growth were poorly distributed.[3] A small elite of robber barons and large farmers reaped the advantages of state subsidies, whereas most Pakistanis suffered as prices rose, real incomes declined and the absolute number of poor people increased. The distribution of wealth between the two wings also showed a widening gap. Although the Ayub regime increased the allocation of public funds to East Pakistan, private investments remained low at about 22 per cent of all investments. In West Pakistan annual growth rates rose from 3.2 per cent in the late 1950s to 7.2 per cent in the early 1960s. In East Pakistan these figures were 1.7 and 5.2, respectively.[4] In other words, the military regime's emphasis on growth intensified the existing inequalities in Pakistan. Not surprisingly, economic disparities became a major issue in inter-wing relations. The Bengal delta's elite began to demand regional economic autonomy by means of a 'two-economy policy'. This implied that the economy of each wing should be treated as completely separate and that an appropriate policy should be devised for each.

All this was related to an important change: Pakistan's development policy had become linked to funding from abroad. In the early 1950s the Cold War had made government-to-government aid a useful geopolitical tool, and there was a strong belief among experts that aid would accelerate economic growth. The new state of Pakistan soon established aid links with the United States and at the same time it became a member of US-dominated international security arrangements. West Pakistan received more than five times as much US aid as did East Pakistan, and most US funds were spent on military, industrial and infrastructural development.[5] The little that reached East Pakistan agriculture – the wing's major economic sector – was used to set up community development programmes, for example the Village Agricultural and Industrial Development (V-AID) programme, which started in 1953 (Plate 15.1).[6] It foundered and was followed by a new initiative in 1955: the establishment of an Academy for Rural Development in Comilla.

THE COMILLA MODEL

The Academy for Rural Development was given a county (*thānā*) in the eastern delta as a 'laboratory area for experiments in local government and economic development'.[7] The main idea at this time was that villages formed

Plate 15.1 Women attending a V-AID-funded embroidery class. Doulotpur village,
c. 1955.

communities that had to be approached as units through which to introduce
'modernisation'. Intermediaries between these communities and the academy were the 'village organiser' and the 'model farmer'. Despite 'a history of
dismal failure of cooperatives in this part of the world', the academy set up
cooperative societies once again and developed a range of training, research
and extension activities. What made these initiatives unusual was that they
emphasised that development was not just the dissemination of expert
knowledge to agriculturists but also needed the input of local knowledge.
The enthusiastic director of the academy, Akhter Hameed Khan, saw the
crux of development as spreading knowledge and changing people's
attitudes:

The desire for practical involvement, the belief that old knowledge must be tested
and new knowledge acquired through unending research, the urgency to make
scientific knowledge useful by extension – these are the basic attitudes which
developed in the United States, and could start the same process for us, too.[8]

After the 1958 coup the Comilla academy became a linchpin in the military regime's attempts to win legitimacy in the rural areas. A significant element of the basic democracies was the public works programme.[9] The objective of this programme, largely conceived by US advisers, was to make use of underutilised manpower in rural areas to work on 'nation-building' activities – constructing embankments, roads, schools and irrigation schemes – and to pay the workers mainly in US surplus wheat.[10] Akhter Hameed Khan, who was actively involved in shaping the works programme, saw it as an important instrument to legitimise the regime. He wrote to the government: 'Frustration, bitterness and cynicism will disappear … as millions of low income rural people go to work in the slack farm season … [and] the protective works … will be omnipresent symbols of a good government.'[11] Critics of the works programme were quick to point out that it was more successful as a propaganda tool for the regime internationally than as an infrastructural improvement. In their opinion, the works programme did provide more employment, but the public works themselves were mainly mud roads and small bridges, poorly planned, executed and maintained, and without local participation or proper accounting.[12]

In the 1960s the academy received many international visitors. Its formula for rural development, now known as the Comilla model, was hailed as a breakthrough and as a humane alternative to China's compulsory people's communes. The Comilla model included family-planning programmes, irrigation and electrification schemes, credit facilities, women's training, and programmes for storing, processing and marketing agricultural produce. From the beginning there were three concerns about the programme: its heavy dependence on the efforts of a single individual (its energetic and well-connected director); its doubtful sustainability if international funding dried up; and the difficulty of reproducing the programme beyond the 'laboratory area'. There was also scepticism as to whether villages in the Bengal delta could be seen as communities. Did co-residence really mean shared interests and loyalties? Despite these misgivings, the Comilla model set the agenda for future rural development programmes in Bangladesh up to the present day. With great enthusiasm and support, innumerable pricey 'pilot projects' and 'model schemes' would be set up, each attempting to create a minuscule development utopia aspiring to blossom into a replicable national or international one.

Between 1959 and 1969 the inflow of external aid resources grew sixfold.[13] From 1960 onwards, most foreign aid – half of which came from the United States – was channelled through the World Bank's Aid-to-Pakistan consortium. This group consisted of the United States, West Germany, the United Kingdom, Canada, France, Japan, Belgium, the Netherlands and Italy.[14] By sharply increasing its commitment, the consortium signalled its support for Pakistan's military regime and became a partner in its development strategy:

It is important to note that the growth of inequality in Pakistan was not the unintended or unconscious by-product of Pakistan's development strategy. Pakistan's policy makers actively pursued policies which promoted inequality ... The flow of foreign aid took place within the framework of this particular set of socio-economic objectives, and helped to facilitate the implementation of growth through inequality.[15]

Thus increasing inequality in Pakistan – both in terms of poverty and in terms of regional exploitation – was sanctioned by the world's wealthiest states. Pakistan's development policy was decidedly authoritarian and top-down. In this sense the plugging of the Comilla experiment as East Pakistan's signature programme of rural development was misleading. Most development policies were conceived and implemented with scant regard for local sensibilities or local knowledge. We have seen how Pakistan's development regime widened the gap between rich and poor and between the country's two wings, fuelling mass discontent in East

Plate 15.2 The Kaptai dam, 1964–5.

Pakistan. But within East Pakistan it also initiated a regional disparity that was to have serious political fallout after East Pakistan became Bangladesh. This was most acute in the case of the Kaptai dam, a massive engineering work in the Chittagong hills (Plate 15.2).

THE DAM IN THE HILLS

One of East Pakistan's early problems was a scarcity of power. It had to import most of its energy. This changed in the 1950s, when exploitable quantities of natural gas were found in the eastern districts of Sylhet and Comilla and foreign aid made it possible to use these to run a cement factory and a fertiliser factory in the region. More energy was needed, however, and Pakistan's planners scored a great success when they persuaded foreign aid-givers to finance a huge hydroelectric project in the Chittagong Hill Tracts. The plan to create an artificial lake in the Chittagong hills actually dated back to 1906, but the work could be taken up seriously with foreign funds only in the 1950s. The project brought thousands of Bengali workers from the plains and engineers from North America and Europe to this non-Bengali area. By 1961 a dam had been constructed across the Karnaphuli river at a village named Kaptai. It was widely celebrated as a triumph of modernity. Before its powerhouse could begin producing electricity for faraway cities and industries, however, the immense (650 km²) and weirdly shaped Kaptai lake had to fill up. The lake submerged many villages and forests and 40 per cent of the arable land in the Chittagong Hill Tracts. Displacing about 100,000 people and devastating wildlife, it was a typical example of top-down development (see box 'Shilabrata and the Great Exodus').

Shilabrata and the Great Exodus

Shilabrata Tangchangya was completely unprepared when the Kaptai dam uprooted his small village (Plate 15.3):

'I still hear the booming sounds of the dam gate closing that continued throughout the night. By the morning, the water had reached our door-steps. We set free our cows and goats, hens and ducks, and then began the rush with the affected people to take their rice, paddy, furniture and whatever else possible to the nearby hills ... Though every possible belonging was taken to the hill top, many still went to their houses to spend the night. But many of them had to rush out of their houses at dead of night when the swelling waters touched them while they slept.'

Nripati Ranjan Tripura, who used to live in Kellamura village, remembers:

Plate 15.3 Hilltops sticking out of Kaptai Lake, 1965.

'Our village was also devoured. We first took shelter on an adjacent hill. The hill was not affected by the inundation in the first year. The water came up to the base of the hill and stopped. During that time it looked like an island. But gradually, in the following months, the sides of the hill began to erode as the waves hit them. It completely went under water in the second year. We had no choice but to move.'

Those who were displaced remember the construction of the Kaptai dam not as a triumph of development but as the Boro Porong (*baṛa paraṃ*; Great Exodus). To them it was 'grotesque and monstrously iniquitous ... We had no guns so we wept in silence, in humiliation and in anger.' Meanwhile, the electricity generated by the Kaptai project reached the cities in the plains, but not the villages of the Chittagong Hill Tracts.

Almost none of the affected people received any compensation, nor did the new project generate employment for them. Some settled around the lake but most were forced to seek refuge in other parts of the Chittagong hills. Tens of thousands could not find a niche and fled to India and Myanmar (Burma). The Indian government settled these development victims in the far-off state of Arunachal Pradesh in the 1960s. Today they and their descendants live there as barely tolerated and effectively stateless people, eking out a very uncertain existence.[16]

AID DEPENDENCE

The Pakistan period saw the establishment of a pattern in which economic development in the Bengal delta was sustained by foreign aid, not by mobilising resources internally. Involvement of intended beneficiaries in development planning was negligible and development administrators were accountable to external patrons, not to local voters. The system, inherently undemocratic and top-down, worked best in a firmly controlled environment. Not surprisingly, it flourished under the well-funded post-1958 military dictatorship. Pakistan's state elite became progressively addicted to foreign aid and – as aid strengthened state institutions – the country's rulers allowed their development priorities to be set by foreign donors.

These donors were confident that support for Pakistan's strongest economic sectors and enterprises would lead most effectively to rapid economic growth, and that the wealth so generated would gradually trickle down to the poor and to weaker economic sectors. This policy of betting on the strong worked out especially unfavourably in East Bengal, where it failed utterly in narrowing the gap with West Pakistan, discouraged the development of a local entrepreneurial class and kept tens of millions in poverty. The political crises that rocked the Bengal delta in the late 1960s were a response to this failure. Two economists summarising Pakistan's development performance on the eve of the Bangladesh Liberation War pointed out that while domestic policy-makers certainly were to blame, 'foreign donors will bear a substantial burden of responsibility for the outcome of Pakistan's struggle in the years ahead'.[17]

CHAPTER 16

A New Elite and Cultural Renewal

After 1947 the inhabitants of the Bengal delta had a lot of rethinking to do. What did it mean to be a Bengali, now that the old centre of Bengali culture, Kolkata, had become inaccessible and many educated Hindus had left for India?

This rethinking was most intense among a new group of professionals who began to come up in the larger towns and cities of the delta. Unlike their predecessors, who had been largely part of the old landowning gentry, or bhodrolok, these newcomers shared a lower- or middle-class background and usually came from villages or small delta towns. Taking advantage of new educational and job opportunities and educated entirely in Bengali, this provincial (mofussil) elite developed a cultural style of its own. It differed consciously from the ways of the Kolkata-based urban professionals as well as from the cultural universe of the landholding gentry, not to speak of the ways of the new West Pakistani leaders. What set this emerging elite apart was that they were not bilingual (Bengali–English or Bengali–Urdu) and that their frame of reference was the Bengal delta, not the entire subcontinent or all of Pakistan. Their new cultural style was shaped by the very provincial Muslim sensibilities that the older elite groups had always looked down upon. It was popular rather than aristocratic, open-minded rather than orthodox, and delta-focused rather than national. Most importantly, it was expressed in the Bengali language.

Dhaka and other rapidly growing towns in East Pakistan became centres of this cultural renewal. The new elite's most vibrant activities centred on student organisations, and the language movement provided them with an issue that was universally popular. Rounaq Jahan has observed that the '1952 language movement created myths, symbols and slogans that consolidated the vernacular elite'.[1] Many of these myths, symbols and slogans remain highly relevant in Bangladesh today.

The language movement was directed not only against the cultural dominance of the West Pakistani rulers but also against that of upper-class

Muslim immigrants from Kolkata and other parts of West Bengal. Often English-educated, these newcomers shared many characteristics with both immigrant Muhajirs from northern India and old aristocratic (and Urdu-speaking) families who resided near the former nawab's court in old Dhaka. These groups formed political alliances, mainly within the Muslim League, and imagined themselves to be the leaders of East Pakistan. After the elections of 1954 had broken their power, however, popular culture in East Pakistan became unambiguously East Bengali in its orientation.

The second half of the twentieth century thus witnessed the emergence of a regional culture that gradually discarded both Kolkata-centred and West Pakistan-controlled cultural models and became more and more self-confident.[2] This self-confidence expressed itself in many ways, for example in the popular weekly *Begom* (*begam*; lady), which provided a forum for women writers (Plate 16.1), and in the cultural organisation Chhayanot (*chāyānaṭ*; a musical mode), which began to celebrate Bengali New Year

Plate 16.1 The cover of the weekly *Begom*, 1969.

with an annual open-air concert in 1963 and continues this tradition today. Bengali New Year (Pohela Boishakh; *pahelā baiśākh* (15 April)) had always been important – for example, it was a time for settling your debts – but now it became a public tradition with strong political overtones.

The new self-confidence also found expression in other institutions that are still active, such as the Bulbul Academy for Fine Arts (which trains dancers, singers and musicians) and the Bangla Academy (which promotes Bengali language and literature), both established in 1955. Another influential institution, the College of Arts and Crafts (now the Faculty of Fine Arts, University of Dhaka), educates painters and sculptors (Plate 16.2). It is also well known for its building (designed by Muzharul Islam and constructed during 1953–5), which is considered the first embodiment of a new architectural school, 'Bengali modernism'.

Modernism came to be linked with another theme: a reappraisal of the Bengal delta's rich folk traditions. For example, film-makers realised that

Plate 16.2 Hamidur Rahman, a student at the College of Arts and Crafts in 1948–50, became an influential painter and art teacher. This work is entitled *Thinker* (1960).[3]

Plate 16.3 A theatre performance in Dhaka in 1962. The Arts Council Drama Group
is performing Abu Sayeed's *The Thing*. After Bangladesh gained independence in
1971, the (East Pakistan) Arts Council became the Bangladesh Shilpokola Academy
(*śilpakalā*; National Academy of Fine and Performing Arts).

commercial success depended on capturing the imagination of rural audiences who were used to village operas (*jātrā*). The first film employing the
artistic conventions of this genre – entitled *Rupbān* (1965) – was a runaway
success and allowed the Dhaka film industry to expand from only five films
that year to thirty-nine in 1970.[4] Rural themes were also prominent in the
theatre, for example in *The Thing,* a play set on a cyclone-hit island in the
Bay of Bengal (Plate 16.3).

During the Pakistan period, radios began to spread in the rural areas.
This was a slow process, because less than 1 per cent of all villages had
electricity and radios were luxury items.[5] The government soon recognised
the power of this new medium – in terms of entertainment, education and
propaganda – in a largely illiterate society. In the mid-1960s it donated
transistor radios to community centres all over the delta.[6] Radio was very
important in creating a sense of unity-in-diversity, as people experienced
the dialects and cultural expressions of other parts of East Pakistan. Folk
music was especially popular with listeners. Regional genres came to be
appreciated across the region, such as the wistful love songs from the

north – bhaoaya (*bhāoyāyā*), made particularly popular by Abbasuddin Ahmed – and the haunting boat songs – bhatiali (*bhāṭiyālī*) – from the east and south (Plate 16.4). Among the more modern songs, those by Kazi Nazrul Islam and Rabindranath Tagore were highly admired among the elite, and film songs were all the rage with young people.

The spread of radios turned out to be a double-edged sword: it allowed state propaganda to reach the rural population but it also provided a powerful tool in the hands of those who struggled against West Pakistani dominance. The rural population was largely illiterate and steeped in rich traditions of oral communication. This made them very receptive to messages of unity among Bengalis, and tales of state violence, that were conveyed by means of songs, recited poetry and music, as well as theatre, dance and cinema.[7]

Throughout the Pakistan period, formal education remained the preserve of a select few. The 1961 population census reported that 82 per cent

Plate 16.4 Live broadcast of folk music on Radio Pakistan, Dhaka, 1961. This group is performing a song of lamentation (*jārigān*).[8] The lead singer, Abdul Gani Bayati of Borishal district, has just received the governor's gold medal for his outstanding performance.

of the people of East Pakistan were illiterate (that is, unable to read a short statement on everyday life). Colonial policy had focused on higher education, leaving primary and secondary education largely to private initiative. As a result, primary education was poorly developed, especially in the rural areas, where four out of five villages had no primary school and teachers were badly trained and poorly paid. Drop-out rates were high: half of the children who attended school left before grade five, and only one in five made it to secondary school. A parallel system of Islamic schools (*maktab, mādrāsā*) provided teaching in Arabic and Islamic studies. The departure of the British did not mark an abrupt policy change. Despite strong popular demand, the East Pakistan government was largely indifferent to mass education. Although it did introduce a new curriculum to replace the colonial one, it spent little on primary and secondary schools or on adult education. By the end of the Pakistan period, hardly any headway had been made.

For those who lived in urban areas and could afford expensive (mostly private) schooling, however, good primary and secondary education was available in English, Urdu and Bengali. The system of higher education expanded more rapidly than the lower levels of education.[9] The number of colleges grew steadily, and four new universities were added to the colonial-era University of Dhaka: the University of Rajshahi (1954), the Agricultural University of Mymensingh (1961), the University of Chittagong (1961) and the University of Engineering and Technology in Dhaka (1962).

The expanding system of higher education produced more graduates than the labour market could absorb. This led to widespread unemployment and frustration among the younger generation of the emerging elite. It was not surprising that the universities became centres of both cultural creativity and political contestation. For a new breed of student activists, the dream of an autonomous Bengal delta promised both economic and cultural emancipation.

The new elite that found its voice, vision and rural support base during the 1950s and 1960s was not without its inner divisions. Most members came from eastern and central parts of the delta – districts such as Comilla, Dhaka, Noakhali and Chittagong, which had the highest concentrations of literate Muslim families. This region had more educational facilities and better infrastructure than the north and west, and it sported the delta's capital (Dhaka), largest port (Chittagong) and foremost industrial city (Narayanganj). It was, in short, more developed than the northern and western delta. As Dhaka mushroomed and became the cultural and economic hub of East Pakistan, east-central dominance began to rankle with many people in the north and west. They developed a sense of regional deprivation that is still noticeable today.

It was by appealing to shared cultural symbols that the emerging vernacular elite was able to stay connected with the rural population at a time when they were distancing themselves economically and physically. The elite's complicated political relationship with the Pakistan state – keen to join but held at arm's length – was reflected in the ambiguous relationship between the new East Bengali culture and Pakistan's attempts at nation-building. Sometimes it was antagonistic and rebellious; at other times it was complicit and supportive. Throughout the Pakistan experiment, however, East Bengali culture acted as a domain that West Pakistanis could neither penetrate nor manipulate – a collective resource that fuelled Bengali solidarity across divisions of class, region and religion. And it was this, more than anything, which gave coherence to demands for autonomy and ultimately independence. Whenever political struggles for emancipation petered out or were repressed, cultural struggles would continue unabated, far less visible to the rulers' eyes. As the state tried to harness the dispersed political power in the East Pakistan countryside by means of its system of basic democracies, it found it impossible to win rural hearts and minds. The vernacular elite, on the other hand, could use its personal and cultural links much more effectively to mobilise the rural population for its vision of cultural renewal, political autonomy and social development.

This is what underlay the extraordinary outcome of the first general elections in 1970. The Awami League, by now largely representing the vernacular elite's aspirations, had captured the vision of the Bengal delta's renewal, autonomy and development in its motto 'Shonar Bangla' (*sonār bāṃlā*; Golden Bengal). This motto was cleverly chosen because it was the title of a song that Rabindranath Tagore had written in 1905 and that the Pakistan government had banned. It thus evoked not only the life-giving and beloved motherland but also a defiant Bengaliness: 'My Golden Bengal, I love you – forever your skies, your air set my heart in tune as if it were a flute.' The song was performed at nationalist meetings, and its promise of a glorious future for the Bengal delta fired the imagination of millions during the ill-fated final days of united Pakistan.

PART IV

War and the Birth of Bangladesh

Part IV Detail of a mural mosaic depicting the language movement of 1952. This street mural at Ramna, Dhaka, is entitled *From 1952 to 1971*; it was made by S. R. Shamim in 1998.

CHAPTER 17

Armed Conflict

The Liberation War of 1971 was the delta's third big shock of the twentieth century. After the devastating famine of 1943/4 and the Partition of 1947, it was now armed conflict that engulfed the delta.

Telling the story of the war is not easy because so many things were happening at the same time – and so much is still fiercely contested. There is a vast literature on what came to pass between March and December 1971, ranging from news reports and propaganda to victims' diaries, military and political memoirs, academic studies, creative writing and films, and inquiry commission reports. Half a century after the event, the flood of publications shows no sign of diminishing – an indication that the war remains sharply etched into the nation's mind and that the 'legacy of this bloodshed smolders in Bangladesh's politics today'.[1]

What emerges is a multilayered story. The main thread is the violent struggle between the Pakistan armed forces and East Bengali nationalists. But interwoven with this chronicle of national liberation are many other themes: the victimisation of specific groups (women, Hindus, ethnic minorities); local vendettas and the settling of personal scores; tensions between nationalists of different hues; regional variation in violence and destruction as well as in population displacement; and thousands of stories of personal courage and sacrifice. Equally important is the fact that the war was part of two larger geopolitical games: the rivalry between India and Pakistan and the struggle between Cold War superpowers. It is these that splashed the conflict across the front pages of the world press throughout 1971 and turned 'Bangladesh' into a household word all over the globe. Never before, or since, has the Bengal delta attracted so much international attention.

PAKISTAN'S 'FINAL SOLUTION'

The twenty-fifth of March 1971 was a fateful day for the delta. As Pakistan's dictator furtively took his last plane out of Dhaka (Chapter 13), he left instructions for a full-blown army attack on East Pakistani citizens. It was a punitive operation to eliminate Bengali nationalism and reassert West Pakistan's dominance over East Pakistan. Yahya Khan put it like this in his radio broadcast from West Pakistan the next day: 'it is the duty of the Pakistan Armed Forces to ensure the integrity, solidarity and security of Pakistan. I have ordered them to do their duty and fully restore the authority of Government ... I appeal to my countrymen to appreciate the gravity of the situation for which the blame rests entirely on the anti-Pakistan and secessionist elements.'[2] The armed assault (codenamed 'Operation Searchlight') was led by General Tikka Khan, soon to be known as the Butcher of Bengal.

It was a brutal onslaught on what the military rulers thought of as the main centres of Bengali opposition. Tanks, armoured personnel carriers and troops fanned out to crush the two Bengali organisations in Dhaka that could offer serious armed resistance: the police and the paramilitary East Pakistan Rifles. These were overwhelmed after fierce fighting. Next, the army homed in on slums: flame-throwers set them ablaze and the army gunned down fleeing inhabitants. A third target was Dhaka University, which had been closed during the civil disobedience of the previous weeks, so fortunately many students had gone home. The troops rampaged through campus, using mortars on dormitories and killing students, faculty and anybody else who was around. And last but not least the army, demolishing hastily put-up barricades, went for the two main symbols of East Bengali nationalist aspirations. The first, the Shohid Minar (Martyrs' Monument), was razed to the ground. The second was Sheikh Mujibur Rahman. Unlike most other Awami League leaders, Mujib chose not to go into hiding. The army, fearful of turning him into a martyr, refrained from killing him. Instead, it arrested him at his home with a view to taking him to West Pakistan. He was then accused of treason for unleashing the civil disobedience movement (see box 'Launching a war').

Launching a war

Here is an eyewitness account of the first moments of the assault on Dhaka, as told by Siddiq Salik, a junior officer in the Pakistan Army:

The first column from the cantonment met resistance at Farm Gate, about one kilometre from the cantonment. The column was halted by a huge tree trunk freshly felled across the road. The side gaps were covered with the hulks of old cars and a disabled steam-roller. On the city side of the barricade stood several hundred Awami Leaguers shouting Joi Bangla [Victory to Bangladesh] slogans. I heard their spirited shouts while standing on the verandah of General Tikka's headquarters. Soon some rifle shots mingled with the Joi Bangla slogans. A little later, a burst of fire from an automatic weapon shrilled through the air. Thereafter, it was a mixed affair of firing and fiery slogans, punctuated with the occasional chatter of a light machine gun. Fifteen minutes later the noise began to subside and the slogans started dying down. Apparently, the weapons had triumphed. The army column moved on to the city . . . The gates of hell had been cast open . . .

As the commandos approached Mujib's house, they drew fire from the armed guard posted at his gate. The guards were quickly neutralized. Then up raced the fifty tough soldiers [to] climb the four-foot high compound wall. They announced their arrival in the courtyard by firing a stengun burst and shouted for Mujib to come out. But there was no response. Scrambling across the verandah and up the stairs, they finally discovered the door to Mujib's bedroom. It was locked from outside. A bullet pierced the hanging metal, and it dangled down. Whereupon Mujib readily emerged, offering himself for arrest. He seemed to be waiting for it. The raiding party rounded up everybody in the house and brought them to the Second Capital in army jeeps. Minutes later, Major Jaffar, Brigade Major of 57 Brigade, was on the wireless. I could hear his crisp voice saying 'BIG BIRD IN THE CAGE . . . OTHERS NOT IN THEIR NESTS . . . OVER.'

As soon as the message ended, I saw the big bird in a white shirt being driven in an army jeep to the cantonment for safe custody. Somebody asked General Tikka if he would like him to be produced before him. He said firmly, 'I don't want to see his face.'[3]

In these first gruesome hours of army terror, people all over Dhaka were picked up from their homes and 'dispatched to Bangladesh' – the army's euphemism for summary execution. There were verbal and later written orders to shoot Hindu citizens.[4] Dhaka's old artisan neighbourhood of Shankharipotti (*śākhāripoṭṭi*; conch-shell-makers' area) was attacked and Hindu inhabitants murdered. Many prominent Hindus were sought out and put to death. When dawn broke over Dhaka after a night of extreme state violence, it revealed a ghost city (see box 'Childhood memories').

Childhood memories

Odhir Chandra Dey remembers how Pakistan Army soldiers murdered his next of kin on the first day of the war. He was seven years old and lived on the campus of Dhaka University, where his father ran a small restaurant.

"I woke up from my slumber with a sudden shock at about 11.30 p.m. [on 25 March 1971], hearing heavy gunfire and ammunition. My parents, my brother and his wife, and my siblings all woke up. They moved the curtain a little and peeped out to see what was happening. I joined them and watched Jagannath Hall in high flames and saw that people were screaming for rescue, 'Help! Help!' . . . Our quarter was between Jagannath Hall and 'Shiva Bari.' After the brutal devastation of both places, I saw them marching towards our building. Now it was our turn . . . All of a sudden the 'Pak hanadar' [raiders] started to kick the door terribly and ordered us to open it with abusive words in Urdu. The heavy blows on the door interrupted my father's prayer and baffled him. He could not understand whether he should open the door or not. Mother rushed to my father and muttered something. My brothers and sisters and I all started trembling in fear. When the door was about to be broken, my father opened it. As soon as he opened it, they pointed their guns to my father. As per international law, there is a rule not to kill the person who surrenders. My father might have known it. So, with a twinkle in his eyes, he surrendered by raising his hands. Even after surrendering two soldiers grasped his hands and snatched him with a sudden pull. My father was a very tall and healthy person. With the jerk he tumbled onto the corridor of the house next door. The door of the house was wide open, as the members of it had already been seized by the army."

"By that time, six to seven soldiers had gotten into our house and they started destroying all our belongings. We screamed and rushed back to hide ourselves. Some of us took shelter under a cot, some of us in the toilet, and some hid inside the almira [cupboard]. Ranjit Dey, our eldest brother, fled to the third floor. Our house was on the second floor. Then the bloody brute saw my newly married boudi [sister-in-law, wife of Ranjit]. She started running to and fro within the house. When they were about to catch her, my sister screamed and called my brother to rescue my boudi from the clutch of the brute. Ranjit-da rushed to the spot and said, 'Rina! Rina! Hold up your hands!' Boudi's name was Rina. As soon as he said it, the soldiers turned back and shot him. My sister Ranu was very near to my brother. The bullet pierced my brother's chest and came out through his back, and then it hit the cheek of Ranu-didi. Dada (my brother) fell down on the floor at once. The floor around him was soaked with blood. After that, the military shot my boudi. She was pregnant then. The bullet hit her chest. I saw the dead body leaning against the wall and it seemed to me that it was not bullet but panic that was responsible for her death. Then they snatched the earrings of my boudi from her ears."

"After that they went back to kill my father in the [flat next to ours]. My younger brothers and sisters and I were all sobbing bitterly on seeing the merciless treatment by the hanadar bahini [army raiders]. My mother got horrified seeing the bloody dead bodies of Ranjit-da and boudi. When the military aimed their gun to shoot my father, my mother ran to him and stood in front of him spreading her hands. She begged the military, 'You have ruined me! You killed my son, my daughter-in-law. Don't kill him, I beg for his life!' They did not pay any heed to her appeal, and instead ordered her to go away. They tried to drag her forcibly but failed. Lastly, out of rage, they cut both of her hands with a bayonet. Her hands got totally dispersed and were hanging just on the skin. Then they shot her. The bullet hit her throat, and her tongue got exposed. Even after she died, they shot her body several times in front of my father. Father also got shot. Both bodies were wet with blood. [W]e did not realize that my father was still alive."[5]

Elsewhere in East Pakistan the army onslaught was equally excessive and vengeful. As a post-war Pakistan government commission reported, during the Comilla cantonment massacre of 27–28 March, 'seventeen Bengali Officers and 915 men were just slain by the flick of one Officer's fingers'.[6] But not everywhere did the army succeed in establishing control. In Chittagong, Bengali troops of the East Bengal Regiment, hearing about the events in Dhaka, killed their Pakistani officers, moved out of town and put up resistance. It was from a small radio station in Kalurghat near Chittagong on 26 March that one of these ex-officers, Ziaur Rahman, broadcast a call to 'the people of Bangladesh' to resist the attacking army. The station had a very limited range and was soon silenced by an air raid. As a result, the world was at first unaware of the events in East Pakistan and of what later became known as the declaration of independence. The army occupied radio stations and telephone exchanges, destroyed the offices of *Ittefaq* and other newspapers and confined foreign correspondents to the single luxury hotel in Dhaka. Although these correspondents could observe the burning city all around them, they had no way of communicating with the outside world.

Despite the suddenness and fierceness of the army attack, there was popular resistance all over the Bengal delta. In some places it was rapidly crushed, but in others – for instance Kushtia, Jessore, Sylhet and the northern districts – it continued for weeks. It was not until the end of May that the Pakistan army felt confident that it controlled most towns.[7]

In the wake of the military action, an exodus of panic-stricken refugees took place. Many thousands fled the cities and towns, where the army was most active, to weather the storm with relatives in villages. But the army attacked villages as well. One eyewitness reported:

After the army crackdown for the first few days, the area was under the control of the Freedom Fighters. Then started the bombings by the Pakistani Air Force. I escaped [from the eastern town of Brahmanbaria] to the countryside with my family. It was a harrowing experience. We could not stay in any particular village for any length of time . . . The Pakistani Army was burning down the villages one after another . . . We spent a night in a village but next morning we heard that the troops were headed for that village. Again we left along with the owner of that house. After a couple of days when we returned, we found the whole village burnt to ashes. Many of the people who could not escape were killed. The carcasses of livestock were strewn all over. The stench was unbearable. It was hell![8]

Others felt so insecure that they crossed the border into India. The Indian authorities reported that by May 1971 more than 1.5 million refugees had arrived and that 60,000 new ones were coming in every day. By the end of the war many more had fled to India – a figure of 10 million refugees is usually quoted, although it is impossible to verify.

THE BANGLADESHI RESPONSE

By May the first phase of the war was over. The army had established a semblance of control over most of the terrified delta, although resistance had not died down. Meanwhile the Awami League leadership had regrouped in India, where they formed a government-in-exile. With Indian support they formally proclaimed Bangladesh to be an independent state on 17 April 1971. The proclamation read in part:

Whereas free elections were held in Bangladesh . . . and

Whereas at these elections the people of Bangladesh elected 167 out of 169 representatives belonging to the Awami League, and . . .

Whereas instead of fulfilling their promise and while still conferring with the representatives of the people of Bangladesh, Pakistan authorities declared an unjust and treacherous war, and . . .

Whereas in the conduct of a ruthless and savage war the Pakistani authorities committed and are still continuously committing numerous acts of genocide and unprecedented tortures, amongst others on the civilian and unarmed people of Bangladesh . . .

We the elected representatives of the people of Bangladesh, . . . in order to ensure for the people of Bangladesh equality, human dignity and social justice, declare and constitute Bangladesh to be a sovereign Peoples' Republic.

The venue of the proclamation, a mango grove near Meherpur, just inside Bangladesh, was renamed Mujibnogor (*mujibnagar*; Mujib Town).[9] Information about these events was broadcast across the delta by a new underground radio station, Independent Bangla Radio.

Initial resistance to the army assault had been largely uncoordinated and spontaneous, but gradually a more organised plan developed. All over the delta young men and women were quietly slipping away to join what became known as the Freedom Fighters or Mukti Bahini (*mukti joddhā, mukti bāhinī*). Right from the beginning the freedom fighters received support and training from India, and most of their camps were just across the border in India. Many people in Bangladesh were struggling to survive in an environment that had suddenly turned into a cauldron of violence. Even so, they were often keen to lend a hand to the guerrilla effort by sheltering, feeding and guiding fighters. The delta's best-known literati composed patriotic poems and songs for them (see box 'No more time for braiding your hair').

No more time for braiding your hair

Sufia Kamal (1911–99) was one of East Pakistan's leading literary figures. A poet, magazine editor and cultural activist, she was particularly prominent in women's organisations and protests against the suppression of Bengali language and culture. During the war of 1971 she stayed in the country, keeping a diary and supporting the freedom fighters. In this wartime poem she exhorted women to take an active part in the struggle.

No More Time for Braiding Your Hair[10]

There's no more time for braiding your hair in patterns,
Or for being concerned with the glamorous border of your *saris*,
The *tip* mark on your forehead, your mascara or lipstick.
No more time, no more time – for the battle for life is on!

There's no more laughter in blossoming girls, or in young widows.
Their mouths and lips are firmly pursed in stern resolve.
Restless now, like the sharp edge of a sword
Are the tender eyes, now piercing and raised.
Not like the frightened doe are these eyes any more.
They are searching, like a hunting hawk.
Their bitter hearts have turned cold, savage, hard,
To take revenge on the brute ravagers.

The women have shed their coy, delicate gentility
To wreak vengeance for the sorrow of their lost dear ones.
In their slender bodies and hearts is gathered
The courage of lions.
Boundless strength they hold – these valiant women.

No more mere love songs – instead,
They sing: 'Victory for my motherland,
My people, the heroic fighters!'
Dipping their *onchol* in the martyrs' blood
Spilled in the street, they repay their debt
To Mother Earth in blood.

sari (*sāṛī*): woman's dress

tip (*ṭip*): coloured dot on the forehead

onchol (*añcal*): loose end of the sari

As the Bangladeshi response was taking shape, the monsoon arrived and the delta became covered in mud and water. This made conventional warfare hard and favoured guerrilla tactics. Through the middle months of 1971 the Pakistan army and groups of freedom fighters were playing a lethal cat-and-mouse game all over the delta (Plate 17.1). Many more people were displaced – according to some guesstimates there were 20 million internally displaced persons during the war – and fears grew that the extensive disruption of rice cultivation and trade would lead to widespread famine.

Plate 17.1 Freedom fighters, 1971.

Groups of freedom fighters now operated in eleven geographically defined 'sectors' under the command of the Mukti Bahini, headquartered in Kolkata. The commander-in-chief of the new Bangladesh Armed Forces was General Osmany. Some had experience in the Pakistan armed forces, but most were newcomers to armed combat and needed basic training. There were also various local groups of freedom fighters joining battle with the Pakistan army. These remained outside the Mukti Bahini but often collaborated with them. Among the many groups were the Kader Bahini in Tangail, the Afsar Bahini in Mymensingh, the Ohidur Bahini in the northwest, and the Siraj Sikdar group in Borishal.[11]

It soon became clear that the freedom fighters were unable to defeat the Pakistan military in open confrontation. As they operated all over the delta, however, they 'represented a ubiquitous menace, constantly harassing their opponents with ambushes, raids, sabotage, and propaganda. Their activities exhausted the Pakistani troops while creating an enervating sense of constant uncertainty and danger.'[12] By November 1971 the various groups of freedom fighters had some 100,000 members, half of them inside Bangladesh/East Pakistan, and they had established control of more than ten liberated areas along the borders. The largest of these were in the Chittagong Hill Tracts, the Dinajpur–Rangpur area and Sylhet.[13]

The Pakistan army sought to counter the freedom fighters by creating civilian groups (Peace Committees) and later paramilitary groups (Razakar, Al-Shams, Al-Badr) under Pakistani command. These provided symbolic support (see Plate 17.2) and also acted as death squads and providers of counterinsurgency intelligence.

INTERNATIONAL INVOLVEMENT

Pakistan's rulers had planned a swift crushing of Bengali political ambition in East Pakistan, followed by an equally swift return to normality. Throughout 1971 the muzzled press persisted in this myth of a minor domestic malfunction soon mended (Plate 17.3).

In reality, however, Pakistan's rulers immediately lost the plot. They got bogged down in a guerrilla war that drew international attention and were utterly unable to convince the world that this was merely a domestic matter. As millions of refugees poured across the border into India, carrying stories of atrocities, the international press began to speak of genocide,[14] Bangladesh support groups mushroomed in many places across the world and Bengali staff of Pakistan embassies fled or were kicked out.[15] International exposure reached its peak with the 'Concert for Bangladesh',

Plate 17.2 In the middle of the war, supporters of Pakistan hold a procession in
Sylhet to mark the twenty-fourth Independence Day of Pakistan, 14 August 1971.
They are carrying a garlanded portrait of M. A. Jinnah and a Pakistani flag.

a mass benefit performance for the children of Bangladesh, which was held
in New York in August 1971 and featured celebrities such as George
Harrison, Bob Dylan and Ravi Shankar. By then, world opinion strongly
condemned Pakistan's ruling elite.

The political response was, however, far more complicated. At the level
of the region things were fairly straightforward. Pakistan and India shared a
'legacy of misperception' and had standard negative interpretations of each
other's motives and actions.[16] As a result, the two states found themselves
opposing each other on any South Asian issue, and 1971 was no exception.
In one corner was India, which presented itself as the champion of
Bangladesh's right to self-determination, supporting it by means of diplo-
macy, military training, hospitality, refugee care, propaganda and artillery
support of freedom fighters' cross-border forays. In the opposite corner was
Pakistan, which insisted that it was defending the united Islamic homeland
and decried India's intolerable interference in its internal affairs. The threat
of war between the two countries loomed large once again (after wars in

Plate 17.3 War propaganda. Life in the delta is returning to normal, according to an army-controlled newspaper in Dhaka on 16 May 1971.

1948 and 1965), and both sides were preparing for a showdown that each thought they could win.

This regional South Asian scenario was embedded in a global political game. The Bangladesh war broke out in the middle of the Cold War, and this meant that the world's superpowers became involved. The line-up was as follows: the Soviet Union backed India and supported the Bangladesh liberation movement, while the United States and China allied themselves with the Pakistan cause. Pakistan also received support from many Muslim-majority states. This division meant that the conflict could not be resolved by diplomatic means – discussions in the United Nations stalled, and bilateral consultations effected no change of position. On the contrary, as the war was allowed to drag on throughout 1971, India and the Soviet Union drew closer together and their support for the Bangladesh side intensified. At the same time the United States and China were re-establishing communication with one another after decades of diplomatic frost, and Pakistan was valuable to them as a go-between on several occasions. The war in East Pakistan/Bangladesh could not be allowed to throw a spanner in these far more important works.[17] As Richard Nixon, the US president, famously scribbled on an order to his staff on 2 May 1971: 'To all hands. Don't squeeze Yahya at this time. RN.'[18]

By October, after the rainy season had ended, it was obvious that the Pakistan army was unable to regain control of the delta, but that the freedom fighters could not win a military victory either. India – which had stopped referring to the delta as 'East Pakistan' and now called it 'East Bengal' – began to inch towards full-scale military invasion. It stepped up its international propaganda campaign and, in November, put an Indian general in charge of the joint command of freedom fighters and Indian troops. Also in November, it expanded its military operations inside East Pakistan/Bangladesh, but, fearful of the geopolitical consequences, desisted from declaring war. Its opportunity came on 3 December 1971, when the Pakistan air force carried out raids from West Pakistan, bombing a number of airfields in northwestern India. India sprang into action, and the (third) India–Pakistan War was on (Plate 17.4).

The Indian armed forces, and the freedom fighters who battled along-side them, had all the advantages. Marching into the delta from every direction, they were better armed than the Pakistanis, had control of the air and the sea and were welcomed as liberators by most of the local population. Still, the invasion was no walkover: the Pakistanis put up fierce resistance and there were many casualties. The final days of the war also saw a last assault on leading Bengali intellectuals. Members of the pro-Pakistan Al-Badr militia rounded up writers, professors, artists, doctors and other professionals in Dhaka, blindfolded them and butchered them. A couple of days later, on 16 December, the Pakistani administration crumbled, and the army was forced to surrender.[19] In West Pakistan,

Plate 17.4 Indian armoured vehicle on the way to Khulna, Bangladesh, December 1971.

Plate 17.5 Mukti Bahini (freedom fighters) marching into Dhaka, 17 December 1971.

some leaders wanted to continue the war, but president Yahya Khan reportedly remarked: 'Leave them. We cannot put West Pakistan in danger because of those black Bengalis.'[20] The war was over, and an independent state had come into being (Plate 17.5).

Pakistan's rulers never apologised for the atrocities they had ordered their armed forces to commit, although later some Pakistani citizens did.[21] Most Pakistanis pictured themselves as victims rather than aggressors and tried to forget the war, which they framed in terms of betrayal and humiliation by India. Henceforth most histories of Pakistan conveniently erased the role that the eastern wing had played in shaping Pakistan's state and society and the wealth it had generated for the western wing.

CHAPTER 18

A State Is Born

The sixteenth of December 1971 was a moment of supreme emotion. The day of Pakistan's capitulation became Bangladesh's Victory Day (Bijoy Dibosh; *bijay dibas*). As liberation and independent statehood became realities, a mood of exuberance took hold of the delta. Now 'Golden Bengal' – that promised happy land – finally was within reach.

Indian forces hurriedly installed an interim government, rounded up Pakistani soldiers and tried to establish a semblance of order. It was a turbulent time. All over the delta people were violently settling scores, and millions of displaced people were returning to often devastated and looted homes. There were three immediate issues confronting the young state: how to cope with collaborators, how to rehabilitate war victims and how to repair the damage caused by the war.

DEALING WITH THE ENEMY WITHIN

What to do with those who had been on the Pakistan side and who remained in the delta? One group consisted of some 90,000 Pakistani prisoners of war and civil internees who were taken away by India. They would spend several years in camps in India before being returned to Pakistan.[1]

A second group consisted of collaborators who remained in Bangladesh: members of paramilitary groups, death squads, citizens' committees, looters and informers. In January 1972 it was decided that these would be brought before a Collaborators' Tribunal and tried for war crimes. This never happened, however, because the Bangladesh government declared an amnesty in 1973 – in return for Pakistan's diplomatic recognition of Bangladesh and the repatriation of several hundreds of thousands of Bengalis held in Pakistan. The issue remained alive, however, and from the 1990s the demand for justice would be revived.[2]

A third and much larger group were the non-Bengali Muslims who had migrated to the delta after 1947 and who had then been welcomed as Muhajirs. They identified strongly with the idea of Pakistan, and it was not surprising that most – but not all – sided with the Pakistan authorities in their conflict with the Bengali nationalists. Bengalis called them 'Biharis', even though not all of them were from Bihar. In the period leading up to the Liberation War, nationalist mobs had killed Biharis, during the war many Biharis had helped the armed forces and, now that the war was over, Biharis were collectively branded as Pakistani collaborators. Severe retribution followed, leading to a counter-genocide of thousands of non-Bengalis and forcing more than a million to leave their homes and seek refuge in hundreds of overcrowded slum-like settlements all over the country.[3] Some sought and received Bangladeshi citizenship after the war, but most described themselves as stranded Pakistanis and demanded to be 'repatriated' to Pakistan. Although a number of them managed to reach Pakistan, the 'Bihari issue' was never resolved. Over time, legal decisions gave them more rights. In 2008 the Bangladesh High Court directed the issuing of national identity cards, and this is usually interpreted as affirming their citizenship. Even so, the stranded Pakistanis, who now prefer to be called Urdu-speaking Bangladeshis, have not gained full citizenship rights. Today the majority continue to be ostracised, living in poverty, isolation and uncertainty.[4]

WAR VICTIMS

The number of people who were victimised during the Bangladesh Liberation War remains unknown. The total number of internally displaced persons and refugees to India ran into the millions. Estimates of the number of war dead vary enormously, from the official Bangladeshi figure of 3 million to the official Pakistani figure of 26,000. One source, compiling numerous guesstimates, suggests that about 1.7 million lives may have been lost.[5] In the absence of any reliable assessment after the war, however, the actual number will never be even remotely certain (Plate 18.1).

In addition to those who died, there were many others who were maimed or traumatised.[6] An important group consisted of numerous women who were raped by Pakistani, Bihari and Bengali men. These women – whom the state honoured with the title 'brave heroines' (birangona; *bīrāṅganā*) – encountered grave discrimination in post-war Bangladesh, as did their children.[7] Initially, efforts were made to help war victims regain their footing in society, but soon they were left to their own devices.

WAR DAMAGE

The war caused enormous material damage. Hundreds of road and railway bridges had been destroyed, the six airports were not functioning, Chittagong – the main port – was full of mines and wrecks, and the telecommunications network was out of action. Countless schools, health centres and houses had been damaged. Both Pakistani and Indian soldiers had looted material goods from Bangladesh and carried them home.[8] Agricultural production had also suffered terribly, because millions had not been able to till their land with the loving care that was required to get a good harvest. Bullocks had been slaughtered, stocks of seeds lost and irrigation pumps and tools damaged. Fishermen had to find new boats and nets. One estimate put the total destruction at more than 40 per cent of the country's annual gross national product.[9] This grim war legacy was counterbalanced by the intense excitement of independence. The efforts of tens of millions of anonymous Bangladeshis struggling to survive and restore their working lives brought about a recovery of the delta's economy and staved off the famine that had been feared during the war. They were helped by an enormous international relief and reconstruction effort, partly coordinated by the United Nations.

Plate 18.1 After the war, Bangladesh became covered in memorial sites, ranging from national monuments to private graves such as this one in the western village of Bholahat. It marks the death of freedom fighter Mohammad Kamaluddin, killed by Pakistani bullets on 6 October 1971.

A MODERATE GOVERNMENT

Who was to take charge of the new state of Bangladesh? One of the concerns that had propelled India into invading the delta and installing a new government was a fear of radicalisation among the freedom fighters. The Indian regions surrounding Bangladesh were politically unstable: in West Bengal Maoist revolutionaries, known as Naxalites, were active and so were various groups (for example Nagas, Mizos) fighting for independence in northeastern India. During the war many freedom fighters had begun to imagine a liberated Bangladesh not just as an independent state but also as a socialist society. This prospect worried India's policy-makers for two reasons. First, it might provide the Naxalites and other leftist rebels with strategic cross-border links; and second, nationalisation of land in Bangladesh could lead to an exodus of dispossessed landholders to India. Ensuring a non-radical government policy in Bangladesh was high on India's wish list, and this is why it threw its support squarely behind the Awami League leaders who had formed the Bangladesh government-in-exile in India during the war. Their authority was, however, not acceptable to many freedom fighters, who had done the actual fighting and considered the leaders in exile a 'do-nothing group living in luxury in Calcutta', out of touch with realities in Bangladesh.[10]

In January 1972 Sheikh Mujibur Rahman (who had been sentenced to death in Pakistan in December 1971) was released from Pakistani captivity.[11] He returned to Bangladesh, received a hero's welcome, assumed the leadership and promulgated a parliamentary form of government. Ever since the uprising of 1968–9, however, leftist forces had been gaining strength, both within and outside the Awami League. The party's election manifesto of 1970 had spoken of nationalisation, land reform and the abolition of land tax. Now, after the war, the Awami League leadership was under enormous pressure from radical and armed freedom fighters who demanded revolutionary change. Mujib – now known as the 'Father of the Nation' (Jatir Jonok; *jātir janak*) – disregarded appeals to form a 'national government' with representation from all political parties (except the pro-Pakistan Islamist rightists, who were now banned). Instead, relying on 'his legend . . . his charismatic appeal and his hypnotic hold over the Bengalis', he formed an Awami League government.[12] By March, India was satisfied that the new government was sufficiently in charge of civil administration for the Indian troops to withdraw. India's prime minister, Indira Gandhi, paid a triumphant visit (Plate 18.2).

Plate 18.2 'A New Sun Has Risen in the Sky': Indira Gandhi visits independent
Bangladesh.

Immediately afterwards, the government nationalised banks, insurance
corporations, shipping companies, and textile, jute and sugar mills. It did
not touch land ownership, however, although it formally fixed a ceiling of
13.5 hectares (100 *bighā*) on landholdings and exempted landholdings of
less than 3.4 hectares (25 *bighā*) from taxation. Later that year Bangladesh
declared itself a 'people's republic' with a parliamentary system. Its constitution asserted that the republic was based on the principles of 'nationalism, socialism, democracy and secularism'.[13] Rabindranath Tagore's song
'My Golden Bengal' became the national anthem.

PARTY OVER STATE

After the war the institutions of state were weak and in disarray. Many
senior positions in the bureaucracy and armed forces lay vacant because

their occupants had been from West Pakistan. These institutions, as well as the political parties, now became arenas of factional struggle between those who had actively supported independence from exile in India and those who had tried to weather the storm of 1971 inside Bangladesh. The weak new state was confronted with enormous challenges: it needed to disarm groups of freedom fighters and establish law and order, run the newly nationalised industries, restore the wrecked infrastructure and become a player in the international state system. Most importantly, the state had to deliver economic development. The promise of emancipation from political domination by Pakistan had been fulfilled; now the government would be judged on its performance regarding its other promise: to emancipate the delta from economic exploitation, poverty and stagnation.

In a feeble state confronted with high popular expectations, the role of a charismatic leader is crucial. Mujib relied on his personal popularity and political intuition to tackle the new challenges. It was an almost impossible balancing act, and it soon became clear that he had been far more effective as an opposition leader than he was as a statesman – fiery rhetoric was more his style than forceful governance. He was unable to transform his personal relationship with his followers into an established authority structure independent of his personal qualifications.[14]

In an eerie replay of the late 1940s and early 1950s – when the Muslim League had been unable to switch from being the engine of the movement for Pakistan to being an effective ruling party – the early 1970s saw a steep erosion of the popularity of the Awami League. Among the reasons were a blossoming personality cult (which reminded people of the Ayub era), the attempt to dub the state ideology 'Mujibism' (*mujibbād*), charges of undue Indian influence in Bangladesh, and reports of widespread corruption and nepotism in the party. But these were not the main reason: the government squandered its popularity chiefly because it was seen to contribute to a deep malaise in the economy.

After the war many Bangladeshis, expecting a rapid recovery of the economy, were shocked to see that the standard of living of the majority of the population did not improve. On the contrary, it kept on falling. Economic productivity lagged far behind the pre-war level, and by 1973 agricultural and industrial production had declined to 84 and 66 per cent respectively of what they had been just before the war. The real income of agricultural and industrial labourers went down drastically: the cost of living for agricultural labourers increased by 150 per cent as overall real incomes slumped to 87 per cent of what they had been in 1970.

What was going on? Partly, it was a matter of inexperience. Many top positions in the state were now occupied by politicians and bureaucrats who had been suddenly promoted from the middle ranks of a provincial government to the highest rank of a national one; they needed time to learn their jobs. Another factor was that most members of the power elite had not seriously planned for post-independence policy-making. They had assumed that the removal of Pakistani exploitation would by itself lead to an economic resurgence, and hence they paid more attention to political, legal and diplomatic matters than to economic ones. Third, the economic circumstances had changed enormously. Gone were Pakistan's 'twenty-two families' and their allies, the landlords and armed forces. Instead, economic power was now in the hands of the delta's surplus farmers, small-scale entrepreneurs and industrial trade unions. Each expected that its support for the Awami League would translate into greatly expanded economic opportunities.[15]

These dynamics exacerbated the economic muddle and prevented the new regime from developing a social agenda. Further problems arose from its failure to create a professional, politically neutral state bureaucracy that could have implemented its policies effectively. Instead, it engaged in an abundant politics of patronage that continues to plague the Bangladesh state machinery today. In independent Bangladesh, ruling-party loyalty supersedes state interest. Rulers use the state to further their party rather than the other way around.

The Awami League was plagued by internal rivalries and sought to secure its members' commitment by creating networks of patronage that colonised the state. It appointed party loyalists, often irrespective of their administrative competence, to key positions in the state bureaucracy. This dominance of party-political considerations forestalled any coherent economic policy, let alone its implementation. Awami League ideologues could not reach a consensus over the correct national and socialist development policies and, worse, despite high-minded rhetoric and much suffering during the Pakistan period and the Liberation War, the Awami League 'had not imbued its leaders or members with idealism to work selflessly for the reconstruction of the war-ravaged country'.[16]

Awami League rule soon turned out to be a case of party over state. Management of the nationalised enterprises was handed to inexperienced political activists, leading to a sharp drop in production and a sharp rise in managerial wealth. Similarly, import licences, distributed among Awami League protégés, became a rich source of illegal pickings, partly by means of smuggling imported goods, jute and rice to India. Thugs with connections in the Awami League became notorious for extortion, and Awami League leaders used a new paramilitary force – the Rokkhi Bahini (*jātiya rakṣī bāhinī*; National Security Force) – to spread fear through intimidation and torture. Mujib was aware of the 'blatant abuse of power and corrupt practices of his party people', but, always the party loyalist, did nothing to stop them.[17]

The delta suffered not only from inadequate economic policy, mismanagement and plunder. Its economic woes were also compounded by Bangladesh's new currency, the taka (*ṭākā*), which was printed in such lavish quantities that it led to inflation and hardship. On the other hand, an inflow of international relief and rehabilitation masked these economic shortcomings until the end of 1973, when the United Nations Relief Organisation in Bangladesh (UNROB) closed down.

BANGLADESH'S FIRST ELECTIONS

In March 1973 Bangladesh held its first general elections. Mujib still retained much of his enormous personal popularity, but 'a store of resentment had built up among the electorate against the Awami League and it was bound to be reflected in the elections'.[18] The Islamic right-wing parties were banned, so all opposition parties stood to the left of the Awami League. Among these were the JSD (*Jātiya Samājtāntrik Dal*; National Socialist Party), a recent offshoot of the Awami League; the 'Islamic socialist' National Awami Party (NAP) of Maulana Bhashani; and a number of pro-USSR and pro-China communist groups. The elections were marred by Awami League attempts to secure a total victory by means of kidnapping, coercion, vote rigging and the stealing of ballot boxes. When the Awami League announced that it had garnered 97 per cent of the seats in parliament, it ensured that the delta's tradition of election irregularities was extended into the Bangladesh era.[19]

Frustration now spilled onto the city streets and village pathways. The opposition parties, feeling that they had been swindled out of their parliamentary role, returned to the street politics that had been so effective in Pakistan times. General strikes (*hartāl*) and mass encirclements (*gherāo*) reappeared, and the government's reaction resembled that of the erstwhile Pakistan government. For example, an Awami League mob set fire to the headquarters of the JSD, the JSD newspaper was taken over by the government and hundreds of party members were arrested.

Now an inescapable dynamic set in. The state's strong-arm tactics left little room for open opposition and pushed many dissenters underground. A plethora of leftist groups, all out to complete what they saw as

Bangladesh's unfinished or aborted revolution, began to wage armed resistance in the countryside. Leftist guerrilla fighters became active in different parts of the delta, attacking police stations and killing Awami League workers all over the country, most frequently in the districts of Borishal, Kushtia, Rajshahi and Dhaka.[20] The government, attempting to regain control, commenced combing operations against these opponents, now branded 'miscreants' and 'antisocial elements', and passed the Special Powers Act (February 1974) to give itself far-reaching formal powers to suppress individual liberty and press freedom.

THE FAMINE OF 1974

By 1974 the dream of a Golden Bengal had turned out to be a chimera. Two years after independence the country was in profound economic and political crisis, and for most people the situation had become almost unbearable. Deeply disillusioned with the Awami League and its sponsor, India, and much poorer than before the war, they had to struggle to make ends meet. The rice harvest of December 1973 was good, but afterwards rice prices kept rising, a situation blamed largely on politically well-connected traders and speculators. By March 1974 starvation, begging and distress migration were on the rise. In these desperate circumstances, nature struck a blow: the summer brought deep, long and damaging floods, pushing many more people over the edge. By the end of August 1974,

the whole of Bangladesh turned into an agonizing spectacle of confusion and human suffering ... it was 1943 re-enacted. Streams of hungry people (men, women, and children), who were nothing but skeletons, trekked into towns in search of food. Most of them were half-naked ... We were all personally witnessing these things in despair. There was very little support available for the destitutes in urban centers except for some private charity ... after a few days of 'wandering' around the streets of the city they simply collapsed and died ... I myself saw an average of three to five unclaimed bodies a day in August on my way to my office, which was only a five minute walk.[21]

Rice prices continued to go up throughout this period, but the treasury was so empty that the government could not import rice. The United States had put an embargo on food aid because Bangladesh had begun to export jute to Cuba, a country on the US blacklist. Relief from other sources was pilfered. After initial denials that anything serious was happening, the government ordered the Bangladesh army to apprehend hoarders and prevent smuggling of rice to India. But the military had to be pulled up sharply when they arrested hoarders 'who were either Awami Leaguers or enjoyed their protection ... Mujib had to give protection to his arrested party men, under pressure of his party colleagues, even when they were patently guilty.'[22]

There was a strong reaction from civil society: Bangladeshis acted in many ways to help the famine victims. Private voluntary organisations all over the country began providing free cooked food and relief, and government-sponsored gruel kitchens followed a little later. These efforts saved the lives of millions. Even so, it is thought that the excess mortality resulting from the 1974 famine may have been near 1.5 million.[23] In demographic terms it was quite as stunning a disaster as the war of 1971.

By the end of the year, the Bangladesh government stood exposed as inept, indifferent and heartless. All its political credit had vanished. Seventy distinguished Bangladeshi economists, lawyers and writers issued a statement saying that the famine was man-made and had resulted from 'shameless plunder, exploitation, terrorisation, flattery, fraudulence and misrule'. They added that the government was 'clearly dominated by and ... representative of smugglers and profiteers'.[24]

AUTHORITARIAN RULE

Disenchanted with the turn of events, Mujib felt that a fresh start was called for. He understood that the rapidly emerging *nouveau riche* group that formed the backbone of the Awami League had become thoroughly discredited. Violent opposition to his rule was spreading. The economy was in a shambles. What Mujib did not realise, however, was that he had lost his charismatic hold over the population. On the contrary, his political intuition told him that there was only one way to counter the slide into anarchy: an autocratic regime that could achieve a breakthrough to an 'exploitation-free' society.[25]

In December 1974 the Bangladesh government proclaimed a state of emergency and suspended all fundamental rights conferred by the two-year-old constitution. In early 1975 it turned the constitution upside down by an amendment introducing a single-party presidential system. Mujib was sworn in as president of Bangladesh and launched a new party, BAKSAL (*Bāṃlādeś Kṛṣak Śramik Āoyāmi Līg*; Bangladesh Peasants, Workers and People's League). He was now an all-powerful head of state who had discarded accountability, democracy and the separation of powers. His aim was to initiate a social revolution from above, rather like what

Tanzania's president, Julius Nyerere, was doing at the time. His new project of civilian autocracy was presented as 'the second revolution'.

For a while, things went well for the new regime. The winter harvest was good and rice prices were coming down. Demonetisation of all 100-taka notes reduced the money supply and slowed down inflation. And the police had arrested and killed Siraj Sikdar, leader of the Shorbohara Party (*Sarbahārā Pārṭi*; Proletarian Party), one of Mujib's most influential underground opponents. But it was not only leftists who bitterly resented Mujib's new incarnation as an autocrat. Another, far more dangerous group felt deeply affronted: the army.

THE ARMY TAKES ACTION

The Bangladesh army of some 55,000 men consisted of Pakistan-era professional soldiers who had joined the freedom fighters, Bengali military personnel who had been stranded in West Pakistan during the war and new recruits from the ranks of various wartime guerrilla groups. In the early 1970s there was not a great deal for them to do, and they felt increasingly unhappy. Their resentment originated in the final days of the war of 1971. According to them, the Indian army had robbed the Bangladeshi fighters of the glory of liberating Bangladesh, walking in when the freedom fighters had already finished the job, and had taken away to India all sophisticated weaponry and vehicles captured from the Pakistanis. The post-war creation of a well-funded parallel force, the Rokkhi Bahini, deepened their sense of neglect, and they also felt bitter about Mujib's closeness to India, which, they thought, undermined the sovereignty of Bangladesh. By 1973 many in the army were both anti-Indian and anti-Mujib; in the elections that year the garrisons voted solidly for opposition candidates.

The army's first real operation came during the famine of 1974. Mujib ordered them to get rid of hoarders and smugglers, but then pulled them back to protect Awami League supporters. It was at this time that army unrest began to translate into acute anger and a sense that the army was the only organisation in the country able to remove Mujib from power. A plot began to take shape. By the spring of 1975 the Indians knew about it and warned Mujib, but he laughed at the suggestion that any Bengali could raise his hand against him: 'No, no. They're all my children.'[26] He was wrong. Just after midnight on 15 August 1975 three strike forces headed by junior officers left Dhaka's main cantonment and within a few hours they had assassinated Mujib and more than forty members of his family.[27] Bangladesh's long-cherished dream of popular democracy had first turned into a nightmare of civilian autocracy and now into military rule.

CHAPTER 19

Imagining a New Nation

The immediate post-war period was a time of national jubilation. In 1972 and 1973 anything seemed possible. The nation had finally won its own state and could now design its own future. The mood was oddly reminiscent of that other moment of euphoria, twenty-five years earlier, when the people of the Bengal delta had joined the Pakistani nation. Then, too, the future had looked bright, and there had been high hopes that the disappearance of detested overlords would usher in a social revolution.

But there was a crucial difference between the two moments. In the late 1940s it was an Islamic vision that had fuelled the sense of nation. The people of the delta were joining other Muslims of South Asia to create the homeland of Pakistan. Muslims first and Bengalis next, they imagined the future society as being in accordance with an Islamic sense of order and justice, adapted to local conditions. By contrast, the national identity that animated them in the early 1970s was a regional one. They were Bengalis first and Muslims next. The new society should be ordered in accordance with principles that had been developed in the West and could be adapted to local circumstances: democracy, socialism and secularism. In Bangladesh, being secular was (and is) understood not as being without religion but as having a neutral, impartial attitude to all religions (dhormo-niropekkho, *dharma-nirapekṣa*).[1] In other words, Islam was important as part of the majority culture and as a matter of personal faith, but it was not part of national identity. Within twenty-five years, they had moved from an image of themselves as Bengali *Muslims* to one of themselves as Muslim *Bengalis*. This remarkable feat was possible only because, as we have seen, a dual Bengali–Islamic identity had roots going back centuries in the Bengal delta.

Moreover, the new nationalism was distinctly 'deltaic': it was limited to East Bengal/Bangladesh, the region where the Bengali–Muslim identity was most salient. Certainly, deep currents of empathy connected Bengalis

208

in Bangladesh with their counterparts in India, but Bangladeshi nationalism definitely did not envisage reunification. Some Indian observers underestimated the strength of this feeling of 'separate Bengaliness'. Insufficiently aware of how East Bengalis remembered British colonial social arrangements, how the Pakistan experience had moulded their identity and how they felt that the Bengali cultural centre of gravity had shifted eastwards, these observers were taken aback when their tentative suggestions of more intimate ties with India met with firm rebuttals.

Thus began a misunderstanding that continues today. Two narratives began to develop. The Indian story stressed Bangladeshi ingratitude. It ran like this: India created Bangladesh. Its armed forces liberated Bangladesh from Pakistan and suffered many casualties in the process. India provided copious support and advice to the newborn country and was clearly entitled to Bangladeshi gratitude, trust and cooperation. While this was indeed the attitude of Bangladeshis immediately after the war, soon, inexplicably, they became hypersensitive, suspicious and uncooperative, if not downright hostile.

By contrast, the Bangladeshi story stressed Indian bossiness. It ran like this: Bangladesh liberated itself, with enormous support from India. Bangladeshis were (and remain) very grateful for this. But the Indian armed forces did not behave like angels in Bangladesh, nor did Indian officials always treat their Bangladeshi counterparts with the respect due to representatives of a sovereign entity. Bangladesh had struggled in order to free itself from Pakistan, not to become a satellite of India. It wanted to live in amity with its huge and richer neighbour but could not tolerate high-handed behaviour.

These stories gelled into a legacy of misperception that is now ingrained in relations between India and Bangladesh. These have been touchy and difficult ever since, although personal relations between Bengalis on both sides of the border are usually remarkably cordial. Major Bangladeshi complaints are that India diverts river water to its own territory and constructs a border fence around Bangladesh. India, for its part, blames Bangladesh for not stopping illegal migration to India, giving shelter to insurgents from Northeast India, refusing to export gas to India and not allowing transit traffic.[2] Over time, the two states have been able to resolve some issues, however, notably the location of their maritime border in the Bay of Bengal in 2014 and the exchange of over a hundred enclaves and territories in 'adverse possession' in 2015.[3]

The new Bangladeshi elite imagined the society that was taking shape in the delta as distinctly Bengali. They thought of Bangladesh as a true nation-state, a homeland to the Bengali community that had been denied justice in Pakistan (see box 'We are all Bengalis!'). This was wonderful news for the delta's Bengalis – tens of millions of Muslims, millions of Hindus, hundreds of thousands of Christians and tens of thousands of Buddhists – but less so for those who were not Bengalis. Triumphant Bengali nationalism had no time for non-Bengali Muslims or the many indigenous communities who had never identified themselves as either Bengalis or Muslims.

We are all Bengalis!

After the war of 1971 the dominant mood in the Bengal delta was one of generosity and inclusion. This was expressed well in a popular poster of the time which read:

> Bengal's Hindus,
> Bengal's Christians,
> Bengal's Buddhists,
> Bengal's Muslims
> We Are All Bengalis!

Showing a Hindu temple, a mosque, a pagoda and a church – linked in unity – the poster emphasised that the time when religion could be used to divide Bengalis was over. The new state of Bangladesh would treat all inhabitants of the Bengal delta as entitled to full citizenship (Plate 19.1).

Plate 19.1 'We Are All Bengalis.'

This Bengali-centrism became painfully clear when Sheikh Mujibur Rahman visited the Chittagong Hill Tracts, where the population was overwhelmingly non-Bengali and non-Muslim. He addressed them 'as brethren and told them to become Bengalis, to forget the colonial past and join the mainstream of Bengali culture'.[4] The locals left the meeting in protest, and the event became as significant in the Chittagong Hill Tracts as Mohammad Ali Jinnah's ill-starred 'Urdu-will-be-the-state-language-of-Pakistan' address had been in East Pakistan a generation earlier. The Pakistan government's inflexibility had fuelled a language movement that had ended in violent conflict. Now the new Bangladesh government showed exactly the same insensitivity to the delta's minority cultures – and it would soon reap armed resistance as well.

A NATIONAL CULTURE

Independence brought cultural autonomy to the delta and a new project of nation-building. Now its inhabitants were invited to imagine themselves as Bangladeshis. For people who were then in their sixties and who had lived in the delta all their lives this was the third invitation to join a nation. They had been born as British Indian subjects, had grown up with the Indian nationalist movement and had become Pakistanis in their thirties. Now they were Bangladeshis, and they saw a new national culture taking shape. Its main pillars were language, a regional style and a search for modernity.

Pride in the Bengali language had fired the national movement, so it was hardly surprising that language took a front seat in nation-building. In the public sphere the Urdu script disappeared overnight and English became rarer. There was a sharp shift to Bengali in the educational system and the Bengali-language press flourished (see box 'Innovation in print').[5]

Innovation in print

It was near-heaven to be young, talented and middle class in early 1970s Dhaka. You were in the midst of an explosion of optimism and creativity. Freed from decades of censorship, the middle class could express itself as never before. One of its most successful platforms, the weekly *Bichitra*, was founded in 1972. This magazine shook up the media landscape of Bangladesh and soon had a circulation that put many established daily newspapers to shame.

Bichitra attracted a group of gifted and outspoken young writers. Modernist and secular, they were convinced of the power of good journalism to change society. They set a new standard for independent reporting and introduced a style of anti-establishment writing that was totally new in mainstream media. The magazine combined investigative journalism with portraits of important cultural and political personalities, independent editorials, testimonies of social injustice, stories of life abroad by expatriate Bangladeshis, a readers' forum, creative writing, and information on sport and fashion. This mix appealed to a large, mainly young readership, and in this way *Bichitra* was very influential in forging a self-confident and enlightened national middle class (Plates 19.2 and 19.3).

Not surprisingly, however, it soon ran into trouble with a state that became increasingly intolerant of independent voices. From the mid-1970s it had a rocky career, but it survived until the government closed it down in 1997. By that time its format had been copied by numerous other magazines in Bangladesh.

Plates 19.2 and 19.3 Covers of *Bichitra*, 1975.

The Bangla Academy, an institution established in the 1950s in the wake of the language movement, now came into its own as the national academy of arts and literature and a major publisher of textbooks, dictionaries, folk literature, translations, cultural research and creative writing. It also was important as a focal point of three annual national events, the month-long festival of *Ekushe* (cultural events commemorating the language movement), the *Ekushe* Book Fair, and the celebration of Bengali New Year in mid-April.

The Bangla Academy is housed in a Dhaka mansion that embodies the different phases of the delta's twentieth-century history. Constructed by the Maharaja of Burdwan (hence its name, Burdwan House) at the time of the division of Bengal in 1905, it is redolent with memories of colonial Bengal's aristocratic landlordism. After Partition it became the seat of East Pakistan's chief minister, who presided over the killings of Bengali language activists in 1952, thus making it a perfect location for Bangladesh's prime symbol of post-Pakistan cultural autonomy.

Bangladesh's new national culture celebrated the delta's folk music, dance and pictorial traditions and at the same time sought to develop and upgrade them. Many projects were put in place to foster handicraft production; the 1970s became a period in which decorative jute-rope pot-hangers, bamboo-cane stools, embroidered quilts and block-printed fabrics were ubiquitous.

The cultural elite of Bangladesh sought to develop a national culture that combined local authenticity with modern appeal. Religious symbols disappeared. Instead, the country's official national symbols referred to the delta's natural beauty and abundance (Plate 19.4). The new flag (a red disc

Plate 19.4 One-taka note (1974), showing a hand holding ripe paddy and the water-lily-shaped national emblem.

Plate 19.5 National Monument for the Martyrs in Savar, initiated in 1972 and completed in 1982.

on a bottle-green background) and the national monument were simple and modernist (Plate 19.5).

A NATIONAL HISTORY

The sense of history that now dominated was fiercely nationalist. It focused on how the people of the delta had been victimised by British imperialists, Hindu landlords and West Pakistani usurpers, and how their struggles had finally led to their emancipation as a recognised and independent nation. It was a story of political activism and democratic motivation.

A national narrative of the delta was constructed to give meaning and legitimacy to the new state. Not surprisingly, its heroes were those who had died for the Bengali language during the Pakistan period and in the Liberation War. They were honoured in a new Liberation War Museum (Muktijuddho Jadughor; *muktijuddha jādughar*) in Dhaka. Suddenly the mainstay of the Pakistan nationalist narrative – the Partition of 1947 – was no longer a focal point, and the aspirations and joys of the Pakistan period became an 'actively forgotten world'.[6]

This was an important departure, because henceforth Bangladeshi perspectives on national history would differ radically from Indian and Pakistani ones. In both India and Pakistan the Partition of 1947 remains the pivot of national consciousness and the bedrock of nationalist historical understanding. In Bangladesh it has been resolutely displaced by the events of 1971. Whereas historians of India and Pakistan present 1947 as the end of colonialism and the coming of national independence, historians of Bangladesh stress that, in the Bengal delta, colonial rule continued until 1971, followed by national independence. In this way, Bangladesh nationalist history serves a dual purpose. On the one hand it legitimises the Bangladesh state and, on the other, it challenges the hegemony of Indo-Pakistani understandings of modern South Asian history.

PART V

Independent Bangladesh

Part V Street scene at New Market, Dhaka, in the 1980s.

CHAPTER 20

Shaping a Political System

In early 1975 Bangladesh was in deep crisis. Its economy was struggling, and there were real fears that the country might slide into anarchy. Bangladesh stood at a crossroads: what was the best way forward? There were three answers to this question. Mujib (and a dwindling group around him) prescribed a stronger dose of the medicine that he had administered in the previous years. Critics to the left were convinced, however, that this would not resolve the country's problems. They insisted that Bangladesh required a social revolution, a thoroughgoing land reform and state socialism. Diametrically opposed were those who saw the solution in economic liberalisation and state support for the private sector.

It was the struggle over these irreconcilable visions of the future that shook the edifice of the Bangladesh state in 1975. First came Mujib's constitutional *coup d'état* of January, establishing civilian autocracy. Immediately counter-forces built up, resulting in Mujib's assassination on 15 August and the installation of a military-backed government. This in turn was overthrown by a second military coup on 3 November, followed by a third on 7 November.[1] The man who now emerged as Bangladesh's ruler was Major-General Ziaur Rahman (popularly known as Zia). One of his first acts was to ban political parties and crack down on the JSD. This was the leftist party that had inspired radical soldiers to carry out the last coup, planned as a soldiers' revolution in the service of the oppressed classes. Zia had its leader, Colonel Abu Taher, hanged – a killing that still inspires literary echoes.[2]

MILITARY RULE (1975–90)

By the end of 1975 Bangladesh had turned its back on both Mujib's vision and the revolutionary path. The new regime of Ziaur Rahman (1975–81) marked a decisive break in the country's economic policies. It handed nationalised enterprises back to their former owners, favoured the private sector and export-oriented growth, and sought to boost agriculture by introducing subsidies and a wide range of development projects. The foreign funds needed for these policies flowed in, propping up the Zia regime and making it possible for the Bangladesh economy to recover. These policies set the country on a course of liberalisation from which it has not deviated since.

The regime of Ziaur Rahman also marked two decisive breaks with the vision of Bangladesh that had triumphed after the Liberation War. Both these breaks meant reverting to patterns that had been established during Pakistan rule and that most Bengalis had detested – few had expected these ever to re-emerge in post-independence Bangladesh. The first was military dictatorship and the second the political exploitation of Islam. Generals would rule Bangladesh for the next fifteen years, and, even after a popular uprising overthrew military rule in 1990, the army never really went back to the barracks. It has continued to loom as the life-or-death-dispensing power behind the throne of successive civilian governments up to the present. The political exploitation of religion also easily outlasted army rule. It has been a major tool for power-seekers and the state elite ever since.

THE ROOTS OF BANGLADESHI DICTATORSHIP

The militarisation of the Bangladesh state so soon after the country's birth as a democratically ruled unit needs an explanation. Military dominance was not rooted in the history of the Bengal delta, but it had been an important feature in the colonial history of Punjab, the faraway, dominant region of Pakistan. In the late nineteenth century the British had developed an ideology that categorised certain South Asian populations as 'martial races', who were considered better fighting material than others. Punjabis were seen as martial (and Bengalis as non-martial), and several regions of Punjab became prime recruiting areas for the Indian army. Ruled by a civil–military bureaucracy, Punjab became 'the garrison province of the Raj'.[3] After 1947 this experience gave the Punjabi Muslim elite the edge in the struggle for power in Pakistan. Initially there were three main groups who thought they would be the leaders of the new state of Pakistan: Bengalis, Muhajirs (Muslim immigrants from India) and Punjabis (see Chapter 12). The Bengalis lost out almost immediately, and the Muhajirs were sidelined in the course of the 1950s. With the ascent of Punjabi power within Pakistan, civil institutions gave way to military ones. The armed forces were a Punjabi institution to begin with: in 1947, Punjabis made up 77 per cent of the Pakistan army.[4] As the army carried out its first coup in the late 1950s, Punjabi dominance reached its peak. The military–bureaucratic elite that now ruled Pakistan perpetuated the paternalistic authoritarianism that had been the hallmark of British colonial control over Punjab.

What did this mean for the Bengal delta, now renamed East Pakistan? Part of the story is well known. As the Pakistan state took on the military–authoritarian features that the British had perfected in Punjab, it turned East Pakistan into an internal colony. The Bengali elite's exclusion from an effective say in state affairs – let alone in the army – eventually forced an end to Pakistan. But state-building was a more continuous process. The colonial garrison state of Punjab, transmuted into the military state of Pakistan, bequeathed its martial traditions to the Bangladesh state.

In Bangladesh, the 1970s were in many ways a replay of the 1950s: high hopes for democratic control were soon dashed as the state struggled through increasingly authoritarian civil rule before finding its feet after an army takeover. Bangladesh was to be under military dictatorships, modelled closely on Pakistan's Ayub–Yahya regime, from 1975 to 1990.[5] Arguably, from the 1950s to the present, military rule has not been the exception to the civilian norm in the Bengal delta but its equal: military men controlled the state for thirty years from 1958 – thirteen years during the Pakistan period and seventeen during the Bangladesh period. These seventeen years include two years in the twenty-first century (2007–9) when once more the armed forces grabbed state power and installed an 'interim government'. One area in Bangladesh, the Chittagong Hill Tracts, has been under continuous military control from 1975 to the present.

How was it possible for Punjabi colonial traditions to be grafted onto those of the Bengal delta? And why did they continue to hold after 1971, without the support of anything resembling the Punjabi elite? Independence from Pakistan had put new, local masters in charge of the delta, but it had not brought a social revolution or an organisational overhaul of the state. In many ways the Bangladesh state was the Pakistan state by another name. Even the armed forces, the state institutions that had been shaken up most by the 1971 war, soon regained their balance by reverting to the Pakistani model. And with this came their self-appointed role as arbiters in state affairs and usurpers of executive power (see box 'Pakistani-trained strongmen of Bangladesh (1975–90)').

The regime of Ziaur Rahman was followed by that of another general, Hussain Muhammad Ershad (1982–90). In both cases a military man seized power, cancelled basic rights and banned political parties in return for promises of swift development and a squeaky-clean administration. In both cases a dictator tried to build legitimacy by creating a political party and have himself elected as president of Bangladesh with sweeping powers. And then, suddenly, he was removed from the scene. This happened in the most drastic fashion to Ziaur Rahman, who was assassinated in a botched military coup during a visit to Chittagong in 1981. A military-backed civilian government took over for some months before Chief of Staff Ershad overthrew it, thus becoming Bangladesh's second dictator. Ershad was forced out of power by a popular uprising in 1990. Since then the military have left the top positions in the state to civilians, although, as we have seen, from 2007 to 2009 they stepped in again to intervene in the running of an 'interim government'.

Pakistani-trained strongmen of Bangladesh (1975–90)

The officers who seized state power in the Bengal delta after 1975 had built their careers during Pakistan's military dictatorships (1958–71). Disdainful of civilian politics, they saw themselves as more capable and deserving of running the state than politicians.

Ziaur Rahman (Plate 20.1) ruled from 1975 until 1981, when he was murdered. Zia's father had been a chemist in Kolkata at the time of Zia's birth in 1936. The family moved to Karachi, where Zia graduated from the Pakistan Military Academy in 1955 and joined the Pakistan army as a teenager.

Plate 20.1 General Zia at a state ceremony.

During the Ayub period he worked in military intelligence. When war broke out in 1971, he happened to be posted in Chittagong. He threw in his lot with the Bangladesh side, rebelled, declared independence on the radio, joined the freedom fighters, fled to India and gained a reputation for valour. After independence he was appointed the deputy chief of staff of Bangladesh's armed forces. His takeover in 1975 echoed that of General Ayub Khan in 1958, almost down to the script of his address to the nation: 'The Government [is] committed not to continue with the Martial Law beyond the time needed . . . I am not a politician. I am a soldier . . . I would like to make it clear I have no connection whatsoever with politics and ours is a completely non-party and non-political Government.'[6] He doubled the size of the armed forces and the police, created a political party and continued to rule the country until he was assassinated over five years later.

After an interlude of months following Zia's assassination, Lieutenant-General Hussain Muhammad Ershad (Plate 20.2) usurped power in 1982. Ershad controlled Bangladesh until 1990, when he was toppled by a popular uprising. Born in Rangpur in 1930 or thereabouts (his birth date is contested), he was commissioned in the Pakistan army in 1952, rising through the ranks.

Plate 20.2 'Martial Law enforced in the entire country.' General Ershad's coup, 1982.[7]

During the Bangladesh Liberation War he was in West Pakistan, but, unlike many other Bengali officers, Ershad did not leave the service of the Pakistan army during that war. He was repatriated to Bangladesh in 1973, joined the Bangladesh army and was made chief of staff during Zia's rule. When he addressed the people of Bangladesh immediately after he had seized state power on 24 March 1982, he justified his act by arguing that the country's national security, independence and sovereignty were threatened 'due to social and political indiscipline, unprecedented corruption, devastated economy, administrative stalemate, extreme deterioration of law and order and frightening economic and food crisis'.[8] In his view, his countrymen needed military discipline, and he was the person to give it to them. One of the lasting effects of the Ershad regime is the Jatiyo Party, the political vehicle that he created to give his rule a democratic appearance. Another is administrative decentralisation in the form of a proliferation of districts. There had been eighteen when Bangladesh came into existence but by the mid-1980s these had been subdivided into sixty-four districts. Each of these units was made up of numerous upozilas (*upajelā*), almost 500 in all. It was the new name for what used to be called thanas.

Like many powerful persons in Bangladesh, Ershad regularly sought the advice of a Sufi spiritual guide. This man, known as the Pir of Atroshi, is thought to have gained considerable power over cabinet appointments and promotions of army staff.[9] In 1988 Ershad amended the constitution of Bangladesh to proclaim Islam the state religion, a hotly contested move.

The political system that evolved in Bangladesh between 1975 and 1990 was one in which the judicial and legislative branches became hostage to military-controlled executive power. In this period civil rights were much more curtailed than they had been in the initial years after independence. This was something that many citizens of Bangladesh refused to accept. Their aspirations for the future expressed themselves in continual struggles to improve the quality of their lives and to increase their influence over the state. Throughout this fifteen-year period of military rule, many Bangladeshis strove for a return to parliamentary democracy against forces that tried hard to shield the state from popular influence (Plate 20.3).[10] Their efforts culminated in a prolonged and widespread campaign of agitation in 1990, which finally managed to dislodge military rule, topple the Ershad regime, and force a return to parliamentary democracy.

Plate 20.3 'Set democracy free!' Nur Hossain had this text on his back, and 'Down with autocracy!' on his chest, during a mass protest against the Ershad regime in 1987. Police shot him dead, turning him into a lasting icon of the struggle for democracy in Bangladesh.

PARLIAMENTARY DEMOCRACY

The return to civilian rule in 1990 was widely celebrated in Bangladesh. Many saw it as a clean break with the immediate past and a fresh start for a truly democratic Bangladesh. And indeed, within months the country had a democratically elected parliament and a popular government eager to usher in a better future. Even so, it had to deal with many continuities stemming from the period of military rule.

The main political legacy of the period of military rule was the emergence of an alternative view of the nation and its embodiment in a major political party. Zia had sought to gain legitimacy for his military regime by constructing a political party and having it stand in elections that he controlled. The party that Zia created, in 1978, was the Bangladesh Nationalist Party (*Bāṃlādeś Jātīyatābādī Dal*, or BNP). Its ideology was nationalist conservatism. Sometime after Zia's death in 1981 his widow, Khaleda Zia (who had married him at the age of fifteen in 1960), was appointed as the leader and despite her political inexperience she held most of the party together. Under her leadership the BNP grew into a formidable political force.

In the same way, Zia's successor, Ershad, created his own party, more right-wing than the BNP. It took the name Jatiyo (National) Party in 1986. Unlike Zia, Ershad survived his dictatorship. After his demise in 1990 he was jailed for corruption and spent years in and out of prison, meanwhile continuing to lead a faction of his party and winning some seats in parliament. Unlike the BNP, the Jatiyo Party never played more than a minor role after parliamentary democracy was restored. Ershad continued to lead his party until his death in 2019.

After Ershad's fall, elections for the national parliament (Jatiyo Shongshod; *jātiya saṃsad*) were held in 1991. A multitude of parties participated, and the result was open and unpredictable. Two parties clearly dominated the outcome, however: the BNP of Ziaur Rahman (now run by his widow, Khaleda Zia) and the Awami League (run by Sheikh Mujibur Rahman's daughter, Sheikh Hasina). The BNP won 31 per cent of the vote and the Awami League 28 per cent. Consequently, Khaleda Zia put together the new government and became the prime minister of Bangladesh.

Since then parliamentary elections have been held in 1996, 2001, 2008, 2014 and 2018 – each time amid much violence and political drama, high voter turnout (except in 2014), and accusations of rigging and irregularities. These elections cemented the dominance of the two leading parties and their leaders. The Awami League won in 1996, the BNP in 2001, and the Awami League in 2008, 2014 and 2018.

The three most recent elections were especially controversial. Widespread violence preceding elections planned for early 2007 prompted the military to step in (behind the thinnest possible veneer of an 'interim government'), suspending all political activities. They ruled Bangladesh for almost two years and tried to 'clean up' the political system by breaking up the two-party status quo and removing Sheikh Hasina and Khaleda Zia from the scene. They failed on both counts and allowed the election to take place in late 2008.[11] As the Awami League settled into power, however, another military irruption occurred. In early 2009, border guards (Bangladesh Rifles, or BDR; now renamed Border Guards Bangladesh (BGB)) revolted against their army officers in their headquarters in central Dhaka. This bloody BDR mutiny ended after two days with seventy dead. Subsequently, 3,500 border guards were charged, and 139 were given the death penalty.[12]

The elections of 2014 were a shambles: they took place after a chaotic period of nationwide strikes, violence, shutting down of media, the banning of the largest Islamist party (Jamaat-e-Islami) and a crackdown on other opposition parties. As a result, the BNP boycotted the elections, allowing the Awami League to sweep back into power with questionable legitimacy.[13] The elections of 2018 – marred by violence, voter intimidation, accusations of vote-rigging and other irregularities – resulted in the Awami League winning 96 per cent of parliamentary seats amid, once again, serious concerns about the validity of the results and the growth of civilian autocracy. In a replay of previous phases in which authoritarian rule took hold of the country, foreign powers remained largely silent about – and thereby supportive of – democracy's decay in the People's Republic of Bangladesh.

The Bangladesh political system in eleven phases

1. *Parliamentary democracy (1971–75)*

Dominant political figure:	Sheikh Mujibur Rahman
Dominant party:	Awami League (created in 1949)
Ended in:	Civilian *coup d'état* by Sheikh Mujibur Rahman

2. *Civilian autocracy (1975)*

Dominant political figure:	Sheikh Mujibur Rahman
Dominant party:	BAKSAL (created by Sheikh Mujibur Rahman)
Ended in:	Assassination of Sheikh Mujibur Rahman, military *coups d'état*)

3. *Military autocracy (1975–81)*

Dominant political figure:	Ziaur Rahman

	Dominant political party:	Bangladesh Nationalist Party (BNP, created by Ziaur Rahman)
	Ended in:	Assassination of Ziaur Rahman

4. *Military autocracy (1982–90)*

	Dominant political figure:	Hussain Muhammad Ershad
	Dominant political party:	Jatiyo Party (created by Hussain Muhammad Ershad)
	Ended in:	Popular uprising, Ershad forced to step down

5. *Parliamentary democracy (1991–6)*

	Dominant political figure:	Khaleda Zia
	Dominant political party:	Bangladesh Nationalist Party (BNP)
	Ended in:	Elections

6. *Parliamentary democracy (1996–2001)*

	Dominant political figure:	Sheikh Hasina
	Dominant political party:	Awami League
	Ended in:	Elections

7. *Parliamentary democracy (2001–6)*

	Dominant political figure:	Khaleda Zia
	Dominant political party:	Bangladesh Nationalist Party (BNP)
	Ended in:	Takeover by military-backed interim government

8. *Military-backed interim government (2007–9)*

	Dominant political figure:	Fakhruddin Ahmed
	Ended in:	Elections

9. *Parliamentary democracy (2009–14)*

	Dominant political figure:	Sheikh Hasina
	Dominant political party:	Awami League
	Ended in:	Elections

10. *Parliamentary democracy (2014–18)*

	Dominant political figure:	Sheikh Hasina
	Dominant political party:	Awami League
	Ended in:	Elections

11. *Parliamentary democracy (2019–)*

	Dominant political figure:	Sheikh Hasina
	Dominant political party:	Awami League

The post-1990 political system featured dictator-born parties, but it was also clearly rooted in the rural political traditions of the Bengal delta. As we have seen in Chapter 1, Bangladeshi villages have never been tightly organised communities under a single village head. Village life is dominated by unstable and continually shifting alliances of family and hamlet leaders. This flexible pattern, which developed as a response to life on the frontier of land and water, is also visible in national politics. David Lewis characterises Bangladesh as a 'patron state'. He argues that in Bangladesh patron–client relations are a cornerstone of society: better-placed people extract services, labour and loyalty from lower-placed people in exchange for protection, employment and support. The result is hierarchical webs of relationships that are unstable – they shift when clients feel that they are not sufficiently rewarded, or when patrons see fit to transfer their resources to another group of clients. In these circumstances it is difficult for clients to build, and maintain, horizontal relationships based on class or locality.[14]

The national political system operates on the same principle and shows the same instability. The political parties are hardly inspired by lofty visions or moral principles, although they certainly exploit ideological symbols to attract voters. Instead, they are vehicles to coordinate 'competing efforts of dominant groups to claim and control resources'. These groups form coalitions of 'local sovereigns' that mobilise a 'factional base of clients, but once mobilised these inevitably disintegrate when it becomes clear that not all groups can be adequately rewarded ... Bangladesh's political parties are, therefore, highly factional and regularly split into groups led by dominant charismatic individuals.'[15]

Despite recurring elections, then, the People's Republic of Bangladesh is not democratically ruled.[16] The power elite of this society of 170 million people is remarkably small and surprisingly connected by family ties, even across party lines.[17] Each time, a tight-knit coterie of familiar power holders comes out on top. It is telling that the two dominant parties still have the same leaders that they had thirty-five years ago and that both tend towards the dynastic family model that is the hallmark of village and regional local politics.[18] In the absence of a grand vision of Bangladesh's future, each party is likely to fracture without the charisma of Sheikh Hasina (leader of the Awami League since 1981) and Khaleda Zia (leader of the BNP since 1984). These leaders effectively use the histrionics of confrontation to keep their parties united and their voters mesmerised, and to obscure the fact that they both bolster a system that not only excludes most citizens from decision-making, but also promotes the power coteries' joint control, as well as growing inequalities and authoritarianism.

This growing authoritarianism of the political system is helped by the fact that the state is only partly decolonised. It still retains many aspects of the repressive British colonial state, from the application of sedition laws, gag rules (section 144 of the Code of Criminal Procedure 1898) and a ban on sexual acts 'against the order of nature' (section 377 of the Penal Code) to overbearing state institutions such as the Forest Department. Many of these have been only marginally dismantled, and some have been updated in tune with the autocratic ethos of the colonial period – for example the Digital Security Act 2018, which has been described as 'draconian' because it 'treats peaceful critics as criminals'.[19]

In other words, despite much rhetoric to the contrary, the nation has never really been able to take possession of the state, even though, for a moment in the early 1970s, it had seemed to be possible. Perhaps most noticeable of all is the enduring bureaucratic culture. State officials tend to be bossy and condescending towards ordinary Bangladeshis, making them feel more like subjects than citizens. Non-elite Bangladeshis often need to resort to the tactics of colonial subjects (obsequiousness, handing over bribes, cajoling and offering petitions) to move officials to pay attention to their needs.

This entrenched character of the state has facilitated the emergence of a political system that is now described as an 'illiberal democracy'. 'Political and legal institutions are subject to partisan politics, and state power is misused for personal and political gain. Politics has become a competition to control the state in order to serve partisan interests within a "winner-takes-all" system.'[20] Bangladesh has been described as a 'partyarchy', or 'party-state'.[21]

But how do these politicians retain a semblance of legitimacy? As we shall see in the next chapter, shrewd calculations of material gain get translated into the language of identity politics.

CHAPTER 21

The Triumph of Identity Politics

The Bengal delta has a tradition of identity politics that reaches back to the early twentieth century. Such politics seek to mobilise people on the basis of their religious or ethnic identity, often by using the language of kinship. Over the past hundred years or so, this trend has progressively chipped away at the inclusive, overarching regional culture that had evolved over many previous centuries (see Chapter 3). Some cultural identities were turned into razor-sharp tools that proved effective in new, sometimes lethal power struggles. Other identities came under attack or were relegated to the political margins. Identity politics reworked the social fabric and created new fault lines that to many Bangladeshis now appear to be natural, inescapable and age-old.

In the early twentieth century political parties began to be formed around religious identity; and from the mid-twentieth century identity politics also crystallised around ethnicity. These were emancipation movements. They were based on a shared experience of injustice and discrimination against Muslims, and against Bengalis, respectively.

The basic assumption was that a shared group identity implies shared political interest. This strategy proved highly successful. First it mobilised mass support for the construct of a 'Pakistan nation' – which presumed that Muslims in British India had shared interests – and then for the construct of a 'Bangladesh nation' – which presumed the same for the inhabitants in East Pakistan. Nationalism was an intense form of identity politics that contributed greatly to the establishment of both Pakistan and Bangladesh. But it did not go unchallenged. It was confronted by oppositional class politics that cut across religious or ethnic categories and sought to organise people on the basis of a shared experience of economic exploitation and poverty.

Class politics also developed in the early twentieth century but could not play a major role in the Bengal delta except during two periods of social crisis. The first was from the 1930s to the 1950s, when communists and other left-wing activists mobilised large groups of sharecroppers and tenants to claim a better deal from their landlords. This emancipation movement was especially effective during the late 1940s but collapsed soon after the establishment of the state of Pakistan (see Chapter 9). The second wave of left-wing success began in the late 1960s, as the Pakistan state was faltering, and it continued vigorously during the early years of Bangladesh – until it was crushed and marginalised in the late 1970s (see Chapters 13 and 18).

During the early years of independent Bangladesh, the dominant political mood favoured identity politics based on a mix of language pride, celebration of regional non-communalist cultural traditions, and Third Worldism. This was the period in which an ardent nationalism became firmly established in people's minds as well as in public institutions. But class-based contestation was strong enough to promote policies such as the insertion of 'socialism' into the constitution, the nationalisation of industries and the legal imposition of a land ceiling.

The return of military dictatorship in 1975 sounded the death knell for class-based politics. Although many left-wing organisations continued to exist (some were outlawed and went underground), their hold on national politics was over. Identity politics was triumphantly back in the saddle and has been there ever since. The mood had changed, however, and soon cracks were appearing in the national celebration of Bengaliness. As politicians began successfully to exploit other identities, several of these cracks widened to create chasms of resentment and violent confrontations that continue to the present day. Here we will look at three of these: the retooling of 'Bengaliness' versus 'Bangladeshiness', the struggle over global Islamic identities versus regional linguistic ones, and the confrontation between minority identities and Bengali claims to cultural superiority.

BENGALIS OR BANGLADESHIS?

The distinction between Bengaliness and Bangladeshiness developed under military dictatorship (1975–90) and became embedded in the parliamentary political system afterwards. The post-1990 scenario is quite remarkable in that it has been dominated by two towering politicians whose appeal is based on 'inherited charisma'. Sometimes referred to as the Two Begoms (ladies), they cooperated in the successful campaign to oust Ershad, in which they were frequently detained and harassed, and they have posed as implacable adversaries ever since. The first is Khaleda Zia, widow of Ziaur Rahman and leader of the Bangladesh Nationalist Party

(BNP). As we have seen, she emerged as prime minister after the first post-Ershad elections in 1991 and governed until 1996. Losing elections that year, she swept back into power after elections in 2001, this time serving until 2006.

Between 1996 and 2001 her arch-rival, Hasina Wazed, also known as Sheikh Hasina, served as prime minister. She returned in 2009 and has remained Bangladesh's prime minister until today. She is the eldest daughter of Sheikh Mujibur Rahman and had survived the assassination of her family in 1975 merely because she happened to be abroad. After the Awami League had reassembled, she became its leader and returned from self-exile shortly after Ziaur Rahman's death in 1981.

It is through these two politicians that a crucial set of unresolved tensions in Bangladesh's political system has taken shape. This is the wrangle over the identity of the nation and the correct national ideology. It gave a new twist to the long history of dual Bengali–Islamic identities in the Bengal delta. As discussed in Chapter 8, the division of Bengal in 1905 had made many inhabitants of the delta aware of a new rift between their Bengali and Muslim selves. For the first time, they felt, they had to choose which was the dominant one. The dilemma became a persistent topic of discussion all through the twentieth century and continues to be a vexed question today. Those who supported the movement for Pakistan chose to highlight their Muslim identity, but during the Pakistan period, when nation-building was predicated upon Muslimness, opposition to West Pakistani dominance over the delta made full use of linguistic and regional symbols.

'Bengaliness'

From the 1950s to the 1970s, the delta's vernacular elite had imagined Bangladesh as the homeland of Bengalis who were denied justice and representation under Pakistan. To them, the Bengali nation stood for much more than a linguistic community. The nation's spirit expressed itself in particular cultural sensibilities, devotional traditions and humanist aspirations that suffused the delta's folk songs and Baul mysticism as deeply as the poetry of Rabindranath Tagore and Kazi Nazrul Islam. The favourite visual representation of the nation was a landscape of bountiful green fields dotted with rustic, peaceful riverside villages. The popular poet Jasimuddin captured this sensibility in his book-length poem 'The Field of the Embroidered Quilt'. The opening lines are:

A village here, a village there,
And a broad field in between
A page to read all written over
With crops and rice so green.[1]

The heyday of this vision of the nation as a rural idyll coincided with the period in which the delta's intelligentsia dominated the political scene, from the Awami League's Six-Point Programme after the India–Pakistan War (1965) to Ziaur Rahman's army take-over (1975). During this eventful ten-year period, many members of the delta's intelligentsia believed that they could shape an autonomous Bangladesh in their own image. Post-1975 events showed this belief to have been gravely mistaken. Political newcomers with different ideas about the essence of the nation sidelined the intelligentsia, which was left with strong feelings of nostalgia for the lost spirit of the late 1960s and early 1970s. It fell to Sheikh Hasina and her supporters to salvage what was left of this version of the nation.

'Bangladeshiness'

With the collapse of Awami League control of the state in 1975, a new narrative of the nation developed to prop up the military regime of Ziaur Rahman. Making a distinction between 'Bengalis' and 'Bangladeshis', it accentuated the religious dimension once more. It held that the independent nation that emerged from the 1971 war was overwhelmingly and *essentially* Muslim.[2] This was an audacious move only a few years after the war, because until then anyone suggesting that Muslim identity might prevail over Bengali identity had been exposed to the charge of being pro-Pakistan and anti-Bangladesh. This new 'narrative of Bangladeshiness' deflected any charges of high treason, however, by idolising the heroic role of Ziaur Rahman in the 1971 war.

In this way, it anchored its claim for legitimacy in the moment of the nation's birth, just like its contender, the older 'narrative of Bengaliness'. But whereas the latter saw the nation as originating in the language movement and the 1971 war, the narrative of Bangladeshiness saw the nation as originating in the movement for Pakistan and the 1971 war. It did not see the creation of Pakistan as a misstep that had been rectified with the emergence of Bangladesh. On the contrary, it stated that the Bangladeshi nation was the

Plate 21.1 The Mausoleum of the Three Leaders (*Tin Netār Mājār*) in Dhaka was constructed in the 1980s. It honours three prominent politicians who were active in the early Pakistan period: A. K. Fazlul Huq (1873–1962), H. S. Suhrawardy (1892–1963) and Khwaja Nazimuddin (1894–1964). The mausoleum's architect was S. A. K. Masud Ahmed. A Mughal-era mosque can be seen in the background.

ultimate manifestation of the delta's Muslim–Bengali identity, which had been maturing during the British and Pakistan periods (Plate 21.1).

In other words, 1947 had been necessary for 1971 to happen: the creation of Pakistan had enabled the emergence of Bangladesh. Zia reintroduced Islamic symbols in political life and he purged secularism from the Bangladesh constitution, instead inserting Islam in its preamble. After his death in 1981, it fell to Khaleda Zia and her supporters to propagate this version of the nation.

The narrative of Bangladeshiness proved attractive to many at the more conservative and religious-minded end of the political spectrum. Their slogan, '*Bangladesh Zindabad!*' (Long live Bangladesh!), became a challenge to the '*Joy Bangla!*' (Victory to Bengal!) that had been the rallying cry until then (Plates 21.2 and 21.3).

Plate 21.2 *'Joy Bangla!'* Poster depicting Sheikh Hasina as a stateswoman surrounded by symbols of her party and the nation: her father, flags, a rural boat. She is described as the 'Jewel of the Land, Leader of the People and Daughter of Sheikh Mujibur Rahman, the Friend of Bengal and Forever Supreme Father of the Bengali Nation' (c. 2005).

In 1991 the outcome of the first democratic elections after military rule showed clearly that the narrative of Bangladeshiness had voter appeal and that the narrative of Bengaliness was on the defensive. It also demonstrated that other narratives of the nation, such as various leftist ones, were almost completely sidelined (see box 'Nonagenarian on the warpath').

Plate 21.3 *'Bangladesh Zindabad!'* The student wing of the BNP celebrated its twenty-seventh birthday in 2006. Chief guest was Khaleda Zia, who is described on this poster as 'Leader of the Country' and is depicted with her assassinated husband, General Ziaur Rahman.

Nonagenarian on the warpath

Since 1947 the Bengal delta had been in political turmoil, and numerous politicians had come and gone. But there was one constant factor: Maulana Bhashani (c. 1880–1976). Bhashani was the only prominent leader who was village-based. For much of his very long life he lived in Santosh, a village in Tangail district not far from where he was born. He started life as Abdul Hamid Khan, earning the title of Maulana (*maolānā*; Islamic scholar) on account of his training and teaching, and the epithet Bhashani for his efforts to protect Bengali settlers on Bhashan Chor (an island in the Brahmaputra in Assam) from floods in the 1930s.

A nonconformist and mercurial leader with an uncanny feeling for the popular mood, he became an important player in East Pakistan.[3] Even though he never held state office, his inimitable interventions often influenced the political course. A long-time supporter of Pakistan, he broke away from the Muslim League in 1949 to form the Awami (Muslim) League and became one of the leaders of the language movement. In 1957, he broke away from the Awami League to form the left-wing National Awami Party (NAP). At this point he became the main ideologue of an Islamic leftist trend in Pakistan. Jailed for his beliefs on several occasions, he was very popular among the peasantry, who saw him as their champion. When the left all over the world

split into pro-Moscow and pro-China factions, the NAP split too and
Bhashani headed its pro-China wing. In 1970 he once again played a crucial
role when he decided that the NAP would not contest the first general elections
in Pakistan, leaving the field wide open for a landslide victory for the Awami
League, now headed by Sheikh Mujibur Rahman. His parting shot came in
1976, when he organised a 'Long March' from Rajshahi to the Indian border to
protest against India's Farakka barrage that would deprive Bangladesh of its
share of the Ganges waters. Since his death, Bangladesh has not had a left-wing
leader with broad national appeal – but there is renewed interest in his
progressive Islamic legacy (Plate 21.4).[4]

Plate 21.4 Maulana Bhashani.

BANGLADESHIS OR MUSLIMS?

The idea of 'Bangladeshiness' is the first persistent legacy of military rule in
Bangladesh. The second is the resurgence of Islamist politicians. Their
main political vehicle is the Jamaat-e-Islami Bangladesh.

The Jamaat-e-Islami (Islamic Gathering) is a political party that traces its
roots to the British period. Founded in 1941 by Maulana Maududi from
Aurangabad in southern India, the Jamaat split into national chapters after
Partition. Maududi migrated to Pakistan and headed the party until 1972.
The Jamaat holds that the sovereignty of God and the sovereignty of the

people are mutually exclusive and that 'Islamic democracy' demands that an Islamic government must accept the supremacy of (the Jamaat's interpretation of) Islamic law over all aspects of political and religious life.

These ambitions led Maududi to clash frequently with the rulers of Pakistan, who were not in favour of a theocratic state, and made him an implacable opponent to the autonomy movement in East Pakistan. Consequently, after the 1971 war, the Jamaat's leaders in Bangladesh were utterly discredited and fled to Pakistan. The Bangladesh government banned the party for collaboration with the Pakistan army. In 1978, however, Ziaur Rahman allowed them to return and resume political activities. There is a distinct connection between military rule and Islamism in Bangladesh. Like Ayub before him, Ziaur Rahman used Islamists to prop up his own power, thereby politically validating an austere and intolerant version of Islam. After General Ershad usurped state power in 1982, he went a step further and used Islamic symbols and contacts even more freely than Zia. To widespread protests from secularists – and applause from Islamists – he amended the constitution, abandoning state secularism and declaring Islam the state religion (Plate 21.5).[5]

After 1990, when Bangladesh returned to an electoral system, the Jamaat-e-Islami fielded candidates for parliament, securing 12 per cent of the vote. After 2000, its popularity never exceeded 4 per cent, and yet it played a central role in what many saw as the creeping Islamisation of Bangladesh politics. In

Plate 21.5 'Using religion in politics is unacceptable!' Women's organisations protesting against the Ershad regime's declaration of Islam as the state religion of Bangladesh, 1988.

2001 the BNP entered into a coalition with it to form the government.[6] When the Awami League returned to power in 2009, the Jamaat had to face a headwind, and it has been banned from elections since 2013.

ISLAMIC RADICALISM

The Jamaat is widely thought to have ties with underground activists who aim for an Islamist revolution in Bangladesh. The rise of radical Islamism became apparent in the early 1990s, expressing itself first in its insistence on gender difference. Clerics began using fatwas (religious verdicts) to condone the maltreatment of women.[7] The power of Bangladesh's fatwa-issuing clerics attracted international attention when a group of them demanded the death of feminist writer Taslima Nasrin. In 1993 she had published a novel titled *Lojja* (*lajjā*; shame) about anti-Hindu violence in Bangladesh, which had occurred the previous year in response to the destruction of the Babri Mosque in Ayodhya (India). The Bangladesh government banned the novel; its author had to flee the country.[8]

Encouraged, Islamic radicals now availed themselves of an old tradition in the Bengal delta – terror. Up to then, terrorist tactics – the use of spectacular public violence to instil fear and destabilise the social order – had been the preserve of progressive politicians. Terror had first been used in the service of freedom from British colonial rule (see Chapter 8).[9] The 'Bengal terrorists' of the early twentieth century lived on as national heroes in Bangladesh, and they had inspired many a freedom fighter during the 1971 war. After independence, radical leftist organisations had applied terrorist tactics as they attempted to trigger a Marxist revolution in Bangladesh. Now this political instrument was appropriated by activists who dreamed of establishing an Islamic state and who turned against secularism and non-Muslims (see box 'Osama's fan club').[10]

Osama's fan club

Terror in the name of Islam took off in the 1990s, partly inspired by Bangladeshi veterans of the anti-Soviet jihad in Afghanistan. The attempt on the life of Shamsur Rahman, a celebrated elderly poet, is a typical example. In 1999 members of Harkat-ul-Jihad-al-Islami Bangladesh (a radical Islamist group reportedly founded with aid from Osama bin Laden)[11] attacked him with axes in his apartment. He was saved by his wife, who stood in their way. The 'Ramna bomb blast' is another example. The cultural organisation Chhayanot had been celebrating Bengali New Year with an open-air concert in the Ramna area of Dhaka every year from 1963. In April 2001 (Bengali New Year 1408) a bomb exploded in the middle of the festive crowd and another blast occurred forty-five minutes later. Nine people were killed and dozens injured. A few months later twenty-one people were killed and many injured in a bomb attack on the offices of the Awami League in Narayanganj.

Later that year the World Trade Center in New York was attacked. Bin Laden, thought to have masterminded the assault, shot to global notoriety. He also became an instant hero among the Islamist fringe in Bangladesh, who saw him as a champion of resistance against Western imperialism and depravity (Plate 21.6). Operational linkages with a number of foreign Islamist groups grew further, and Islamic warriors (*jihādī*) were reportedly trained in camps in Bangladesh, for example in the vicinity of Ukhia in the southeast.[12]

Plate 21.6 Calendar featuring Osama bin Laden for sale in a shop in Rangamati, 2001.

Shootings, knifings, bomb explosions and grenade attacks now became more frequent. Some were indiscriminate. In 2002 at least seventeen people were killed and more than a hundred injured in a series of bomb blasts in four crowded cinemas in Mymensingh. In 2005 over 300 explosions took place simultaneously in fifty cities and towns across Bangladesh.

Other attacks were clearly targeted. For example, anti-Ahmadi agitations started from 2003. The Ahmadi(yyas) are a Muslim sect with about 100,000 members in Bangladesh. Islamist radicals terrorise Ahmadis and demand that the Bangladesh government declare the sect to be non-Muslim. They killed Shah Alam (a preacher in Jessore) and bombed and set ablaze Ahmadi mosques in Nator and Brahmanbaria.[13] Other groups that the Islamists target are Hindus, Christians and Buddhists. These formed an organisation, the Bangladesh Hindu Buddhist Christian Unity Council, which keeps detailed accounts of attacks and discrimination. Jihadi killers also targeted well-known personalities in literature (Humayun Azad), politics (Shah Kibria, Sheikh Hasina), human rights advocacy (Shahriar Kabir) and academia (Muhammad Yunus). Bangladeshi cartoonist Tanmoy depicted the anger and confusion that Bangladeshi Islamists felt at the killing of Osama bin Laden in Pakistan in an image of lookalikes receiving the news (Plate 21.7).

Plate 21.7 'Bin Laden is dead!' Cartoon by Tanmoy, 2011.

Global events increasingly influenced Islamist identity politics in Bangladesh. News of the attack on the World Trade Center in New York in 2001 and the wars in Afghanistan, Iraq and Syria reached tens of millions of Bangladeshis via rapidly expanding mass media. Television was now widely available and information technology, mainly by means of mobile phones, made social media accessible throughout the country. In addition, more Bangladeshis had first-hand knowledge of social life in the traditional heartland of Islam – as migrant labourers in the Gulf, as pilgrims to the holy sites, or as fighters in the wars. These developments strengthened a sense of belonging to a global community of Muslims (*ummah*) that shared an experience of victimisation – a perfect breeding ground for identity politics.

This sense of belonging expressed itself in many forms – from lifestyle to orthodox interpretations of textual Islam. In a way, what was happening was nothing new. It was the latest of several waves of religious 'purification' that had swept over the Bengal delta since confrontation with European rule had called for cultural introspection across the region (see Chapters 6 and 8).The current rethink about what it takes to be a good Muslim in twenty-first-century Bangladesh, and the move to more doctrinaire interpretations, is part of a long historical process. It stands in the tradition of 'rectifying movements' that have always rejected the notion that Islam could have multiple, equivalent, local forms, and struggled against Sufi-inspired, locally embedded spirituality. There are certainly important differences between early-nineteenth-century movements, such as Faraizi and Tariqah-i-Muhammadiyah, and the current forms of reformist puritanism, but they are inspired by the same urge.

It is essential to distinguish between this moral and ritual repositioning (which is often apolitical and concerned with personal rectitude)[14] and the ambitions of Islamism, which seeks to establish a theocratic political order, not just in Bangladesh but worldwide. It is also important to distinguish Islamism from Jihadism (Islamist militancy), which seeks to launch that theocratic order by violent means. These differences are visualised in Plate 21.8. We see the new moon that marks the end of the holy month of Ramadan and the beginning of the festival of Eid. To the left are variously dressed Muslim Bengalis painting it white, to the right is a lone Jihadist painting it black.

The confrontation between progressive activists and Islamists reached a climax in 2013 and, not surprisingly, over issues related to the 1971 war of independence. The Awami League won elections in 2008 and came to power on a promise to establish an international war crimes tribunal to prosecute those responsible for wartime atrocities. The tribunal had first been legalised in 1973, but the law had never been implemented (see Chapter 18). Now, thirty-seven years later, the tribunal began to function.

In 2013, when a high official of the Jamaat-e-Islami was given a life sentence for war crimes and crimes against humanity, the country became the scene of a very public face-off between Islamists and nationalists. First the Jamaat called a general strike in Dhaka that turned violent. Then a large-

Plate 21.8 'This Eid and our spirit.' Cartoon by Mehedi Haque in the *Daily New Age*, 2016.

scale peaceful sit-in began, initiated by progressive bloggers and cultural activists. Tens of thousands gathered spontaneously at the Shahbag intersection in Dhaka, a number that grew with each passing day. They demanded that all those convicted of war crimes be given the death penalty. The 'Shahbag movement' was born (Plate 21.9).[15] It spread to cities and towns across the country, giving new hope to those who had feared that retribution for the perpetrators would never come – and who felt that the political class had squandered the ideals of the 1971 war enshrined in the constitution: nationalism, socialism, democracy and secularism.

But this was not the only movement in response to the tribunal. It also marked the beginning of a new period of Islamist militancy. Hardline Islamists regrouped under the banner of a madrasha-based organisation styled Hefazat-e-Islam and marched on Dhaka for mass street demonstrations. They demanded, among other things, a blasphemy law, severe punishment for atheists and bloggers, and an end to infiltration by 'alien culture'. They clashed violently with security forces and ruling-party activists, resulting in many dead and wounded. In the aftermath of this confrontation, the government made some concessions to their demands.

Plate 21.9 'Death to the Razakars [war criminals]!' Against a backdrop of
Bangladeshi flags, a 2013 Shahbag activist replicates the body-paint protest depicted
in Plate 20.3.

At the same time, the government also had to deal with newly reinvigo-
rated Jihadist groups. An earlier wave of terrorist attacks had peaked around
2005 (see box 'Osama's fan club') but then had tapered off as a result of state
action. But Jihadists – better integrated than before into transnational
networks – were soon becoming more active again. In late 2012 they burned
old Buddhist temples and houses in Ramu (Cox's Bazar) and they used the
political effect of terrorist acts by murdering members of non-Muslim
minorities, Shia and Ahmadi Muslims, secular activists and foreigners.
Online confrontations led to real-life assassinations of several progressive
bloggers – and others were forced to flee the country.[16] In 2016 a spectacular
Jihadist attack on a stylish café in Gulshan, one of Dhaka's poshest neighbourhoods, caused national alarm. What shocked public opinion was the
audacity of the attack, which killed more than twenty people, but also the
fact that the perpetrators did not fit the popular stereotype of Islamist
fanatics. These were not traditionally dressed, madrasha-educated and
socially disadvantaged men but youngsters from elite families with excellent
prospects.

THE CHITTAGONG HILL TRACTS WAR (1975–97)

The third persistent legacy from the period of military rule – in addition to
the struggle between 'Bengaliness' and 'Bangladeshiness' and the rise of

Islamist politics – is an inability to accommodate regional autonomy and cultural diversity. We have seen that this is not a new problem in the history of the Bengal delta. In the late-colonial period the Congress Party had refused to accept the notion of post-colonial regional autonomy for Bengal under the Muslim League, thereby forcing the partitioning of Bengal and the creation of East Pakistan (see Chapter 9). After 1947, the Pakistan state elite had rejected the demands of the autonomy movement in East Pakistan, thereby forcing it into increasingly radical positions, before attempting unsuccessfully to crush it by military means (see Chapter 12). Mohammad Ali Jinnah had wanted some sort of confederation but ended up leading an independent Pakistan. Sheikh Mujibur Rahman had pictured himself as the future prime minister of Pakistan right up to the army crackdown of March 1971 but ended up leading an independent Bangladesh.

Demands for regional autonomy and respect for cultural diversity within Bangladesh surfaced soon after the state had come into existence. They fell on deaf ears. Neither triumphant Bengali nationalism nor the more Islamic interpretations of the nation that emerged from the late 1970s held much promise for those citizens of Bangladesh who did not identify as Bengali and/or Muslim. National debates first ignored the rights of the country's many indigenous communities and then actively sought to silence them.

The experience of a delegation from the Chittagong Hill Tracts, meeting with Sheikh Mujibur Rahman in 1972, set the tone. The group, headed by a member of parliament, wished to hand Mujib a memorandum seeking retention of the autonomy safeguarded in the Chittagong Hill Tracts Regulation of 1900 as well as a ban on the influx of non-hill people.[17] Mujib refused to accept the memorandum and dismissed it out of hand. When the first Bangladesh constitution was promulgated later that year, there was no longer a special provision for the Chittagong Hill Tracts: the new rulers of Bangladesh rejected the model of minority autonomy that had been developed in the British period and that today survives in the constitution of India. Their insensitivity to the country's minority cultures and to their charge of internal colonialism was all the more astonishing in view of their own long struggle for self-determination. It was in this context that the hill people began referring to themselves collectively as 'Jumma' (*jummā*) – a sobriquet denoting their links with hill agriculture (*jhum*)[18] – and in 1972 formed a political party, the United People's Party, or JSS (Jono Shonghoti Shomiti; *pārbatya chaṭṭagrām jana saṃhati samiti*).

The coups of 1975 made it impossible for the JSS to operate as a political party and led to insurgent activity in the Chittagong Hill Tracts that India (which opposed the Zia regime) began to support. Ziaur Rahman thought that he could eliminate the movement by military force, but this policy backfired spectacularly. The armed wing of the JSS, the Shanti Bahini (*sānti bāhinī*; Peace Force), fought the Bangladesh army and soon a full-blown regional war was underway (Plate 21.10). The Chittagong Hill Tracts became heavily militarised, and local people were herded into 'cluster villages' around army camps. The regime also sponsored Bengali migration into the hills, where it provided poor settlers with transport, land grants, rations, cash and armed protection. As the Shanti Bahini attacked army camps and Bengali settlements, Bangladesh armed forces and groups of armed settlers carried out reprisal killings on Jumma villages, leading to a string of massacres and to tens of thousands of Jumma refugees fleeing to India. In 1986 India established six refugee camps to cope with the influx of hill people who refused to be returned to Bangladesh. The Chittagong Hill Tracts War continued under the Ershad (1982–90) and Khaleda Zia (1991–6) regimes, but when an Awami League government returned to power in Bangladesh in 1996, India withdrew its support for the autonomy

Plate 21.10 Fighting the Bangladesh armed forces. Members of the Shanti Bahini guerrilla army in the Chittagong Hill Tracts pose for a picture in their jungle hideout, 1986.

movement and this opened the door for a peace settlement between the JSS and the Dhaka government, signed in 1997. The settlement affirmed that administrative arrangements in the Chittagong Hill Tracts would continue to differ somewhat from those in the rest of the country, although far less than the autonomists had demanded. The Chittagong Hill Tracts retained some regional peculiarities – or an internal state frontier (see Chapter 3) – in the form of vestiges of indirect rule (the office of three chiefs, or rajas), a local system of taxation and land rights, and special forms of representation such as a regional council and a national Ministry of Chittagong Hill Tracts Affairs.[19]

Despite the settlement, however, peace did not return to the region. The massacres and abductions of the previous years remained uninvestigated and unpunished (see box 'Kolpona Chakma'), and ex-JSS members who opposed the settlement continued to fight, now as the United People's Democratic Front (UPDF). Furthermore, successive Bangladesh governments have failed to implement the most important provisions of the settlement.[20] These include the rehabilitation of all returned refugees and internally displaced people, restoration of land confiscated from the hill people during the war, withdrawal of non-permanent army camps from the Chittagong Hill Tracts and transfer of power to the local administration.[21] As a result, the Chittagong Hill Tracts (now broken up into three districts) is the only part of Bangladesh that has persistently remained under tight military control since 1975, even though the rest of Bangladesh has long returned to civilian rule. Jumma nationalism continues to throw up a strong regional challenge to countrywide debates about national selfhood and democracy. Meanwhile, both indigenous people and Bengali immigrants struggled with economic precarity, insecurity, political volatility and military high-handedness. As a result, their mutual relationships were complex and alternated between violent confrontation, accommodation and conviviality.[22]

Kolpona Chakma

Kolpona Chakma was a young and energetic women's rights activist. As the organising secretary of the Hill Women's Federation, she had been publicly criticising the harassment to which personnel of the Bangladesh armed forces subjected Jumma women (Plate 21.11). In June 1996 parliamentary elections were held in Bangladesh, and Kolpona was lobbying for an independent candidate who had the support of the JSS.

On the night before the ballot boxes opened she was woken up. Strangers had come to her home in the village of Lallyaghona in the northern Chittagong

Hill Tracts. They entered the house, shone a strong torchlight on the sleeping family and took away Kolpona and her two brothers. Their abductors turned out to be the commander of a nearby army camp, Lieutenant Ferdous, and other plain-clothes agents. Some time before, Kolpona had had an argument with Ferdous about an incident in which soldiers from his camp had wounded some Jumma people and set their houses on fire.

Now the men blindfolded and tied up their three captives. The brothers managed to escape by jumping into water while being fired at. Kolpona screamed: '*Da, da, mahre baja!*' (Brother, brother, rescue me!). The next morning her brothers, accompanied by others, went to the local army camp and police station but received no help. The army began a botched disinformation campaign. Soon the abduction became a national issue, as Bangladeshi women's organisations and human rights campaigners took it up, holding demonstrations, petitioning the home minister and pointing out that abduction and rape of Jumma women had occurred before. The case also received wide international publicity. The UN special rapporteur on violence against women approached the Bangladesh government, Amnesty International called for an impartial inquiry and the European Parliament passed a resolution.[23] But Kolpona was never seen again and the case remains open.[24]

Plate 21.11 Kolpona Chakma speaks in public, Khagrachhari, 1995.

The Bangladesh state elite's refusal to countenance cultural diversity occurred at a time when a worldwide movement of identity politics based on 'indigeneity' was taking off. Activists from the Chittagong Hill

Tracts, and later from other parts of Bangladesh, connected with this movement. Soon they were rejecting the condescending Bengali epithet 'upozati' (*upajāti*; tribe). A more acceptable term was 'indigenous peoples', or, in translation, 'adibashi' (*ādibāsi*; adivasi, aboriginal inhabitants). Indigeneity became a new political resource, backed up by UN institutions and initiatives such as the International Day of the World's Indigenous Peoples (Plate 21.12).

The Bangladesh Indigenous People's Forum (or Bangladesh Adivasi Forum) was established in 2001 and it started campaigning nationally and internationally against discrimination, land grabbing and state hostility, and for constitutional recognition of the more than fifty indigenous peoples and languages in the country. Successive Bangladesh governments took the position that there are no indigenous people in the country, although a constitutional amendment in 2011 conceded the existence of 'small ethnic groups' (khudro nrigosthi; *kṣudra nṛgōṣṭhī*).[25] Over time, the indigenous movement gained power and legitimacy and attracted backers among the Bengali majority population.[26]

Indigenous activists have been particularly energetic in campaigning for recognition of their political and cultural rights, and education in their mother tongues. They challenge the popular understanding that only (Muslim-)Bengalis can be true citizens of Bangladesh and that exclusion of ethnic and religious minorities is therefore legitimate. At the same time, they campaign against physical oppression and land grabbing by rubber plantations, tea estates, brick fields, the armed forces, the Forest Department, border guards and private citizens in different parts of the country.[27]

THE BANGLADESH POLITICAL SYSTEM

Three competing visions of the nation – Bengali, Bangladeshi, Muslim – and two models of government – autocracy and parliamentary democracy – have towered over political life in Bangladesh ever since the mid-1970s. The tensions between them have resulted in variable and sometimes capricious alliances between the country's political parties during periods of both military and civilian rule (see Chapter 20). They have also influenced the type of leadership that flourishes in the Bangladesh political system. Whatever party or military ruler is in power, the basic character of leadership remains the same. It is always highly personalised, 'based on patrimonial authority and loyalty, and maintained through a complex, informal network of patron-client relations'.[28] The result is a political

বিশ্বের সকল আদিবাসী   এক হও, এক হও

"আন্তর্জাতিক আদিবাসী দিবস" উপলক্ষ্যে

বিশাল আদিবাসী সমাবেশ

১১ আগস্ট, ২০০৩
স্থান ঃ লোকভবন (টাউন হল), দিনাজপুর

কর্মসূচি ঃ
সকাল ঃ ১১:০০ ঘটিকায় র‍্যালী শেষে জেলা প্রশাসক, দিনাজপুর-এর নিকট স্মারকলিপি প্রদান
দুপুর   ঃ ১:০০ ঘটিকায় আলোচনা সভা
দুপুর   ঃ ২:০০ ঘটিকায় আদিবাসী সাংস্কৃতিক অনুষ্ঠান

সহযোগিতায় ঃ গ্রাম বিকাশ কেন্দ্র, কারিতাস, আরডিআরএস বাংলাদেশ, বিএনইএলসি, ডিএফ, জিকেপি, এমএসএনবি, ডিএলপি, এইচআরডিএফ

Plate 21.12 'Indigenous peoples of the world, unite!' A call to join the celebration of the International Day of the World's Indigenous Peoples 2003, in the northern town of Dinajpur.

landscape crowded with tugs of war between large egos, in the form of either furtive negotiations or public displays such as mass demonstrations, general strikes and police charges.[29] These leave most Bangladeshis with a sense of anguish about the country's lack of guidance and direction. Many feel that the politicians have recklessly gambled away the great opportunities that offered themselves after the 1971 war.

Remembering the Liberation War

In 1971 nobody could have predicted that the war would still be such a political juggernaut half a century later. The country's major political groupings continue to exploit its memory to legitimise themselves and to set the tinderbox of national politics ablaze whenever they see an advantage. How these groupings seek to remember (or forget) the war is of direct relevance to their struggles for power today. Between 1975 and 1996, successive governments discouraged scrutiny of the war as a living and contested experience, choosing instead to embalm it in the pomp and circumstance of state ritual. The sacrifices of the freedom fighters, extolled under the Awami League regime up to 1975, were later downplayed, and state support to needy freedom fighters was stopped (Plate 21.13).

The plight of the forgotten freedom fighters occasionally surfaced, however, in opposition parties' attempts to drum up popular support. Plate 21.14 shows an example. This poster, based on a wartime image of heroic fighters, is an invitation to the public to join a 'special reunion and meeting of guerrilla and freedom fighters' at a central green in Dhaka in 1994, organised by a left-wing party's student group.

Sometimes it was not the political parties but other groups that were able to influence public perceptions of the war. The Shahbag movement of 2013 (mentioned earlier in this chapter) was in many ways a replay of earlier citizens' attempts to shake up the political system. In 1992 a group of 'pro-liberation' activists headed by Jahanara Imam formed the Nirmul Committee (or Committee for the Uprooting of Traitors and Collaborators of 1971; *ekāttarer ghātak-dālāl nirmūl kamiṭi*). They staged a people's court (gono adalot; *gaṇa ādālat*) to get the people's verdict on the leader of the Jamaat-e-Islami, whom they accused of war crimes and treason (Plate 21.15). In this way they sought to force the issue of the stalled prosecution of war criminals back onto the political agenda. The government reacted by charging the organisers of the people's court with treason. Nevertheless, the Nirmul Committee (now styled the Forum for Secular Bangladesh) survived and became an important rallying point for secular and anti-fundamentalist forces in Bangladesh.[30] Another significant event shaping public perceptions of the 1971 war during this period was the release of the documentary film *Song of Freedom* (*Muktir Gan*) in 1995.

চিন্‌লেন না স্যার, আপনি
ছিলেন কমাণ্ডার; আমি
ছিলাম মুক্তিযোদ্ধা ·······

Plate 21.13 'Don't you recognise me, sir? You were my commander; I was a freedom fighter.' Cartoon (1981) criticising the political elite's treatment of those who had risked their lives for the nation's independence a decade earlier.

With its sequel, *Words of Freedom* (*Muktir Kotha*), it generated a public debate about the need to inform the post-war generation about many unknown aspects of the war.[31]

When in 1996, after a gap of twenty-one years, the Awami League once again managed to become the dominant force in the Bangladesh political system, there was a sharp upswing in the public visibility of the Liberation War and the party's role in it. This visibility diminished noticeably once the Awami League was relegated to the opposition after 2001 but it resurfaced after the party swept back into power in 2009. Since then, the

Plate 21.14 'Respect the ideals of the Liberation War.' Poster, 1994.

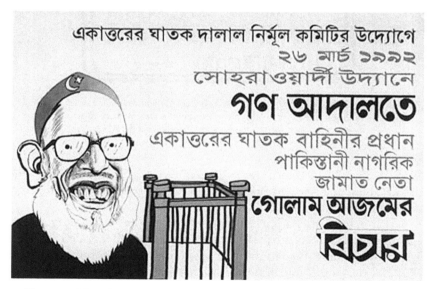

Plate 21.15 Nirmul Committee poster announcing the people's trial of Golam Azam ('head of death squads of 1971, citizen of Pakistan, and leader of the Jamaat') on 26 March 1992.

party has made energetic political use of its interpretation of the Liberation War to stabilise its rule.

When Bangladesh came into existence in 1971, many observers doubted that it could survive. Nevertheless, independent Bangladesh has not become a failed state. On the contrary, from uncertain beginnings and through many permutations, the state has grown, and it has strengthened its control over the Bengal delta in many ways (although not in all – for example, it still lacks a functioning system to register births and deaths).[32] It has developed a political system that proved remarkably crisis-resistant and increasingly able to deliver services to its citizens. This solidity has not been entirely home-grown, however. International support to the young state has been an absolutely crucial ingredient in the mix, as we will see in the next chapter.

CHAPTER 22

Transnational Linkages

In 1971, after four centuries of foreign rule, it was once again a local elite who took charge of the Bengal delta. We have seen that these new rulers were a remarkably small and inexperienced group. The delta's elite had been decimated twice within a generation. In 1947 many upper-class, professional and entrepreneurial Hindus had left for India, and they had been largely replaced by newcomers from West Pakistan. In 1971 these newcomers retreated to Pakistan amidst targeted killings of the delta's professionals and intellectuals. As a result, independent Bangladesh started out with only a few people who had any experience in running state institutions or large enterprises. They needed all the help they could get.

Luckily, newborn Bangladesh had many well-wishers. The midwives of its independence, India and the Soviet Union, were keen to nurture it, and emergency aid to overcome the wholesale war devastation was flooding in from all over the world. Dhaka, now a national capital, became dotted with embassies. Suddenly the delta's elite had to perform on the global stage. As a result, Bangladesh society rapidly developed new transnational links that would shape its future course. Especially influential were foreign aid and investment, mass migration and rapid advances in connectivity.

FOREIGN AID

As we have seen in Chapter 15, in the 1950s and 1960s economic development in the Bengal delta had been sustained by foreign aid, not by mobilising resources internally. Pakistan's state elite had become progressively addicted to foreign assistance and had allowed their development priorities to be set by foreign donors. These followed a policy of betting on the strong on the assumption that benefits would trickle down to poorer people and weaker sectors of the economy. This had worked out unfavourably in the Bengal delta and had contributed to the political crises that rocked the region in the late 1960s. The delta's autonomy movement had been fuelled by the hope that a larger share of the foreign aid to Pakistan would reach the local economy.

Thrust into independence, Bangladesh inherited an impoverished, war-damaged and overwhelmingly rural economy. Nine out of ten Bangladeshis made their living in the countryside. As over 80 per cent of the population lived below the poverty line (defined as consuming under 2,150 calories a day), there was little capacity for internal resource generation. Moreover, there was no real scope for the state to extract a surplus from those who could have generated it – big farmers and entrepreneurs – because these were its main supporters and vote brokers. This political reality ruled out a structural transformation of rural society, a move feared by India (because it would produce cross-border refugees) but advocated by leftists.

No wonder Bangladesh's leaders were keen to cash in on the global climate of sympathy towards the country and international imaginings of Bangladesh as a helpless, poor, deserving society. Aid was easier to come by than ever before. Many people across the world felt that the international community had a duty to help war-ravaged Bangladesh back on its feet. In addition, 'the dominant powers also saw [aid] as an opportunity to recoup their diminished credibility with the people of Bangladesh due to their support for the erstwhile Pakistani ruling elite'.[1] Finally, Cold War logic also dictated aid from the West as an instrument to make sure Bangladesh would not join the communist bloc.

Aid commitments grew by leaps and bounds, and Bangladesh became a celebrated test case of aid-propelled development.[2] Just before the war, foreign aid to East Pakistan had amounted to US$4 per inhabitant. By the mid-1970s it had tripled, and it continued to rise during the years of military rule until it reached an all-time high of US$20 per Bangladeshi in 1990, after which it declined. By the late 2010s the share of foreign aid in the country's gross national product (GDP) was only around 2 per cent (or 5 per cent of the country's capital formation, down from over 70 per cent in the 1970s).[3]

Foreign aid contributed very substantially to the delta's economic recovery, and donors used this instrument to induce post-1975 governments to privatise and liberalise the economy.[4] The social and political implications were far-reaching. Thousands of foreign expatriates – consultants, volunteers, aid administrators, diplomats and technical support staff – descended on Bangladesh. Their role was to tutor, advise and cajole the new state elite, manage the aid accounts and assist in the rehabilitation of the delta's society. They were the local representatives of foreign governments, international organisations, commercial enterprises, humanitarian

Plate 22.1 Bangladeshi official receiving bags of money (marked 'pounds', 'dollars', 'yen', 'riyals' and 'debts') while holding up a sign reading 'We must be self-reliant!' Cartoon by Nazrul, 1979.

bodies and voluntary societies. Many different interests coalesced here, from visionary zeal to hard-boiled salesmanship and from geopolitical manoeuvring to unselfish benevolence. Taken together, and backed up by the large sums of money that they controlled, these visitors were a formidable presence.[5]

If the Pakistan elite of the 1960s had been aid-dependent, the much poorer Bangladesh elite of the 1970s and 1980s was even more addicted. In fact, it was the aid regime that allowed them to emerge, stabilise and sustain themselves (Plate 22.1). Many found employment in aid-funded state institutions, non-governmental organisations and development projects. Aid-sponsored schools, clinics and infrastructural works improved their quality of life. Not a few grew rich by embezzling aid. Largely freed from the necessity to mobilise internal resources, Bangladesh's elite came to rely more on transnational partners than on the Bangladesh citizenry at large. They created a world of their own in the posh neighbourhoods of Dhaka that they shared with the expatriate community. And last but not least, the aid regime was crucial in propping up military and undemocratic institutions – aid commitments kept on rising under military rule.

A PROLIFERATION OF NGOS

Foreign aid also produced a major new form of organisation in the delta, the non-governmental organisation, or NGO. The Bangladesh state had limited capacity to process the aid flows, and international donors often felt that their money could be spent less wastefully, more promptly, more effectively and more creatively through private organisations. As a result, NGOs emerged as a prime channel for implementing all kinds of 'development policy'.[6] Soon the social landscape was cluttered with thousands of aid-supported NGOs, from tiny pop-and-mom ventures in charge of a neighbourhood development project to huge enterprises with international ambitions. Some acted as extensions of the state, others set themselves up against the state – and then there were a few who came to look rather like states within the state. One of these was BRAC. This started out as a small-scale donor-funded relief organisation, the Bangladesh Rural Advancement Committee, in Sulla (Sylhet district) in 1972. Thirty-five years later it described itself as:

an independent, virtually self-financed paradigm in sustainable human development. It is the largest in the world employing 97,192 people, with the twin objectives of poverty alleviation and empowerment of the poor. Through experiential learning, BRAC today provides and protects livelihoods of around 100 million people in Bangladesh ... BRAC's outreach covers all sixty-four districts of the country and ... [BRAC] has been called upon to assist a number of countries including Afghanistan and Sri Lanka.[7]

Over the years BRAC became a giant corporation that spawned activities as varied as national health programmes, upmarket crafts shops, a tea company, a bank, a university, internet services and an ombudsperson's office.

Another NGO that started out as a local project and developed into an international movement was the Grameen Bank (*grāmīn*; rural). It began life in the 1970s as an innovative action research project on credit delivery in a few villages near Chittagong and became an independent bank by 1983. Designed to challenge conventional banking practices, the Grameen Bank lent small amounts of money to groups of poor women without collateral or formal contracts. This approach, dubbed 'microcredit', proved extraordinarily productive, and in 1995 the bank stopped taking donor funds. By 2018 the Grameen Bank had disbursed more than US$25 billion in loans, had more than 9 million borrowers in Bangladesh – almost all women – and reached over 95 per cent of all villages in the country. Like BRAC, it had grown into a powerful corporation with numerous offshoots, from the country's major mobile phone company to textile mills.[8] Building on what had been achieved in Bangladesh, microcredit (or microfinance) programmes were set up in many countries around the world. In 2006 the Grameen Bank and its founder Muhammad Yunus received the Nobel Peace Prize.

There were many other forms in which local initiatives played a part in how development took place. Bangladeshis engaged in lively debates on the pros and cons of the inflow of foreign assistance, how these funds should be spent and what various development programmes actually contributed to the country's welfare. In some cases they managed to prevent the implementation of programmes that they considered harmful or ill-considered. The most celebrated case was a nationwide campaign against the Flood Action Plan.

After the devastating floods of 1988 (see Chapter 1), donors proposed truly gargantuan engineering works to stop flooding once and for all. In response, meetings were organised in Bangladesh and abroad to challenge the assumptions underlying the plan: that flood control is desirable, that it is possible to tame the delta's major rivers sustainably by means of huge embankments, and that such vast interventions can be planned in isolation from the people for whom they are intended and without recognition of the environmental costs. The ideas that developed during the campaign focused on flood mitigation rather than control, people's participation in the planning process, improved drainage through dredging, regional solutions rather than a national master plan, and environmental assessment. Several of these ideas became integrated into Bangladesh's official policy. The large-scale works originally proposed were never implemented, but in 2018 the government adopted a new, retooled and heavily aid-dependent 'Bangladesh Delta Plan 2100'.[9]

Compared to foreign aid, investments by foreign companies in the Bangladesh economy remained modest. Bangladesh was attractive for its cheap and abundant labour, and, beginning with the regime of Ziaur Rahman (1975–81), it tried hard to attract investments. But its mercurial politics, lack of transparency and shaky infrastructure made it a risky destination for investors. For decades, foreign direct investments (in energy, textiles, pharmaceuticals and mobile phones) were less than half the amount of foreign assistance, but they gradually grew to equal foreign assistance in the late 2010s. Among foreign investments, China rapidly became more important in the 2010s, drawing the Bangladesh state into new geopolitical skirmishes. A case in point is the 2010 agreement between the Bangladesh and Chinese governments for a major Chinese-financed deep-sea port at Sonadia, near Chittagong. In 2016, Bangladesh suddenly pulled out, reportedly following 'intense political pressure from India and the United States, both of whom are concerned over China's growing influence in the Indian Ocean region'. Japan was also said to be keen to establish a deep-sea port in Bangladesh.[10]

The contribution of foreign aid in shaping post-1971 Bangladesh society has been very considerable. It allowed new initiatives to become successful, gave stability to a fledgling state and provided a new generation with unexpected opportunities. It decisively improved the quality of life for millions of Bangladeshis by providing better protection from natural hazards, more healthcare, safer drinking water, new employment opportunities, higher productivity, better schooling, vastly improved infrastructure (see box 'Bridging the delta') and many other benefits.

Bridging the delta

One of the most celebrated engineering feats in Bangladesh is the enormous Jamuna Bridge. After half a century of deliberations and calculations, this 4.8-km-long bridge could finally be constructed with lavish international support. Most funds were provided by the Japanese government, the Asian Development Bank and the International Development Agency – the Bangladesh government contributed one third of the costs. Korean engineers and many subcontractors were involved, as well as thousands of Bangladeshi workers. The bridge features road and rail connections and also carries telecommunications cables and a pipeline for natural gas (Plate 22.2).

Plate 22.2 Buses crossing the Jamuna Bridge, 2003.

The bridge spans the waters of the treacherous and wandering Jamuna (Brahmaputra) river. It was opened in 1998 and has been the pride of Bangladesh ever since. Now, for the first time in history, northern Bangladesh had a direct land link with the rest of the country. Before the bridge was opened, travellers between central and northern Bangladesh had to use ferries to navigate the Jamuna. The bridge cut travelling times by two-thirds and opened up new produce and labour markets for the inhabitants of the northern delta.

By the 1990s the importance of foreign aid as a powerhouse of change began to diminish because other sources of wealth were becoming available. Some of these were generated internally, by the corporate NGOs and the state, and others transnationally. A major new source of wealth was remittances by migrants.

MIGRATION

International migration was nothing new in the Bengal delta, which has been a crossroads with a highly mobile population for millennia. The cities of Bengal had always been cosmopolitan centres, and Bengali communities had long been established overseas (see Chapter 4). In Chapter 3 we saw how, in the nineteenth century, the agrarian frontier had begun to move decisively beyond the delta as a steady flow of settlers left for Assam and Myanmar (Burma). And Chapter 11 examined mass population exchange resulting from Partition.[11] In the 1990s, however, the consequences of out-migration from the delta changed significantly: migrants' remittances rapidly increased and they soon emerged as a major support for the national economy. Official figures – which represent only a fraction of the real figures – show the trend: foreign remittances recorded by the Bangladesh Bank soared from US$0.2 billion around 1980 to US$1 billion in the early 1990s, US$5 billion in 2006 and US$15 billion in 2015.[12]

It is useful to distinguish three different types of emigration, each standing in a long tradition. The first was overseas labour migration. Sailors from Bangladesh (especially from the districts of Sylhet, Noakhali and Chittagong) had been employed on British ships for centuries, and from the eighteenth century stranded sailors (loshkor; *laskar*) had formed communities in port cities such as London and New York. By the mid-twentieth century the British economy faced labour shortages and began to import cheap labour, mostly from South Asia and the Caribbean. Within Bangladesh, Sylhet became the prime sending area. From the early 1960s, thousands of men went to industrial towns all over Britain to work in factories. They returned home with success stories, thereby prompting further migration. As Britain tightened its immigration laws, however, it became more difficult to travel back and forth, and

Sylheti labourers settled permanently in Britain. Today Britain's large Bengali population is overwhelmingly Sylheti in origin.[13] From the mid-1970s a somewhat similar pattern of labour migration developed when the economies of the oil-rich states in West Asia began to expand rapidly and required large amounts of cheap labour. This migration, partly state-organised, involved millions of mostly low-skilled workers from all over Bangladesh who were brought over on short-term contracts, especially to Saudi Arabia, the United Arab Emirates, Kuwait, Oman, Libya and (up to 1990) Iraq. Later on, groups of Bangladeshi workers were also offered contracts in Malaysia, Singapore and South Korea (Plate 22.3).[14] Some Bangladeshi labour migrants got caught up in war or revolution in their places of work and had to escape (Plate 22.4). Most

Plate 22.3 Bangladeshi contract labourer arriving at Kuala Lumpur airport, 2007.

Plate 22.4 'Reception centre for returned migrant workers from Libya.' Signboard at Dhaka airport, 2011. When civil war broke out in Libya in 2011, foreign labourers had to flee post-haste.

others tried to stay, or move on to other destinations, after their contracts expired, joining a global fraternity of undocumented labour nomads.[15]

Wherever these labour migrants were able to find work and create fairly stable communities, they formed organisations that continued to link them to their homes. These could be associations of people from a particular district, but also cultural groups and religious organisations. Soon, providers of legal and financial services would appear on the scene, and so did local chapters of Bangladeshi political parties (Plates 22.5 and 22.6).

The second type of migration built on the tradition of the delta's middle-class families educating their children in important centres of learning. In the British period, this had meant Dhaka, Kolkata or Britain; and in the Pakistan period, Dhaka, West Pakistan, Britain or the United States. In the first years of Bangladesh, it was very hard for most families to send their children abroad, but by the early 1990s the national elite had undergone a transformation. It was now much larger, more affluent and far more self-assured and cosmopolitan. Higher education abroad had become not only a possibility, but also a much-coveted status symbol.

Plate 22.5 This 'Bangla Agency' sported a façade in the bottle-green and red colours of the Bangladeshi flag. Using the slogan 'we are committed to serving you', it claimed to offer 'all immigration-related services'. Naples (Italy), 2015.

Now the University of Dhaka – which their parents a generation ago had extolled as 'the Oxford of the East' – was no longer good enough for their children.[16] Young people, fed on media images of middle-class affluence and well-being in rich countries, craved a life away from the restrictions of Bangladesh. As opportunities for settling abroad opened up, many better-off families were becoming transcontinental entities with footholds in North America, Australia, Europe or the Gulf. Their migrant members often managed to secure well-paid jobs in the world's richest economies while continuing to cherish their Bangladeshi roots (Plate 22.7).[17] They could afford to send substantial amounts of money back home. This in turn allowed their relatives in Bangladesh to wean themselves from their excessive dependence on foreign aid.

The third type of migration was at the opposite end of the spectrum. It involved by far the largest and poorest group of Bangladeshis. The cheapest way of leaving Bangladesh was by crossing the border into India, often on foot, and becoming unauthorised immigrants there. Cross-border migration networks predated the border – countless Bangladeshi settlers and workers had migrated to Assam, Tripura and Arakan before the Partition of 1947 – and many refugees from the delta had settled in India after 1947.

Plate 22.6 The office of the Bangladesh Nationalist Party (BNP) in Athens, Greece,
2018.

It is unknown how many Bangladeshis have moved to India without state
authorisation since 25 March 1971 (the date before which the two countries decided that Bangladesh would not be held responsible for such
unauthorised settlement), but they were many. Among them were
families fleeing discrimination and oppression; environmental refugees;
political exiles; trafficked women, men and children; and destitute people
in search of a decent life.[18] In India, they had a mixed reception. There
were many employers and politicians who welcomed their cheap labour
and votes, but strong anti-immigrant movements developed as well,
notably in Northeast India and among supporters of Hindu fundamen-
talist parties.[19] In 2003 the Indian government claimed that a stunning
20 million Bangladeshis were residing illegally in India (see box 'Noori

Plate 22.7 'Forming a bridge between tradition and the new generation abroad.'
Poster announcing the annual convention of the Federation of Bangladeshi
Associations of North America, 2007.

returns'). Even though many of these migrants were extremely poor, their sheer numbers made the remittances they sent home considerable.

Noori returns

Noori was just one of the millions of resourceful poor Bangladeshis who migrated to India. With her husband and five children she made her living in a Delhi slum. As an unauthorised migrant, her life was difficult. Regularly the police would organise campaigns of deportation, and suspected Bangladeshis would be taken to the border and 'pushed back' into Bangladesh territory. Sometimes you could pay the police a bribe in the hope of being let off. Noori had been deported to the India–Bangladesh border on seven different occasions. Every time she had returned triumphantly.

As she told a researcher in Delhi in 1998: 'They have deported me many times. But each time after they left me at the border, I returned after a while. Even the police were astonished. They said, "There goes Atiya's amma [mother]. She is back again. Didn't we deport her just last week?" After they deported me twice, I told them clearly, "I will not pay you the bribe, but I will come back. You just wait and see. And I did!"'[20]

Bangladesh refuses to take back deportees from India, claiming that India cannot prove that they are actually Bangladeshi citizens, so these unfortunate migrants are caught between two states, one that refuses to let them earn a living on its territory, the other disowning them as citizens (Plate 22.8).[21]

Plate 22.8 Deported migrants with an Indian border guard intent on driving them across the border into Bangladesh (seen in the background). Bangladeshi border guards refused the deportees entry, forcing hundreds of them to camp out in the no man's land between the two countries. Lalmonirhat/Cooch Behar border, 2003.

The three kinds of migration – overseas labour migration, middle-class educational and job migration, and unauthorised labour migration to India – became such important sources of wealth for the delta economy because of the strength of kinship ideology among Bangladeshis.[22] Going abroad was often not an individual decision but one taken by a family, or by its most powerful members, on the basis of who could earn most and send money back home. In other words, remittances were material proof of the strength of kinship ties and the transnational obligations they implied. It is to be expected that the flow of remittances will continue as more and more Bangladeshis go abroad to make a living. We can also expect, however, that remittances will stagnate or taper off when the migrants themselves grow old. In most cases their foreign-born children do not have the same allegiance to their relatives in Bangladesh.

A special form of transnational linkages and remittances developed from the late 1980s, when Bangladesh's second military dictator, Hussain Muhammad Ershad, was in power. He involved the Bangladesh armed forces and police in UN peacekeeping operations around the world. Their deployment turned out to be a rich source of remittances, and it gave the armed forces prestige abroad (Plate 22.9).[23] Today, Bangladesh is the third largest contributor of army and police personnel to UN peacekeeping operations, mostly in conflict zones in Africa.

Plate 22.9 Bangladeshi soldiers leaving for a UN peacekeeping mission in Sudan, Dhaka airport, 2013.

By the late 2010s, officially recorded remittances to Bangladesh were five times greater than all foreign aid going to Bangladesh, amounting to close to US$90 per inhabitant. These figures do not include the vast amounts of money that migrants send back through non-official channels, bypassing the banking system. Most migrants prefer the more reliable, cheaper and faster system of money transfers through trusted informal money changers. This system – known as hundi or hawala (*huṇḍi, hāoyālā*) – predates the modern banking sector, but it has undergone a vigorous revival as millions of Bangladeshis became transnational migrants. If we add these informal remittances, invisible to the state, to the official figures, it is clear that migrants have become Bangladesh's major donors. The Bangladesh economy is now remittance-dependent rather than aid-dependent.

REFUGEES FROM THE SOUTH: THE ROHINGYAS

There were also people who crossed the border *into* Bangladesh. Among them were well-heeled expats involved in business and service jobs, and also moderate numbers of international tourists – transnationals who brought wealth to the Bangladesh economy. But this was not the case with the best-known group of newcomers: refugees from the coastal plain of Arakan (Rakhine State) in neighbouring Myanmar (Burma). Known as Rohingyas, they are a mostly Muslim community and speak a language related to Bengali. The presence of Rohingyas in Arakan can be traced back for centuries. There is a spirited debate among scholars and activists about their historical roots and identity formation.[24]

It is important to remember that the narrow coastal plain of Chittagong/Arakan, squeezed by mountains to the east, is a multi-ethnic geographical unit that has a long history of connectedness. For example, around 1600 CE the port of Chittagong was the naval garrison town of the Arakan kingdom, where trilingual coins (Arakanese, Arabic and Bengali) were minted.[25] And in 1799 a Scottish visitor described 'three dialects, spoken in the *Burma* Empire, but evidently derived from the language of the *Hindu* nation. The first is that spoken by the *Mohammedans*, who have long settled in *Arakan*, and who call themselves *Rooinga*, or natives of *Arakan*.'[26] During the British period, these Rohingya were joined by seasonal migrants from the northern part of the coastal plain. The British encouraged this flow to overcome labour shortages in Arakan's agriculture, especially in harvesting its abundant paddy crop. Some of these migrants from rural Chittagong settled down in Arakan and mingled with the older groups.

A new situation developed in 1947 when the British left. Now an international border was imposed on the multi-ethnic landscape. It separated Chittagong (in Pakistan) from Arakan (in Myanmar). Many Arakanese-speaking Buddhists (Rakhain) found themselves north of the border – in the Muslim homeland of Pakistan – just as Muslim Rohingyas found themselves south of the border, in Myanmar. This marked the end of the region's interlinked past and the beginning of a double process of minority harassment.

In Pakistan (and later in Bangladesh), the Rakhain were categorised as a 'tribe' and progressively marginalised. As their livelihoods were threatened, many felt compelled to leave. In 1953 a report stated: 'being unable to cope with the changed conditions [the Rakhain] have already begun in hundreds to migrate to Burma against their will just in an attempt to save their lives'.[27] Rakhain migration from Pakistan/Bangladesh has continued ever since, and many of these refugees were able to become fully-fledged Myanmar (Burmese) citizens.[28] This process was occasionally quickened by violent attacks, such as the looting and torching of borderland Buddhist temples in and around Ramu in 2012.[29]

On the Myanmar side of the border, the Rohingyas experienced even more vigorous marginalisation. In 1949 Myanmar descended into civil war and the turbulent borderland became the scene of complex cross-border migrations, including flows of Rohingya refugees. Rohingyas were not included in the list of 'national races' that defined Myanmar citizenship and therefore lacked basic rights.[30] This became increasingly clear as new legal instruments, identity documents and registration drives came about, and oppression and land-grabbing became commonplace. The first major conflict and mass flight occurred in 1978 (when some 220,000 Rohingyas arrived in Bangladesh), followed by new waves in 1991–92 (250,000) and in 2012. Many ended up in overcrowded refugee camps near the Naf river on the Bangladesh side of the border. Tens of thousands settled unobtrusively in Bangladeshi villages and cities (Plate 22.10), or moved on to India, Pakistan or Southeast Asia. Others were allowed to return home.

A renewed military crackdown in 2017–18 saw the majority of the remaining Rohingya population being driven out of Myanmar. Some 700,000 of them have found rudimentary shelter in enormous camps in Bangladesh.[31] It was only at this point that the world seriously took notice. Numerous international aid organisations descended upon the camps – and international media started speaking of 'ethnic cleansing', a 'humanitarian crisis' and 'the most persecuted minority in the world',

Plate 22.10 A Rohingya refugee stallholder selling Myanmar goods in a border village near Teknaf, Bangladesh, 2001.

effectively turning the plight of the Rohingyas into a global spectacle of suffering.

Bangladesh was not happy with this massive influx of destitute refugees. Relations between the governments of Bangladesh and Myanmar had never been close, and serious tensions arose over the refugee issue. It did not help that, over time, Myanmar official discourse had shed the term 'Rohingya', instead referring to this group as 'Bengalis', or 'illegal immigrants from Bangladesh'. But Bangladesh does not recognise them as its citizens, and relations between Rohingya refugees and local Bangladeshis are often fraught. Despite official negotiations, a return of the refugees seems highly unlikely, and they cannot look forward to resettlement. Their transnational lives are in a state of suspended animation.

CONNECTIVITY

Foreign aid, foreign investments, migration and flows of refugees forged powerful transnational links, but nothing demonstrates better the sheer speed of change than the advances made in telecommunications. The delta had long been neglected in this respect. For example, in the 1970s it was a familiar experience to see a high official pick up one of several brightly coloured telephones on his desk and start shouting at the top of his voice in an attempt to make his words reach a colleague in the same city over the crackle of static and cross-wired conversations. Thirty years later, it was almost as common to see an illiterate village woman saunter over from her hut with no electricity to a neighbour's house, switch on a mobile phone and talk quietly to her son in Dubai. Within a generation, the way information travelled around the Bengal delta had been revolutionised. In the 1970s most Bangladeshis depended on word of mouth, newspapers, letters, telegrams and radio. A non-local telephone call took hours to arrange, and television was beyond the means of middle-class families. By the 1980s television came within their reach and began to spread to the rural areas, followed by mobile phones and all kinds of portable electronic devices. Electricity had not reached many parts of the countryside – even today only half the population has access to the grid – but towns are connected and information about the outside world spreads much more rapidly than before. The Bangladesh middle classes are enthusiastic participants in global cyberspace and social media. Today numerous Bengali fonts are available online, and Bangladeshi websites, blogs and discussion groups are multiplying rapidly.

Independent Bangladesh has forged transnational links with breath-taking speed. It would certainly be a mistake to think of contemporary Bangladesh society as spatially contained within its territorial boundaries. All kinds of Bangladeshi citizens – both urban and rural, both working class and middle class – now lead lives that take them well beyond the national territory. There are Bangladeshi communities all over the world, and they are in close touch with compatriots back home. As brokers of new ideas and wealth, they contribute to the fresh dynamism that has suffused the social and economic life of the Bengal delta.

CHAPTER 23

Boom or Bust?

As soon as Bangladesh was born, it became an object of intense international scrutiny. Was this new country actually viable? How could it overcome its problems, if at all?

Instantly, Bangladesh became a poster child for 'development' and a testing ground for successive fads in the field. This led to burgeoning research funds and a veritable explosion of studies on the country. The bulk of these were, and continue to be, in the field of development studies and 'much of the writing that is produced originates from within the "aid industry", even today'.[1] Summarising the huge body of knowledge that these studies represent is well beyond the scope of this chapter.[2] The same is true of exploring how these studies are rooted in colonial studies and in geopolitical strategising (see Chapter 15). Instead, we will highlight some twists and turns in the post-1971 trajectory and contextualise these in the longer history of the Bengal delta.

Although in the 1970s many observers despaired of Bangladesh's ability to escape from the depth of mass starvation, war damage, political chaos and neocolonialism, they were in for a surprise. Their fears of stagnation proved to be unfounded. The five decades since independence witnessed enormous change in the Bengal delta as it experienced new economic vitality, brisk population growth and unprecedented urbanisation. Humans put pressure on the environment as never before, however, and it was clear that this was a society bursting at the seams. Now a breathtaking race was on: was the delta headed for boom or bust?

One basic change was the expansion of urban life. Towns are not new in the Bengal delta, where urban centres go back over 2,000 years. Even so, the vast majority of people have always lived in villages. As recently as 1970, over 90 per cent of Bangladeshis lived in the countryside, and today 65 per cent of Bangladeshis still do so. Meanwhile the population of

Bangladesh has grown from 70 million to 170 million, so today rural crowding is more acute than ever before.

It is no surprise, then, that many Bangladeshis decided to try their luck in the cities and that these grew at an astonishing rate. At the birth of Bangladesh, the new capital, Dhaka, had 1 million inhabitants; by 1990 it had 6 million and in 2020 it is estimated at some 21 million. This very steep rise makes it one of the fastest-growing cities in the world and – with at least 300,000 mostly poor Bangladeshis moving to Dhaka every year – expectations are that the city will reach 27 million inhabitants in 2030. By that time, it will have joined the select club of the world's true megacities: it is predicted that by 2035 it will be the fourth largest in the world. And Dhaka is not alone. Other cities are growing rapidly as well: Chittagong had 0.8 million inhabitants in 1971 and 5 million in 2019.

Population growth has been a major factor in shaping twentieth-century Bangladesh society, and, if predictions are to be believed, it will continue to do so well into the twenty-first century. The current ballpark figure for the year 2050 is a population of over 200 million, three times the population of 1970. In view of the fact that such sustained growth is a strain on any economy, Bangladesh has done remarkably well.[3] It has made a number of surprising advances. In 1971 the average Bangladeshi could expect to live for forty-four years; today life expectancy is seventy-two years, the world average. Infant and under-five mortality have declined, and, very impressively, total fertility has halved.[4] Equally notable is the fact that food production has grown at a higher rate than the population. The adult literacy rate went up from 26 per cent in 1974 to over 50 per cent in 2018. The economy of Bangladesh grew by less than 2 per cent until the 1990s and then accelerated, reaching 7 per cent growth rates in the late 2010s. Per capita income (GDP per capita) rose from a record low of US$317 in 1972 to a record high of US$1,100 in 2019. These are no mean feats. Enormous advances occurred in a relatively short time.

Looking back, the turn of the twenty-first century marked a gradual escape from the bear hug of stagnation and frustration that had enveloped the Bengal delta for decades. The vicelike grip of a 'low-level equilibrium trap' began to relax, and life became better for millions of Bangladeshis. Poverty levels declined spectacularly in terms of income – halving between the 1990s and the 2010s – but considerably less so in terms of deprivation.[5] Poverty reduction occurred more in urban areas than in rural ones (where extreme poverty remained concentrated), and more in some regions of the delta than in others.

Despite the advances, it is important to realise that the Bengal delta has experienced increased economic inequality. A growing number of (super) rich people call Bangladesh home, and both income and wealth inequality are glaring and increasing (Plate 23.1).[6] But half a century after Bangladesh was born, tens of millions of citizens continue to be forced to live lives mired in deep poverty and deprivation, even if they are fully employed. Today, poor Bangladeshis are more numerous than the *entire* population of the delta in the 1960s.

Inequalities are stark in agriculture, a sector that used to dominate the delta's economy but is rapidly dwindling in economic importance. Since Bangladesh became independent, many cultivators have been dispossessed by 'development' in the form of land-grabbing, urbanisation, industrialisation, plantations, aquaculture and mining. There can be no doubt, however, that agriculture has been quite dynamic: both investments and productivity have risen significantly since 1971. But productivity remains relatively low, the proportion of Bangladeshis earning their living from agriculture is declining and, today, agriculture generates no more than one-seventh of the gross domestic product.[7]

Plate 23.1 Inequality in twenty-first century Bangladesh. Cartoon by Mehedi Haque in the *Daily New Age*, 2013.

A RICE BOOM

Rice continues to be the mainstay of the delta's agriculture, providing 80 per cent of the value of agricultural output and 70 per cent of the calorie intake of the average Bangladeshi – higher than in any other country where rice is the staple food.

Over the generations, rice producers have been unable to invest much in improving the technology of rice production, which continues to rely heavily on wooden ploughs, underfed bullocks, local seeds and fertilisers, and much loving care (Plate 23.2). They have long sought to increase yields by bringing new land under the plough, but this strategy came to an end with the closing of the agrarian frontier in the British colonial period. Cultivators then tried to push up agrarian output per land unit by means of multiple cropping, intensifying cultivation and reducing post-harvest crop losses. They also curtailed their consumption and diversified their sources of income by taking to wage labour and petty trade.[8]

Despite very small land holdings and little state investment in agriculture, the delta's cultivators were thus able to increase rice yields from 900 to 1,100 kg of clean rice per hectare during the Pakistan period. The Bangladesh period saw a very significant improvement. Rice production increased sharply, mainly as a result of concerted efforts by state and

Plate 23.2 Ploughing, Dhaka district, 1981.

international institutions to invest in agriculture. These investments had two main effects.

First, winter cropping expanded. Up to the 1970s, winter rice could grow only on some of the lowest-lying plots, or with irrigation, because hardly any rain falls in winter. There was a long tradition of lifting water from rivers and ponds by wooden scoops and swing baskets, but when engine-driven pumps became available these proved to be far more effective. In addition, tube-wells were installed all over the delta to pump up irrigation water from deep aquifers. Now, irrigated winter rice (*boro*) began to expand rapidly and soon provided half of Bangladesh's total rice production.

Second, high-yielding rice varieties were introduced to replace local ones, pushing up output in all three seasons – autumn (*āman*), winter (*boro*) and summer (*āus*). These varieties required increased use of chemical fertilisers and pesticides. These two interventions – combined with further agrarian involution (millions of smallholders applying even more labour to rice production) – began to push up rice yields from the late 1970s. The area devoted to rice production remained stable, but yields reached 2,000 kg of clean rice per hectare around the turn of the century and 3,000 kg per hectare by 2015. Although this is still fairly low by world standards, the delta now produces three times as much rice per land unit as in the middle of the twentieth century. Bangladesh's annual rice production rose from 12 million tons in the 1970s to 23 million in 2000 (when the country produced a surplus of food grains for the first time in its modern history) and to 34 million in 2015.[9]

This is a very imposing achievement indeed. Still, many observers see it as only a temporary boon of 'green revolution' technology and no guarantee for self-sufficiency in the years to come. Every year Bangladesh still needs to import rice. Future growth in rice (and other cereal) production has to be achieved with decreasing resources (land, groundwater and labour) and even smaller farm sizes. It also has to cope with the unintended effects of the adopted modern technology, notably severe loss of rice biodiversity, declines in soil fertility and water contamination. The effects of future climate change are hard to predict. In short, there are serious worries that the rice boom, which prevented mass starvation but failed to raise the living standards of rice producers in Bangladesh during the late twentieth century, will not be sustainable. Food security remains a basic challenge in this highly fertile land.[10]

JUTE LINGERS ON

The story of jute provides a study in contrasts. Since the mid-nineteenth century, this natural fibre had been the delta's main export crop, but by the 1970s it was in deep trouble, chiefly because of competition from synthetic fibres. Its production stagnated and exports were flat. As the country's other exports grew, jute's share fell precipitously, from 80 per cent in the early 1970s to 5 per cent thirty years later. However, it remains a crop that gives employment to millions, both growers and jute factory workers. By 2007 the government decided, amid much labour unrest, to close loss-making and obsolete jute factories, laying off thousands of workers. The future of the industry looks uncertain but there is a palpable 'nostalgia for jute' in Bangladesh.[11] Jute production increased a little during the 2010s and the government showed some interest in reviving the jute industry. But despite hopes that this cheap, strong natural fibre will find new markets in an increasingly eco-conscious world, global jute consumption is not growing (Plate 23.3).[12]

Plate 23.3 Workers at the People's Jute Mill in Khulna, some months before this state-owned factory was closed in 2007.

ANOTHER BOOM: SHRIMPS

In the early 1980s businessmen discovered the export market for frogs and shrimps. Tens of millions of bullfrogs were caught in the delta's fields, ponds and marshes to be exported as frogs' legs. It was a very lucrative trade, with adverse ecological and economic effects. As frogs disappeared from the rice fields, insects flourished and so did insect-related diseases. In the end, the cost of pesticides imported to kill the insects outstripped the income from frogs' legs. In 1989 Bangladesh banned the trade in frogs.

Unlike frogs, however, shrimps can be bred. Entrepreneurs began to buy low-lying arable land in the tidal lower delta and flood it with brackish water (Plate 23.4). Shrimp farming proved to be more profitable than crop agriculture, and soon (frozen) shrimps became the country's third-largest foreign income earner. Today the sector provides employment for hundreds of thousands of labourers. It also causes the destruction of trees and crops, raises soil salinity and triggers population displacement and violent clashes over land and subsistence rights.[13] Here, too, sustainability is a key concern.

A RUN ON THE CITIES

After 1971 agriculture and fisheries became more dynamic, but they could not provide adequate employment for the millions who needed jobs there.

Plate 23.4 Labourers at work in a shrimp enclosure, Bagerhat, 2006.

The result is extremely low rural wages and widespread deprivation. Nevertheless, no nationwide famines have hit Bangladesh since 1974, although there are frequent reports of regional ones – which the authorities refer to as monga (*maṅgā*; near-famine) – especially in northern Bangladesh.[14] Many chose migration to the cities, or abroad, as their escape route. The mobility that had always characterised the people of the Bengal delta is now more urban than ever.

What do the cities have to offer the poor migrant? Clearly, rapid urbanisation provides a wide and growing range of employment opportunities for large numbers of newcomers. New arrivals in the cities enter a labour market that is highly gendered. For decades, low-skilled men have been able to find employment in a variety of poorly paid and often dangerous menial jobs in transport (cycle rickshaws or pushcarts), construction, public works and service, as well as informal trade (Plates 23.5 and 23.6). Similarly, dirty and highly dangerous jobs opened up in industries such as ship-breaking in Chittagong.[15]

For low-skilled women, the options are more restricted, although two types of employment are of importance because these are expanding: industrial labour and domestic work.[16] In the 1980s, a ready-made garments industry took off in Bangladesh. Foreign buyers subcontracted to Bangladeshi entrepreneurs to produce shirts, trousers, T-shirts and sweaters

Plate 23.5 Day labourers with pushcarts waiting for custom, Gulshan, Dhaka, 1981.

Plate 23.6 Garbage collector in Dhaka, 2018.

for export, mostly to North America and the European Union. After a lapse of some two centuries – and under vastly changed conditions – Bengalis were once again producing textiles for the world market. The industry expanded rapidly, and soon it became the country's prime export earner. By 1990 garments accounted for half of all registered exports from Bangladesh – replacing jute and jute goods as top export goods – and by 2018 for 85 per cent. As Bangladesh became the world's second-largest apparel exporter, garments factories proliferated in urban centres all over the delta. By 2018 the industry's 5,000 factories employed over 4 million workers, overwhelmingly women (Plate 23.7). Conditions in these factories are appalling in terms of working hours, wages, health risks, security, sexual harassment, worker organisation and child labour – and there are international campaigns that seek to ameliorate these. Still, women flock to the garments factories because there are no other opportunities for them to earn the equivalent of US$20 per month. The hazards of the garments industry became well-known in Bangladesh after recurrent factory fires that killed many workers, but they did not gain worldwide notoriety and outrage until 2013, when a factory called Rana Plaza collapsed, resulting in the death of over 1,100 people.[17]

The other major employment for women is domestic work. The lifestyle of the Bangladesh middle class depends heavily on household servants, and

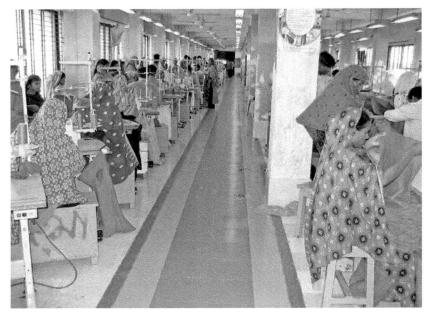

Plate 23.7 Workers in a clothing factory in Savar, 2005.

from the 1970s the middle class has been growing in both size and wealth, providing many new opportunities for domestic workers. Wages are lower in this sector, and working conditions vary enormously.

The cities grow haphazardly. Their brisk and largely unplanned expansion has landed them in serious trouble: traffic jams, air pollution, power cuts, lack of earthquake-proofing and severely overstretched services. The inflow of migrants is so large that many cannot immediately find jobs or housing.[18] The result is a large floating population of homeless people surviving on alms, odd jobs or crime (Plate 23.8).[19]

The capital city of Dhaka is changing rapidly because here most wealth accumulates and this attracts numerous migrants in search of opportunities, real or imagined. Today Dhaka is struggling to keep up its electricity and water supply, and it still lacks an adequate system of public transport. Although efforts are being made to fight extreme air pollution and get a metro system working by the late 2020s, Dhaka regularly shows up on lists of the world's most polluted and 'least liveable' cities. As one-third of its inhabitants live in densely packed slums, the rich have begun to retreat to newly developed urban enclaves with gated apartment buildings, private

Plate 23.8 Young scrap-paper collectors waking up on the pavement, Dhaka, 1983.

security and shopping malls that cater to extravagant consumerism (Plates 23.9 and 23.10). Old parts of the city are largely neglected and dilapidated, but a movement to conserve Dhaka's architectural heritage is gathering pace.[20]

New middle-class wealth has pushed up domestic consumption in many ways. One form it took was the rapid expansion of domestic tourism. This new phenomenon built on an older tradition of group picnics and pilgrimages. By the early 2000s it had spawned a booming leisure industry that provided employment for many thousands. It featured amusement parks, fancy hotels, 'tribal' tours in the Chittagong Hill Tracts, Sundarban safaris, excursions to Chittagong's infamous ship-breaking yards, nature retreats and beach resorts (Plate 23.11).[21] And it was not long before growing numbers of Bangladeshi tourists were able to go abroad.

WATER

Thirty million people were living in the delta in 1901; a little over a century later, there are almost six times as many. Within a century, the number of people per square kilometre has risen from 200 to over 1,200, and two-fifths have to make their living from agriculture. As all these Bangladeshis

Plate 23.9 The city is coming. High-rises of Dhaka's new suburb, Boshundhara City, closing in on older dwellings, 2006.

Plate 23.10 'Beware of the dog!' Private security squad guarding an upscale office building in Gulshan, Dhaka, 2018.

Plate 23.11 Tourists renting beach chairs at Kuakata, Bay of Bengal, 2019.

crowd together, they are inevitably putting more and more pressure on their environment. But it is not primarily population growth that affects the delta's environment. Industrial production and lifestyles have become far more damaging and wasteful. The delta now has to cope with huge amounts of plastics and other non-biodegradable rubbish, artificial fertilisers, pesticides and industrial waste. Some of these wash down the many rivers flowing into Bangladesh from India. These noxious substances tend to end up in the surface water, which is already a rich source of pathogens, because, in the absence of sewerage, some 90 per cent of Bangladesh's human waste ends up in the delta's rivers and lakes. There is just one sewer system in the entire country. Not surprisingly, it is in Dhaka – but it treats only 2 per cent of that city's sewage.[22]

Soon after independence Bangladesh launched a very successful drive to provide better sanitation in the form of hand pumps. Before long, consumption of surface water from rivers, ponds and wells went down. Today most Bangladeshis drink pumped-up groundwater, which has enormously benefited their health (Plate 23.12). But this intervention also had unintended consequences: in 1993 it was discovered that groundwater could be just as dangerous. In many parts of the delta, and especially in the southern belt and the northeast, groundwater is contaminated with naturally occurring arsenic. This poison also finds its

Plate 23.12 Hundreds of hand pumps are stacked up in a supplier's courtyard in Dhaka, ready to be dispatched to the countryside, 1983.

way into the rice that is such a crucial component of the Bangladeshi diet. There is no cure for arsenic poisoning and no immediate safe alternative for what a World Health Organization report described as 'the largest mass poisoning of a population in history', affecting between 35 and 77 million people.[23] Piped water is unavailable to these people, but even that is not safe: 'piped water, an exclusive asset for rich urban populations [in Bangladesh], seldom faces issues of arsenic or salinity, yet it is still highly contaminated with fecal bacteria'.[24]

Another major water problem is of a different kind. In Bangladesh it is known as the Farakka issue. Farakka is a village on the western border between India and Bangladesh. It is here that the Ganges enters Bangladesh as it branches out to form its delta. Just before entering Bangladesh, the first spill channel branches off the main river and flows down to Kolkata. This branch, the Bhagirathi-Hooghly, used to be the main channel before the river moved eastwards in the Mughal period (see Map 2.1 in Chapter 2). Now it is no longer part of the active delta and there have long been serious concerns that Kolkata's port is silting up.

Partition provided India with an opportunity to redress the long-standing eastward shift of the Bengal delta without worrying too much about adverse effects on the eastern delta, now a foreign country. Since 1947 India and Pakistan/Bangladesh have been quarrelling over their rights to use the waters of the Ganges. In 1961 Pakistan objected strongly to the Indian government's announcement that it had decided to construct a barrage at Farakka to divert Ganges water to Kolkata during the dry season. India argued that it needed the water to flush silt from Kolkata's port. Pakistan countered that such a diversion would leave insufficient water in the main channel to maintain East Pakistan's agriculture and economy. Even so, India completed the barrage in 1975. By this time East Pakistan had become Bangladesh, and complex negotiations about water sharing finally resulted in a thirty-year agreement in 1996.[25]

The adverse effects of the Farakka barrage on the ecology and economy of southwestern Bangladesh have been hotly debated ever since, especially regarding low water levels – hindering navigation, fisheries and irrigation – diminished soil moisture, salinisation and poor drinking-water quality. It has also been argued that Farakka created a boomerang effect in India when numerous environmental refugees began arriving there from Bangladesh.[26] Other Indian plans to divert river water by means of link canals – notably projects to connect the Brahmaputra, Ganges and Tista rivers – and dams – notably the Tipaimukh dam on the Barak river – stir up further indignation and worries in Bangladesh, and they lead to cross-border alliances of environmental activists.[27]

The Bengal delta has always prided itself on being one of the world's wettest places. Its rivers running down from the pristine Himalayas contain overabundant, pure, life-giving water. Monsoon rainwater is often so plentiful that it leads to floods. Yet today the delta is facing an unprecedented water crisis – its surface water polluted, much of its groundwater suspect and the demand for water skyrocketing. Agriculture has become very dependent on irrigation, a burgeoning rural population consumes much more water and cities bursting at the seams are without an adequate water supply. The problem is not so much a lack of water as an acute lack of safe water.

CLIMATE CHANGE

By the 1990s many Bangladeshis had become aware of threats to their natural world. A vocal environmental movement began to focus on a wide variety of issues, from the health risks of air and water pollution to land degradation, loss of biodiversity and the effects of global climate change.[28] Bangladeshis have never been able to lull themselves into a false belief that they controlled nature (Chapter 1), and they are used to an unpredictable climate with large variations from year to year. But by the beginning of the twenty-first century they realised that there were new perils to the natural order. Bangladesh may be particularly vulnerable to six effects of global warming: sea-level rise, deeper flooding, drought, more frequent cyclones, urban heat stress and crop loss resulting from higher temperatures.[29]

In debates on global warming, deltaic Bangladesh is often held up as an example of calamitous victimhood. As sea levels rise, saltwater inundation will soon make large parts uninhabitable. Such dire predictions do not take account of a basic fact: the Bangladesh coast is diverse and forever changing. Each year the eastern delta is expanding as the major rivers deposit vast amounts of silt that push the coastline further into the Bay of Bengal. Annual land gains may continue to exceed land loss resulting from erosion and rising sea levels.[30] In the western delta both land gains and land losses are minimal and here rising sea levels may have more effects, such as soil salinity. But Bangladeshis certainly are not like rabbits caught in the headlights:

The Bengali people have generations of experience of adapting to changing environmental conditions caused by shifting river channels, land creation and erosion, and the impacts of floods, cyclones and storm surges. . . . They continued to adapt during the period of rapid change since the 1950s when the first major flood embankments were constructed and, later, with the spread of dry-season irrigation and the introduction of high-yielding crop varieties. The country's government, too, has long experience of managing change, including measures to cope with recurrent natural disasters. Bangladesh is not helpless, therefore, against coping with sea-level rise, but it might need financial and technical assistance with providing practical mitigation measures.[31]

Apart from an array of strategic household-level adaptations, such measures could include diverting water from the main rivers to improve freshwater flows and sediment accretion in southwestern Bangladesh, reclaiming land in low-lying areas, or constructing cross-river barriers to prevent saltwater intrusion.[32]

Higher temperatures may well lead to other effects, notably more intense and longer-lasting monsoon rains, more frequent droughts and cyclones, and crop loss. Current evidence shows that Bangladeshis living in densely packed urban areas are now suffering seasonally from dangerously increasing heat stress.[33] The consequences of climate change may be further complicated by the natural subsidence of parts of the delta's land mass.[34]

Current predictions are highly tentative, however. Some suggest that Bangladesh should be prepared to deal with millions of environmental refugees from its coastal areas by the middle of the century. On the other hand, migration for environmental reasons is nothing new in Bangladesh; it goes back centuries and remains important. In this vast, unsettled delta, subject to unruly nature and marked by stark social inequalities, people have always been very mobile. In this sense, there have always been 'climate refugees', and any predictions about 'climate *change* refugees' should take account of the factors that have been driving this historical process.[35] As we have seen in Chapter 1, available evidence does not support popular assumptions that global warming has already seriously enhanced Bangladesh's susceptibility to floods, tropical cyclones and drought.

Even so, the global climate panic is already having a very real impact on Bangladesh. It informs an emergent development paradigm of climate security that is turning the Bengal delta into a test site for technologies to pre-empt climate chaos.[36] The fear is that hordes of climate exiles will fan out across the world and become a planetary security threat. Not surprisingly, '[a]larmist discourses about climate-related mass migration and resulting insecurity, conflict and chaos ... often find their origin in the more affluent countries'.[37] Current 'climate-smart' development schemes turn Bangladesh (and its bemused citizens) into a spectacle for 'an anxious Western world' as these schemes seek to demonstrate that technocratic interventions will 'keep people in (their) place'.[38]

ENERGY

Bangladesh's environmental movement also focused its energies on more immediate issues. It enjoyed an early triumph in the 1990s, when it successfully opposed the massive Flood Action Plan (Chapter 22), and another in 2002, when the government decided to ban the production and use of polythene bags. Initially this was a resounding success, but gradually bags from illegal polythene factories have crept back into the market. Two areas in which the environmental movement's impact is especially visible are the country's energy policy and the loss of biodiversity.

Bangladeshis have long depended on biomass for their energy needs: stoves run on dry leaves, wood, rice husks, jute stalks and dried cow-dung, much of it collected by household members. Today half of the country's energy is still provided by non-commercial biomass. Commercial sources of energy came later: kerosene and candles for lamps, diesel for irrigation pumps, fuel for cars, electricity and natural gas. Despite their rapid spread, demand still far outstrips supply: by the late 2010s only one out of ten people had access to hydrocarbons (liquid fuels and gas) and roughly one out of two to electricity. Electricity supplies suffered from frequent power cuts ('load-shedding') and low voltage.[39]

As the demand for energy increased, successive governments have tried to expand supplies. In the 1960s the government inaugurated the Kaptai hydroelectric complex and floated plans for a nuclear power plant in Rooppur (Pabna). Then the discovery of large reserves of natural gas turned all attention to this source of energy. Prospecting for natural gas and oil by international corporations goes back a century in Bangladesh, especially in the Sitakund area (Chittagong) and in eastern Sylhet. The first commercially useful gas field was discovered in Haripur (Sylhet) in 1955. Dozens more were later found in the eastern belt, some of them offshore in the Bay of Bengal. Industrial use of gas started in 1959 with a cement factory, followed by a fertiliser factory and a power plant. In the late 1960s piped natural gas became available for some domestic users in Dhaka and later for many more. However, the supply of natural gas for cooking and other domestic uses remained restricted to a few cities and semi-urban areas. The discovery of further reserves fuelled a debate about the desirability of exporting gas, especially to India, and about the social effects of gas extraction on local populations.[40]

As the demand for energy rose steeply, however, policies changed. Bangladesh began to import gas and coal to feed its power plants and, in conjunction with private companies and foreign governments, it began to explore alternate sources of energy, notably nuclear, solar and wind power, as well as biogas conversion. Even so, by the 2010s these new sources were still of minor importance.[41] Wind and sunshine are readily available in the delta; wind power had been essential to propel throngs of sailing boats on the many rivers from the earliest times up to the late twentieth century, when engine-powered river traffic became the norm.

Open-pit coal mining in the northern border zones, notably the Phulbari mine, led to organised resistance in which environmental activists participated.[42] There was also a growing awareness of the deleterious effects of stone quarrying in the Chittagong Hill Tracts and Sylhet,[43] and a growing concern about the environmental risks involved in a nuclear power plant being constructed in Rooppur and a coal-powered thermal plant in Rampal, next to the Sundarban mangrove forest.[44] Environmentalists took the lead in these discussions, reminding the public of the ecological disasters that had resulted from the Kaptai project (see Chapter 15) and emphasising the need for a national energy policy that is ecologically sound. They were especially vocal in warning against ill-considered solutions driven by a desire for short-term commercial or political gain.

ENDANGERED BIODIVERSITY

The environmental movement has also been successful in spreading awareness of the fragility of the delta's ecosystem. For example, human interference affects the delta's rich water habitat, leading to the collapse of many aquatic life forms. The story of the black soft-shell turtle is instructive. In the 1700s an Islamic spiritual guide, Bayazid Bostami, had a large pond dug near Chittagong and put some of these freshwater turtles in it. After his death the adjacent shrine became a centre of pilgrimage. The turtles and fish in the pond were venerated, fed and protected. As the turtles became rarer in their natural habitat (which may have covered the eastern delta and Arakan), the captive population in the artificial pond took on a new significance. Today the black soft-shell turtle (*Aspideretes nigricans*) is extinct in the wild; the few hundred individuals in the Bostami pond are the only survivors. But they are not safe there. In 2004 they became victims of Islamist terror. In a calculated attack on the old, authentically Bengali Muslim practice of venerating animals, Islamists put pesticide in the Bostami pond. Most of the fish died, but a host of volunteers were able to rescue the turtles.

Another example is the decline of the hilsa (*ilis*), a fish that has long been a cultural icon and the essence of deliciousness in Bengali cuisine. It is the official 'national fish' of Bangladesh, even though it spends much of its life at sea, only migrating up the estuarine rivers to spawn during the flood season. Highly prized and seasonally plentiful in the delta's rivers, hilsa is also an important export to West Bengal and to expatriate Bengali communities around the world. Its stocks, which used to be superabundant, have been declining. The reasons for this are the construction of dams for irrigation and flood control (blocking migration), overfishing of egg-bearing hilsa at the points where their migration gets blocked, siltation of rivers and pollution of surface water. For years, Bangladeshi consumers have been lamenting the scarcity of hilsa and its ever-rising price.[45]

It is not just amphibians and fish that are vulnerable. Three species of vultures experienced an incredibly steep decline in the 1990s and almost became extinct. They used to be a common sight all over the delta until a human painkiller (diclofenac) came into use in Bangladesh, spread into the environment and killed them off. In the 2010s, the Bangladesh government banned the painkiller and established two 'vulture safe zones' in an attempt to revive vulture populations.

The environmental movement also engages with marine habitats (see box 'Coral and turtles'), but most attention goes to land habitats that need protection. The Bengalian rainforest that once covered the entire delta is long gone, replaced by rice fields stretching in all directions. The lakes (*hāor, bil*) of the delta still act as important staging places for migratory birds from as far away as Siberia, the Himalayan region and Europe. Here and there small patches of wooded land remain, but rescuing the remnants of the old flora and fauna is an uphill task. An old forest in central Bangladesh, Modhupur, is now described as 'dying'. Only two marginal regions are still forested: the Chittagong Hill Tracts in the southeast and the Sundarban wetlands in the southwest, and both are in serious decline.[46]

Coral and turtles

Some 10 km beyond the southernmost spit of land of Bangladesh lies a small island in the Bay of Bengal. It faces the coast of Myanmar (Burma). This is Narikel Jinjira, better known to the outside world as St. Martin's Island.

It stands out because it is quite unlike the many alluvial islands that fringe the sea coast. Narikel Jinjira is not a silt-flat. It is the only island in Bangladesh that has coral reefs. It boasts very distinctive ecosystems and all of these – marine, land and tidal lagoon – are seriously endangered by human activity such as overfishing, coral and shell collection, reclamation, agriculture and tourism. The island is inhabited by some 600 families who subsist mostly on seasonal fishing and dried-fish production. In the late 1980s local elders came together to sign a conservation declaration, and in the 1990s an environmental NGO was set up. The Bangladesh government, pressurised by conservationists at home and abroad, declared the island an 'ecologically critical area' and initiated several projects to protect its biodiversity – but implementation is poor and degradation continues.[47]

One of the projects is a hatchery for sea turtles who visit the beaches to lay their eggs (Plate 23.13). Each year hundreds of olive ridley and green turtles deposit thousands of eggs. These are severely threatened and need protection from humans as well as dogs. They are collected with loving care and hatched in safety before the hatchlings are released in the sea.

Plate 23.13 The sea-turtle hatchery in Narikel Jinjira, 2001. The buildings in the background are cyclone shelters, not a luxury for the inhabitants of this exposed, low-lying island in the path of the tropical storms that develop seasonally over the Bay of Bengal.

Deforestation of the Chittagong Hill Tracts became an acute problem from the 1960s. Population growth had led to land shortages and the soil was getting exhausted because slash-and-burn cycles were unsustainably shortened – hill fields have to lie fallow for many years in order to regain their fertility. Yields began to drop. Then the Kaptai dam led to massive loss of arable land and forced many cultivators to find new fields on which to practise hill agriculture (see Chapter 15). This situation worsened after the birth of Bangladesh. Deforestation and ecocide accelerated notably after 1975, when the Chittagong Hill Tracts War broke out and the politically motivated

settlement of plainspeople commenced (see Chapter 21). The area became
dotted with military outposts, perched on denuded hill tops. Army personnel
and outside contractors established lucrative partnerships, and soon logging
and extraction of bamboo, other forest resources and stones were out of
control (Plate 23.14). This in turn led to erosion and declining soil fertility.
Policy decisions intended to offset the resulting decline in productive

Plate 23.14 Deforestation in action: timber from reserved forests in the Chittagong
Hill Tracts being brought ashore in Rangamati, 2001.

capacity – notably the establishment of teak and rubber plantations – inadvertently further aggravated the environmental damage.[48]

By comparison, the salt-tolerant mangrove habitat of the Sundarbans ('beautiful forest' or 'forest of *sundrī* trees') fared somewhat better. It used to be three times bigger, spreading across the delta's entire seaward fringe. Over the generations, hardy cultivators in search of a living have pushed the agricultural frontier deeper into this risky environment. The process accelerated in the early colonial period, when a revenue-hungry state encouraged land-hungry settlers.[49] The entire forest might well have disappeared but for an awareness among colonial administrators that there was a growing need to provide nearby urban centres with timber and fuelwood. Locally, income from wood became as vital a resource to the colonial state as income from agricultural production. In the 1870s large tracts of the Sundarbans were assigned to the Forest Department, and they 'became and remained a production unit run as a state monopoly industry in lower Bengal' (Plate 23.15).[50]

In 1947 the area was divided between India and Pakistan, with the largest part, in the district of Khulna, going to Pakistan. Management of forest resources continued under Pakistan and Bangladesh. Woodcutters, honey collectors, fishermen and hunters enter the Sundarbans, with or without government licences. Long-term degradation is well documented:[51]

Plate 23.15 Creek filling up with the incoming tide, Sundarbans, 2006.

the density and luxuriance of the vegetation, and the diversity and abundance of animals and fish, is far less than what it was two centuries ago. Within the Sundarbans, the Javan rhinoceros was last recorded in 1870, and the last wild buffalo shot in 1890. The muntjac and fishing cat are also locally extinct. Crocodiles, monkeys and other animals have been much depleted even in the Reserves since independence. Remnants of the threatened Bengal tiger population survive on the Reserves in both nations. But some of their prey (the swamp deer, hog deer, and gaur) are gone.[52]

After 1971 the Sundarbans became the focus of Bangladesh's budding ecotourism industry. Playing to tourist images of pristine nature, the Sundarbans are packaged as the last unspoiled forest, teeming with wildlife. The area's furtive top predator, the Bengal tiger, has become the tourist industry's darling. Declared to be Bangladesh's 'national animal', it finds itself thrust into the role of pin-up and crowd-puller. It has become an emblem of environmental awareness, national pride, tourism potential and exotic adventure (Plate 23.16).[53]

In a relatively short time the environmental movement, riding the waves of a global anxiety, has been able to place issues of ecological degradation on Bangladesh's political agenda. Here it has to compete with a strong lobby of transnational and local entrepreneurs who tempt politicians, officials and military personnel with quick financial returns from logging and environmentally harmful development projects.

Significant economic change and population growth have characterised post-1971 Bangladesh. It has been a period in which the delta's society more than doubled in numbers and its economy kept pace. Impressively, both economic growth and food security have held up despite predictions to the contrary. Still, economists and agronomists

Plate 23.16 'Our national prowess – save the tiger – stop hunting tiger.'
Bangladesh stamps, 1974.

express serious concern as to whether food security will be sustainable in the near future. Demographers have begun to consider the long-term economic effects of lower fertility and rising life expectancy, resulting in an ageing population. Environmentalists, for their part, speak of the horrendous consequences of human pressure and poor resource management on the delta's ecosystem and natural resources. In addition, experts project that rising average temperatures will depress per capita income by over 10 per cent in the years ahead.[54] Is the delta headed for boom or bust?

CHAPTER 24

Gender Movements

The Bengal delta has never been a place of serene tranquillity. On the contrary, the turmoil of social movements and emancipatory struggle has shaped its long history. We have seen that these movements were of many kinds. Historians have studied them under the rubrics of religious innovation, peasant insurgency, anti-colonialism, nationalism and class struggle. But so far historians have paid little attention to the historical roots of social movements that began to manifest themselves with increasing vigour towards the end of the twentieth century.

As Bangladesh society forged new transnational linkages and became more urban and educated, many Bangladeshis began to re-examine and challenge conventional ideas. A reassessment of the relationship between human beings and their natural surroundings led to the vibrant environmental movement (see Chapter 23). Ethnic minorities came together in the movement that demanded more rights and respect for non-Bengali citizens (see Chapter 21). In this chapter, we look at yet other movements: those that began to challenge the entangled systems of gender, kinship and sexuality – the ideological bedrock of society. They focused on social – rather than economic – change, and they were often initiated by middle-class activists.

GENDER

As far as we know, patriarchal values and heterosexual norms have always been dominant in the social fabric of the Bengal delta. But this dominance was neither constant nor complete. Bangladeshi women have never been helpless victims of all-powerful men (Chapter 3). It is certainly true that there are often stark power differences between men and women in private and public life, but these differences have varied with time, class, religious community and ethnicity.[1] The Bengal delta's cultural repertoire has been rich in challenges to prevailing gender roles, from formidable goddesses, literary heroines and 'anti-husband tirades' to female rulers, artists and entrepreneurs.[2] Such characters challenged ideological constructions of women as demure homemakers, objects of male sexual desire, dutiful daughters and self-sacrificing mothers. Local concepts of gender could vary enormously. Some have been studied in detail, for example the ideas underlying the literary expressions and sexual rituals of the Baul community. These point to a universe that challenges patriarchy and in which males cannot attain perfection unless they absorb a woman's femaleness.[3]

We need to know more about how colonial conquest disrupted the pre-colonial gender orders of the Bengal delta and how it created new ones. It is clear that the British period produced many voices that opposed patriarchal gender relations and viewed them as being upheld not just by men but also by women. An example is Rashsundari Debi (c. 1809–99), a housewife in Faridpur, who rebelled against the tradition that women should stay illiterate. She secretly taught herself to read, and she became the first Bengali woman (and the first Bengali) to write a full-length autobiography. She observed: 'Really, how cross those old housewives would be if they saw a woman with as much as a piece of paper in her hands. So, how was I to learn anything? But my heart would not accept this, it was forever yearning.'[4]

Many other women expressed their hunger for emancipation and education. In Chapter 8 we encountered a famous example, Rokeya Sakhawat Hossain.[5] In the 1920s a group of village women in Manikganj (central Bangladesh) invited Shudha Mazumdar, the wife of a colonial official, to visit, and a very old lady told her:

'Our needs are many ... But the first thing we want is education. We must have knowledge for only this can give us the power to break our fetters of ignorance and superstition and then the women of India will be able to regain the honoured position that was theirs in the golden days of the Vedic age.' The next speaker was a bright teenage daughter of the house. Eager to learn all that the modern world offered, she was convinced the deterioration of Bengal was closely related to the backwardness of her daughters. Education to equip them for service in the home and perhaps later in spheres beyond the home was badly needed.[6]

Female education always lagged behind male education. As late as 1974, population census data showed that around 85 per cent of all women were illiterate, as against 67 per cent of men. In some districts, fewer than 10 per cent of women could read.[7] These figures from the 1970s improved rapidly as female education became a policy focus for the first time. By the 2010s women had almost caught up with men: school attendance had gone up and 50 per cent of women (against 54 per cent of men) were literate.[8] Even so, half of all citizens of Bangladesh were still illiterate.[9]

Schooled women could imagine other futures for themselves than getting married young and living lives dominated by mothers-in-law and husbands, and hemmed in by childcare and housework. In the same period other important changes occurred: contraceptives became more widely available and so did employment opportunities for both married and unmarried women outside their homes. Incomes rose and birth rates declined sharply from seven children per woman of reproductive age in the early 1970s to about two in the 2010s.

In this evolving scenario, which also included better connectivity, migration to urban jobs or educational facilities was a way to avoid, or at least postpone, being drawn into restricting kinship obligations.[10] A new sense of individuality began to develop among more young women. Now the romantic notion of a 'love marriage' and the dream of a meaningful job seemed more attainable than ever, and this led to frictions between daughters and parents over the selection of their spouses and careers. The kinship systems – several coexist in Bangladesh – had always been a contested terrain, but also the only safeguard against calamity, disrepute and destitution. Now women pushed to rework kin ideology to allow them more personal choice. For most women, however, this was an uphill task because poverty left them very little wiggle room – the vast majority of adult women remained economically dependent on their husband's income.

Urban middle- and upper-class women were in the best position to voice the new awareness and some of them began openly to challenge the patriarchal hierarchy. Gender-specific victimisation during the Liberation War of 1971, as well as the role of female freedom fighters, were contributing factors that intensified the challenge. There had been many women's organisations in the past, but now new ones, such as Bangladesh Mohila Porishad (*mahilā pariṣad*; Women's Association, founded in 1970), Women for Women (1973), Naripokkho (*nārīpakṣa*; Women's Panel, 1983) and many others, shaped and supported the budding women's movement (Plate 24.1).

A feminist sensibility began to permeate public discussions in Bangladesh, notably regarding gender inequality, sexual exploitation, violence against women, representations of femininity and masculinity, discrimination on the basis of skin colour and the commodification of women's bodies.[11] Even the most conservative discourses, such as that of Jamaat-i-Islami leaders, began to shift.[12] But feminist activists found themselves in a difficult position.[13] As Firdous Azim explained:

Plate 24.1 A poster from the National Association of Women Lawyers informs
Bangladeshi Muslim women about their legal rights in divorce, 1998.

Women's movements in countries such as Bangladesh can be seen to operate
within a cleft stick – under the shadow of a growing Islamization, on the one
hand, and under Western eyes on the other. Women's movements have to

grapple with issues such as violence, women's subordination, the special religious strictures on women, as well as social practices that keep women in a position of subservience. As women highlight incidences of dowry death or acid-throwing, or of women being stoned to death, the Western representation of eastern or 'Islamic' societies as backward and barbaric seems to be vindicated. At the same time, feminists are branded as Western within their own societies, and as complicit with the Western stereotyping of women from 'Islamic' and 'third world' countries.[14]

Another challenge to the patriarchal order came from a different group of women: female sex workers who, in the 1990s, began to organise against evictions, state violence and negative stereotypes. They rejected the common sobriquet of potita (*patitā*; fallen woman, bad girl), stressed their identity as workers, and demanded respect. Their mobilisation was facilitated by international development agencies concerned with the global spread of HIV/AIDS. Feminists took up their cause but debated whether sex workers should be considered primarily as victims of sexual exploitation or as working women.[15]

Historians have neglected the histories of masculinity among the diverse ethnic and religious groupings in Bangladesh. The one group that they did focus on were colonial Bengali elite men known as bhodrolok (gentlefolk, see Chapter 6). These cultural brokers between ordinary Bengalis and the British overlords (not just in Kolkata but also in the provincial towns and zamindari mansions of the eastern Bengal countryside) had been the target of colonial prejudice. The British stereotyped these men as effeminate, weak and unfit for manly activities such as warfare. This specific aspersion on elite Bengali manliness – on top of the standard injuries to masculinity inflicted on elite men in colonised societies more generally – continues to reverberate in the historical literature.[16] But the fragility of bhodrolok masculinity played little role in Bangladesh after the exodus of this group to India as a result of the Partition of 1947. This is not to say, however, that Bengali manliness was not degraded during the following decades, when Bangladesh was known as East Pakistan (1947–71). Generally speaking, West Pakistani attitudes towards Bengali men were condescending, stereotyped and often racialised. Pakistan's British-trained military rulers in particular inherited colonial prejudices about the physical frailty and mental weakness of Bengali males – and their uselessness in warlike pursuits. These rulers considered themselves 'superior to the Bengalis in everything – in looks, in brains, the way they spoke English and the stylish way in which they lived'. In their eyes, Bengalis were 'black', and needed to overcome their 'docility and softness' and 'all the inhibitions of downtrodden races' before they could become 'equal partners and prove an asset'.[17]

Although the historical permutations of non-elite masculinities in the Bengal delta remain understudied, it is evident that being a good man revolved around being married, a protector of the family honour, a good income earner, and someone who wielded authority both inside and outside the household. The ideal also included physical strength, sexual potency, healthiness and the ability to produce sons (Plate 24.2). All-encompassing kinship ties framed and regimented these qualities. They provided men with remarkable economic, physical and ideological power

Plate 24.2 A rooftop advertisement shows the healthy male body that will result from a healer's treatment of conditions as varied as sexual malfunctioning, arthritis, sexually transmitted diseases, skin problems and dysentery. Khulna, 2006.

over dependents – younger siblings, widowed or divorced mothers and sisters, wives, children and grandchildren – but they also saddled them with the responsibility of providing material support, controlling women's sexuality, defending the family's honour, and steering dependents' lives towards well-being and fulfilment.[18] In a society that offered few collective forms of protection, the family acted as a safe haven that gave security from outside danger. Kinship ideology provided the regulatory framework for relations within family groups, although in practice powerful members – usually adult men – could abuse their position without outside interference.

Kinship should be understood as the grammar of social life in contemporary Bangladesh more generally, because it spreads far beyond the family to structure wider social, economic and political relationships. Non-relatives are habitually approached as if they were relatives. When you address some powerful bureaucrat or politician as your father's younger brother (chacha; *chāchā*), greet a total stranger as if he were your elder brother (bhai; *bhāi*), or call the wife of your spouse's boss your elder sister (apa; *āpā*), you attempt to draw them into the regulatory realm of kin closeness, hierarchy and respect. This fictive kinship provides a tool to make behaviour more predictable, and, in this way, patriarchal ideas reach far beyond the family. They form a template that regulates everyday interpersonal relations. Powerful webs of fictive kinship connect Bangladeshis across the country and wherever they are in the world.

Patriarchy is never static. It is clear that urbanisation, education, access to new media, transnational migration, and the adulation of sport celebrities and movie stars have affected masculinities in Bangladesh. These appear to have become more diverse, especially among young urban men. Many young men in rural areas dream of escaping from their kin-inflected universe. In nearby towns their elders can still monitor them, but not in Dhaka, which they see as a 'colourful' metropolis where they can enjoy individual freedom and have access to money, sex and new lifestyles.[19]

Even so, masculinity research shows that there is much continuity as well. Performing the patriarchal gender ideology remains central to most men's selves, which they understand in terms of 'money, sexual prowess, being a good "provider", and having regular paid work outside the home'.[20] In poor families, however, it is almost impossible to attain this ideal; poor men often aim to offset their powerlessness outside the house with dominance within their family. In many cases this leads to physical violence against wives and children.[21] It is important to realise that patriarchal ideologies, including violent practices within families, are not necessarily 'traditional' but may have been co-produced by the violence of colonial and post-colonial rule. Patriarchal attitudes are also not restricted to men. Many women subscribe to them, for example Karimon, a poor woman in Netrakona, who expressed her feelings like this: 'Women should obey their husbands . . . A husband has the right to protect as well as to rule over his wife . . . and most of the time problems arise when both the husband and the wife argue with each other . . . in such situations, one should maintain silence . . . the wife should do this.'[22] In addition, research suggests that mothers may be more often perpetrators of violence against children than fathers.[23]

The women's movement has been successful in questioning gender relations and supporting programmes to empower women, leading to changing gender norms. Masculinities are in flux. Some men feel threatened by women moving about 'in unruly ways' and 'consider[ing] themselves as men', but others welcome the change: 'Now women are joining the society, going here and there. In the past, women never got out of the house. But in the past, people starved to death too. Now no one is starving to death.'[24]

SEXUALITIES

Another movement that began to challenge the entangled systems of gender, kinship and sexuality in Bangladesh was the campaign for the recognition of non-heterosexual sexualities and gender pluralism. The history of this pluralism remains to be written, but it is clear that the pre-colonial gender orders of the Bengal delta were complex and allowed for multiple sexual practices that today would be labelled same-sex, bisexual and transgender. Currently available evidence is largely circumstantial, but it appears to conform to wider South Asian patterns. For example, Ruth Vanita analyses fourteenth-century devotional texts from Bengal that 'celebrate sexual love between co-wives by representing it as divinely planned and blessed, as structured by kinship, and as contributing to the welfare of the patriarchal family, the community of the living, their ancestors, and their posterity'.[25] Another form of same-sex relations, between socially unequal partners, was predicated upon an ancient trade. For many centuries, starting well before the twelfth century CE, Bengal (and, according to the sources, notably Sylhet) was known for its slave boys and eunuchs, who were sold to rulers and other powerful men for various services, including sexual ones. This trade is thought to have continued into the nineteenth century.[26]

Better known is a category of people who are hard to describe because they comprise a range of gender identities, bodily conditions, sexual

Plate 24.3 Hijra and companions in eastern Bengal, around 1860.
(photographer unknown, source: Wikimedia commons)

preferences and social positions. Historically lumped together under terms such as 'third gender' and 'hijra' (*hijṛā*), in contemporary parlance they are sometimes represented as transgender persons. They are historically well documented across South Asia as a culturally recognised gender category forming distinct communities with their own linguistic code (*ulṭi*), and they are living proof of the complexity of Bangladesh's sexual landscape (Plate 24.3).

Bodily male persons, who identify and dress as women, their sexuality is usually assumed to be either non-existent or same-sex, but it can be situational – '[u]nlike the stereotyped image of *hijra*, many *hijra* in Dhaka are in fact heterosexually married men who simultaneously perform the role of "macho" householding men and that of *hijra*'.[27] In recent decades public discourse began to pay more attention to hijra, leading to the Bangladesh government officially recognising them as a 'third gender' in 2013. As Adnan Hossain explains, this recognition was based on the misapprehension that hijra were 'individuals sexually disabled since birth', who were eligible for disability benefits.[28]

The early twenty-first century saw another sexual emancipation movement take off in the form of same-sex activism. Historically, the hijra had always been visible in public, but bisexual, gay and lesbian Bangladeshis had lived mostly in the shadows, especially after 1860. In that year the British interfered in the sexual landscape of their colony by proscribing consensual (male) homosexuality, and criminalising it by means of section 377 of the Penal Code. This proscription found its way into the Penal Code of Bangladesh. Rarely applied, it backed up social prejudices against men who had sex with other men and against openly gay people and, therefore, self-identification was risky.[29] Self-identification was also less urgent because in Bangladesh society people are expected to have most of their social (non-sexual) relationships with persons of their own sex. This 'homosociality' makes it possible to portray same-sex relationships as close friendships that do not raise suspicion among family and friends.[30]

In the 1990s the worldwide alarm over HIV/AIDS began to change the situation in Bangladesh. Sexual health became a matter of public concern and NGO action, and sexual diversity was beginning to be discussed more openly. It became clear that the sexual landscape was far more diverse than many had assumed: both sexual practices and sexual identities were 'fluid and overlapping' as well as 'contextual and contingent'.[31] In this more open atmosphere – also fostered by new online connectivity – it became possible for urban middle-class gay identities to find voice in publications and websites.[32] These voices included testimonies from the Bangladeshi diaspora.[33] One remarkable creation was a graphic comic story featuring a lesbian character named Dhee (Plate 24.4).[34]

The movement was dealt a severe blow in 2016 when a group of militant Islamists invaded an apartment in Dhaka and killed two prominent members by hacking them to death.[35] These murders point to the fact that sexual emancipation movements in Bangladesh defy a colossal taboo.

Plate 24.4 The Story of Dhee (*Dhee-er Golpo*), 2015.[*]
Courtesy of Boys of Bangladesh.

In Dina Siddiqi's words, 'sexual taboos in society are not so much about sexuality as about bringing into the public domain matters that should remain private'. Indeed, 'a range of sexual behaviours is . . . sanctioned or tolerated or ignored, as long as such activities remain hidden from the public gaze and they do not disrupt the ideal of procreative heterosexual marriage that is more or less mandatory for men and women'.[36]

REORDERING GENDER

In the Bengal delta, ideas about gender and sexuality have never been static or monolithic. They have varied over time and between communities and classes. They played a role in many social movements that were not exclusively concerned with these themes but were nevertheless shot through with notions of gender equality and sexuality beyond the strait-jacket of kinship. Conversely, gender and sexuality were also at the core of movements that sought to strengthen patriarchal dominance as well as orthodoxies and puritanism of various kinds. There is a need for historical

---

[*] Left: Dhee, a young lesbian woman, is being admonished by her grandmother ('When are you getting married? I want to see my grandchildren before I die'), her mother ('The boy is a banker. And he is handsome. What's to object?') and her sister ('Or do you like somebody else?'). Right: She imagines how her relatives would react to her telling them that she is in love with another woman: '*What* are you saying, Dhee!?', 'We should take her to the doctor', 'Yeah, tell her'.

scholarship to tease out these aspects as well as the actual practices that people in the Bengal delta engaged in.

The current gender and sexuality movements are more focused and explicit, but it is essential to realise that they build upon local cultural precursors. Distinctly Bangladeshi in character, they develop in constant dialogue with global debates about gender and sexuality, just as their forerunners were also linked to wider concerns and campaigns.[37] The same is true of their counterparts whose puritanical and patriarchal urges reflect both local sensibilities and global anxieties. Firdous Azim's image of gender emancipation in Bangladesh finding itself in a 'cleft stick' – under the shadow of a growing puritanical form of Islamisation as well as under Western eyes – is a useful one. As the new movements demonstrate in their engagements with both Islamists and Westerners, reordering gender relations in Bangladesh requires a thorough understanding of local histories of gender and sexuality.

CHAPTER 25

A National Culture?

After independence, Bangladesh underwent spectacular cultural innovation. Young statehood demanded the creation of a national culture, new transnational linkages brought novel ideas, and growing wealth among some groups found expression in new lifestyles. The delta's culture was pulled in different directions, and clashing trends had to accommodate each other. It has been a half-century of renewed idealism and passionate soul-searching.

A MOFUSSIL UPSURGE

The leaders of the movement for Bangladesh had imagined a society based on democracy, socialism, secularism and nationalism. Once freed from its Pakistani fetters, the delta's economy would surge forward, and all would be provided for. These ideals were expressed in the name of the new state – the People's Republic of Bangladesh – and in the romantic evocation of a soon-to-be 'Golden Bengal'. Officially Bangladesh is still a 'people's republic' but to most citizens the old ideals sound pretty hollow. Only nationalism has withstood the ravages of time. Socialism and secularism were ditched in the mid-1970s, and democracy has had a chequered and interrupted career. As for 'Golden Bengal', it is now seen more as the symbol of a visionary past than as a blueprint for the future.

Bangladesh's first leaders failed to deliver on their dreams. This weakened the appeal of their vernacular cultural model – a mix of the refinement embodied in the colonial genteel (bhodrolok) lifestyle and popular East Bengali ways (see Chapter 16). Disillusionment set in, and the rise of military leaders from the mid-1970s created room for a new model, brash and increasingly self-confident. The older elite, who had emancipated themselves from provincial (mofussil) backgrounds a generation before, were faced with a new wave of 'mofussilisation' in the 1970s and 1980s. They considered the new power-holders to be half-educated upstarts on whom the romance of Bengali literature, the subtleties of Tagore songs and the finer things in life were completely lost. The new cultural model was self-consciously *nouveau riche*: clothes had to be flashy, jewellery chunky, houses and their interiors ostentatious. The new cultural hero was no longer the delicate poet, the bashful homemaker or the idealistic student-activist. Now it was the streetwise rowdy, the mostan or mastan (*mastān/ māstān*).

POLITICAL BULLIES

The mostan was not new on the social scene, but he fitted the new mood perfectly. The archetypal mostan was young, urban, armed and testoster-one-charged. He was the product of the country's rapid urbanisation and the elite's inability to control this new environment. He acted officiously as the leader of a locality, pushing aside respected elders and appointed authorities. An upstart, he ruled through fear, sometimes avenging wrongs but more often committing them himself. He emerged as a major figure in Bangladeshi popular culture (Plate 25.1).[1]

How could a petty gangster become a cultural icon? He came to represent a new urbanised society that was more violent, less predictable and less firmly under the control of the old elite. The figure of the mostan was especially attractive to young people who had been disappointed in

Plate 25.1 Film posters in a rural tea shop, 2001. One film is entitled *Munna the Mastan*, another *Women Can Also Be Mastans*.

what independent Bangladesh had to offer; he symbolised rage, promised to avenge injustice and gave a voice to lower-class ambitions.

His growing importance was no figment of the imagination, either. Post-independence political parties had given arms to young men to corner votes for them, to recruit and manage crowds for mass gatherings, to enforce general strikes and to generate party funds. It did not take long for these armed men to form gangs and carve out a power base of their own.[2]

Mostans could be useful cogs in what is usually described as corruption – a system that provides all kinds of public services against payment. Bangladeshis associate this primarily with state personnel. The police, the judiciary, customs and tax officials, and bureaucrats are seen as particularly successful operators. As a pattern of behaviour, corruption has a long history in the delta – for most people it has always been the only way to get an administrator to lend you their ear, a police officer to release your impounded cow, a judge to drop a case, or a nurse to do their job. Development assistance, economic liberalisation and transnational remittances have invigorated the system. Now, if you need fertiliser, a tube-well, a permit, a tax dodge or a successful tender, you have to give 'oil' (a bribe) to the bureaucrat, entrepreneur, politician or NGO person concerned.[3] If necessary, mostans can play the role of enforcers.

Mostans really excel at another transaction, however: they provide neighbourhood security for payment under duress – in other words, they run protection rackets. As armed specialists in extortion (chandabaji; *cãdãbãji*), they straddle the worlds of politics, the bureaucracy, the market and crime.[4] As mostan control of society grew, people began to speak of 'mostanocracy' – gangster rule.

The heyday of urban mostan rule was between the 1980s and late 2000s; after that period, the power elite gained some more control of city life. In a process that David Jackman has called 'party politicisation of criminality', political parties were able to absorb many mostans into their youth, student and labour wings, and drive out those who would not be brought under control. In this way, party political actors of the ruling coalition replaced autonomous mostans as the local political bullies and grassroots enforcers of urban Bangladesh.[5]

ISLAMIC PROPRIETY

Another challenge to the vernacular cultural model emerged from a growing Islamic sensibility. This growth was caused by a combination of forces. On the one hand, there was the return of Islamic symbols in public life during military rule (see Chapter 20), the inflow of global ideas of Islamic decorum brought back by migrants to the Gulf, and financial aid to Islamic groups and institutions provided by rich states in West Asia. On the other hand, it was the way in which an emerging lower-middle class responded to being unable to gain bhodrolok respectability. Finally, it represented a search for more positive values among those who were disgusted with corruption in public life and who sought more security in the urban jungle.

For those who embrace the new Islamic propriety, it is a way of affirming a modernity that is both moral and spiritual – a way of being pure in an impure world. In some ways this new sensibility recalls the nineteenth-century movements that were bent on 'purifying' the religious and social practices of Bengali Muslims. Then, too, it had been new – yet tradition-alist – ideas from the Arabian peninsula that had inspired a rethinking of how to be a 'proper' Muslim in Bengal.

There is another historical parallel as well. The new urban mosques serve the same purpose for migrants from the countryside that the frontier mosques had served for peasants clearing and settling the forests of the eastern delta during Mughal times (see Chapter 3). They offer them community protection and social order. The new mosques are essential institutions in Bangladesh's rushed urbanisation, supplying their congregations with connections, a sense of belonging, and support in finding jobs and lodgings. In Mughal times, the agrarian, religious and state frontiers had fused, and Islam had evolved into an ideology of taming the forest and promoting settled agriculture. In the process, a distinctly Bengali Islam had developed. In the early twenty-first century Islam has evolved into an ideology that helps rural migrants cross the frontier to urban life. In this drive to become the ideology of newly urbanised Bangladesh, the delta's Islam naturally changes to suit the new conditions.

This new Islam is equally Bengali but distinct from its rural forerunner. It has adapted from a religion suited to the multistranded face-to-face interactions of village life to the more single-stranded, anonymous inter-actions in the city. It is more demonstrative and scriptural, and less accepting of local cultural elements.[6] Many organisations have sprung up to promote it. One of the most successful is the Tabligh (Outreach) movement, headquartered in the Kakrail mosque in Dhaka. Its annual gathering at Tongi, north of Dhaka, is known as the Bissho Ijtema (*biśva ijtemā*; World Gathering). Today it is often described as the largest Muslim gathering in the world after the Hajj, drawing over 2 million people.[7]

Plate 25.2 Participants at the Bissho Ijtema, Tongi, 2003.

As Plate 25.2 shows, one of the most visible expressions of Islamic propriety is fashion. Men wear embroidered caps (tupi; *ṭupi*), and their shirts can be so long that they almost obscure the checked lungi (*luṅgi*; sarong) underneath.

Women's outdoor appearance is especially expressive of new notions of Islamic decorum. The 1970s and 1980s had been a period of sari (*sārī*) hegemony. The sari is the long and colourful unstitched garment, draped around the body, which is popular all over South Asia. In Bangladesh it was the dress of choice for adult women, while many young girls would wear a long tunic with pyjama trousers. During the movement for Bangladesh, the sari had become a symbol of Bengali authenticity and a sartorial protest against West Pakistani hegemony. In certain areas (especially in eastern Bangladesh districts such as Noakhali), some Muslim women would wear a tent-like burka (*borkā*) over their sari whenever they left their village. The custom, which was also well established in Dhaka's oldest neighbourhood, was thought to be on the way out (Plate 25.3).

In the 1970s, few would have predicted that the burka would stage a stylish comeback. And yet, with the rise of new ideas of Islamic propriety, this is exactly what happened. Although many Muslim (and

Plate 25.3 Woman in a burka, old Dhaka, 1983.

all non-Muslim) women in Bangladesh reject the new cultural repertoire, an increasing number now wear a variety of scarves, veils and burkas when they appear in public. These garments differ from the old ones in colouring, materials and style. And they are meant to be different: they signal public adherence to the new, self-assured face of Bangladeshi Islam. The burka represents a move 'from private to public patriarchy' and a 'compromise between the need for women to take part in society and the desire to keep them in seclusion' (Plate 25.4).[8]

The trend towards a new austere and patriarchal Islamic cultural repertoire in Bangladesh does not go unchallenged.[9] It does not replace the more liberal vision of what Bangladeshi culture and Islam are all about. On the contrary, the liberal vision denies the Islamist one the right to speak for the nation.

Plate 25.4 Women visiting a new shopping mall in Dhaka display a variety of dress styles, 2006.

A LIBERAL VISION OF BANGLADESH

Since the 1980s a liberal vision of the future has been confronting an austere, expressly Islamic one. Both claim to provide the best guide out of the quandary of injustice, corruption and insecurity that a lot of Bangladeshis face. A basic problem for Bangladeshi liberals is that, unlike Islamists, they had a chance to fulfil their promises, but they failed to deliver a Golden Bengal. Even though they lost their exclusive grip on state power, they strive to defend their vision by institutionalising it in various ways. Old institutions such as the Bangla Academy and the Shilpokola Academy (Academy of Fine and Performing Arts) remain national cultural centres of great importance, and new ones have sprung up. Some of these are state-sponsored, for example the National Museum (opened in 1975), the Children's (shishu; *śiśu)* Academy (1976), and the National Archives and National Library (established in 1973, opened in 1985). Others are private initiatives, for example the Liberation War Museum (opened in 1996), private universities and a plethora of private mass media.

Much liberal energy goes into the creation of NGOs.[10] The big development NGOs such as BRAC and Grameen Bank are squarely in the liberal camp. In addition there are influential advocacy NGOs such as Ain-O-Shalish Kendro (*āin-o-sāliś kendra*; Legal Aid Centre) and Odhikar (*adhikār*; Rights). These organisations focus on raising awareness of legal and human rights. They provide free legal aid and campaign against issues such as domestic violence, acid attacks on women, and discrimination of religious and ethnic minorities.

Rights issues also have been taken up by these groups themselves. The Bangladesh Hindu Buddhist Christian Unity Council was formed in 1988 in protest at the declaration of Islam as the state religion of Bangladesh. The Bangladesh Indigenous People's [now: Adivasi] Forum, bringing together over forty ethnic groups, came together to demand the cancellation of an 'eco-park' that would push indigenous people off their ancestral land.[11] Bangladesh also developed a determined women's movement, with several associations and strong international connections (see Chapter 24).

The liberal interpretation of the delta's future expresses itself in public events as well. Some of these are linked with the national movement, such as the laying of wreaths at memorials to the martyrs all over the country on Victory Day (16 December) and Language Day (Ekushe, 21 February) (Plate 25.5).[12] Each is associated with distinct dress codes: red and green for Victory Day, black and white for Martyred Intellectuals' Day (14 December), and letters of the Bengali alphabet for Language Day (Plate 25.6).

Plate 25.5 Performing patriotic songs at Rajshahi University, Language Day, 2018.

Plate 25.6 A family in festive letter-covered Language Day outfits, 2019.

Others are celebrations of non-communal regional identity. Bangladeshis of different religious backgrounds participate jointly in numerous local festivals and activities, including religious ones.[13] Foremost among these is the celebration of Bengali New Year (14 April), when enormous festive crowds take to the streets of Dhaka to watch brightly coloured floats of huge peacocks and fantastic animals, observe intricate floor decorations (alpona; *ālpanā*), buy painted pots and toys, and listen to songs celebrating the six seasons of the Bengali year (Plate 25.7).[14] Yet other events link up with international celebrations such as International Women's Day and May Day.

A flourishing arts scene also propagates liberal interpretations of Bangladesh culture. The Pakistan period had seen the budding of modernist theatre, visual arts and architecture (see Chapter 16). After 1971 rapid improvements in connectivity and arts education gave a boost to further artistic innovation, especially in Dhaka. New galleries, museums, theatres and arts centres sprang up, and international events such as the Dhaka Art Summit, the International Film Festival and Chobi Mela (a photography

Plate 25.7 Welcoming the New Year in Dhaka, April 2007.

festival) made the transnational arts world sit up.[15] Well-heeled collectors at home and abroad began to notice and appreciate the works of Bangladeshi artists as never before.

By the late twentieth century, a distinct youth culture had begun to take shape in the Bengal delta. One of its distinguishing features was a new music style, band music. The first popular band, Zinga Gosthi, was established by college students in Chittagong in the 1960s. Early bands performed cover versions in English, but by the 1990s most bands wrote their own songs in Bengali, often adapting folk tunes such as the Baul songs. This created a vibrant popular music scene that branched out beyond the familiar patriotic and romantic songs. Unlike the traditional songs, the new music also expresses social criticism as well as darker emotions such as frustration and rage. Rock concert tours and television performances began to shape new tastes among a mass audience of young adults, not only in Bangladesh but also in West Bengal and among Bengalis around the world. As it rejuvenated the delta's rich traditions, Bangladeshi rock went global. The resulting fusion was expressed well in the names of popular bands such as Nogor Baul (Urban Bard) and Lalon Band (Plate 25.8). As Internet access spread, it allowed bands to self-publish their songs and reach new audiences. Contemporary Bangladeshi music combines the

Plate 25.8 Cover of *Baul Soul*, an album by popular singer Rinku, 2006.

delta's musical traditions with international styles – metal, pop, rock, fusion, rap and hip-hop – and its lyrics address political and social injustice. Much of it gives voice to the experiences and emotions of young urban adults in a way that is diametrically opposed to the new puritanical Islamic sensibility.

THE BANGLADESH CULTURE WARS

The liberal and Islamic visions of Bangladesh culture clash on many fronts: language use, dress, gender relations, festivities, music and even the naming of children.[16] The media are a most important battleground, especially the many newspapers, television stations, cinemas and online conversations.[17] Expressing your views in public can be risky, however, and liberal journalists, opinion-makers, activists and bloggers are sometimes attacked and killed.[18] Education is another crucial arena. How secular or Islamic is the school you send your children to? And what kind of Islam is taught there? The Bangladesh educational system has two parallel streams, one ostensibly secular and the other Islamic (*mādrāsā*). At the level of colleges and universities the two merge, and it is here that cultural antagonists regularly cross swords. Campus politics has always been important as a harbinger of the national mood, and in the 1990s it became dominated by the clash between secularists and Islamists. And these were not just symbolic clashes; they were bloody ones that claimed many lives. Student groups with links to national parties were given firearms and bombs, and they used them freely to intimidate, injure and kill fellow students and faculty members. Dormitory-to-dormitory shoot-outs were far from exceptional. Some campuses went to the Islamists. For example, Shibir (*islāmi chātra śibir*; Islamic Students' Camp), the youth organisation of the Jamaat-e-Islami, ruled the roost at the University of Chittagong from 1982 and non-Islamist faculty and students had to tread very carefully. Other campuses were constant battlegrounds or were controlled by secularists (Plate 25.9). In the 2010s, however, Shibir's power diminished as a result of police crackdowns on suspicion of Islamist terrorism.[19]

The new move towards Islamic propriety and the terror tactics of the radical fringe worry liberal Muslims in Bangladesh. But the millions of non-Muslims in the country are infinitely more worried. Among these the Hindus are by far the largest group. Numbering about 10 million in 1971 and 17 million in 2017, they form the third-largest Hindu population in the

Plate 25.9 Bas-relief showing secular symbols on the campus of Jahangirnagar University in Savar, part of the front line in the struggle between Islamist and non-Islamist student organisations in 2006.

world, after India and Nepal.[20] The number of Bangladeshi Hindus has been growing more slowly than that of Bangladeshi Muslims, however, so their proportion has fallen from 13 per cent in the early 1970s to 10 per cent today. The reasons for this relative decline are emigration in the face of state-sponsored discrimination and everyday prejudice as well as low birth rates. Most Hindus are cultivators living all over the country, but there are regional concentrations, for example in the southwest. Hindus are also well represented in certain sectors, such as education and the creative professions. One of them is the much-loved political cartoonist Shishir Bhattacharjee (Plate 25.10). For Bangladeshi Hindus and other non-Muslims alike, the liberal scenario is the only desirable one.

Plate 25.10 Shishir Bhattacharjee is famous for poking fun at the political establishment. In this cartoon we see the prime minister, Sheikh Hasina, misusing national exultation for party-political purposes. In the year 2000 the Bangladesh cricket team achieved 'Test status', a source of great pride in the country. The prime minister, exclaiming 'We are all so happy!', is painting a cricket bat to resemble the waistcoat that her late father, Sheikh Mujib, used to wear – and which became the uniform of Awami League stalwarts.

Today, liberal Bangladeshis feel increasingly embattled. Many are convinced that Islamism is dangerously growing, supported by an accommodating government as well as terrorist intimidation.[21] On the other hand, liberal Bangladesh forms a vibrant, feisty and vocal community with everstronger global links. The further Islamisation, or secularisation, of Bangladesh society is by no means a foregone conclusion. The jury is still out on what new twist the youngest generation in the delta will give to that old hyphenated identity – Bengali-Muslim.

FISH AND RICE

Burka-clad provincials, streetwise rowdies and feminist socialites may disagree violently on issues of identity and morality, but they are very likely to see eye to eye on one cultural topic: food. Bangladesh culture must be one of the most food-centred in the world. The delta has always produced many varieties of food, and over the centuries new crops and new habits have been added to the range. In this way, tomatoes, potatoes and chillies – all early imports from the Americas – became domesticated as daily necessities. The staple food throughout remained rice, eaten in great heaps, with spicy side dishes (torkari; *tarkāri*) cooked in mustard oil.[22] As they say in the region, 'fish and rice make a Bengali' (*māche bhāte bānāli*), and this is true, at least for those who can afford to eat well. Many poor people in Bangladesh eat fish only occasionally and in small portions and meat very rarely indeed, instead adding lentils and other vegetable dishes, or just chillies, to their rice. Men usually get the best food, so women eat less fish and meat than men.[23] Bangladeshi cuisine sports an enormous array of intricate dishes, varying from region to region, from community to community, from class to class, and from family to family. For example, the Hindu and Muslim versions of Bangladeshi cooking are quite distinct, people in the coastal areas have a special liking for dried sea fish (shuntki machh; *śūṭki mach*), a mix of rice and lentils (khichuri; *khicuri*) is traditionally poor people's food, and each non-Bengali community has its own distinct gastronomic style.

Growing up with this culinary wealth, the inhabitants of the delta are well known for their discerning palates. Food is a serious business: it is treasured and critically appraised.[24] But the national focus on food has always gone well beyond nourishment, taste and the passing on of gastronomic skills. Food was, and continues to be, central in notions of hospitality, social networking, business deals, respectability and well-being (Plate 25.11). Dinner invitations (daoat; *dāoyāt*), and accepting or refusing

Plate 25.11 Sharing a meal during a picnic, a Bangladeshi institution. Nator, 2006.

them, are most important social currencies. Hosts will try to impress their guests with the lavishness of the spread. Afterwards, guests will carefully evaluate the quality of the food, the number and types of dishes, and the hosts' insistence on offering even more food. On their part, hosts will be disappointed and unhappy with guests who eat little.

Among the changes in food habits that the Bangladesh period has brought is the consumption of wheat, mostly in the form of flatbread for breakfast (ruti, *ruṭi*; porota, *paroṭā*). It replaces older rice-based breakfast foods such as cooked rice soaked in water overnight and lightly fermented, served with salt and an onion or lime (panta bhat; *pāntā bhāt*). Another important change is that people have begun to buy far more packaged and processed food, relieving housewives and servants of the laborious tasks of husking rice and grinding spices (Plate 25.12). The plonking of the foot-pedalled wooden rice-husker (dhenki; *ḍhēki*), commonplace in the delta's villages until a generation ago, has been gradually replaced by the clanking of the mechanical rice-mill.

Tea is another item of consumption that was a rare luxury outside the middle class in the 1970s but has become more popular over time. The delta's many local fruits – from the highly prized mango (am; *ām*) and

Plate 25.12 Various brands of packaged flatbread for sale in a newly opened super-market in an upscale neighbourhood of Dhaka, 2014.

jackfruit (kanthal; *kãthãl*) to the lowly sour plum (kul; *kul*) and blackberry (jam; *jãm*) – have been joined by imported fruits such as grapes, oranges and apples. Certain foods have become rare or have disappeared, however. When it was discovered that a popular pulse (kheshari; *khesãri*; grass pea), when eaten over long periods, causes paralysis (lathyrism), its consumption declined steeply.[25]

Throughout the period there has been only one thing that rivals rice as archetypal of the Bengal delta's food habits: the mishti, or sweet. More than rice, its recent fortunes are linked to the history of state formation (see box 'Sweet addiction'; Plates 25.13 and 25.14).

Sweet addiction

The inhabitants of Bangladesh are famous for their sweet tooth. Their traditional addiction is to milk-based sweets (mishti; *miṣṭi*). These have been around for many centuries, being prepared at home and by specialised professionals. From the mid-nineteenth century onwards, urban sweetshops appeared to cater to the refined tastes of the elite. The top-ranking confectioners were overwhelmingly Hindus. The Partition of Bengal in 1947 meant that many of them left for India, creating a crisis in the supply of sweets to the middle classes in East Pakistan. Some Hindu sweet-makers stayed on, however, and soon Muslim sweet-makers entered the scene. The Bangladesh

War led to a further shift and adaptation. The increasing wealth of
Bangladesh's middle classes in the late twentieth century lay at the basis of
a remarkable development of the sweets sector: turnovers rose rapidly, and
chains of swanky sweetshops mushroomed in smart neighbourhoods and
around army cantonments.

   Mishti are more than an addiction. Large boxes of sweets are a must to take
along as gifts when you visit family or friends. Religious festivals and life-cycle
events are unthinkable without sweets. And after a trip to another town you are
expected to return with that locality's particular sweet. There are dozens of
local specialities. For example, Comilla prides itself on its roshmalai (*rasmālāi*;
sweet curd balls in thickened milk), Rajshahi glories in its roshkodom
(*raskadam*; curd balls covered with large white beads of sugar) and Bogra's
claim to fame is its creamy yoghurt-like doi (*dai, dahi*). There are also standard

Plate 25.13 Professional mishti-maker draining bags of fresh curd in Nator, 2006.

sweets – roshogolla (*rasagollā*; sponge curd balls boiled in sugar syrup) or shondesh (*sandeś*; dry curd-paste squares) – that are eaten all over the country (and in neighbouring India).

Curd sweets are merely the best known of an amazingly large assortment of confections and sweet desserts. Many are rice-based and continue to be homemade. Rice-flour cakes (pitha; *piṭhā*) – which come with fillings such as coconut, molasses or date juice – are winter-harvest favourites. A Muslim thanksgiving (milad; *milād*) is not complete without a tray of fresh coil-like sweets known as jilapi (*jilāpi*). And then there is paesh (*pāyes*; rice boiled in sugared milk with cardamom and pistachios), shemai (*semāi*; wheat noodles boiled in sugared milk with cinnamon and cassia leaf (tezpata; *tejpātā*)) and so on. Sweets are a national love affair – but tucking into sweets has lost its innocence now that many Bangladeshis are aware of rising trends of obesity, diabetes and heart disease among the middle classes.

Plate 25.14 Filling a gift box at a sweet shop in Rajshahi, 2018.

SPORTS

Another passion that unites the nation is sport. The delta has a long history of local sports. Seasonal boat races in long-boats – each with sixty or more rowers spurred on by a large drum and riverside crowds – are still a living tradition. Bolikhela (*balīkhelā*), a form of wrestling, flourished in Chittagong district, where it took on anti-colonial overtones in the first half of the twentieth century. The popular team sport of hadudu (*hāḍuḍu*) – also known as kobadi (*kabāḍi*) – was declared Bangladesh's national sport in 1972.

Two sports have played an especially important role in supporting the national culture of Bangladesh. The first is football. The earliest football clubs in Bengal were formed in the late nineteenth century and soon became anti-British bodies. The role of football in politics became even more significant in the 1930s and 1940s when it became communalised. Muslim and Hindu clubs played against each other in an increasingly bitter atmosphere of divided loyalties.[26] After Partition, football remained the most popular sport and it helped strengthen identification with the Pakistan nation. When the Bangladesh Liberation War broke out in 1971, the Bangladesh government in exile immediately formed the Shadhin Bangla (Independent Bangladesh, *swādhīn bāṃlā*) football team, which toured India to whip up support for the freedom struggle. After the war, football established itself as the prime mass spectator sport for Bangladeshis.

Although powerfully symbolic in the national arena, football did not allow Bangladeshis to project themselves as a sporting nation internationally. During football world cups, they root for others: whole neighbourhoods get festooned with the flags of Argentina or Brazil. But from the turn of the twenty-first century another sport made Bangladeshis proud. The national cricket team defeated Pakistan and went on to reach 'Test status'. Heavily supported by jubilant ruling-class and entrepreneurial elites as well as by impassioned national media, cricket soon surpassed football as a source of national sporting self-respect (Plate 25.15; see also Plate 25.10).[27]

In Bangladesh the role of sports as a unifying force has become of paramount importance. Sporting successes inspire intense pride in being Bangladeshi and they are also pursued to inspire respect. In the 2010s several Bangladeshi men and women set out to make their country proud by planting the national flag on Mount Everest and other towering mountains around the world. On their return they were fêted as national heroes. Bangladesh has 'few widely accepted, non-partisan heroes to build a national identity around'. This is why those who excel in sports – whether as mountaineers or cricketers – are particularly valuable as consensus symbols of the nation's achievements.[28]

Plate 25.15 This colossal bat-wielding gorilla cheered on the national team during the 2011 Cricket World Cup, co-hosted by Bangladesh.

REDEFINING NATIONAL CULTURE

The Bangladesh period has seen a quickening of cultural change in the Bengal delta. Independent nationhood and new lifestyles have put its inhabitants in touch with global cultural transformations as never before. They have responded creatively, but their responses do not all point in the same direction. The delta resounds with heated debates on what national culture is all about. What does it mean to be a person living in these great floodplains in the twenty-first century? How can the rich cultural heritage best be engaged to face the future?

Even though most Bangladeshis share a deep sense of belonging and attachment to their delta environment, for a growing number the national context is not their only frame of reference. Whether living in Bangladesh or fanned out across the globe, they are in touch with transnational cultural visions that vary from secular to orthodox, from radical to moderate, from democratic to authoritarian, and from conservative to avant-garde. The result is an extraordinarily complex, fragmented and vibrant cultural scene, in which markedly different public and private presentations of self are possible. Being a Bangladeshi today means consciously making cultural choices all the time. Yet a multilayered culture has always been the hallmark of the Bengal delta. The delta's history of multiple, moving frontiers has simply entered a new and exciting phase.

Conclusion

History lives in the every day. When a boy stoops down to plant rice seedlings in Mahasthan, he can be sure that others have performed the same act, in the same field, for at least 3,000 years. When a honey collector bows to the goddess Bonbibi before entering the Sundarban wetlands, they stand in a millennia-long tradition. And when a woman sees floodwater submerging her home, she knows that, for tens of thousands of years, her forebears have had the same experience.

In this old land many things have a long history. Bangladesh may be a fairly young state, but its social arrangements result from a lengthy and turbulent past. In this book we have taken a bird's-eye view, sketching the contours but leaving out most details. The idea was to explain contemporary Bangladesh by showing its historical roots. Some of these reach back to an ancient past. Ever since humans settled in this region, making a living in a flood-prone tropical delta has been a constant challenge. Even today, humankind's technological prowess is dwarfed by the awesome power of nature to grant abundance or wreak havoc.

A constant factor has been the Bengal delta's openness. Ideas, peoples and goods have met and mingled at this major crossroads since time immemorial, leaving innumerable cultural, economic and genetic traces, and creating a distinct regional culture. It is from such mingling and cross-fertilisation that modern Bangladeshi identities have gradually emerged – never monolithic, often conflicted, and in perpetual flux.

Long-term processes have shaped the deep structure of contemporary Bangladesh – its settlement patterns, agricultural ways, kinship ideology, musical traditions, culinary style and religious diversity. It is these that set the region apart. But the Bengal delta also shares much with its surroundings, for example a centuries-old history of imperial control, first by the northern Indian Mughals (1610–1713) and then by the British (1757–1947). These periods brought economic restructuring and administrative changes, many of which endure. They also created new elite groups and

333

gave fresh layers of meaning to old cultural practices that continue to be relevant in Bangladesh today.

Finally, the twentieth century saw political ferment, demographic jolts and geopolitical shifts that would result in a new state, Bangladesh. Three shocks in particular shaped the course of events: famine in 1943, partition in 1947 and war in 1971 – each in turn largely replacing its precursor in popular memory.

This modern history is the stuff of everyday life in twenty-first-century Bangladesh, a fiercely contested legacy that is far from being settled, because opposing groups use it in their quest for recognition and power. It is a history that is very much alive. A heady mix of memory, myth-making, propaganda, amnesia and scholarly history-writing, the importance of this most recent historical trajectory is obvious to all Bangladeshis – although perhaps not always its deeper historical underpinnings. It created the vigorous political system that dominates their lives, it underlies the current economic and ecological struggles, and it gave rise to the country's animated culture wars. Today's inhabitants of the Bengal delta cope – often magnificently – by bringing into play a flexible, upbeat resilience that is one of the region's most valuable historical legacies.

Map B   Bangladesh districts since 1984.

Key Political Figures since 1947

These sketches are ordered by date of birth.

Mohammad Ali Jinnah (1876–1948) is best known as the architect of Pakistan. The son of a prosperous merchant, he was born in Karachi. He trained as a lawyer in London and practised law in Mumbai (Bombay) before entering politics in 1896. He joined the Indian National Congress, but later headed the All-India Muslim League, which strove to establish the state of Pakistan as a homeland for India's Muslims. When Pakistan was born in 1947, Jinnah became its first governor-general. During his first visit to East Pakistan he gave a speech declaring that Urdu would be Pakistan's state language, incensing the Bengali-speaking majority. He died shortly afterwards.

(Maulana) Abdul Hamid Khan Bhashani (c. 1880–1976) was a very influential politician who never held state office. Born in Dhanpara (Sirajganj district), he was a religious personality (maulana; *maolānā*; Muslim scholar) who developed into a firebrand village-based politician fighting for the interests of peasants and labourers. In the late 1930s he moved to Assam, where he became active in the Muslim League and worked among Bengali settlers. In 1948 he came to Pakistan, and in 1949, disillusioned with the Muslim League, he founded the East Pakistan Awami Muslim League. Then he became prominent in the language movement. During his long career he was enormously influential as a leftist Islamic politician, and he was gaoled several times for his outspoken positions. One of his last actions was a 'long march' against the Farakka dam near Rajshahi in 1976.

Abdul Monem Khan (1899–1971) was an extremely unpopular governor of East Pakistan (1962–69). Born in Humayunpur (Kishorganj district), he obtained a law degree from Dhaka University in 1924. He joined the Muslim League in 1935 and was an active political organiser

in Mymensingh. After the birth of Pakistan he held various administrative positions. He was particularly close to General Ayub Khan and joined his cabinet as a minister before being appointed as governor of East Pakistan in 1962. He persecuted and arrested political opponents, tightened control over the media and created an atmosphere of fear. He renewed the attack on the Bengali language – infamously banning songs by Rabindranath Tagore, the most revered poet, from Radio Pakistan – and thereby revived the politics of language. As his protector Ayub fell in 1969, Monem Khan lost his position as well. During the 1971 war freedom fighters killed him in an attack on his home.

(General) Ayub Khan (1908–74) was Pakistan's first military dictator, from 1958 to 1969. He was born in the North-West Frontier Province (now in Pakistan) and was trained at the Royal Military College at Sandhurst (UK). In 1928 he joined the British Indian army. During the Second World War he served in Myanmar (Burma), and at Partition he joined the Pakistan army. In 1948 he was sent to East Pakistan as general officer commanding, responsible for the country's entire eastern wing. In 1951 he became commander-in-chief of the Pakistan army. In 1958 he staged a bloodless *coup d'état*, becoming Pakistan's military ruler for over ten years. He changed the constitution and set up a system of 'representational dictatorship' known as basic democracies. Economic growth accelerated under his regime, but distribution of wealth was highly skewed. He aligned Pakistan closely with the United States and later with China as well. After war with India in 1965 (during which he promoted himself to the rank of field marshal), his repressive regime began to unravel. The movement for the autonomy of East Pakistan gathered strength, and finally, after large-scale popular protests in both West and East Pakistan, the army deposed him in March 1969. His place was taken by General Yahya Khan.

(General) Tikka Khan (1915–2002). Born in the Punjab and trained at the Indian Military Academy, Tikka Khan fought in Myanmar (Burma) and North Africa during the Second World War and became an instructor at the Pakistan Military Academy in 1947. He fought in the India–Pakistan War of 1965 and earned a reputation for ruthlessness which was borne out when Yahya Khan appointed him military commander of East Pakistan in March 1971. Tikka Khan was the architect of Operation Searchlight, the massive military campaign to crush the movement for Bangladesh on 25 March 1971, causing many civilian deaths. Having earned the epithet 'Butcher of Bengal', he was replaced that April and called back to West Pakistan in September. Considered a major war criminal in

Bangladesh, he continued to be patronised by the Pakistan political elite. Zulfikar Ali Bhutto made him army chief in 1972 and sent him to quell the separatist movement in Baluchistan, where his mercilessness earned him a second title, 'Butcher of Baluchistan'. After retiring from the army, he joined the Pakistan People's Party, acting as special assistant on national security to Bhutto and being appointed as governor of Punjab under prime minister Benazir Bhutto in 1988.

(General) Yahya Khan (1917–80) was Pakistan's second military dictator, from 1969 to 1971. Born in Peshawar, he attended Punjab University and the Indian Military Academy before joining the British Indian army in 1938. During the Second World War he served in Iraq and North Africa, where he was captured by Axis forces in 1942. Joining the Pakistan army in 1947 and rising through the ranks, he became commander-in-chief in 1966. In 1969 he succeeded Ayub Khan as military ruler. His style differed from his predecessor's, and he organised Pakistan's first general parliamentary elections in December 1970. After the surprise outcome, he presided over complicated negotiations between East Pakistan's Awami League (headed by Sheikh Mujibur Rahman) and West Pakistan's Pakistan People's Party (headed by Zulfikar Ali Bhutto). When these talks did not produce a compromise and the situation in East Pakistan reached boiling-point in March 1971, he ordered the armed forces to crush the movement for autonomy/independence of East Pakistan. This ignited the Bangladesh Liberation War, which resulted in Pakistan losing its entire eastern wing. Yahya Khan had to hand power over the remaining western wing to Bhutto on 20 December 1971.

(General) Mohammad Ataul Ghani Osmany (1918–84) was the commander-in-chief of the Bangladesh liberation forces in 1971. He was born in Sunamganj and educated in Sylhet, Aligarh and at the Indian Military Academy at Dehra Dun before joining the British Indian army in 1940 and the Pakistan army in 1947. He joined the Awami League in 1970 and became a member of parliament the same year. When war broke out, he was made the commander of the Bangladesh forces, and after the war he became a general in the Bangladesh army. He retired in 1972 to become a minister in the Awami League cabinet. He resigned when Mujib introduced civilian autocracy. Later he created his own party and unsuccessfully contested two presidential elections.

Sheikh Mujibur Rahman (Mujib) (1920–75) was the charismatic leader of the movement for Bangladesh and the country's first president. He was

born in Tungipara (Gopalganj district) as the son of a minor official in a civil court. Sent to Kolkata for his college education, he became a political activist, first for the Muslim League and then for the Awami (Muslim) League in 1949. His oratory and organisational skills were his greatest assets. He was active in the language movement, and from 1953 to 1966 he was the general secretary of the Awami League. In the mid-1950s he was elected to East Bengal's Provincial Assembly and he served briefly as a minister in the provincial government. He became East Pakistan's undisputed symbol of national aspiration in the second half of the 1960s, when he fielded a political manifesto (the Six-Point Programme) and was gaoled for the Agartala conspiracy. His party, the Awami League, won a landslide victory in the national parliamentary elections of 1970, and Mujib was widely seen as Pakistan's next prime minister. This was vehemently opposed by West Pakistani politicians (notably Z. A. Bhutto) and army leaders. Political stalemate ended in the army's attempt to crush the Awami League, leading to the Bangladesh Liberation War (1971). Mujib was arrested in the first hours of the war, flown to West Pakistan and sentenced to death in a secret trial. After the war Mujib was allowed to return to Bangladesh, where he assumed the state leadership in early 1972. He favoured a secular nationalism and nationalised key industries. His party won another large victory in Bangladesh's first parliamentary elections in 1973 but lost popular support soon after. In early 1975 Mujib declared a 'second revolution' and installed himself as Bangladesh's first autocratic ruler. He was killed in an army coup on 15 August 1975.

Golam Azam (1922–2014) was an Islamist politician who became notorious as a collaborator with Pakistan forces during the Bangladesh Liberation War. Born into a family of Dhaka preachers, he studied political science at Dhaka University and taught in Rangpur in the early 1950s. He became secretary-general of the Jamaat-e-Islami East Pakistan in 1957 and its leader (or 'amir') in 1969. He strongly opposed the movement for Bangladesh and was a prominent supporter of the Pakistan army during the war of 1971. He fled to Pakistan at the end of the war and sought support in the Middle East to topple the Bangladesh government. Ziaur Rahman allowed him to return to Bangladesh in 1978, and he became leader of the Jamaat-e-Islami Bangladesh (technically this was illegal because he did not have Bangladeshi citizenship until 1994). The people's court organised by Jahanara Imam and others in 1992 accused him of collaboration and having headed death squads during the war of 1971. In 2000 he retired from active politics. In 2013 a special tribunal found him

guilty of war crimes during the Bangladesh Liberation War of 1971 and stated that he deserved the death sentence. However, in view of his advanced age and poor health it gave him a ninety-year prison sentence. He died a prisoner in 2014.

Ila Mitra (1925–2002) was a communist activist who was one of the leaders of the Tebhaga/Nachol uprising (1946–50). Born into a Kolkata bhodrolok family, she married Ramendra Mitra, a communist member of a landlord family in Chapai Nawabganj. After moving there, she began to organise local peasants (mostly Santals) to fight for their rights. After the creation of Pakistan, she decided to stay on. The Nachol movement radicalised after the Pakistan government banned the Communist Party in 1948. After a serious clash in 1950 the Pakistan army crushed the movement, and Ila Mitra was among those who were arrested. Her statement in the Rajshahi court exposed police and army brutality and torture, thus adding to a general disgruntlement with the Muslim League government among residents of East Pakistan. Serving a life sentence, she benefited from a change of government in 1954. Her very poor health moved the new government to allow her to go to Kolkata for medical treatment. She did not return until after Bangladesh had gained independence. Each time she returned, she was given a heroine's welcome.

Zulfikar Ali Bhutto (1928–79) was a Pakistani politician who played a decisive role in the country's break-up in 1971. Born into a wealthy and powerful landlord family in Larkana (now in Pakistan), he studied political science in California and law in Oxford. In 1958 General Ayub Khan appointed him as cabinet minister, and Bhutto became the dictator's trusted adviser. He became foreign minister in 1963, but resigned in 1967, turned against Ayub Khan and founded the Pakistan People's Party. In the wave of anti-Ayub unrest he rose to prominence, was briefly arrested in 1968 and demanded Ayub's resignation. After Yahya Khan came to power (1969), Bhutto positioned himself as the hardline spokesman for West Pakistani interests. After parliamentary elections in 1970, in which his party won most West Pakistan seats, but the Awami League won the outright majority, he refused to countenance an Awami League government and more autonomy for East Pakistan. He torpedoed all attempts at political conciliation and fully supported the March 1971 army crackdown on his political opponents in East Pakistan. After the war he took over power in (West) Pakistan from Yahya Khan on 20 December 1971 and became truncated Pakistan's president, army commander-in-chief and first civilian chief martial law administrator. In January 1972 he released Sheikh

Mujibur Rahman, who was held in a Pakistani gaol and had been sentenced to death. He did not recognise Bangladesh as an independent state until June 1973. After a further eventful career, he was arrested and tried by Pakistan's third military dictator, Zia ul Haq, and hanged in 1979.

Jahanara Imam (1929–94) was a writer who shot into the political limelight as an organiser of the people's court (Gono Adalot) in 1992. She was born in Murshidabad (now in West Bengal, India), the daughter of a deputy magistrate. Schooled at home, she worked as a schoolteacher in Mymensingh and Dhaka after her marriage and undertook further studies at Dhaka University and in the United States. In 1971 her son joined the freedom fighters and she expressed her experiences and worries in a diary that was published after the war as *Ekattorer Dinguli* (Days of '71). Vexed at the absence of punishment for war criminals and the neglect of the ideals that had inspired the freedom fighters, she co-organised a public people's court as a symbolic condemnation of war criminals and collaborators in 1992.

(General) Hussain Muhammad Ershad (c. 1930–2019) was Bangladesh's second military dictator, from 1982 to 1990. He was born in Rangpur and joined the Pakistan army in 1952. During the Bangladesh Liberation War Ershad was in West Pakistan, but, unlike many other Bengali officers who resigned, he stayed with the army throughout the war. He was repatriated to Bangladesh in 1973, joined the Bangladesh army and was made chief of staff during Zia's rule. In 1982, some months after Zia's assassination, he staged a bloodless coup. He declared himself president of Bangladesh the following year and created the Jatiyo Party in 1986. More right-wing than Zia, he leaned heavily on Islamic rhetoric. In 1988 he declared Islam to be the state religion of Bangladesh. Opposition to his regime grew into a broad-based popular movement led by Khaleda Zia and Sheikh Hasina, and after violent clashes he was forced to resign in 1990. He was imprisoned for corruption and spent years in and out of prison but continued to lead a faction of his party.

(Raja) Tridiv Roy (1933–2012) was the main political figure in the Chittagong Hill Tracts up to 1971. He was born in Rangamati, the son of the Chakma chief, Raja Nalinaksha Roy, whom he succeeded at the age of nineteen in 1953. He was also a magistrate, revenue collector, politician and occasionally a member of official delegations abroad. In 1962 he became an environmental refugee as the Kaptai hydroelectric project was completed and a huge lake flooded the central valleys of the Chittagong Hill Tracts. Raja Tridiv's palace was one of thousands of homes that

disappeared under water. He was elected to the National Assembly in 1970 as one of only two independent candidates from East Pakistan. He did not join the movement for Bangladesh, largely because he thought the regional autonomy of the Chittagong Hill Tracts would be more threatened in an independent Bangladesh than in Pakistan. When the Bangladesh Liberation War broke out, he sought to stay neutral but ultimately sided with Pakistan, acting as its envoy on a goodwill trip to Sri Lanka and Southeast Asia and serving as a wartime minister in the army-dominated provincial government. At the end of the war, he left for Pakistan. The Bangladesh government regarded him as a traitor and deposed him. Raja Tridiv became a minister in the post-war Pakistan cabinet headed by Z. A. Bhutto and later served as Pakistan's ambassador to Argentina and other countries. He died in Islamabad in 2012.

(General) Ziaur Rahman (Zia) (1936–81), Bangladesh's first military dictator, from 1975 to 1981, was born in Bagbari (Bogra district). His father was working as a chemist in Kolkata at the time. After the creation of Pakistan the family moved to Karachi. Zia graduated from the Pakistan Military Academy in 1955 and joined the Pakistan army as a teenager. During the Ayub period he worked in military intelligence. In 1960 he married Khaleda Zia (who would later become prime minister, see her entry later in this section). When war broke out in 1971, he happened to be posted in Chittagong. He threw in his lot with the Bangladesh side, rebelled, declared independence on the radio, joined the freedom fighters, fled to India and gained a reputation for valour. After independence he was appointed deputy chief of staff of Bangladesh's armed forces. After three military coups in 1975 Zia took control of the state and ran a repressive regime. He denationalised industries and favoured private enterprise. He appointed himself president of Bangladesh in 1977. The following year he created the Bangladesh Nationalist Party (BNP) and allowed other parties to resume their activities. He reintroduced Islamic elements in politics and promoted the concept of 'Bangladeshiness'. Zia was assassinated in an abortive army coup in 1981.

(Colonel) Abu Taher (1938–76) was a military officer and radical political activist. He was born in Assam and taught at a high school near Chittagong before joining the Pakistan army in 1960. Trained as a commando, he fought in the India–Pakistan War of 1965 and was serving in West Pakistan when the 1971 war broke out. He left the army in protest at the crackdown in East Pakistan/Bangladesh, made his way there and became an influential sector commander of freedom fighters in the Mymensingh-Rangpur

region. He lost a leg during an attack on Pakistan forces in November 1971. After medical treatment in India he returned to Bangladesh in 1972, joined the Bangladesh army and was decorated. He also joined the new National Socialist Party (JSD or Jatiyo Shomajtantrik Dol), which emerged as the major leftist party of Bangladesh. In 1975 coup and counter-coup followed each other and there was much restiveness in the army. Abu Taher used this to organise a leftist soldiers' revolt on 7 November 1975. This coup brought Ziaur Rahman to power rather than Abu Taher. Zia had Abu Taher arrested and tried by a military tribunal in Dhaka Central Jail. He was sentenced to death and hanged in 1976.

Manabendra Narayan Larma (1941–83) was the main exponent of Jumma nationalism. Born in Khagrachhari district (Chittagong Hill Tracts), he trained as a lawyer in Chittagong and took part in regional student activities from an early age. He organised a movement to demand proper compensation for the thousands of people who were displaced by the Kaptai hydroelectric project in 1960, for which he was imprisoned for two years. He was elected to the East Pakistan Provincial Assembly in 1970 as an independent. Shortly after Bangladesh gained independence, Larma presented demands for regional autonomy for the Chittagong Hills to the committee drafting the new constitution. When these were ignored, he established the JSS (Jono Shonghoti Shomiti; Chittagong Hill Tracts United People's Party). After Mujib's fall in 1975, Larma fled to India, from where he directed the Shanti Bahini, the armed wing of the JSS, in guerrilla warfare. Ideological conflict broke out within the JSS between leftists and nationalists and this resulted in the assassination of Larma in 1983. His younger brother, **Jyotirindra Bodhipriya (Shantu) Larma** (born in 1944), then assumed the leadership of the JSS. Shantu Larma played a central role in negotiating the Chittagong Hill Tracts Peace Accord of December 1997. This ended the twenty-five-year regional war but led to a split in the JSS. Those who did not agree with the accord and wanted to continue the armed fight against the authorities in Dhaka formed a new party, the United People's Democratic Front (UPDF). Peace did not come to the Chittagong hills, as JSS, UPDF and the Bangladesh armed forces continued to commit many acts of violence.

Siraj Sikdar (1944–75) was a revolutionary politician. Born in Bhedarganj (Shariatpur district), he trained as an engineer and became involved in leftist politics. In 1968 he established a 'Mao Tse Tung Research Centre' in Dhaka, which was soon closed by the authorities. During the 1971 war he formed his own guerrilla group in the Borishal

region. He lost a leg during an attack on Pakistan forces in November 1971. After medical treatment in India he returned to Bangladesh in 1972, joined the Bangladesh army and was decorated. He also joined the new National Socialist Party (JSD or Jatiyo Shomajtantrik Dol), which emerged as the major leftist party of Bangladesh. In 1975 coup and counter-coup followed each other and there was much restiveness in the army. Abu Taher used this to organise a leftist soldiers' revolt on 7 November 1975. This coup brought Ziaur Rahman to power rather than Abu Taher. Zia had Abu Taher arrested and tried by a military tribunal in Dhaka Central Jail. He was sentenced to death and hanged in 1976.

Manabendra Narayan Larma (1941–83) was the main exponent of Jumma nationalism. Born in Khagrachhari district (Chittagong Hill Tracts), he trained as a lawyer in Chittagong and took part in regional student activities from an early age. He organised a movement to demand proper compensation for the thousands of people who were displaced by the Kaptai hydroelectric project in 1960, for which he was imprisoned for two years. He was elected to the East Pakistan Provincial Assembly in 1970 as an independent. Shortly after Bangladesh gained independence, Larma presented demands for regional autonomy for the Chittagong Hills to the committee drafting the new constitution. When these were ignored, he established the JSS (Jono Shonghoti Shomiti; Chittagong Hill Tracts United People's Party). After Mujib's fall in 1975, Larma fled to India, from where he directed the Shanti Bahini, the armed wing of the JSS, in guerrilla warfare. Ideological conflict broke out within the JSS between leftists and nationalists and this resulted in the assassination of Larma in 1983. His younger brother, **Jyotirindra Bodhipriya (Shantu) Larma** (born in 1944), then assumed the leadership of the JSS. Shantu Larma played a central role in negotiating the Chittagong Hill Tracts Peace Accord of December 1997. This ended the twenty-five-year regional war but led to a split in the JSS. Those who did not agree with the accord and wanted to continue the armed fight against the authorities in Dhaka formed a new party, the United People's Democratic Front (UPDF). Peace did not come to the Chittagong hills, as JSS, UPDF and the Bangladesh armed forces continued to commit many acts of violence.

Siraj Sikdar (1944–75) was a revolutionary politician. Born in Bhedarganj (Shariatpur district), he trained as an engineer and became involved in leftist politics. In 1968 he established a 'Mao Tse Tung Research Centre' in Dhaka, which was soon closed by the authorities. During the 1971 war he formed his own guerrilla group in the Borishal

disappeared under water. He was elected to the National Assembly in 1970 as one of only two independent candidates from East Pakistan. He did not join the movement for Bangladesh, largely because he thought the regional autonomy of the Chittagong Hill Tracts would be more threatened in an independent Bangladesh than in Pakistan. When the Bangladesh Liberation War broke out, he sought to stay neutral but ultimately sided with Pakistan, acting as its envoy on a goodwill trip to Sri Lanka and Southeast Asia and serving as a wartime minister in the army-dominated provincial government. At the end of the war, he left for Pakistan. The Bangladesh government regarded him as a traitor and deposed him. Raja Tridiv became a minister in the post-war Pakistan cabinet headed by Z. A. Bhutto and later served as Pakistan's ambassador to Argentina and other countries. He died in Islamabad in 2012.

(General) Ziaur Rahman (Zia) (1936–81), Bangladesh's first military dictator, from 1975 to 1981, was born in Bagbari (Bogra district). His father was working as a chemist in Kolkata at the time. After the creation of Pakistan the family moved to Karachi. Zia graduated from the Pakistan Military Academy in 1955 and joined the Pakistan army as a teenager. During the Ayub period he worked in military intelligence. In 1960 he married Khaleda Zia (who would later become prime minister, see her entry later in this section). When war broke out in 1971, he happened to be posted in Chittagong. He threw in his lot with the Bangladesh side, rebelled, declared independence on the radio, joined the freedom fighters, fled to India and gained a reputation for valour. After independence he was appointed deputy chief of staff of Bangladesh's armed forces. After three military coups in 1975 Zia took control of the state and ran a repressive regime. He denationalised industries and favoured private enterprise. He appointed himself president of Bangladesh in 1977. The following year he created the Bangladesh Nationalist Party (BNP) and allowed other parties to resume their activities. He reintroduced Islamic elements in politics and promoted the concept of 'Bangladeshiness'. Zia was assassinated in an abortive army coup in 1981.

(Colonel) Abu Taher (1938–76) was a military officer and radical political activist. He was born in Assam and taught at a high school near Chittagong before joining the Pakistan army in 1960. Trained as a commando, he fought in the India–Pakistan War of 1965 and was serving in West Pakistan when the 1971 war broke out. He left the army in protest at the crackdown in East Pakistan/Bangladesh, made his way there and became an influential sector commander of freedom fighters in the Mymensingh-Rangpur

Bangladesh District Maps

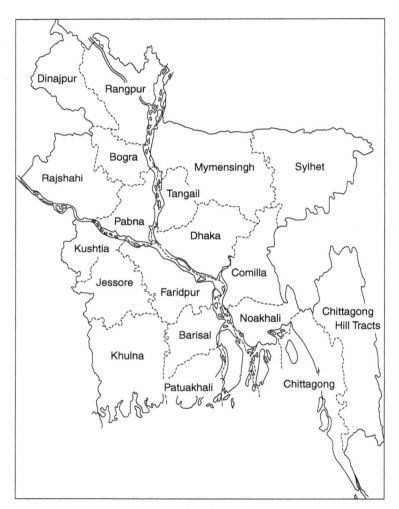

Map A Bangladesh districts 1971–84.

335

(Barisal) region and established a new party, the Shorbohara Party or East Bengal Proletarian Party. In 1973 he became president of the National Liberation Front of East Bengal, a combination of eleven radical organisations that launched an armed struggle against the Bangladesh government in several parts of the country. Their aim was to complete the unfinished revolution and establish proletarian rule. These attacks destabilised the Awami League regime and contributed to Mujib's decision to promulgate a state of emergency in late 1974. Sikdar went underground but was arrested in Chittagong and killed by police gunfire on his way to detention in Dhaka in January 1975.

(Begum) Khaleda Zia (born in 1945) was prime minister of Bangladesh twice (1991–6 and 2001–6). The daughter of a businessman in Dinajpur, at the age of fifteen she married Ziaur Rahman (then a captain, later military ruler of Bangladesh) and joined him in West Pakistan in 1965. Later he was posted to East Pakistan. When the 1971 war broke out, he chose to fight for the Bangladesh side, and the Pakistan army arrested Khaleda. After her husband was assassinated in 1981 his party, the BNP, was in danger of falling apart. Khaleda was chosen as its vice-president and in 1984 she became BNP chairperson, a position she still holds. In alliance with Sheikh Hasina and others she spearheaded a resistance movement against the Ershad regime, forcing it to an end in 1990. Elections the following year made her Bangladesh's first woman prime minister and Sheikh Hasina leader of the opposition. They changed places after elections in 1996 and once again in 2001. The coalition government that Khaleda then led included Islamist parties, notably the Jamaat-e-Islami. During her first stint as prime minister, Bangladesh introduced free, compulsory primary education and tuition-free education for girls up to class ten. Her second stint was marked by rising Islamist terror, to which the government responded meekly. The decision to ban Ahmadi publications in 2004 was seen as an indication of the power of Islamist forces in the cabinet. In 2007, after elections were postponed and an interim government took over, Khaleda and her two sons were arrested on charges of corruption. In 2018 she began a five-year jail sentence for corruption and was barred from standing in general elections later that year.

Sheikh Hasina Wazed (born in 1947) was prime minister of Bangladesh from 1996 to 2001, and from 2009 to today. She is the daughter of Sheikh Mujibur Rahman and survived the family's assassination in 1975 because she was abroad. In 1981, while living in exile in Delhi, she became president of the Awami League, a position she has occupied ever since. She returned to

Bangladesh shortly afterwards and became a central figure in the resistance movement against the Ershad regime. Elections in 1986 made her the leader of the opposition in parliament, and, forming an alliance with other politicians, notably Khaleda Zia, she organised a mass movement that forced Ershad to step down. Since then she and Khaleda have dominated the political scene in Bangladesh. Hasina returned as the leader of the opposition after elections in 1991, and Khaleda became prime minister. New elections in 1996 brought Hasina's party victory and she became prime minister of a coalition government. She negotiated a thirty-year treaty with India for sharing the waters of the Ganges and a peace accord in the Chittagong Hill Tracts. Parliamentary elections in 2001 returned her as the leader of the opposition once again and Khaleda as prime minister. In 2004 grenades were hurled at her as she was addressing a public rally – fourteen people were killed and 300 injured but Hasina escaped unhurt. Elections due in 2007 were postponed as an interim government took over. In mid-2007 Hasina was arrested on charges of graft and extortion but general elections in 2008 saw her return to the position of prime minister. During the 2010s her rule became increasingly authoritarian and her son Sajeeb Wazed Joy (born in 1971) became politically active. She organised general elections in 2014 amid violence and an opposition boycott, so the legitimacy of her mandate was widely questioned both domestically and internationally. She concluded a Land Boundary Agreement with India in 2015. In 2018 she organised new elections that were marred by voter intimidation, vote rigging and a crackdown on opposition candidates. She won 96 per cent of the parliamentary seats – but she lost even more credibility as a democratically elected leader.

Glossary of Bengali Terms

adibashi	indigenous people	*ādibāsi*
ajlaf	low-born	*ājlāph*
alpona	floor decoration	*ālpanā*
am	mango	*ām*
amon	autumn rice	*āman*
apa	elder sister	*āpā*
arai	2½	*āṛāi*
ashraf	aristocratic	*āśrāph*
atrap	low-born	*ātrāp*
aush	spring rice	*āuś*
bangal	East Bengali	*bāṅāl*
Bangla	Bengali	*bāṃlā*
Bangladesh	Bangladesh	*bāṃlādeś*
baro bhuiya	twelve chiefs	*bāra bhũiyā*
Baul	devotional community	*bāul*
begom	lady	*begam*
bhai	elder brother	*bhāi*
bhaoaya	folk song	*bhāoyāyā*
bhasha andolon	language movement	*bhāsā āndalan*
bhat	cooked rice	*bhāt*
bhatiali	boat song	*bhāṭiyāli*
bhodrolok	gentlefolk	*bhadralok*
bhodromohila	gentlewoman	*bhadramahilā*
bhita	homestead	*bhiṭā*
bigha	0.14 hectare	*bighā*
Bijoy Dibosh	Victory Day	*bijay dibas*
bil	low land, lake	*bil*
birangona	(war) heroine	*bīrāṅganā*
Bissho Ijtema	world gathering	*biśva ijtemā*
bolikhela	a form of wrestling	*balīkhelā*

Bongobondhu	Friend of Bengal	*baṅgabandhu*
boro	winter rice	*boro*
Boro Porong	Great Exodus	*baṛa paraṃ*
burka, borka	tent-like garment	*borkā*
chacha	father's younger brother, uncle	*cācā*
chandabaji	extortion	*cãdābāji*
chaul	husked rice	*cāul* or *cāl*
chhayanot	a musical mode	*chāyānaṭ*
chhotolok	lowly people	*choṭalok*
chor	silt-bank, island	*car*
dak bangla	resthouse for officials	*ḍāk bāṃlā*
Dalit	lowest-caste groups (Hindu)	*dalit*
danga	high land	*ḍāṅgā*
daoat	invitation	*dāoyāt*
der	1½	*der*
dhan	unhusked rice	*dhān*
dhenki	rice-husker	*ḍhẽki*
dhormo-niropekkho	secular	*dharma-nirapekṣa*
didi	elder sister	*didi*
diwan	chief revenue collector	*deoyān, dioyān*
doba	waterhole	*ḍobā*
doi	sweet yoghurt	*dai, dahi*
dorga	tomb-shrine	*dargā*
ekushe	21 (February)	*ekuśe*
Firingi	Europeans	*phiriṅgi*
ghat	landing place	*ghāṭ*
gherao	surrounding	*gherāo*
ghoti	West Bengali	*ghaṭi*
gonj	market town	*gañj*
gono adalot	people's court	*gaṇa ādālat*
gramer lok	village people	*grāmer lok*
gramin, grameen	rural	*grāmīn*
hadudu	a team sport	*hāḍuḍu*
hal	plough	*hāl*
haor	low land, lake	*hāor*
hawala	banking system	*hāoyālā*
hijra (1)	hegira, migration	*hijrā*
hijra (2)	transgender person	*hijṛā*

hore-dore hatu jol	knee-deep in water, whatever you do	*hare-dare hãṭu jal*
hortal	general strike	*hartāl*
hundi	banking system	*huṇḍi*
ilish	hilsa (a fish)	*iliś*
jal	fishing net	*jāl*
jam	blackberry	*jām*
jarigan	lament	*jārigān*
Jatiyo Shongshod	national parliament	*jātiya saṃsad*
Jatir Jonok	Father of the Nation	*jātir janak*
jatra	village opera	*jātrā*
jhum	hill agriculture	*jhum*
jihadi	Islamic warrior	*jihādī*
jilapi	a sweet	*jilāpi*
jolidhan	floating rice	*jalidhān*
jongol	forest	*jaṅgal*
Joy Bangla!	Victory to Bengal!	*jay bāṃlā*
kacha	mud-made	*kãcā*
kanthal	jackfruit	*kãṭhāl*
kheshari	grass pea	*khesāri*
khichuri	rice–lentil mix	*khicuri*
khola	open land	*kholā*
khudro nrigosthi	small ethnic group	*kṣudra nṛgōṣṭhī*
kobadi	a team sport	*kabāḍi*
kori	cowrie shell	*kaṛi*
kul	sour plum	*kul*
kuri	20	*kuṛi*
krishok	peasant	*kṛṣak*
Lalon-giti	Baul songs	*lālan-gīti*
langol	plough	*lāṅgal*
lojja	shame	*lajjā*
loshkor	sailor, lascar	*laśkar*
lungi	men's sarong	*luṅgi*
madrasha	Islamic school	*mādrāsā*
mastan	rowdy, gangster	*māstān*
maulana	Muslim scholar	*maolānā*
mazar	tomb-shrine	*mājār*
milad	thanksgiving	*milād*
mishti	sweet	*miṣṭi*
mofussil	countryside	*maphasval*
mojlish	village gathering	*majliś*
monga	near-famine	*maṅgā*

mongolkabbo	poem praising deities	*maṅgalkābya*
mostan	rowdy, gangster	*mastān*
mouza	revenue village	*maujā*
Muhajir, Mohajir	immigrant	*muhājir*
Mujibbad	Mujibism	*mujibbād*
Mukti Bahini	freedom fighters	*mukti bāhinī*
mukti joddha	freedom fighter	*mukti joddhā*
nobab	nawab, ruler	*nabāb*
olondaz	Dutch; pirate	*olandāj*
panta bhat	soaked rice	*pāntā bhāt*
para	hamlet	*pāṛā*
paesh	a sweet dish	*pāyes*
pir, pirani	spiritual guide	*pīr, pīrani*
pitha	rice-flour cake	*piṭhā*
Pohela Boishakh	Bengali New Year	*pahelā baiśākh*
porgona	subdivision	*parganā*
porota	flatbread	*paroṭā*
poti-ninda	anti-husband tirade	*pati-nindā*
potti	village	*paṭṭi*
pottonidari	sub-infeudation	*pattanidāri*
pukur	pond	*pukur*
raiyot	tenant	*rāiyat*
rastrobhasha	national language	*rāṣṭrabhāsā*
razbari	palace	*rājbāṛi*
Rokkhi Bahini	Security Force	*rakṣī bāhinī*
roshkodom	a sweet	*raskadam*
roshmalai	a sweet	*rasmālāi*
roshogolla	a sweet	*rasagollā*
ruti	flatbread	*ruṭi*
shadhin	independent	*swādhīn*
shai	religious guide	*sãi*
Shanti Bahini	Peace Force	*śānti bāhinī*
shankari	conch-shell-maker	*śãkhāri*
shari	saree/sari	*śāṛī*
shemai	a sweet dish	*semāi*
shishu (1)	river dolphin	*śiśu; śuśuk*
shishu (2)	child	*śiśu*
shobha	association	*sabhā*
shodeshi	own-country	*swadeśi*
shohid minar	martyrs' memorial	*śahīd minār*
shomaz	congregation	*samāj*
Shonar Bangla	Golden Bengal	*sonār bāṃlā*

shondesh	a sweet	*sandeś*
shorkar	government	*sarkār*
shuba	province	*subā*
shuntki machh	dried fish	*śũṭki mach*
swadeshi	see: shodeshi	
Taka	Bangladesh currency	*ṭākā*
tebhaga	three shares	*tebhāgā*
tezpata	cassia leaf	*tejpātā*
thana	police station; county	*thānā*
tonka	silver coin	*ṭaṅkā*
torkari	side dish	*tarkāri*
tupi	cap	*ṭupi*
ulti	hijra argot	*ulṭi*
upozati	tribe	*upajāti*
upozila	sub-district	*upajelā*
urs	pir's death anniversary	*urs, orch*
zamindar	landlord/tax collector	*jamindār* or *jamidār*
zindabad!	long live!	*jindābād*

Notes

1 A LAND OF WATER AND SILT

1 Whitcombe (2012), 2223; Brammer (2016a).
2 Darian (1978).
3 Bergmann (2018); Straume et al. (2019).
4 J. Bandyopadhyay (1995); Brammer (2004).
5 Brammer (2016b).
6 S. M. I. Huq and Shoaib (2013).
7 Sommer and Mosley (1973).
8 Mirza (2003); cf. Philip et al. (2019).
9 N. Hossain (2018a).
10 Bertocci (1970; 1996).
11 Brammer (2014; 2016b); T. Rashid (2014).

2 JUNGLE, FIELDS, CITIES AND STATES

1 Magon de Clos-Doré (1822); Guhathakurta and Van Schendel (2013), 80–2.
2 Creative Conservation Alliance (2016).
3 Basak and Srivastava (2017); Van Driem (2016); M. Hazarika (2017); G. Sultana et al. (2015); Boivin et al. (2013); Gazi et al. (2013).
4 This has remained true for most rural dwellings across the millennia. Iftekhar Ahmed (2012).
5 D. K. Chakrabarti (1992); Swadhin Sen (2002); Mitri and Neog (2016); Basak and Srivastava (2017); S. H. Jahan (2018).
6 For overviews, see R. Chakravarti (2018); M. S. Rashid (2018). For a chronology of the region since the establishment of agriculture, see K. Chakrabarti and S. Chakrabarti (2013), xxiii–xxxii.
7 Civáň et al. (2016); Van Driem (2017); P. Roy (2019).
8 District-wise lists of rice cultivars can be found in Hunter (1876); Travis et al. (2015).
9 A. Akmam (2011); Rayhan (2012); S. M. Rahman et al. (2018).
10 Glassie (1997).
11 G. Sengupta et al. (2007).
12 Shariful Islam (2018).

13 Salles (2018); P. Roy (2019).
14 Bautze (1995).
15 Goswami, n.d.; Shamsuddin (2015).
16 Samaren Roy (1981); Li et al. (2018).
17 Eaton (1993), 3.
18 Clark (1955), 511.
19 Eaton (1993), 4.
20 M. Hazarika (2012; 2017); H. P. Ray (2006); Swadhin Sen (2015; 2017).
21 Darian (1978), 138.
22 Darian (1978).
23 Knutson (2012); Furui (2017b); A. M. Chowdhury and Chakravarti (2018), 499–898.
24 A. M. Chowdhury (2003a; 2003b).
25 Panja (2003); Swadhin Sen et al. (2014).

3 A REGION OF MULTIPLE FRONTIERS

1 Nicholas (2001); Eaton (1990; 1993).
2 Sopher (1964); Misbahuzzaman (2016).
3 Fleming (2013), 578. Also Furui (2017a; 2017b); Griffiths (2018).
4 Magon de Clos-Doré (1822), 76, 80 (my translation); Guhathakurta and Van Schendel (2013), 80–2.
5 Sugata Bose (1993), 8–37.
6 Geertz (1963).
7 Leach (1960).
8 Van Schendel et al. (2000); T. M. Chowdhury (2016); N. Uddin and Gerharz (2017).
9 Chowdhury and Chakravarti (2018), 2:271–352.
10 Xuanzang (tr. Samuel Beal) in: Guhathakurta and Van Schendel (2013), 37–9.
11 Nicholas (1981; 2003); Dimock (1989); Curley (2001); Nandy (2001); K. Chatterjee (2008; 2013); Lorea (2018b).
12 Clark (1955), 506.
13 Dimock (1963); W. L. Smith (1980).
14 Clark (1955).
15 Van Schendel (2015a).
16 Eaton (1993), xxi.
17 Sirajul Islam (2003b).
18 Shah Jalal's birthplace is disputed. Here I follow A. Karim (2003), who bases himself on an inscription found in Sylhet.
19 Mackintosh-Smith (2002), 253–4.
20 Eaton (2001), 36. Cf. Stewart (2001).
21 Eaton (1993), 267; Stewart (2001); Nicholas (2001); S. M. Uddin (2006).
22 Eaton (1993), 303; Hatley (2007).
23 Ludden (2003b).

24 Lewin (1869); Dalton (1872); Bernot (1967); Brauns and Löffler (1990); M. Zakaria (2017); Peterson (2019).
25 Bal (2007); Qureshi (1984); Gain (1995).
26 Sukumar Sen (1960).
27 Dimock (1963), 5.
28 Van Schendel (1992b).
29 For example, Marma is written in Burmese script and Mro (Mru) in both Latin script and a new Mro script, developed in the 1980s. Recently the Chak (Sak) have also developed their own script. Cf. www .ethnologue.com/country/BD; https://independent.academia.edu /huziwarakeisuke.
30 The Bengali and Assamese languages share the Eastern Nagari script (*pūrbī nāgarī lipi*), with minor variations. This script has also been widely used for Sylheti, Chakma, Chittagonian and Rohingya. In recent decades, however, campaigns to abandon this script and to (re) introduce the Sylheti *[Jalalabadi] Nagri* script, the Chakma *Ojhopath* script and the Rohingya *Hanifi* script have been variously successful. For examples of the Sylheti script, see https://eap.bl.uk/project/EAP071.
31 Stewart (2004), 6; Dimock (1963).
32 Nasrin (1993).
33 W. L. Smith (1979).
34 A. Roy (2001); Jalais (2010).
35 Togawa (2008); Callan (2008); Bertocci (2006); Harder (2011).
36 W. Ahmed (2003).
37 Stewart (2004; 2013a); S. Zakaria (2013); K. Chatterjee (2013); S. Choudhury (1979); Jalais (2010); N. Khan (2016); Sudipta Sen (2017).
38 P. Hasan (2014).
39 S. J. Ahmed (2009): Mukharji (2011).
40 S. Zakaria (2013); S. J. Ahmed (2006).
41 N. Chaudhuri (1951), 31–4. Also Togawa (2008).
42 Stewart (2013a), x.
43 Openshaw (2002); Dimock (1989); F. Bhattacharya (2003); Knight (2011); Solomon et al. (2017).
44   Tomār path dhāikyāchhe mandire masjide,
    tomār dāk śuni, sāi, chalte nā pāi,
    ruiksya dāṛāy gurute morshede. . .,
    tor duyāre nānān tālā, purān korān tasbi mālā.
    hāy guru, ei biṣam jwālā, kãindya madan mare khede.
            Adapted from Shamsuzzaman Khan (1987), 1:297. Also Solomon et al. (2017).
45 Nandi (2014); Swaraj Basu (2003).

4 THE DELTA AS A CROSSROADS

1 Mackintosh-Smith (2002), 254.
2 P. C. Chakravarti (1930); Berthet (2015).
3 H. P. Ray (2003), 80; Suchandra Ghosh (2017).
4 W. L. Smith (1980), 90.
5 R. Chakravarti (2003), 183; H. P. Ray (2003); Suchandra Ghosh (2017).
6 Moudud (1992); Shahed (2018). Also Guhathakurta and Van Schendel (2013), 40–1.
7 Moudud (1992), 61; R. Sultana (1994), 77.
8 Deyell (2010); Basu Majumdar (2018); Ludden (2019).
9 H. P. Ray (2003), 83.
10 Schoff (1912).
11 Van Schendel (2015a).
12 Quoted in Eaton (2009), 200.
13 R. Chakravarti (2003), 184.
14 Ludden (2019); Yang (2004).
15 R. Chakravarti (2003); Chaudhury (2003); Suchandra Ghosh (2017).
16 Prakash (1985), 27–34; Prakash (2004), 451.
17 H. P. Ray (2003), 30–6; Deyell (2010).
18 Hambly (1974).
19 Church (2004).
20 Chaudhury (2003), 188; cf. Prakash (1985), 28.
21 Hall (2004), 251.
22 K. N. Chaudhuri (1990), 311–12.
23 Chaudhury (2003), 188.
24 Deyell (2010), 90.
25 A. Ray (2003); Campos (1919), 26–43, 66–80; Chadha (2005); Zami and Lorea (2016).
26 Van Schendel (2015a).
27 Prakash (1985), 258.
28 Prakash (1985), 53, 75, 118–41.
29 Detail of the drawing by Fouquet de Champigny titled 'Plan du comptoir de Dacca et de tous les terrains qui en dependent'. Fonds Ministériels, Série Géographique, CP 2PL/530. Archives Nationales d'Outre-Mer, Aix-en-Provence, France.
30 Ridley (2004). Cf. Sirajul Islam (2004).
31 Prakash (2004), 453.
32 Van Schendel (2005), 274–5.
33 Prakash (2004), 453.
34 Chaudhury (1995b).
35 Raychaudhuri (1969), 32–3, 192–211.
36 Chaudhury (1995a); Prakash (1985), 221–34, 256, 259.
37 Van der Heijden (1681). Also Guhathakurta and Van Schendel (2013), 59–64.

38　Raychaudhuri (1969), 237.
39　Campos (1919), 90, 100–11; Zami and Lorea (2016).

5 FROM THE MUGHAL EMPIRE TO THE BRITISH EMPIRE

1　J. Sarkar (1976); Tarafdar (1965).
2　Karim (1964); M. S. Hossain (2013).
3　T. M. Chowdhury (2016).
4　Raychaudhuri (1969), 38–9.
5　Schouten (1775); T. Chakraborty (2019).
6　Nathan (1936), 1:130–1; Raychaudhuri (1969), 82–4, 112–14.
7　S. Misra (2018), 10; Cederlöf (2014).
8　Raychaudhuri (1969), 113.
9　d'Hubert (2018; 2019a; 2019b).
10　Raychaudhuri (1969), 86. On cotton production, see S. Misra (2018), 15–25.
11　Raychaudhuri (1969), 223–4; Ludden (2017), 328–9.
12　Habib (1982); Raychaudhuri (1969), 204–11.
13　Solvyns (1804).
14　Chaudhury (1995a), 306–35; Chaudhury (2000).

6 BRITISH LEGACIES

1　Hunter (1868), 1:26–7, 29–30.
2　Sugata Bose (1993).
3　Cederlöf (2014b), 31.
4　T. Sengupta (2012), 62–5.
5　U. Bhattacharya (2017); T. Ghosh (2018).
6　Guha (1963); Sirajul Islam (1979); Sartori (2011).
7　Kawai (1987); Sirajul Islam (2003a); Taniguchi et al. (2007).
8　Iliopoulou (2001).
9　Sirajul Islam (1988).
10　S. U. Ahmed (1986), 75–7.
11　*Annual Report* (1934); Mevissen (2005).
12　Cederlöf (2019).
13　Van Schendel (1995), 38–70; Iqbal (2010; 2017).
14　B. B. Chaudhuri (2003).
15　T. O. Ali (2018).
16　Bose (1993).
17　T. O. Ali (2018), 95–102.
18　Giunchi (2010).
19　Long (1868), 92–111; Acharya (1978); Kakkar (2017).
20　M. M. Kabir (2009).
21　'Medical Education' (1855/2006), 39.
22　Prasad (2015).
23　Iqbal (2010), 117–39; Klein (2001); Whitcombe (2012).

24 Eaton (1990).
25 Landell Mills (1998); Mukul et al. (2012).
26 The intellectual connections and antecedents of these movements are complex. They were inspired by the teachings of Muhammad Ibn 'Abd al-Wahhab in Arabia, Shah Wali Allah in Delhi and Sayyid Ahmad Barelwi in Patna. Yarrington (2010), 73–80.
27 Later purification movements have also been influenced by the Deoband school, which developed in north India in the second half of the nineteenth century. Yarrington (2010), 77–9.
28 S. Bandyopadhyay (1990; 1997); S. Zakaria (2013), 121–6; Guhathakurta and Van Schendel (2013), 109–12; Lorea (2017); Mukherjee (2018).
29 N. Bose (2014a); Daechsel (2015); M. Sarkar (2015); S. Bandyopadhyay (1990).
30 Broomfield (1968); Chatterji (1995); Sartori (2008).
31 Tagore (1919); N. C. Chaudhuri (1951); Mazumdar (1977); P. Chatterjee (2002); T. Sengupta (2013).
32 Iftikhar-ul-Awwal (1992).
33 S. U. Ahmed (1986); Mamoon (1993).

7 A CLOSING AGRARIAN FRONTIER

1 Sugata Bose (1993); B. B. Chaudhuri (2003); M. Mufakharul Islam (2003); T. O. Ali (2018).
2 Ludden (2017); Iqbal (2014).
3 Van Schendel (2005), 191–255; Alexander et al. (2016).
4 Van Schendel (1981/1982), 64–7.
5 Van Schendel (1986).
6 Van Schendel (1991), 302–4.
7 https://esa.un.org/unpd/wpp/. Figures for 2020.
8 Iqbal (2010), 140–59; Iqbal (2005; 2009).
9 T. O. Ali (2018).
10 Van Schendel and Faraizi (1984).
11 Van Schendel (2012; 2015b; 2017).
12 Gain et al. (2005), 47–69; Gain (2009).
13 Greenough (1982), 309; A. Sen (1981), 52–85; Iqbal (2011).
14

> *Sā-re-gā-mā-pā-dhā-ni,*
> *Bōm phelechhe Jāpāni,*
> *Bōmār maidhe keuṭe sāp,*
> *Briṭiś bale bāp-re-bāp.*

Adapted from Shahed (1993), 155.

15 Greenough (1982), 89.
16 Greenough (1982), 85, 97, 307; A. Sen (1981); M. Mufakharul Islam (2007).
17 Jahangir (1993); Sarkar (1998); Sunderason (2017).

8 COLONIAL CONFLICTS

1 Cederlöf (2009).
2 M. H. Khan (2003); S. Roy (1980); A. Bhattacharya (2014); Bhattacharyya (2016).
3 R. L. Chakraborty (1977); Lees (2015); Van Schendel (1985).
4 Mamoon (1985–2000).
5 Kling (1966).
6 J. M. Tagore, cited in Sugata Bose (1993), 158.
7 Mamoon (2007).
8 S. Sarkar (1973).
9 Laushey (1975); Heehs (1993).
10 *Chottogram Jubobidroho* (2001); J. Sengupta (2003).
11 Sil (2002), 126; Chakrabarty (2004).
12 Dutta and Robinson (1997), 487.
13 S. Bandyopadhyay (1990).
14 T. M. Murshid (1995).
15 R. Ahmed (2001), 7.
16 R. Ahmed (1981).
17 Chatterji (1995).
18 T. O. Ali (2017), 1338; Banerjee (2017).
19 Das (1991); S. Bandyopadhyay (2003).
20 Hossein (1908/2005); R. S. Hossain (2005); Quayum (2016).
21 S. S. Islam (1992).

9 TOWARDS PARTITION

1 'Presidential Address' (1993).
2 Jalal (1985).
3 N. Bose (2014a); Custers (2010).
4 Cooper (1988).
5 Hore (1990).
6 Franda (1970), 588; Umar (2004).
7 Umar (2004), 138–44.
8 Gandhian activist Suhasini Das, quoted in Ashfaque Hossain (2013), 276.
9 Chatterji (1995).
10 Hashmi (1992).
11 Sugata Bose and Jalal (1998), 188.

10 PARTITION

1 Ashfaque Hossain (2013).
2 Van Schendel (2002; 2005).
3 Shewly (2017).
4 Van Schendel (2005), 296–331; Sur (2016).
5 Chatterji (1999); Ludden (2003b).

6 Chatterji (1999); A. Saikia (2016).
7 A. Kamal (2009), 11, citing Tapan Roy Chowdhury.

11 POPULATION EXCHANGE

1 Gardner (1995); Bald (2015); Alexander et al. (2016).
2 Imtiaz Ahmed et al. (2004); Alexander et al. (2016), esp. 52–101.
3 M. M. Rahman and Van Schendel (2003); Chatterji (2007b), 105–208; H. Roy (2012).
4 Nasrin (2002). Also Guhathakurta and Van Schendel (2013), 175–6.
5 Bal (2004); Leider (2016b).
6 S. Bandyopadhyay (2004), 191–239; D. Sen (2012).
7 A. Kamal (2009), 24–5, quoting Ajoy Bhattacharya and Troilokyanath Chakrabarty, respectively.
8 M. Ray (2002); P. K. Chakrabarti (1999); H. Roy (2012).
9 Lorea (2017), 4. Also S. Bandyopadhyay (1990; 1997); Chatterji (2007a); Anwesha Sengupta (2017); Mukherjee (2018).
10 For an attempt to estimate two-way flows in one district on the basis of official statistics, see Subhrashi Ghosh (2014).
11 Chakrabarty (1996); U. Sen (2014).
12 N. Zaman (1999), 127–56; A. J. Kabir (2018).
13 Guhathakurta (2000–1).
14 Jalais (2013), 262; cf. B. Roy (1994).

12 THE PAKISTAN EXPERIMENT

1 Maswani (1979), 84–5.
2 *Five Years of Pakistan* (1952), 243.
3 Muhammad A. Khan (1967), 22.
4 Zaheer (1994), 21.
5 R. Jahan (1972), 12. Also Toor (2009).
6 A. Kamal (2009), 22.
7 Anisuzzaman (1993), 91–116; Toor (2009).
8 Zaidi (2003); Oldenburg (1985).
9 A. Kamal (2009).
10 Khasru and Zami (2016).
11 East Pakistan (1958), 35.
12 Rashiduzzaman (1970); Umar (2004); Custers (2010).
13 S. M. Uddin (2006).
14 Ahmed identifies the performance of Munier Chowdhury's play *Kabar* ('The Grave') as '*the* defining moment in the narration of the nation (Bangladesh now) in its theatrical context'. This play was first performed surreptitiously by inmates of Dhaka Central Jail on 21 February 1953 to commemorate the real-life confrontation of the previous 21 February. S. J. Ahmed (2014).
15 Saleem (n.d. [2006]); Maniruzzaman (1967); Talbot (1998); Toor (2009).

16 Zaheer (1994), 26.
17 Park and Wheeler (1954); M. M. Rahman (1999).
18 'Muslim League Debacle' (1954).
19 Callard (1957).
20 Custers (2010), 243.
21 Jalal (1995a, 295–6; 1995b).
22 Muhammad A. Khan (1967), 187.
23 Singhal (1962). For the very similar words of his successor as a dictator, Yahya Khan, see A. R. Siddiqi (2004), 14–15.
24 I borrow this term from Timothy Brittain-Catlin (2014).

13 PAKISTAN FALLS APART

1 Ataur Rahman Khan, *Swairacharer Dash Bachar* (Dhaka, 1974), 45, quoted in A. Kamal (2009), 27.
2 Anisuzzaman (2008).
3 Maniruzzaman (1967).
4 Rashiduzzaman (1970); R. Khan (1999).
5 Umar (2004); Singh (1983–92); Van Schendel (2014).
6 T. Ali (1970); Custers (2010).
7 Mohammad A. Khan (1983), 28.
8 A. R. Siddiqi (2004), 46; cf. 47–9. Also N. Hossain (2018a).
9 Baxter (1971); R. Jahan (1972); Mujahid (1971).
10 R. T. Roy (2003); Van Schendel et al. (2000).
11 Salim (2001).
12 A. R. Siddiqi (2004), 58; S. A. Karim (2005), 172–203.

14 EAST PAKISTANI LIVELIHOODS

1 For a classic study of kinship in rural East Pakistan, see Hara (1991).
2 *Statistical Pocket-Book* (1970); *Statistical Digest* (1973); T. M. Khan and Bergan (1966); Andrus et al. (1951), 61; K. Ahmad (1969); Boyce (1987).
3 Jalal (1990), 3.
4 Dewey (1991); A. M. Huq (1958); K. P. Misra (1972); Bajwa (1996), 240.
5 Brecher and Abbas (1972).
6 K. P. Misra (1972); R. Jahan (1972), 36; Nurul Islam (1972); Sobhan (1971).
7 Andrus and Mohammed (1966), 270; S. R. Bose (1968).
8 R. Jahan (1972), 30–6.
9 Nurul Islam (1972).
10 Lambert (1959).
11 P. M. M. Rahman (1994), 73.
12 Van Schendel (1991), 306–7.
13 Van Schendel (2005), 157–60; Anwesha Sengupta (2018); T. O. Ali (2018), 176–93.
14 Van Schendel (2005), 147–90. Cf. M. M. Rahman and Van Schendel (1997).

15 Brecher and Abbas (1972), 101–2; Van Schendel (1995).
16 Gallagher (1992), 637; cf. Kirkpatrick (2003).

15 THE ROOTS OF AID DEPENDENCE

1 Van Schendel (1995), 38–70; Iqbal (2010; 2017).
2 Jalal (1990), 158.
3 Wilcox (1969).
4 Talbot (1998), 170–1; R. Jahan (1972), 68–85.
5 Brecher and Abbas (1972), 62; Swinnerton (1953); Jabeen and Mazhar (2011).
6 Bhuiyan et al. (2005); M. N. Islam (1960), 12.
7 Raper (1970), 14–15.
8 Raper (1970), 18.
9 Rashiduzzaman (1968).
10 Nurul Islam (1972).
11 A. H. Khan (1963), 133–4, quoted in R. Jahan (1972), 114.
12 Sobhan (1968); Raper (1970), 98–125.
13 Sobhan (1982), 2.
14 Lerski (1968), 404; Brecher and Abbas (1972).
15 Nurul Islam (1972), 519.
16 H. Chakma et al. (1995); Van Schendel et al. (2000); S. Chakma (2018).
17 Brecher and Abbas (1972), 171.

16 A NEW ELITE AND CULTURAL RENEWAL

1 R. Jahan (1972), 44.
2 N. Bose (2018); Iqbal (2018).
3 S. Ahmad (1960).
4 Alamgir Kabir (1979).
5 Kapp et al. (1975), 101.
6 Rashiduzzaman (1968), 93; Raper (1970), 5.
7 For example the 'Ekushe' songs, eulogising the sacrifices of 21 February 1952 (see Plate 12.1). See also N. Ahmed (2014); Raju (2012).
8 S. J. Ahmed (2006), 80–3; S. Zakaria (2013), 31–44.
9 Z. R. Siddiqui (1997).

17 ARMED CONFLICT

1 Bass (2016), 140. See also the sharp rebuttals by Mandal and Mookherjee (2007) and Mohaiemen (2011a; 2011b) of Sarmila Bose's interventions, culminating in her book (2011a; cf. 2011b).
2 'Political Activities Banned' (1971).
3 Salik (1984b), 7:4–8. Also Guhathakurta and Van Schendel (2013), 231–6.
4 *Hamoodur Rahman Commission Report* (1974).

5 Imtiaz Ahmed (2009), 76–8. Also Guhathakurta and Van Schendel (2013), 237–40.

6 *Hamoodur Rahman Commission Report* (1974). Also M. Siddiki (2018).

7 J. H. Gill (2003), 11; M. M. Rahman (2005).

8 J. Imam (1986/1990), entry for 9 May 1971.

9 Biswas (2005).

10 Translated by Abrar Ahmad, in N. Zaman (2003), 9–10. Cf. N. Zaman (2001); Anam (2007); Dulal (1987).

11 For example Mizan (2018).

12 J. H. Gill (2003), 21.

13 For a description of events in a part of the Chittagong Hill Tracts that stayed under Pakistani control until the very end of the war, see Van Schendel (2016).

14 *The Events in East Pakistan* (1972); W. Akmam (2002).

15 Quaderi (1972); Quadir (1997).

16 Sisson and Rose (1990); Raghavan (2013).

17 Hersh (1983), 444–64.

18 Hersh (1983), 449. Both Bass (2013) and Raghavan (2013) provide detailed accounts of the complexity of the international context.

19 Salik (1998); A. R. Siddiqi (2004); Zaheer (1994); Niazi (1999).

20 As told by his one-time advisor Roedad Khan in the documentary 'Asian Century: The Rise and Fall of Mujib', directed by Shehzad Hameed Ahmad (2017).

21 Salim (2012).

18 A STATE IS BORN

1 Salik (1984a); Memon (1983); Niazi (1999), 232–51.

2 *Ekattorer Ghatok* (1987); S. A. Karim (2005), 296–8; D'Costa and Hossain (2010); Bass (2016).

3 Matiur Rahman and Hasan (1980), 10–34.

4 Redclift (2013; 2016); Haider (2018).

5 Rummel (1998), 153–63.

6 Biswas (2007); Afsan Chowdhury (2007).

7 Ibrahim (1998); S. Akhtar et al. (2001); D'Costa (2010); D'Costa and Hossain (2010); Y. Saikia (2011); Mookherjee (2015); Mookherjee and Keya (2019).

8 O. Ahmad (2003), 252; Y. Saikia (2011), 175.

9 Oliver (1978), xvi.

10 Jahan (1973, 200; 2005).

11 S. A. Karim (2005), 249–55.

12 Maniruzzaman (1980), 155.

13 *Gonoprojatontri Bangladesher Shongbidhan* (1972), 12; B. Siddiqi (2018).

14 Z. R. Khan (1984), 106.

15 Nurul Islam (1977).

16 Maniruzzaman (1980), 159.

17 S. A. Karim (2005), 272–3, 283–90.

18 S. A. Karim (2005), 305.

19 S. A. Karim (2005), 303–9.
20 Maniruzzaman (1975).
21 M. Alamgir (1980), 128–9.
22 S. A. Karim (2005), 336, cf. 367.
23 M. Alamgir (1980), 143; A. Sen (1981), 131–53.
24 Weinraub (1974).
25 S. A. Karim (2005), 345.
26 J. Sengupta (1981), 91.
27 Maniruzzaman (1976); Lifschultz (1979).

19 IMAGINING A NEW NATION

1 Various meanings of secularism in Bangladesh are analysed in Riaz (2016, 199–218) and D. M. Siddiqi (2018).
2 Sobhan (2002); Bhasin (2003); Van Schendel (2005).
3 Permanent Court of Arbitration (2014); Anderson (2015); *India & Bangladesh* (2015); Mishra (2016); Shewly (2017); Ferdoush and Jones (2018); M. M. Hasan and Jian (2019).
4 A. B. Chakma (1984), 58.
5 S. R. Imam (2005).
6 Hoek (2014b), 101. Cf. Mookherjee (2019).

20 SHAPING A POLITICAL SYSTEM

1 Maniruzzaman (1976).
2 Lifschultz (1979). A biographical novel on Colonel Taher's life (Shahaduzzaman, 2010) inspired a popular play by theatre company BotTala in 2016.
3 Tan (2005).
4 Jaffrelot (2002), 69.
5 Ahamad (1988); G. Hossain (1988); Amin (1991); Riaz (1994).
6 'Be Vigilant' (1975).
7 'Shara Deshe' (1982).
8 'Martial Law' (1982).
9 Landell Mills (1998).
10 Muhammed (1993).
11 Lewis (2011), 75–108.
12 Orgeret and Sobhan (2012); 'BDR Carnage' (2017).
13 Riaz (2014).
14 Lewis (2011), 99–102. Also Kochanek (2000).
15 Lewis (2011), 100.
16 Ali Riaz distinguished four eras: the rise and demise of authoritarianism (1972–90), hope and despair (1991–2006), democracy deficit (2007–8), and polarisation and democracy's retreat (since 2009). Riaz (2016), 4–5.
17 Sabur (2010).
18 Ruud and Islam (2016); Ruud (2018).

19 R. Hasan (2018); Adams (2019).
20 Lewis (2011), 107–8.
21 *State of Governance* (2006); Suykens (2017).

21 THE TRIUMPH OF IDENTITY POLITICS

1 Jasimuddin (1975/1986).
2 Choudhuri (1995); S. M. Uddin (2006).
3 Umar (2004).
4 Custers (2010); Mubashar Hasan (2017).
5 Muhammed (1993).
6 I. Hossain and Siddiquee (2004).
7 Nargis and Pereira (2002); *Eclipse* (1994).
8 Nasrin (1997); T. M. Murshid (2004); Rashiduzzaman (1994); Zafar (2005).
9 Heehs (1993).
10 Riaz (2008).
11 Rajamohan (2002); K. P. S. Gill (2004).
12 Rajamohan (2002); Lintner (2002).
13 'Breach of Faith' (2005).
14 M. Huq (2009); Samia Huq (2011).
15 Sabur (2013); D'Costa (2013); Zeitlyn (2014).
16 *Countering Jihadist Militancy* (2018); *Mapping* (2015); Saaz (2017).
17 R. D. Roy et al. (2000). Cf. D. M. Siddiqi (2018), 246–9.
18 Van Schendel (1992a).
19 *'Life Is Not Ours'* (2000).
20 Braithwaite and D'Costa (2018), 321–62; M. S. Chowdhury and Chakma (2018), 97–104.
21 Adnan and Dastidar (2011).
22 F. Alamgir (2017); Siraj and Bal (2017); Bal and Siraj (2017); R. Datta (2018).
23 Coomaraswamy (1997); *'Life Is Not Ours'* (1997). Cf. Mohsin (1997); L. Karim (1998).
24 M. S. Chowdhury and Chakma (2018), 67–70.
25 N. Uddin (2018).
26 M. S. Chowdhury and Chakma (2018).
27 Bal and Siraj (2017); Gerharz (2018).
28 Kochanek (2000), 547. Cf. Riaz (2016).
29 *Judge, Jury, and Executioner* (2006).
30 S. Kabir (1995; 1998); Jahangir (1998).
31 Mohaiemen (2016).
32 M. Uddin et al. (2019).

22 TRANSNATIONAL LINKAGES

1 Sobhan (1982), 7.
2 Faaland and Parkinson (1976).

3 World Bank (2017).

4 Muhammad (2006); Shahzad Uddin (2005).

5 Sobhan (1982); Wood (1994).

6 Feldman (2003); Lewis (2003).

7 BRAC (www.brac.net/about.htm). For its current self-representation, see www.brac.net/who-we-are.

8 Grameen Bank (www.grameen.com).

9 Adnan (1992); Brammer (1990; 2004); Khalequzzaman (2016); Yasmin et al. (2018); *Bangladesh Delta Plan 2100* (2018). For ideas about alternative futures, see https://bengal.institute.

10 Mooney (2016). See also Wahed and Rahman (2018); Liu and Pandit (2018); Chung (2018).

11 Alexander et al. (2016), 52–101.

12 De Bruyn and Kuddus (2005); Sarker and Islam (2018).

13 Gardner and Ahmed (2006); Alexander et al. (2016).

14 T. Siddiqui (2005); Dannecker (2005).

15 Mapril (2014); Sur and Van Meeteren (2018). For visual representations, see, for example, *Deshantori* (2006), *Licu's Holidays* (2007) and *A Life Suspended* (2013).

16 Imtiaz Ahmed and Iqbal (2016).

17 T. Siddiqui (2004); Knights (1996); Sabur (2010; 2014).

18 Akhtar et al. (2001); Van Schendel (2005), 191–255; Sur (2013); Sahana Ghosh (2015); cf. S. Hazarika (2000).

19 G. Ghosh (2015); Shamshad (2017).

20 Ramachandran (1999).

21 Van Schendel (2005).

22 Gardner (2006).

23 Zaman and Biswas (2017).

24 Charney (1999); Farzana (2015); Leider (2016a); Mazumder (2019); Prasse-Freeman and Mausert (2020).

25 Van Schendel (2015a).

26 Buchanan (1799), 237.

27 Chin (1953). See also Van Schendel (2001b), 416.

28 Tun (2015), 155–66.

29 Barman and Neo (2013), 50–2; *Full Report* (2012); Ahrar Ahmad (2013), 80.

30 Cheesman (2017).

31 Guhathakurta (2017); N. Murshid (2018); Berthet (2013).

23 BOOM OR BUST?

1 Lewis (2011), 7.

2 Lewis (2011) provides an exemplary introduction to the political economy of contemporary Bangladesh.

3 Quibria (1997).

4 Kabeer (2001).

5 Shadlee Rahman (2018).

6 *Independent Review* (2018); N. Ahasan (2018).
7 Rogaly et al. (1999); cf. Boyce (1987); H. Rashid (2005), 55–78; Adnan (2016); A. Ahasan and Gardner (2016); Feldman (2016).
8 Van Schendel (1981/1982).
9 *45 Years Agriculture Statistics* (2018).
10 Balcombe et al. (2007); Timsina et al. (2018).
11 T. O. Ali (2018), 195–8.
12 Nuruzzaman (2006); Sanzidur Rahman et al. (2017).
13 A. K. Datta (1998); Guhathakurta (2003); Paprocki and Cons (2014); Abdullah et al. (2017); Akber et al. (2017).
14 Ansari (2013).
15 M. S. Karim (2009); Gregson et al. (2010); S. M. M. Rahman (2016).
16 Ahsan (1997); T. Choudhury (2013).
17 Kabeer (2000); Feldman (2009); D. M. Siddiqi (2015); Ashraf and Prentice (2019).
18 K. Siddiqui et al. (1990); Nazrul Islam and Ahsan (1996); Begum (2007).
19 Conticini and Hulme (2007).
20 M. S. Hossain (2013); Mahbubur Rahman (2016); Rahman and Imon (2017).
21 Parvez and Kashem (2018).
22 World Bank (2018), 3.
23 A. H. Smith et al. (2000), 1093. Cf. World Bank (2018), 26; M. T. A Chowdhury (2016); S. M. I. Huq and Shoaib (2013).
24 World Bank (2018), 2.
25 Crow et al. (1995); I. Hossain (1998); Khalid (2004).
26 Swain (1996).
27 M. S. Islam and Islam (2016).
28 Nazrul Islam (2005); M. S. Karim et al. (2012); Gain (2002).
29 Dastagir (2015); Trotter et al. (2017); Delaporte and Maurel (2018); Jacobs et al. (2019).
30 Brammer (2014). For a long-term comparison, see T. Rashid (2014).
31 Brammer (2014), 59.
32 Brammer (2014), 59–60. Cf. Nicholls et al. (2018).
33 Trotter et al. (2017); Jacobs et al. (2019).
34 Dastagir (2015); Mohammad Ataur Rahman and Rahman (2015); Delaporte and Maurel (2018); Brammer (2014; 2016b).
35 Iqbal (2019).
36 Cons (2018).
37 Stojanov et al. (2017), 358.
38 Cons (2018). Also Paprocki (2018); M. K. Hasan et al. (2018b).
39 Saiful Islam and Khan (2017); Bedi (2018).
40 B. Imam (2003). Gardner et al. (2012); Gardner et al. (2014); Gardner (2018).
41 Gilbert (2015).
42 N. S. Chowdhury (2016); Bedi (2015); M. K. Chakma (2015); Luthfa (2017); Nuremowla (2016).
43 Seddiky (2014); Yousuf (2018).

44 R. Karim (2018); I. A. Siddiki (2015); Bedi (2018).

45 For an introduction to the history of fisheries in Bengal, see Pokrant et al. (2001).

46 Gain (2002), 101–86; Ahammad et al. (2019).

47 Thompson and Islam (2010).

48 Adnan (2004). For a survey of what may be the last toehold of some endangered species in Bangladesh, see Creative Conservation Alliance (2016).

49 Sirajul Islam (1988).

50 Richards and Flint (1990), 27.

51 Iftekhar and Islam (2004); M. Ali et al (2006).

52 Richards and Flint (1990), 30.

53 Khanom and Buckley (2015).

54 Mani et al. (2018), 8, 47.

24 GENDER MOVEMENTS

1 Early gender systems and sexual behaviour are explored in Suchandra Ghosh and Pal (2018), 14–6; Husain (2018); Dasgupta (2018). For gendered power among affluent, cosmopolitan Bangladeshis in the twenty-first century, see Sabur (2010; 2014).

2 Stewart (2004); W. L. Smith (1979); Dimock (1963); Nasrin (1993); S. J. Ahmed (2011).

3 Openshaw (2002); Solomon et al. (2017); Lorea (2018a). Also S. J. Ahmed (2011).

4 T. Sarkar (1999), 169. Originally published as Debi (1897).

5 For more examples, see Southard (1996); K. Sen (2004).

6 Mazumdar (1977), 204. Also Guhathakurta and Van Schendel (2013), 142.

7 *Statistical Pocket Book* (1988), 278.

8 *Education Scenario* (2017), 16.

9 For the complexity of ideas about gender held by a group of illiterate and semi-literate rural women, see Alam (2018).

10 Rozario (2007); U. B. F. Sultana (2015).

11 S. P. Huq (2003); F. D. Chowdhury (2009); S. P. Huq (2012); Panday and Li (2014); N. Hossain (2018b).

12 Shehabuddin (2008).

13 Shehabuddin (2014); E. H. Chowdhury (2009); D. M. Siddiqi (2011a; 2011b); A. J. Kabir (2018).

14 Azim (2005).

15 Azim (2000); R. Chowdhury (2006); H. Sultana (2015). Also Zarina R. Khan and Arefeen (1989).

16 Sinha (1995); Dimeo (2002); Subho Basu and Banerjee (2006). For a general treatment of colonial and post-colonial masculinities, see Connell (2016).

17 H. Rahman (2012), 18; A. R. Siddiqi (2004), 22; Muhammad A. Khan (1967), 187; Roedad Khan in the documentary 'Asian Century: The Rise and Fall of Mujib'. See Mookherjee (2015), 164–5; Adnan Hossain (2019).

18 For example, the diary that Md. Bosharot Ali, a villager in Comilla district, kept from 1923 to 1943. Guhathakurta and Van Schendel (2013), 137–9; M. M. Rahman (2011). Cf. M. M. Rahman and Van Schendel (1997), 268–71; M. E. Khan et al. (2014), 85–132, 155–230; White (2017).

19 Imtiaz (2012). Also Shuchi Karim (2012); Awwal (2018); Adnan Hossain (2019); M. E. Khan et al. (2014), 85–132, 155–230; M. K. Hasan et al. (2019). On substance use (a mostly male and urban phenomenon), see M. Kamal et al. (2018).

20 M. K. Hasan et al. (2018a; 2019), 357. Cf. M. E. Khan and Townsend (2014).

21 Physical violence against wives is thought to be correlated with dowry demand at the time of marriage, an indicator of patriarchal attitudes. Naved and Persson (2010).

22 Imtiaz et al. (2017), 13. Cf. M. E. Khan and Townsend (2014).

23 Imtiaz (2013), 27. For male views, see Yount et al. (2016).

24 Interlocutors quoted in Schuler et al. (2018), 119–20.

25 Vanita (2005), 548.

26 Hambly (1974), 127, 130.

27 Adnan Hossain (2012, 500; 2018, 323–4). For similar findings among hijras in the Sylhet borderland, see Hussain (2013), 77–100. Cf. Hollerbach et al. (2014), 88; Jebin (2018).

28 Adnan Hossain (2017).

29 *Invisible Minority* (2015); Mannan (n.d); Ebert (2012); Hussain (2009a).

30 Shuchi Karim (2012); Hollerbach et al. (2014), 99–100.

31 D. M. Siddiqi (2011c), S5, 5.

32 https://roopbaan.org; www.boysofbangladesh.org; www.dheeblog.com. Also Shuchi Karim (2014); Deb (2011); Alim (2012).

33 An autobiographical account of being Muslim, gay, Bangladeshi, Bengali and British can be found in Momin Rahman (2014), 9–26.

34 S. A. Khan (2016); Felden (2015); Bhadury (2018).

35 'Shattering First-Person Account' (2016); Amundsen (2018); D. M. Siddiqi (2019).

36 D. M. Siddiqi (2011c), 4.

37 E. H. Chowdhury (2009); D. M. Siddiqi (2011a; 2011b; 2011c); Alim (2012); Momin Rahman (2014), 9–26; Mannan (n.d.).

25 A NATIONAL CULTURE?

1 Hoek (2013; 2014a).

2 Ruud (2014); Atkinson-Sheppard (2017); Jackman (2017).

3 *Corruption in Service Sectors* (2018); *Who Gets What and Why* (n.d.); Mamoon and Ray (1998), 245–51; S. Zaman (2005), 196–200; Hassan and Prichard (2016); M. A. Rahman (2018); Hoque and Michelutti (2018).

4 Khan and Afroze (1999); Lewis (2011), 133–4. For aspiring rural mostans, see Hoque and Michelutti (2018).

5 Jackman (2017), 113; Ruud (2014); Kuttig (2019).

6 Wilce (1998); Bertocci (2006); Callan (2007).

7 B. Siddiqi (2018).

8 Feldman (2001), 1116; Rozario (2006), 378.

9 F. E. Ahmed (2011).

10 Cf. Seabrook (2001).

11 Gain (2002), 187–222.

12 Mookherjee (2007).

13 Hussain (2009b); S. Zakaria (2013); Glassie (1997).

14 For an introduction to the aesthetics of these art forms, see Glassie (1997).

15 Among the prominent post-1971 private institutions are the Bengal Foundation, Drik Picture Library, Samdani Art Foundation and Britto Arts Trust, each with their own website. For others, also outside Dhaka, see Akand (2018). Also Selim (2014); S. J. Ahmed (2014).

16 Haque and Abedin (2011). Also Shehabuddin (2011).

17 Raju (2006); Wahid (2007); Shoesmith et al. (2013).

18 Odhikar (www.odhikar.org); Ain o Salish Kendra (www.askbd.org); Reporters without Borders (www.rsf.org).

19 Suykens (2018).

20 Imtiaz Ahmed and Mohsin (2005); Sinha-Kerkhoff (2006).

21 Md. Maidul Islam (2018).

22 Greenough (1982), 70–84.

23 Tetens et al. (2003).

24 Janeja (2010); Mookherjee (2008).

25 A. Haque et al. (1996).

26 Dimeo (2001); K. Bandyopadhyay (2009).

27 K. Bandyopadhyay (2012); Adnan Hossain (2019).

28 Mubashar Hasan (2015), 545.

Bibliography

Abdullah, Abu Nasar, Bronwyn Myers, Natasha Stacey, Kerstin K. Zander and Stephen T. Garnett, 'The Impact of the Expansion of Shrimp Aquaculture on Livelihoods in Coastal Bangladesh', *Environment, Development and Sustainability*, 19 (2017), 2093–114.

Acharya, Poromesh, 'Indigenous Vernacular Education in Pre-British Era: Traditions and Problems', *Economic and Political Weekly*, 13:48 (1978), 1981, 1983–8.

Adams, Brad, 'Bangladesh's Draconian Internet Law Treats Peaceful Critics as Criminals', *Washington Post* (19 July 2019).

Adnan, Shapan, *People's Participation, NGOs, and the Flood Action Plan: An Independent Review* (Dhaka: Research and Advisory Services, 1992).

Migration, Land Alienation and Ethnic Conflict: Causes of Poverty in the Chittagong Hill Tracts of Bangladesh (Dhaka: Research and Advisory Services, 2004).

'Alienation in Neoliberal India and Bangladesh: Diversity of Mechanisms and Theoretical Implications', *Samaj: South Asia Multidisciplinary Academic Journal*, 13 (2016), 1–22.

Adnan, Shapan, and Ranajit Dastidar, *Alienation of the Lands of Indigenous Peoples in the Chittagong Hill Tracts of Bangladesh* (Dhaka: Chittagong Hill Tracts Commission and International Work Group for Indigenous Affairs, 2011).

Ahamad, Emajuddin, *Military Rule and the Myth of Democracy* (Dhaka: University Press Limited, 1988).

Ahammad, Ronju, Natasha Ellen Stacey, Ian M. S. Eddy, Stephanie A. Tomscha and Terry Sunderland, 'Recent Trends of Forest Cover Change and Ecosystem Services in Eastern Upland Region of Bangladesh', *Science of the Total Environment*, 674 (2019), 379–89.

Ahasan, Abu, and Katy Gardner, 'Dispossession by "Development": Corporations, Elites and NGOs in Bangladesh', *Samaj: South Asia Multidisciplinary Academic Journal*, 13 (2016), 1–17.

Ahasan, Nazmul, 'Why Bangladesh's Inequality Is Likely to Rise', *Daily Star* (12 May 2018).

Ahmad, Aftab, *Swadhinota Shonggrame Bangali* [Bengalis in their struggle for independence] (Dhaka: Aftab Ahmad, 1998).

Ahmad, Ahrar, 'Bangladesh in 2012: Economic Growth, Political Under-development', *Asian Survey*, 53:1 (2013), 73–83.

Ahmad, Kamruddin, *Labour Movement in East Pakistan* (Dhaka: Progoti Publishers, 1969).

Ahmad, Oli, 'Revolution, Military Personnel and the Liberation War of Bangladesh' (PhD thesis, Oxford Brookes University, 2003).

Ahmad, Sayeed, 'An Exhibition of Drawings', *Contemporary Arts in Pakistan*, 1:7 (July 1960), 2–6, at 4.

Ahmed, Fauzia Erfan, 'Ijtihad and Lower-Middle-Class Women: Secularism in Rural Bangladesh', *Comparative Studies of South Asia, Africa and the Middle East*, 31:1 (2011), 124–32.

Ahmed, Iftekhar, 'The Courtyard in Rural Homesteads of Bangladesh', *Vernacular Architecture*, 43 (2012), 47–57.

Ahmed, Imtiaz, *Historicizing 1971 Genocide: State Versus Person* (Dhaka: University Press Limited, 2009).

Ahmed, Imtiaz, and Iftekhar Iqbal (eds.), *University of Dhaka: Making Unmaking Remaking* (Dhaka: Prothoma Prokashan, 2016).

Ahmed, Imtiaz, and Amena Mohsin, *The Birth of Minority: State, Society and the Hindu Women of Bangladesh* (Dhaka: Forum on Women in Security and International Affairs, Bangladesh Freedom Foundation, 2005).

Ahmed, Imtiaz, Abhijit Dasgupta and Kathinka Sinha-Kerkhoff (eds.), *State, Society and Displaced People in South Asia* (Dhaka: University Press Limited, 2004).

Ahmed, Nazneen, 'The Poetics of Nationalism: Cultural Resistance and Poetry in East Pakistan/Bangladesh, 1952–71', *Journal of Postcolonial Writing*, 50:3 (2014), 256–68.

Ahmed, Rafiuddin, *The Bengal Muslims 1871–1906: A Quest for Identity* (Delhi: Oxford University Press, 1981).

'Introduction: The Emergence of the Bengal Muslims', in: Rafiuddin Ahmed (ed.), *Understanding the Bengal Muslims: Interpretative Essays* (New Delhi: Oxford University Press, 2001), 1–25.

Ahmed, Reaz (comp. and ed.), *Gonomadhyome Bangladesher Muktijuddho, Kartun, Prothom Khondo/Media and Liberation War of Bangladesh, Cartoons, Vol. 1* (Dhaka: Centre for Bangladesh Studies, 2002).

Ahmed, Sharif Uddin, *Dacca: A Study in Urban History and Development* (London: Curzon Press, 1986).

Ahmed, Syed Jamil, 'Hegemony, Resistance, and Subaltern Silence: Lessons from Indigenous Performances of Bangladesh', *TDR: The Drama Review*, 50:2 (2006), 70–86.

'Performing and Supplicating Mānik Pīr: Infrapolitics in the Domain of Popular Islam', *TDR: The Drama Review*, 53:2 (2009), 51–76.

'A Psychoanalytic Reading of *Mālañcamālā, Rūpbān, Nūr Bānu*, and *Madanamañjarī*: Popular Imaginings of the Wife-Mother by the Bengali People', *Asian Ethnology*, 70:2 (2011), 223–53.

'Designs of Living in the Contemporary Theatre of Bangladesh', in: Ashis Sengupta (ed.), (2014), 135–76.

Ahmed, Wakil, 'Pir', in: Islam and Miah (eds.) (2003), 8:89–90.

Ahsan, Rosie Majid, 'Migration of Female Construction Labourers to Dhaka City, Bangladesh', *International Journal of Population Geography*, 3 (1997), 49–61.

Akand, Shawon, 'Bangladesh', *ArtAsiaPacific Almanac 2018*, 13 (2018), 85–6.

Akber, Md. Ali, Md. Ali Akber, Munir Ahmed, Md. Munsur Rahman and Mohammad Rezaur Rahman, 'Changes of Shrimp Farming in Southwest Coastal Bangladesh', *Aquaculture International*, 25 (2017), 1883–99.

Akhtar, Shahin Suraya Begum, Hameeda Hossein, Sultana Kamal and Meghna Guhathakurta (eds.), *Narir '71 O Juddhoporoborti Kotthokahini* [Women's plain stories of 1971 and the aftermath of the war] (Dhaka: Ain-O-Shalish Kendro, 2001).

Akmam, Afroz, *Early Urban Centres in Bangladesh: An Archaeological Study – 3rd Century B.C. to mid 13th Century A.D.* (Dhaka: Shahitya Prakash, 2011).

Akmam, Wardatul, 'Atrocities against Humanity during the Liberation War of Bangladesh: A Case of Genocide', *Journal of Genocide Research*, 4:4 (2002), 543–59.

Alam, Sarwar, *Perceptions of Self, Power, and Gender Among Muslim Women: Narratives from a Rural Community in Bangladesh* (Dordrecht: Springer, 2018).

Alamgir, Fariba, 'Land Politics in Chittagong Hill Tracts of Bangladesh: Dynamics of Property, Identity and Authority' (PhD thesis, University of East Anglia, 2017).

Alamgir, Mohiuddin, *Famine in South Asia: Political Economy of Mass Starvation* (Cambridge, MA: Oelgeschlager, Gunn and Hain, 1980).

Alexander, Claire, Joya Chatterji and Annu Jalais, *The Bengal Diaspora: Rethinking Muslim Migration* (Abingdon: Routledge, 2016).

Ali, Mohammad, M., Alamgir Kabir and A. T. M. Rafiqul Hoque, 'People's Attitude and Use of Forestland: Co-Evolution of Forest Administration in Bangladesh', *Small-scale Forest Economics, Management and Policy*, 5:2 (2006), 271–86.

Ali, Tariq, *Pakistan: Military Rule or People's Power* (New York: William Morrow, 1970).

Ali, Tariq Omar, 'Agrarian Forms of Islam: Mofussil Discourses on Peasant Religion in the Bengal Delta during the 1920s', *Modern Asian Studies*, 51:5 (2017), 1311–39.

  A Local History of Global Capital: Jute and Peasant Life in the Bengal Delta (Princeton, NJ: Princeton University Press, 2018).

Alim, Tanvir, 'Without Any Window: Series of Interviews with the Gay Community in Bangladesh' (2012). https://globalqueerdesi.wordpress.com

Amin, Rohul (ed.), *Ziaur Rohman Smarok Grontho* [A memento to Ziaur Rahman] (Dhaka: Hira Book Market, 1991).

Amundsen, Inge, 'The Ruins of Bangladesh's LGBT Community', *East Asia Forum* (23 March 2018). www.eastasiaforum.org

Anam, Tahmima, *A Golden Age* (London: John Murray, 2007).

Anderson, D. H., 'Bay of Bengal Maritime Boundary (Bangladesh v. India)', *American Journal of International Law*, 109:1 (2015), 146–54.

Andrus, J. Russell, and Azizali F. Mohammed, *Trade, Finance and Development in Pakistan* (Karachi: Oxford University Press, 1966).

Andrus, J. Russell, Azizali F. Mohammed and Mohammed Afzal, 'State and Private Enterprise in Pakistan', *Far Eastern Survey*, 20:7 (1951), 61–4.

Anisuzzaman, *Creativity, Reality and Identity* (Dhaka: International Centre for Bengal Studies, 1993).

'Claiming and Disclaiming a Cultural Icon: Tagore in East Pakistan and Bangladesh', *University of Toronto Quarterly*, 77:4 (2008), 1058–69.

Annual Report of the Varendra Research Society for 1932–33 and 1933–34 (Rajshahi: Varendra Research Society, 1934).

Ansari, Mohammad Nayeem Aziz, 'Hunger, Place and Seasonality: Understanding Monga Vulnerability in Northwest Bangladesh' (PhD thesis, Durham University, 2013).

Ashraf, Hasan, and Rebecca Prentice, 'Beyond Factory Safety: Labor Unions, Militant Protest, and the Accelerated Ambitions of Bangladesh's Export Garment Industry', *Dialectical Anthropology*, 43 (2019), 93–107.

Atkinson-Sheppard, Sally, '"Mastaans" and the Market for Social Protection: Exploring Mafia Groups in Dhaka, Bangladesh', *Asian Criminology*, 12 (2017), 235–53.

Awwal, Arpana, 'From Villain to Hero: Masculinity and Political Aesthetics in the Films of Bangladeshi Action Star Joshim', *BioScope: South Asian Screen Studies*, 9:1 (2018), 24–45.

Azim, Firdous, 'Women's Movements in Bangladesh', *Feminist Review*, 64 (2000), 119–21.

'Feminist Struggles in Bangladesh', *Feminist Review*, 80 (2005), 194–7.

Bajwa, Farooq Naseem, *Pakistan and the West: The First Decade 1947–1957* (Karachi: Oxford University Press, 1996).

Bal, Ellen, 'An Untold Story of the Partition: The Garos of Northern Mymensingh', in: I. Ahmed et al. (eds.) (2004), 245–79.

They Ask If We Eat Frogs: Garo Ethnicity in Bangladesh (Singapore: Institute of Southeast Asian Studies, 2007).

Bal, Ellen, and Nasrin Siraj, '"We Are the True Citizens of This Country": Vernacularisation of Democracy and Exclusion of Minorities in the Chittagong Hills of Bangladesh', *Asian Journal of Social Science*, 45 (2017), 666–92.

Balcombe, Kevin, Iain Fraser, Mizanur Rahman and Laurence Smith, 'Examining the Technical Efficiency of Rice Producers in Bangladesh', *Journal of International Development*, 19 (2007), 1–16.

Bald, Vivek, *Bengali Harlem and the Lost Histories of South Asian America* (Cambridge, MA: Harvard University Press, 2015).

Bandyopadhyay, Jayanta, 'Water Management in the Ganges–Brahmaputra Basin: Emerging Challenges for the 21st Century', *International Journal of Water Resources Development*, 11:4 (1995), 411–42.

Bandyopadhyay, Kausik, 'In Search of an Identity: The Muslims and Football in Colonial India', *Soccer and Society*, 10:6 (2009), 843–65.

Bangladesh Playing: Sport, Culture, Nation (Dhaka: ICBS Subarna, 2012).

Bandyopadhyay, Sekhar, *Caste, Politics and the Raj: Bengal 1872–1937* (Kolkata: K. P. Bagchi, 1990).

Caste, Protest and Identity in Colonial India: The Namasudras of Bengal, 1872–1947 (Richmond, UK: Curzon, 1997).

(ed.), *Bengal: Rethinking History – Essays on Historiography* (Delhi: International Centre for Bengal Studies, 2001).

'A Namasudra-Muslim Riot in Jessore-Khulna, May 1911: A Case Study in Community Formation and Communal Conflict', in: Bidyut Chakrabarty (ed.), *Communal Identity in India: Its Construction and Articulation in the Twentieth Century* (New Delhi: Oxford University Press, 2003), 214–28.

Caste, Culture and Hegemony: Social Dominance in Colonial Bengal (Delhi: Sage Publications, 2004).

Banerjee, Mou, 'The Tale of the Tailor: Munshi Mohammad Meherullah and Muslim-Christian Apologetics in Bengal, 1885-1907', *South Asian Studies*, 33:2 (2017), 122–36.

Bangla Name Desh [A country named Bangla] (Kolkata: Anondo Publishers, 1972).

Bangladesh Delta Plan 2100 (Bangladesh in the 21st Century) (Dhaka: Bangladesh Planning Commission, Government of the People's Republic of Bangladesh, 2018), 2 vols.

Bangladesh Economic Review 2017 (Dhaka: Finance Division, Ministry of Finance Government of the People's Republic of Bangladesh, 2017).

Bari, M. A., *Muktijuddher Roktim Smriti/Memoirs of a Blood Birth* (Dhaka: Banimahal Prokashoni, c. 1996).

Barman, Dalem Chandra, and Mong Sing Neo (eds.), *Human Rights Report 2012 on Indigenous Peoples in Bangladesh* (Dhaka: Kapaeeng Foundation, 2013).

Barros, João de, *Ásia de João de Barros: Dos feitos que os portugueses fizeram no descobrimento e conquista dos mares e terras do Oriente, Vol 4 (Quartadécada)* [João de Barros's Asia: The achievements of the Portuguese in the discovery and conquest of the seas and lands of the east, Vol. 4 (fourth decade)] (Lisbon, 1777–88).

Basak, Bishnupriya, and Pradeep Srivastava, 'Earliest Dates of Microlithic Industries (42–25 ka) from West Bengal, Eastern India: New Light on Modern Human Occupation in the Indian Subcontinent', *Asian Perspectives*, 56:2 (2017), 237–59.

Bass, Gary J., *The Blood Telegram: Nixon, Kissinger, and a Forgotten Genocide* (New York: Alfred A. Knopf, 2013).

'Bargaining Away Justice: India, Pakistan, and the International Politics of Impunity for the Bangladesh Genocide', *International Security*, 41:2 (2016), 140–87.

Basu, Subho, and Sikata Banerjee, 'The Quest for Manhood: Masculine Hinduism and Nation in Bengal', *Comparative Studies of South Asia, Africa and the Middle East*, 26:3 (2006), 476–90.

Basu, Swaraj, *Dynamics of a Caste Movement: The Rajbansis of North Bengal, 1910–1947* (Delhi: Manohar, 2003).

Basu Majumdar, Susmita, 'Media of Exchange: Reflections on the Monetary History', in: A. M. Chowdhury and Chakravarti (eds.) (2018), 2:233–68.

Bautze, Joachim Karl, *Early Indian Terracottas* (Leiden: E. J. Brill, 1995).

Baxter, Craig, 'Pakistan Votes – 1970', *Asian Survey*, 11:3 (1971), 197–218.

'BDR Carnage Case: HC Confirms Death for 139', *Daily Star* (November 27, 2017).

'Be Vigilant against Self-Seekers: Zia. Martial Law Won't Outlive Its Utility', *Bangladesh Observer* (12 November 1975), 1.

Bedi, Heather Plumridge, 'Right to Food, Right to Mine? Competing Human Rights Claims in Bangladesh', *Geoforum*, 59 (2015), 248–57.

'"Our Energy, Our Rights": National Extraction Legacies and Contested Energy Justice Futures in Bangladesh', *Energy Research and Social Science*, 41 (2018), 168–75.

Begum, Anwara, 'Urban Housing as an Issue of Redistribution through Planning? The Case of Dhaka City', *Social Policy and Administration*, 41:4 (2007), 410–18.

Bernot, Lucien, *Les paysans arakanais du Pakistan Oriental: le monde végétal et l'organisation sociale des réfugiés Marma (Mog)* [The Arakanese peasants of East Pakistan: The plant world and social organisation of the Marma (Mog) refugees] (Paris: Mouton, 1967), 2 vols.

Bergmann, Fenna, 'The Bengal Fan on Different Temporal and Spatial Scales: Integrating Seismoacoustic and IODP Expedition 354 Data to Examine Internal and External Controls on Depositional Processes' (PhD thesis, University of Bremen, 2018).

Berthet, Samuel, 'Les Rohingya à Chittagong (Bangladesh): enjeux d'une invisibilité' [The Rohingyas in Chittagong (Bangladesh): Issues of invisibility], *Moussons: Recherche en sciences humaines sur l'Asie du Sud-Est*, 22 (2013), 75–86.

'Boat Technology and Culture in Chittagong', *Water History*, 7 (2015), 179–97.

Bertocci, Peter J., 'Elusive Villages: Social Structure and Community Organization in Rural East Pakistan' (PhD thesis, Department of Anthropology, Michigan State University, 1970).

The Politics of Community and Culture in Bangladesh: Selected Essays (Dhaka: Centre for Social Studies, 1996).

'A Sufi Movement in Bangladesh: The Maijbhandari Tariqa and Its Followers', *Contributions to Indian Sociology* (NS), 40:1 (2006), 1–28.

Bhadury, Poushali, '"There Is No Such Thing as a Straight Woman": Queer Female Representations in South Asian Graphic Narratives', *Journal of Lesbian Studies*, 11:4 (2018), 1–11.

Bhasin, Avtar Singh (ed.), *Indian–Bangladesh Relations: Documents – 1971–2002* (New Delhi: Geetika Publishers, 2003), 5 vols.

Bhattacharya, Ananda, 'The Peripatetic Sannyasis: A Challenge to Peasant Stability and Colonial Rule?' *Indian Historical Review*, 41:1 (2014), 47–66.

Bhattacharya, France, 'De sang et de sperme : La pratique mystique bāul et son expression métaphorique dans les chants' ('Blood and semen: Bāul mystic practice and its metaphoric expression in song'), in: Véronique Bouillier and Gilles Tarabout (eds.), *Image du corps dans le monde hindou* (Paris: CRNS Éditions, 2003).

Bhattacharya, Ujjayan, 'From Surveys to Management: The Early Colonial State's Intervention in Water Resources of Bengal', *Indian Historical Review*, 44:2 (2017), 225–51.

Bhattacharyya, Ananda, 'The Wandering Fakirs of Bengal: Heroes or Villains?' *South Asia Research*, 36:1 (2016), 1–23.

Bhuiyan, Abul Hossain Ahmed, Aminul Haque Faraizi and Jim McAllister, 'Developmentalism as a Disciplinary Strategy in Bangladesh', *Modern Asian Studies*, 39:2 (2005), 349–68.

Biswas, Sukumar (ed.), *The Bangladesh Liberation War: Mujibnagar Government Documents 1971* (Dhaka: Mowla Brothers, 2005).

(ed.), *History from Below: Accounts of Participants and Eyewitness* (Dhaka: Muktijuddho Gobeshona Kendro, 2007).

Boivin, Nicole, Dorian Q. Fuller, Robin Dennell, Robin Allaby and Michael D. Petraglia, 'Human Dispersal across Diverse Environments of Asia during the Upper Pleistocene', *Quaternary International*, 300 (2013), 32–47.

Bose, Neilesh, 'Purba Pakistan Zindabad: Bengali Visions of Pakistan, 1940–1947', *Modern Asian Studies*, 48:1 (2014a), 1–36.

Recasting the Region: Language, Culture, and Islam in Colonial Bengal (New Delhi: Oxford University Press, 2014b).

'Inheritance and the Idea of "the East" in Banglaphone Thought in the Era of Decolonisation', *South Asia: Journal of South Asian Studies*, 41:4 (2018), 1–13.

Bose, Sarmila, *Dead Reckoning: Memories of the 1971 Bangladesh War* (London: Hurst, 2011a).

'"Dead Reckoning": A Response', *Economic and Political Weekly*, 46:53 (2011b), 76–9.

Bose, Sugata, *Peasant Labour and Colonial Capital: Rural Bengal since 1770* (Cambridge: Cambridge University Press, 1993).

Bose, Sugata, and Ayesha Jalal, *Modern South Asia: History, Culture, Political Economy* (London: Routledge, 1998).

Bose, Swadesh R., 'Trend of Real Income of the Rural Poor in East Pakistan, 1949–66', *Pakistan Development Review*, 8:3 (1968), 452–88.

Boyce, James K., *Agrarian Impasse in Bengal: Institutional Constraints to Technological Change* (Oxford: Oxford University Press, 1987).

Bradley-Birt, F. B., *The Romance of an Eastern Capital* (London: Smith, Elder and Co., 1906).

Braithwaite, John, and Bina D'Costa, *Cascades of Violence: War, Crime and Peacebuilding Across South Asia* (Acton, ACT: Australian National University Press, 2018).

Brammer, Hugh, 'Floods in Bangladesh: II. Flood Mitigation and Environmental Aspects', *Geographical Journal*, 156:2 (1990), 158–65.

Can Bangladesh Be Protected from Floods? (Dhaka: University Press Limited, 2004).

'Bangladesh's Dynamic Coastal Regions and Sea-level Rise', *Climate Risk Management*, 1 (2014), 51–62.

Bangladesh: Landscapes, Soil, Fertility and Climate Change (Dhaka: University Press Limited, 2016a).

'Floods, Cyclones, Drought and Climate Change in Bangladesh: A Reality Check', *International Journal of Environmental Studies*, 73:6 (2016b), 865–86.

Brauns, Claus-Dieter, and Lorenz G. Löffler, *Mru: Hill People on the Border of Bangladesh* (Basle: Birkhauser, 1990).

'Breach of Faith: Persecution of the Ahmadiyya Community in Bangladesh', *Human Rights Watch*, 17:6 (2005), 1–44.

Brecher, Irving, and S. A. Abbas, *Foreign Aid and Industrial Development in Pakistan* (Cambridge: Cambridge University Press, 1972).

Brittain-Catlin, Timothy, 'Dictator Chic', *Architectural Review* (May 2014), 114–5.

Broomfield, J. H., *Elite Conflict in a Plural Society: Twentieth-Century Bengal* (Berkeley: University of California Press, 1968).

Buchanan, Francis, 'A Comparative Vocabulary of Some of the Languages Spoken in the Burma Empire', *Asiatic Researches*, 5 (1799), 219–40.

Callan, Alyson, '"What Else Do We Bengalis Do?" Sorcery, Overseas Migration, and the New Inequalities in Sylhet, Bangladesh', *Journal of the Royal Anthropological Institute* (NS), 13 (2007), 331–43.

'Female Saints and the Practice of Islam in Sylhet, Bangladesh', *American Ethnologist*, 35:3 (2008), 396–412.

Callard, Keith, *Pakistan: A Political Study* (London: George Allen and Unwin, 1957).

Campos, J. J. A., *History of the Portuguese in Bengal* (Kolkata: Butterworth, 1919).

Cederlöf, Gunnel, 'Fixed Boundaries, Fluid Landscapes: British Expansion into Northern East Bengal in the 1820s', *Indian Economic and Social History Review*, 46:4 (2009), 513–40.

Founding an Empire on India's North-Eastern Frontiers, 1790–1840: Climate, Commerce, Polity (Delhi: Oxford University Press, 2014a).

'Monsoon Landscapes: Spatial Politics and Mercantile Colonial Practice in India', *Rachel Carson Center Perspectives*, 3 (2014b), 29–35.

'Poor Man's Crop: Evading Opium Monopoly', *Modern Asian Studies*, 53:2 (2019), 633–59.

Chadha, Radhika, 'Merchants, Renegades and Padres: Portuguese Presence in Bengal in the Sixteenth and Seventeenth Centuries' (PhD thesis, Jawaharlal Nehru University, 2005).

Chakma, A. B., 'Look Back from Exile: A Chakma Experience', in: Mey (ed.) (1984), 35–62.

Chakma, Harikishore, Tapas Chakma, Preyasi Dewan and Mahfuz Ullah, *Bara Parang: The Tale of the Developmental Refugees of the Chittagong Hill Tracts* (Dhaka: Centre for Sustainable Development, 1995).

Chakma, Mangal Kumar, *Mining and Silent Disaster: An Account of Mining-Affected Indigenous Peoples and Environment of Tahirpur, Sunamganj and Bijoypur, Netrokona* (Dhaka: Kapaeeng Foundation, 2015).

Chakma, Samari, *Bor Porong: Kaptai Bandh – Boro Porong Duburider Atmokohon* [The Great Exodus – Kaptai dam – narratives of the submerged] (Dhaka: Comrade Rupak Chakma Memorial Trust, 2018).

Chakrabarti, Dilip K., *Ancient Bangladesh: A Study of the Archaeological Sources* (Delhi: Oxford University Press, 1992).

Chakrabarti, Kunal, and Shubhra Chakrabarti, *Historical Dictionary of the Bengalis* (Lanham, MD: Scarecrow Press, 2013).

Chakrabarti, Prafulla K., *The Marginal Men: The Refugees and the Left Political Syndrome in West Bengal*, 2nd ed. (Kolkata: Naya Udyog, 1999).

Chakrabarty, Dipesh, 'Remembered Villages: Representation of Hindu-Bengali Memories in the Aftermath of Partition', *Economic and Political Weekly*, 31:32 (1996), 2143–51.

'Romantic Archives: Literature and the Politics of Identity in Bengal', *Critical Inquiry*, 30 (2004), 654–82.

Chakraborty, Ratan Lal, 'Chakma Resistance to Early British Rule', *Bangladesh Historical Studies, Journal of the Bangladesh Itihas Samiti*, 2 (1977), 133–56.

Chakraborty, Titas, 'The Household Workers of the East India Company Ports of Pre-Colonial Bengal', *International Review of Social History*, 64 (2019), 71–93.

Chakravarti, Prithwis Chandra, 'Naval Warfare in Ancient India', *Indian Historical Quarterly*, 6:4 (1930), 645–64.

Chakravarti, Ranabir, 'Trade and Commerce – Ancient Period', in: Islam and Miah (eds.) (2003), 10:180–8.

'Economic Life: Agrarian and Non-Agrarian Pursuits', in: A. M. Chowdhury and Chakravarti (eds.) (2018), 2:111–96.

Charney, Michael W., 'Where Jambudipa and Islamdom Converged: Religious Change and the Emergence of Buddhist Communalism in Early Modern Arakan, 15th–19th Centuries' (PhD thesis, Michigan University, 1999).

Chatterjee, Kumkum, 'The Persianization of "Itihasa": Performance Narratives and Mughal Political Culture in Eighteenth-Century Bengal', *Journal of Asian Studies*, 67:2 (2008), 513–43.

'Goddess Encounters: Mughals, Monsters and the Goddess in Bengal', *Modern Asian Studies*, 47:5 (2013), 1435–87.

Chatterjee, Partha, *A Princely Impostor? The Strange and Universal History of the Kumar of Bhawal* (Princeton, NJ: Princeton University Press, 2002).

Chatterji, Joya, *Bengal Divided: Hindu Communalism and Partition, 1932–1947* (New Delhi: Foundation Books, 1995).

'The Fashioning of a Frontier: The Radcliffe Line and Bengal's Border Landscape, 1947–52', *Modern Asian Studies*, 33:1 (1999), 185–242.

'"Dispersal" and the Failure of Rehabilitation: Refugee Camp-dwellers and Squatters in West Bengal', *Modern Asian Studies*, 41:5 (2007a), 995–1032.

The Spoils of Partition: Bengal and India, 1947–1967 (Cambridge: Cambridge University Press, 2007b).

Chaudhuri, Binay Bhushan, 'Commercialisation of Agriculture', in: Islam and Miah (eds.) (2003), 1:371–427.

Chaudhuri, K. N., *Asia before Europe: Economy and Civilisation of the Indian Ocean from the Rise of Islam to 1750* (Cambridge: Cambridge University Press, 1990).

Chaudhuri, Nirad C., *The Autobiography of an Unknown Indian* (Bombay: Jaico Publishing House, 1951).

Chaudhury, Sushil, *From Prosperity to Decline: Eighteenth Century Bengal* (Delhi: Manohar, 1995a).

'International Trade in Bengal Silk and the Comparative Role of Asians and Europeans, circa 1700–1750', *Modern Asian Studies*, 29:2 (1995b), 373–86.

The Prelude to Empire: Plassey Revolution of 1757 (Delhi: Manohar, 2000).

'Trade and Commerce – Medieval Period', in: Islam and Miah (eds.) (2003), 10:188–91.

Cheesman, Nick, 'How in Myanmar "National Races" Came to Surpass Citizenship and Exclude Rohingya', *Journal of Contemporary Asia*, 47:3 (2017), 461–83.

Chin, U, 'Report on the Migration of Arakanese Buddhists to Arakan' (1953), in: Government of East Bengal, Home Ministry, Confidential Records, B. Proceedings, CR 9 M-14/53 (6–54), National Archives of Bangladesh (1953).

Chottogram Jubobidroho 1930–34 Alekhyomala [Pictures of the 1930–4 Youth Revolt in Chittagong] (Kolkata: Biplobtirtho Chottogram Smritishongstha Prokashon, 2001).

Choudhuri, Abdul Gaffar, *Amra Bangladeshi, na Bangali?* [Are we Bangladeshis or Bengalis?] (Dhaka: Okkhorbritto, 1995).

Choudhury, Sujit, 'Badsah: A Hindu Godling with a Muslim Background', in: Mustafa Zaman Abbasi and Bashir Al Helal (eds.), *Folkloric Bangladesh* (Dhaka: Bangladesh Folklore Parishad, 1979), 61–9.

Choudhury, Tanzina, 'Experiences of Women as Workers: A Study of Construction Workers in Bangladesh', *Construction Management and Economics*, 31:8 (2013), 883–98.

Chowdhury, Abdul Momin, 'History: Early Period', in: Islam and Miah (eds.) (2003a), 5:104–11.

'Matsyanyayam', in: Islam and Miah (eds.) (2003b), 6:446.

Chowdhury, Abdul Momin, and Ranabir Chakravarti (eds.), *History of Bangladesh: Early Bengal in Regional Perspectives (up to c. 1200 CE)* (Dhaka: Asiatic Society of Bangladesh, 2018), 2 vols.

Chowdhury, Afsan (ed.), *Bangladesh 1971* (Dhaka: Mowla Brothers, 2007), 4 vols.

Chowdhury, Elora Halim, '"Transnationalism Reversed": Engaging Religion, Development and Women's Organizing in Bangladesh', *Women's Studies International Forum*, 32 (2009), 414–23.

Chowdhury, Farah Deeba, 'Theorising Patriarchy: The Bangladesh Context', *Asian Journal of Social Science*, 37 (2009), 599–622.

Chowdhury, Md. Tanvir Ahmed, 'Arsenic in Bangladeshi Soils Related to Physiographic Regions, Paddy Management, and Geochemical Cycling' (PhD thesis, University of Aberdeen, 2016).

Chowdhury, Mong Shanoo, and Pallab Chakma (eds.), *Human Rights Report 2017 on Indigenous Peoples in Bangladesh* (Dhaka: Kapaeeng Foundation, 2018).

Chowdhury, Nusrat Sabina, 'Mines and Signs: Resource and Political Futures in Bangladesh', *Journal of the Royal Anthropological Institute* (NS), 22 (2016), S87–107.

Chowdhury, Reshmi, '"Outsiders" and Identity Construction in the Sex Workers' Movement in Bangladesh', *Sociological Spectrum*, 26:3 (2006), 335–57.

Chowdhury, Tamina M., 'Raids, Annexation and Plough: Transformation through Territorialisation in Nineteenth-Century Chittagong Hill Tracts', *Indian Economic and Social History Review*, 53:2 (2016), 183–224.

Chung, Chien-peng, 'What Are the Strategic and Economic Implications for South Asia of China's Maritime Silk Road Initiative?' *Pacific Review*, 31:3 (2018), 315–32.

Church, Sally K., 'The Giraffe of Bengal: A Medieval Encounter in Ming China', *Medieval History Journal*, 7:1 (2004), 1–37.

Civáň, Peter, Hayley Craig, Cymon J. Cox and Terence A. Brown, 'Three Geographically Separate Domestications of Asian Rice', *Nature Plants*, 1, Article 15164 (2016), 1–5.

Clark, T. W., 'Evolution of Hinduism in Medieval Bengali Literature: Siva, Candi, Manasa', *Bulletin of the School of Oriental and African Studies, University of London*, 17:3 (1955), 503–18.

Connell, Raewyn, 'Masculinities in Global Perspective: Hegemony, Contestation, and Changing Structures of Power', *Theoretical Sociology*, 45 (2016), 303–18.

Cons, Jason, 'Staging Climate Security: Resilience and Heterodystopia in the Bangladesh Borderlands', *Cultural Anthropology*, 33:2 (2018), 266–94.

Conticini, Alessandro, and David Hulme, 'Escaping Violence, Seeking Freedom: Why Children in Bangladesh Migrate to the Street', *Development and Change*, 38:2 (2007), 201–27.

Coomaraswamy, Radhika, *Report of the Special Rapporteur on Violence against Women, Its Causes and Consequences* (Geneva: Office of the United Nations High Commissioner for Human Rights, 1997).

Cooper, Adrienne, *Sharecropping and Sharecroppers' Struggles in Bengal, 1930–1950* (Kolkata: K. P. Bagchi, 1988).

Corruption in Service Sectors: National Household Survey 2017 (Dhaka: Transparency International Bangladesh, 2018).

Countering Jihadist Militancy in Bangladesh (Brussels: International Crisis Group, 2018).

Creative Conservation Alliance, *A Preliminary Wildlife Survey in Sangu-Matamuhuri Reserve Forest, Chittagong Hill Tracts, Bangladesh: A Report Submitted to the Bangladesh Forest Department* (Dhaka: Creative Conservation Alliance, 2016).

Crow, Ben, with Alan Lindquist and David Wilson, *Sharing the Ganges: The Politics and Technology of River Development* (New Delhi: Sage Publications, 1995).

Curley, David L., 'Marriage, Honor, Agency, and Trials by Ordeal: Women's Gender Roles in Candīmangal', *Modern Asian Studies*, 35:2 (2001), 315–48.

Custers, Peter, 'Maulana Bhashani and the Transition to Secular Politics in East Bengal', *Indian Economic and Social History Review*, 47:2 (2010), 231–59.

Daechsel, Markus, 'Review of *Recasting the Region: Language, Culture and Islam in Colonial Bengal*, by Neilesh Bose' (review no. 1871), *Reviews in History* (2015). www.history.ac.uk/reviews/review/1871

Dalton, Edward T., *Descriptive Ethnology of Bengal* (Kolkata: Office of the Superintendent of Government Printing, 1872).

Dannecker, Petra, 'Transnational Migration and the Transformation of Gender Relations: The Case of Bangladeshi Labour Migrants', *Current Sociology*, 53:4 (2005), 655–74.

Darian, Steven G., *The Ganges in Myth and History* (Honolulu: University Press of Hawaii, 1978).

Das, Suranjan, *Communal Riots in Bengal, 1905–1947* (Delhi: Oxford University Press, 1991).

Dasgupta, Nupur, 'Social History of Women in Ancient Times: Emergent Methodology and Historiographical Issues', in: A. M Chowdhury and Chakravarti (eds.) (2018), 2:91–106.

Dastagir, M. Rehan, 'Modeling Recent Climate Change Induced Extreme Events in Bangladesh: A Review', *Weather and Climate Extremes*, 7 (2015), 49–60.

Datta, Anjan Kumar, *Land and Labour Relations in South-West Bangladesh: Resources, Power and Conflict* (New York: St. Martin's Press, 1998).

Datta, Ranjan, *Land-Water Management and Sustainability in Bangladesh: Indigenous Practices in the Chittagong Hill Tracts* (London: Routledge, 2018).

D'Costa, Bina, *Nationbuilding, Gender and War Crimes in South Asia* (London: Routledge, 2010).

'War Crimes, Justice and the Politics of Memory', *Economic and Political Weekly* 48:12 (2013), 39–43.

D'Costa, Bina, and Sara Hossain, 'Redress for Sexual Violence before the International Crimes Tribunal in Bangladesh: Lessons from History, and Hopes for the Future', *Criminal Law Forum*, 21 (2010), 331–59.

De Bruyn, Tom, and Umbareen Kuddus, *Dynamics of Remittance Utilization in Bangladesh* (Geneva: International Organization for Migration, 2005).

Deb, Arnab, 'Interview with Tanvir Alim' (2011). https://globalqueerdesi.wordpress.com

Debi, Rashsundari, *Amar Jiban* (1897).

Delaporte, Isaure, and Mathilde Maurel, 'Adaptation to Climate Change in Bangladesh', *Climate Policy*, 18:1 (2018), 49–62.

Dewey, Clive, 'The Rural Roots of Pakistani Militarism', in: Low (ed.) (1991), 255–83.

Deyell, John S., 'Cowries and Coins: The Dual Monetary System of the Bengal Sultanate', *Indian Economic and Social History Review*, 47:1 (2010), 63–106.

d'Hubert, Thibaut, *In the Shade of the Golden Palace: Ālāol and Middle Bengali Poetics in Arakan* (Oxford: Oxford University Press, 2018).

'India Beyond the Ganges: Defining Arakanese Buddhism in Persianate Colonial Bengal', *Indian Economic and Social History Review*, 56:1 (2019a), 1–31.

'Persian at the Court or in the Village? The Elusive Presence of Persian in Bengal', in: Nile Green (ed.), *The Persianate World: The Frontiers of a Eurasian Lingua Franca* (Oakland: University of California Press, 2019b), 93–112.

Dimeo, Paul, 'Football and Politics in Bengal: Colonialism, Nationalism, Communalism', *Soccer and Society*, 2:2 (2001), 57–74.

'Colonial Bodies, Colonial Sport: "Martial" Punjabis, "Effeminate" Bengalis and the Development of Indian Football', *International Journal of the History of Sport*, 19:1 (2002), 72–90.

Dimock, Edward C., Jr (ed. and trans.), *The Thief of Love: Bengali Tales from Court and Village* (Chicago: University of Chicago Press, 1963).

The Sound of Silent Guns and Other Essays (Delhi: Oxford University Press, 1989).

Dulal, Shaifullah Mahmud (ed.), *Muktijuddho: Nirbachito Kobita* [Liberation War: Selected poems] (Dhaka: Nawroze Kitabistan, 1987).

Dutta, Krishna, and Andrew Robinson (eds.), *Selected Letters of Rabindranath Tagore* (New York: Foundation Books, 1997).

East Pakistan, Government of, Education Department, *Report of the East Bengal Language Committee, 1949* (Dhaka: Officer on Special Duty (Home Dept.), East Pakistan Govt. Press, 1958).

Eaton, Richard M., 'Human Settlement and Colonization in the Sundarbans, 1200–1750', *Agriculture and Human Values*, 7:2 (1990), 6–16.

The Rise of Islam and the Bengal Frontier, 1204–1760 (Berkeley: University of California Press, 1993).

'Who Are the Bengal Muslims? Conversion and Islamization in Bengal', in: Rafiuddin Ahmed (ed.), *Understanding the Bengal Muslims: Interpretative Essays* (New Delhi: Oxford University Press, 2001), 26–51.

'Shrines, Cultivators, and Muslim "Conversion" in Punjab and Bengal, 1300–1700', *Medieval History Journal* 12:2 (2009), 191–220.

Ebert, Rainer, 'Bangladesh's Invisible Minority' (2012). https://rainerebert.com

Education Scenario in Bangladesh: Gender Perspective (Dhaka: Bangladesh Bureau of Statistics, UCEP Bangladesh and Diakonia Bangladesh, 2017).

Ekattorer Ghatok O Dalalra Ke Kothay [Where are the killers and collaborators of 1971 today?] (Dhaka: Muktijuddho Chetona Bikash Kendro, 1987).

The Events in East Pakistan, 1971: A Legal Study (Geneva: International Commission of Jurists, 1972).

Faaland, Just, and J. R. Parkinson, *Bangladesh: The Test Case of Development* (London: Hurst, 1976).

Farzana, Kazi Fahmida, 'Boundaries in Shaping the Rohingya Identity and the Shifting Context of Borderland Politics', *Studies in Ethnicity and Nationalism*, 15:2 (2015), 292–314.

Felden, Ellen, 'Dhee: Bangladesh's First Lesbian Comic Strip Heroine', *DW.com* (2015). www.dw.com/en/dhee-bangladeshs-first-lesbian-comic-strip-heroine/a-18700028

Feldman, Shelley, 'Exploring Theories of Patriarchy: A Perspective from Contemporary Bangladesh', *Signs*, 26:4 (2001), 1097–127.

'Paradoxes of Institutionalisation: The Depoliticisation of Bangladeshi NGOs', *Development in Practice*, 13:1 (2003), 5–26.

'Historicizing Garment Manufacturing in Bangladesh: Gender, Generation, and New Regulatory Regimes', *Journal of International Women's Studies*, 11:1 (2009), 268–88.

'The Hindu as Other: State, Law, and Land Relations in Contemporary Bangladesh', *Samaj: South Asia Multidisciplinary Academic Journal*, 13 (2016), 1–19.

Ferdoush, Md. Azmeary, and Reece Jones, 'The Decision to Move: Post-Exchange Experiences in the Former Bangladesh-India Border Enclaves', in: Alexander Horstmann, Martin Saxer and Alessandro Rippa (eds.), *Routledge Handbook of Asian Borderlands* (Abingdon: Routledge, 2018), 255–65.

Five Years of Pakistan (August 1947–August 1952) (Karachi: Pakistan Publications, 1952).

Fleming, Benjamin J., 'Making Land Sacred: Inscriptional Evidence for Buddhist Kings and Brahman Priests in Medieval Bengal', *Numen*, 60 (2013), 559–85.

45 Years Agriculture Statistics of Major Crops (Aus, Amon, Boro, Jute, Potato and Wheat) (Dhaka: Bangladesh Bureau of Statistics, 2018).

Franda, Marcus F., 'Communism and Regional Politics in East Pakistan', *Asian Survey*, 10:7 (1970), 588–606.

Full Report of the Human Rights Fact-Finding Team ... after Visiting the Crime Scenes in Cox's Bazar and Chittagong (Dhaka: Odhikar, 2012).

Furui, Ryosuke, 'Variegated Adaptations: State Formation in Bengal from the Fifth to the Seventh Century', in: Noboru Karashima and Masashi Hirosue (eds.), *State Formation and Social Integration in Pre-modern South and Southeast Asia: A Comparative Study of Asian Society* (Tokyo: Toyo Bunko, 2017a), 73–87.

'Subordinate Rulers under the Pālas: Their Diverse Origins and Shifting Power Relation with the King', *Indian Economic and Social History Review*, 54:3 (2017b), 339–59.

Gain, Philip (ed.), *Bangladesh: Land, Forest and Forest People* (Dhaka: Society for Environment and Human Development (SEHD), 1995).

The Last Forests of Bangladesh (Dhaka: Society for Environment and Human Development (SEHD), 2002 [1998]).

(ed.), *The Story of Tea Workers in Bangladesh* (Dhaka: Society for Environment and Human Development (SEHD), 2009).

Gain, Philip, Lucille Sircar and Shamimul Islam, *The Case of Forests, Ethnic Communities and Tea Workers of Bangladesh* (Dhaka: Society for Environment and Human Development (SEHD), 2005).

Gallagher, Rob, *The Rickshaws of Bangladesh* (Dhaka: University Press Limited, 1992).

Gardner, Katy, *Global Migrants, Local Lives: Travel and Transformation in Rural Bangladesh* (Oxford: Clarendon Press, 1995).

'The Transnational Work of Kinship and Caring: Bengali-British Marriages in Historical Perspective', *Global Networks*, 6:4 (2006), 373–87.

'We Demand Work! "Dispossession", Patronage and Village Labour in Bibiyana, Bangladesh', *Journal of Peasant Studies*, 45:7 (2018), 1484–1500.

Gardner, Katy, and Zahir Ahmed, *Place, Social Protection and Migration in Bangladesh: A Londoni Village in Biswanath* (Brighton: Development Research Centre on Migration, Globalisation and Poverty, University of Sussex, 2006).

Gardner, Katy, Zahir Ahmed, Fatema Bashir and Masud Rana, 'Elusive Partnerships: Gas Extraction and CSR in Bangladesh', *Resources Policy*, 37:2 (2012), 168–74.

Gardner, Katy, Zahir Ahmed, Mohammad Masud Rana and Fatema Bashar, 'Field of Dreams: Imagining Development and Un-Development at a Gas Field in Sylhet', *Samaj: South Asia Multidisciplinary Academic Journal*, 9 (2014), 1–4.

Gazi, Nurun Nahar, Rakesh Tamang, Vipin Kumar Singh et al., 'Genetic Structure of Tibeto-Burman Populations of Bangladesh: Evaluating the Gene Flow along the Sides of Bay-of-Bengal', *PLoS ONE* 8:10 (2013), e75064.

Geertz, Clifford, *Agricultural Involution: The Process of Ecological Change in Indonesia* (Berkeley: University of California Press, 1963).

Gerharz, Eva, 'Indigenous Activism Beyond Ethnic Groups: Shifting Boundaries and Constellations of Belonging', in: Gerharz et al. (eds.) (2018), 92–118.

Gerharz, Eva, Nasir Uddin and Pradeep Chakkarath (eds.), *Indigeneity on the Move: Varying Manifestations of a Contested Concept* (New York: Berghahn, 2018).

Ghosh, Gautam, 'An "Infiltration" of Time? Hindu Chauvinism and Bangladeshi Migration in/to Kolkata, India', *Journal of Comparative Research in Anthropology and Sociology*, 6:1 (2015), 263–88.

Ghosh, Sahana, 'Anti-trafficking and Its Discontents: Women's Migrations and Work in an Indian Borderland', *Gender, Place and Culture: A Journal of Feminist Geography*, 22:9 (2015), 1220–35.

Ghosh, Subhrashi, 'Population Movements in West Bengal: A Case Study of Nadia District, 1947–51', *South Asia Research*, 34:2 (2014), 113–32.

Ghosh, Suchandra, 'Water, Water Bodies and Waterscapes in Early Medieval South-Eastern Bengal and Assam: A View from Epigraphs', in: Rila Mukherjee (ed.), *Living with Water: Peoples, Lives, and Livelihoods in Asia and Beyond* (Delhi: Primus Books, 2017), 66–78.

Ghosh, Suchandra, and Sayantani Pal, 'Everyday Life in Early Bengal', in: A. M. Chowdhury and Chakravarti (eds.) (2018), 2:3–42.

Ghosh, Tirthankar, 'Floods and People, Colonial North Bengal, 1871–1922', *Studies in People's History*, 5:1 (2018), 32–47.

Gilbert, Paul Robert, 'Money Mines: An Ethnography of Frontiers, Capital and Extractive Industries in London and Bangladesh' (MA thesis, University of Sussex, 2015).

Gill, John H., *An Atlas of the 1971 India-Pakistan War: The Creation of Bangladesh* (Washington, DC: Near East South Asia Center for Strategic Studies, 2003).

Gill, K. P. S., *Brief on Islamist Extremism and Terrorism in South Asia* (New Delhi: Institute for Conflict Management, 2004).

Giunchi, Elisa, 'The Reinvention of Sharīʿa under the British Raj: In Search of Authenticity and Certainty', *Journal of Asian Studies*, 69:4 (2010). 1119–42.

Glassie, Henry, *Art and Life in Bangladesh* (Bloomington: Indiana University Press, 1997).

Gonoprojatontri Bangladesher Shongbidhan [Constitution of the People's Republic of Bangladesh] (Dhaka: Bangladesh Gonoporishod, 1972).

Goswami, Krishnapada, *Place Names of Bengal* (Kolkata: Jnan Prakasan, n.d. [1984]).

Greenough, Paul R., *Prosperity and Misery in Modern Bengal: The Famine of 1943–44* (New York: Oxford University Press, 1982).

Gregson, N., M. Crang, F. Ahamed, N. Akhter and R. Ferdous, 'Following Things of Rubbish Value: End-of-Life Ships, "Chock-chocky" Furniture and the Bangladeshi Middle Class Consumer', *Geoforum*, 41 (2010), 846–54.

Griffiths, Arlo, 'Four More Gupta-period Copperplate Grants from Bengal', *Pratna Samiksha: A Journal of Archaeology* (NS), 9 (2018), 15–57.

Guha, Ranajit, *A Rule of Property for Bengal* (Paris: Mouton, 1963).

Guhathakurta, Meghna, 'Families, Displacement', *Transeuropéennes*, 19–20 (2000–2001), 131–42.

'Globalization, Class and Gender Relations: The Shrimp Industry in South-Western Bangladesh', *Journal of Social Studies*, 101 (2003), 1–15.

'Understanding Violence, Strategising Protection: Perspectives from Rohingya Refugees in Bangladesh', *Asian Journal of Social Science*, 45 (2017), 639–65.

Guhathakurta, Meghna, and Willem van Schendel (eds.), *The Bangladesh Reader: History, Culture, Politics* (Durham, NC: Duke University Press, 2013).

Habib, Irfan, *An Atlas of the Mughal Empire: Political and Economic Maps with Detailed Notes, Bibliography and Index* (Delhi: Oxford University Press, 1982).

Haider, Zaglul, 'Biharis in Bangladesh and Their Restricted Access to Citizenship Rights', *South Asia Research*, 38:3 (2018), 25S–42S.

Hall, Kenneth, 'Local and International Trade and Traders in the Straits of Melaka Region: 600-1500', *Journal of the Economic and Social History of the Orient*, 47:2 (2004), 213–60.

Hambly, Gavin, 'A Note on the Trade in Eunuchs in Mughal Bengal', *Journal of the American Oriental Society*, 94:1 (1974), 125–30.

Hamoodur Rahman Commission Report (n.p.: Government of Pakistan, 1974).

Haque, A., M. Hossain, G. Wouters and F. Lambein, 'Epidemiological Study of Lathyrism in Northwestern Districts of Bangladesh', *Neuroepidemiology*, 15:2 (1996), 83–91.

Haque, Muhammad Shahriar, and Zainul Abedin, 'The Discursive Construction of (A)moral Names: Religion versus Language', *Multilingua: Journal of Cross-Cultural and Interlanguage Communication*, 30:3–4 (2011), 377–90.

Hara, Tadahiko, *Paribar and Kinship in a Moslem Rural Village in East Pakistan* (Tokyo: Institute for the Study of Languages and Cultures of Asia and Africa, 1991).

Harder, Hans, *Sufism and Saint Veneration in Contemporary Bangladesh: The Maijbhandaris of Chittagong* (New York: Routledge, 2011).

Hasan, Md. Kamrul, Peter Aggleton and Asha Persson, 'The Makings of a Man: Social Generational Masculinities in Bangladesh', *Journal of Gender Studies*, 27:3 (2018a), 347–61.

'Sexual Practices and Sexual Health Among Three Generations of Men in Bangladesh: Exploring Gender- and Sexuality-Assemblages', *Sexuality and Culture*, 23 (2019), 475–93.

Hasan, Md. Kamrul, Sam Desiere, Marijke D'Haese and Lalit Kumar, 'Impact of Climate-smart Agriculture Adoption on the Food Security of Coastal Farmers in Bangladesh', *Food Security*, 10:4 (2018b), 1073–88.

Hasan, Md. Monjur, and He Jian, 'Protracted Maritime Boundary Dispute Resolutions in the Bay of Bengal: Issues and Impacts', *Thalassas: An International Journal of Marine Sciences*, 35 (2019), 323–40.

Hasan, Mubashar, 'Sport as a Critique of Politics: Everest Climbing, Nationalism and the Failure of Politics in Bangladesh', *Global Discourse: An Interdisciplinary Journal of Current Affairs and Applied Contemporary Thought*, 5:4 (2015), 540–52.

'The Diverse Roots of the "Secular" in East Pakistan (1947–71) and the Crisis of "Secularism" in Contemporary Bangladesh', *History and Sociology of South Asia*, 11:2 (2017), 156–73.

Hasan, Perween, 'The Presence of the Past: Tradition, Creativity and Identity in the Architecture of Medieval Bengal', *Studies in People's History*, 1:1 (2014), 31–41.

Hasan, Rashidul, 'Digital Security Bill Passed: Concerns of Journos, Rights Activists Ignored; Opposition MPs Raise Objection; Fear Widespread over Free Speech, Independent Journalism', *Daily Star* (20 September 2018).

Hashmi, Taj ul-Islam, *Pakistan as a Peasant Utopia: The Communalization of Class Politics in East* Bengal, *1920–1947* (Boulder, CO: Westview Press, 1992).

Hassan, Mirza, and Wilson Prichard, 'The Political Economy of Domestic Tax Reform in Bangladesh: Political Settlements, Informal Institutions and the Negotiation of Reform', *Journal of Development Studies*, 52:12 (2016), 1704–21.

Hatley, Shaman, 'Mapping the Esoteric Body in the Islamic Yoga of Bengal', *History of Religions*, 46:4 (2007), 351–68.

Hazarika, Manjil, 'Lithic Industries with Palaeolithic Elements in Northeast India', *Quaternary International*, 269 (2012), 48–58.

Prehistory and Archaeology of Northeast India: Multidisciplinary Investigation in an Archaeological Terra Incognita (Delhi: Oxford University Press, 2017).

Hazarika, Sanjoy, *Rites of Passage: Border Crossings, Imagined Homelands, India's East and Bangladesh* (New Delhi: Penguin Books, 2000).

Heehs, Peter, *The Bomb in Bengal: The Rise of Revolutionary Terrorism in India 1900–1910* (Delhi: Oxford University Press, 1993).

Hersh, Seymour M., *The Price of Power: Kissinger in the Nixon White House* (New York: Summit Books, 1983).

Hoek, Lotte, 'Killer Not Terrorist: Visual Articulations of Terror in Bangladeshi Action Cinema', *South Asian Popular Culture*, 11:2 (2013), 121–32.

Cut-Pieces: Celluloid Obscenity and Popular Cinema in Bangladesh (New York: Columbia University Press, 2014a).

'Cross-wing Filmmaking: East Pakistani Urdu Films and Their Traces in the Bangladesh Film Archive', *BioScope: South Asian Screen Studies*, 5:2 (2014b), 99–118.

Hollerbach, Paula E., Shivananda Khan and Sharful Islam Khan, 'The Construction of Gender and Sexual Identities among Young Men in Dhaka, Bangladesh', in: M. E. Khan et al. (eds.) (2014), 85–112.

Hoque, Ashraf, and Lucia Michelutti, 'Brushing with Organized Crime and Democracy: The Art of Making Do in South Asia', *Journal of Asian Studies*, 77:4 (2018), 991–1011.

Hore, Somenath, *Tebhaga: An Artist's Diary and Sketchbook* (translated from the Bengali by Somnath Zutshi) (Kolkata: Seagull Books, 1990).

Hossain, Adnan, 'Beyond Emasculation: Being Muslim and Becoming *Hijra* in South Asia', *Asian Studies Review*, 36:4 (2012), 495–513.

'The Paradox of Recognition: Hijra, Third Gender and Sexual Rights in Bangladesh', *Culture, Health and Sexuality*, 19:12 (2017), 1418–31.

'De-Indianizing Hijra: Intraregional Effacements and Inequalities in South Asian Queer Space', *TSQ: Transgender Studies Quarterly*, 5:3 (2018), 321–31.

'Sexual Nationalism, Masculinity and the Cultural Politics of Cricket in Bangladesh', *South Asia: Journal of South Asian Studies*, 42:4 (2019), 638–53.

Hossain, Ashfaque, 'The Making and Unmaking of Assam–Bengal Borders and the Sylhet Referendum', *Modern Asian Studies*, 47:1 (2013), 250–87.

Hossain, Golam, *General Ziaur Rahman and the BNP: Political Transformation of a Military Regime* (Dhaka: University Press Limited, 1988).

Hossain, Ishtiaq, 'Bangladesh–India Relations: The Ganges Water Sharing Treaty and Beyond', *Asian Affairs*, 25:3 (1998), 131–50.

Hossain, Ishtiaq, and Noore Alam Siddiquee, 'Islam in Bangladesh Politics: The Role of Ghulam Azam of Jamaat-I-Islami', *Inter-Asia Cultural Studies*, 5:3 (2004), 384–99.

Hossain, Mohammad Sazzad, 'Strategies to Integrate the Mughal Settlements in Old Dhaka', *Frontiers of Architectural Research*, 2 (2013), 420–34.

Hossain, Naomi, 'The 1970 Bhola Cyclone, Nationalist Politics, and the Subsistence Crisis Contract in Bangladesh', *Disasters*, 42:1 (2018a), 187–203.

'Post-Conflict Ruptures and the Space for Women's Empowerment in Bangladesh', *Women's Studies International Forum*, 68 (2018b), 104–12.

Hossain, Rokeya Sakhawat, *Sultana's Dream and Padmarag: Two Feminist Utopias* (translated with an introduction by Barnita Bagchi) (New Delhi: Penguin Books, 2005).

Hossein, R. S., *Sultana's Dream* (Kolkata: S. K. Lahiri, 1908; facsimile edition, Dhaka: Liberation War Museum, 2005).

Hunter, W. W., *The Annals of Rural Bengal* (New York: Leypoldt and Holt, 1868), 3 vols.

A Statistical Account of Bengal (London: Trübner, 1876), 20 vols.

Huq, A. M., 'Reflections on Economic Planning in Pakistan', *Far Eastern Survey*, 27:1 (1958), 1–6.

Huq, Maimuna, 'Talking Jihad and Piety: Reformist Exertions among Islamist Women in Bangladesh', *Journal of the Royal Anthropological Institute* (NS), 15 (2009), S163–82.

Huq, S. M. Imamul, and Jalal Uddin Md. Shoaib, *The Soils of Bangladesh* (Dordrecht: Springer, 2013).

Huq, Samia, 'Piety, Music and Gender Transformation: Reconfiguring Women as Culture Bearing Markers of Modernity and Nationalism in Bangladesh', *Inter-Asia Cultural Studies*, 12:2 (2011), 225–39.

Huq, Shireen P., 'Bodies as Sites of Struggle: Naripokkho and the Movement for Women's Rights in Bangladesh', *Bangladesh Development Studies*, 29:3/4 (2003), 47–65.

'My Body, My Life, Whose Rights?: Bangladeshi Women's Struggle for a Fair Deal', *Contemporary South Asia*, 20:1 (2012), 11–18.

Husain, Shahanara, 'Social Life of Women', in: A. M. Chowdhury and Chakravarti (eds.) (2018), 2:71–90.

Hussain, Delwar, 'Gay, Straight, or MSM?' *Guardian* (6 August 2009a).

'Hindu-Muslim *Bhai Bhai* in a Small Town in Bangladesh', *Economic and Political Weekly*, 44:21 (2009b), 21–4.

Boundaries Undermined: The Ruins of Progress on the Bangladesh–India Border (London: Hurst, 2013).

Ibrahim, Neelima, *Ami Birangona Bolchhi* [This is the war heroine speaking] (Dhaka: Jagroti Prokashon, 1998).

Iftekhar, M. S., and M. R. Islam, 'Degeneration of Bangladesh Sundarbans Mangroves: A Management Issue', *International Forestry Review*, 6 (2004), 123–35.

Iftikhar-ul-Awwal, 'State of Indigenous Industries', in: Sirajul Islam (ed.) (1992), 272–370.

Iliopoulou, Despina, 'The Uncertainty of Private Property: Indigenous versus Colonial Law in the Restructuring of Social Relations in British India', *Dialectical Anthropology*, 26 (2001), 65–88.

Imam, Ayesha, Jenny Morgan and Nira Yuval-Davis, *Warning Signs of Fundamentalisms* (n.p.: Women Living under Muslim Laws, 2004).

Imam, Badrul, 'Gas, Natural', in: Islam and Miah (eds.) (2003), 4:335–42.

Imam, Jahanara, *Ekattorer Dinguli* (Dhaka: Shondhani Prokashoni, 1986). English translation: *Of Blood and Fire: The Untold Story of Bangladesh's War of Independence* (Dhaka: University Press Limited, 1990).

Imam, Syeda Rumnaz, 'English as a Global Language and the Question of Nation-Building Education in Bangladesh', *Comparative Education*, 41:4 (2005), 471–86.

Imtiaz, Sayed Md. Shaikh, 'Young Men in a Colourful City: Masculinity, Young Men's Sexual Practices, and HIV/AIDS in Dhaka, Bangladesh' (PhD thesis, University of Amsterdam, 2012).

Imtiaz, Sayed [Md.] Shaikh, *Understanding Construction of Masculinities at Institution and Extreme Poor Households in Rural Bangladesh* (Dhaka:

CARE Engaging Men Initiative/Centre for Men and Masculinities Studies, 2013).

Imtiaz, Sayed [Md.] Shaikh, Ishrat Jahan Khan, Tahia Rahman and Afsana Islam, *Fatherhood, Couple Relationship and Violence against Children in Extreme Poor Households in Bangladesh: Needs and Strategies to Engage Fathers as Caregivers* (Dhaka: Centre for Men and Masculinities Studies, 2017).

Independent Review of Bangladesh's Development: An Analysis of the National Budget for FY2018–19 (Dhaka: Centre for Policy Dialogue, 2018).

India and Bangladesh Land Boundary Agreement (Delhi: Ministry of External Affairs, Government of India, 2015).

The Invisible Minority: The Situation of the LGBT Community in Bangladesh (The Hague: Global Human Rights Defence/Boys of Bangladesh, 2015).

Iqbal, Iftekhar, 'Towards an Environmental History of Colonial East Bengal: Paradigms and Praxis', *Journal of the Asiatic Society of Bangladesh (Humanities)*, 50:1–2 (2005), 501–18.

'Fighting with a Weed: Water Hyacinth and the State in Colonial Bengal, c. 1910–1947', *Environment and History*, 15:1 (2009), 35–59.

The Bengal Delta: Ecology, State and Social Change, 1840–1943 (London: Palgrave Macmillan, 2010).

'The Boat Denial Policy and the Great Bengal Famine', *Journal of the Asiatic Society of Bangladesh (Humanities)*, 56:1–2 (2011), 271–82.

'Governing the "Wasteland": Ecology and Shifting Political Subjectivities in Colonial Bengal', *Rachel Carson Center Perspectives*, 3 (2014), 39–43.

'Cooperative Credit in Colonial Bengal: An Exploration in Development and Decline, 1905–1947', *Indian Economic and Social History Review*, 54:2 (2017), 221–37.

'State of (the) Mind: The Bengali Intellectual Milieu and Envisioning the State in the Post-Colonial Era', *South Asia: Journal of South Asian Studies*, 41:4 (2018), 876–91.

'Governing Mass Migration to Dhaka: Revisiting Climate Factors', *Economic and Political Weekly*, 54:36 (2019), 26–31.

Islam, M. Mufakharul, 'Agriculture: History', in: Islam and Miah (eds.) (2003), 1:71–82.

'The Great Bengal Famine and the Question of FAD Yet Again', *Modern Asian Studies*, 41:2 (2007), 421–40.

Islam, Md. Maidul, 'Secularism in Bangladesh: An Unfinished Revolution', *South Asia Research*, 38:1 (2018), 20–39.

Islam, Md. Saidul, and Md. Nazrul Islam, '"Environmentalism of the Poor": The Tipaimukh Dam, Ecological Disasters and Environmental Resistance Beyond Borders', *Bandung Journal of the Global South*, 3:27 (2016), 1–16.

Islam, Meherun Nechha, 'Doulotpur Polli Unnoyon Kendro' [The Doulotpur Rural Development Centre], *Begom* (27 March 1960), 123–7.

Islam, Nazrul, 'Background to the Environment Movement in Bangladesh', *Journal of Social Studies*, 107 (2005), 69–86.

Islam, Nazrul, and Rosie Majid Ahsan (eds.), *Urban Bangladesh: Geographical Studies* (Dhaka: Urban Studies Programme, Department of Geography, University of Dhaka, 1996).

Islam, Nurul, 'Foreign Assistance and Economic Development: The Case of Pakistan', *Economic Journal*, 82:325 (1972), 502–30.

Development Planning in Bangladesh: A Study in Political Economy (London: Hurst, 1977).

Islam, Saiful, and Md. Ziaur Rahman Khan, 'A Review of Energy Sector of Bangladesh', *Energy Procedia*, 110 (2017), 611–8.

Islam, Shariful, 'Origin and Development of the Bangla Script', in: A. M. Chowdhury and Chakravarti (eds.) (2018), 2:607–22.

Islam, Sirajul, *The Permanent Settlement in Bengal: A Study of Its Operation* (Dhaka: Bangla Academy, 1979).

Bengal Land Tenure: The Origin and Growth of Intermediate Interests in the 19th Century (Kolkata: K. P. Bagchi, 1988).

(ed.), *History of Bangladesh 1704–1971* (Dhaka: Asiatic Society of Bangladesh, 1992), 3 vols. Bengali edition: *Bangladesher Itihash, 1704–1971* (Dhaka: Asiatic Society of Bangladesh, 1993).

'Permanent Settlement', in: Islam and Miah (eds.) (2003a), 8:34–42.

'State', in: Islam and Miah (eds.) (2003b), 9:420–4.

'American Maritime Activities in Calcutta: Cases of Elephant and Ice', *Journal of the Asiatic Society of Bangladesh (Humanities)*, 49:1 (2004), 41–59.

Islam, Sirajul, and Sajahan Miah (eds.), *Banglapedia: National Encyclopedia of Bangladesh* (Dhaka: Asiatic Society of Bangladesh, 2003), 10 vols.

Islam, Syed Serajul, 'Bengal Legislative Assembly and Constitutional Development', in: Sirajul Islam (ed.), (1992), 276–306.

Jabeen, Mussarat, and Muhammad Saleem Mazhar, 'Security Game: SEATO and CENTO as Instrument of Economic and Military Assistance to Encircle Pakistan', *Pakistan Economic and Social Review*, 49:1 (2011), 109–32.

Jackman, David, 'Living in the Shade of Others: Intermediation, Politics and Violence in Dhaka City' (PhD thesis, University of Bath, 2017).

Jacobs, Cor, Tanya Singh, Ganesh Gorti et al., 'Patterns of Outdoor Exposure to Heat in Three South Asian Cities', *Science of the Total Environment*, 674 (2019), 264–78.

Jaffrelot, Christophe (ed.), *A History of Pakistan and Its Origins* (London: Anthem Press, 2002).

Jahan, Rounaq, *Pakistan: Failure in National Integration* (New York: Columbia University Press, 1972).

'Bangladesh in 1972: Nation-Building in a New State', *Asian Survey*, 13:2 (1973), 199–210.

Bangladesh Politics: Problems and Issues (Dhaka: University Press Limited, 2005).

Jahan, Shahnaj Husne, 'Bangladesh', in: A. M. Chowdhury and Chakravarti (eds.) (2018), 1:80–94.

Jahangir, Burhanuddin Khan, *The Quest of Zainul Abedin*, translated by Meghna Guhathakurta (Dhaka: International Centre for Bengal Studies, 1993).

Hotyar Rajniti O Bangladesh [The politics of killing and Bangladesh] (Dhaka: Shomoy Prokashon, 1998).

Jalais, Annu, *Forest of Tigers: People, Politics and Environment in the Sundarbans* (London: Routledge, 2010).

'Geographies and Identities: Subaltern Partition Stories along Bengal's Southern Frontier', in: David N. Gellner (ed.), *Borderland Lives in Northern South Asia* (Durham, NC: Duke University Press, 2013), 245–65.

Jalal, Ayesha, *The Sole Spokesman: Jinnah, the Muslim League and the Demand for Pakistan* (Cambridge: Cambridge University Press, 1985).

The State of Martial Rule: The Origins of Pakistan's Political Economy of Defence (Cambridge: Cambridge University Press, 1990).

Democracy and Authoritarianism in South Asia: A Comparative and Historical Perspective (Cambridge: Cambridge University Press, 1995a).

'Conjuring Pakistan: History as Official Imagining', *International Journal of Middle East Studies*, 27:1 (1995b), 73–89.

Janeja, Manpreet K., *Transactions in Taste: The Collaborative Lives of Everyday Bengali Food* (London: Routledge, 2010).

Jardine, William (ed.), *The Naturalist's Library, Vol. VII: Mammals. Whales etc.* (by Robert Hamilton) (Edinburgh: W. H. Lizars, 1843).

Jasimuddin, *Nokshi Kanthar Math* (Kolkata: Pabalisarsa, 1975 [1928]). English translation: *The Field of the Embroidered Quilt*, 4th edn (Dhaka: Poet Jasim Uddin Academy, 1986).

Jebin, Lubna, 'Status of Transgender People in Bangladesh: A Socio-economic Analysis', *South Asian Journal of Policy and Governance*, 42:1 (2018), 49–63.

Judge, Jury, and Executioner: Torture and Extrajudicial Killings by Bangladesh's Elite Security Force (New York: Human Rights Watch, 2006).

Kabeer, Naila, *The Power to Choose: Bangladeshi Women Workers and Labour Market Decisions in London and Dhaka* (London: Verso, 2000).

'Ideas, Economics, and "the Sociology of Supply": Explanations for Fertility Decline in Bangladesh', *Journal of Development Studies*, 38:1 (2001), 29–70.

Kabir, Alamgir, *Film in Bangladesh* (Dhaka: Bangla Academy, 1979).

Kabir, Ananya Jahanara, 'Utopias Eroded and Recalled: Intellectual Legacies of East Pakistan', *South Asia: Journal of South Asian Studies*, 41:4 (2018), 1–27.

Kabir, Mohammed Mahbubul, '"Let's Go Back to Go Forward": History and Practice of Schooling in the Indigenous Communities in Chittagong Hill Tracts, Bangladesh' (MA thesis, Faculty of Social Sciences, University of Tromsø, 2009).

Kabir, Shahriar (ed.), *Resist Fundamentalism: Focus on Bangladesh* (Dhaka: Nirmul Committee, 1995).

Bangladeshe Moulobad O Shamprodayikota [Fundamentalism and communalism in Bangladesh] (Dhaka: Ononya, 1998).

Kakkar, Ankur, '"Education, Empire and the Heterogeneity of Investigative Modalities": A Reassessment of Colonial Surveys on Indigenous Indian Education', *Paedagogica Historica*, 53:4 (2017), 381–93.

Kamal, Ahmed, *State Against the Nation: The Decline of the Muslim League in Pre-independence Bangladesh* (Dhaka: University Press Limited, 2009).

Kamal, Mohit, N. Huq, B. Mali, H. Akter and S. M. Y. Arafat, 'Epidemiology of Substance Abuse in Bangladesh: A Narrative Review', *Journal of Mental Disorders and Treatment*, 4:2 (2018), 165–8.

Kapp, K. William, Luc Bigler, Brigitte Janik and Peter Wirth, *Neue Wege fur Bangladesh: Sozio-okonomische Analyse der Entwicklungsaufgaben und – moglichkeiten des neuen Staates* [New directions for Bangladesh: Socio-economic analysis of the development tasks and options of the new state] (Hamburg: Institut fur Asienkunde, 1975).

Karim, Abdul, *Dacca: The Mughal Capital* (Dhaka: Asiatic Society of Pakistan, 1964).

'Shah Jalal (R)', in: Islam and Miah (eds.) (2003), 9:196–8.

Karim, Lamia, 'Pushed to the Margins: Adivasi Peoples in Bangladesh and the Case of Kalpana Chakma', *Contemporary South Asia*, 7:3 (1998), 301–16.

Karim, Md. Saiful, 'Violation of Labour Rights in the Ship-Breaking Yards of Bangladesh: Legal Norms and Reality', *International Journal of Comparative Labour Law and Industrial Relations*, 25:4 (2009), 379–94.

Karim, Md. Saiful, Okechukwu Benjamin Vincents and Mia Mahmudur Rahim, 'Legal Activism for Ensuring Environmental Justice', *Asian Journal of Comparative Law*, 7:1 (2012), 1–44.

Karim, Ridoan, Mohammad Ershadul Karim, Firdaus Muhammad-Sukki et al., 'Nuclear Energy Development in Bangladesh: A Study of Opportunities and Challenges', *Energies*, 11:7 (2018), 1672 (1–15).

Karim, S. A., *Sheikh Mujib: Triumph and Tragedy* (Dhaka: University Press Limited, 2005).

Karim, Shuchi, 'Living Sexualities: Negotiating Heteronormativity in Middle Class Bangladesh' (PhD thesis, Erasmus University Rotterdam, 2012).

'Erotic Desires and Practices in Cyberspace: "Virtual Reality" of the Non-Heterosexual Middle Class in Bangladesh', *Gender, Technology and Development*, 18:1 (2014), 53–76.

Kawai, Akinobu, *'Landlords' and Imperial Rule: Change in Bengal Agrarian Society c. 1885–1940* (Tokyo: Institute for the Study of Languages and Cultures of Asia and Africa, 1987).

Khalequzzaman, Md., 'Bangladesh Delta Plan 2100: Not the Most Practical Proposal', *Daily Star* (21 April 2016).

Khalid, Abu Raihan M., 'The Interlinking of Rivers Project in India and International Water Law: An Overview', *Chinese Journal of International Law*, 3 (2004), 553–70.

Khan, Akhter Hameed, 'The Public Works Programme and a Developmental Proposal for East Pakistan', in: *An Evaluation of the Rural Public Works Programme, East Pakistan, 1962–63* (Comilla: Pakistan Academy for Rural Development, 1963).

Khan, M. E., and John W. Townsend, 'Representation of the "Masculine" Identity in Bangladesh', in: M. E. Khan et al. (eds.) (2014), 113–32.

Khan, M. E., John W. Townsend and Pertti J. Pelto (eds.), *Sexuality, Gender Roles, and Domestic Violence in South Asia* (New York: Population Council, 2014).

Khan, Mohammad Asghar, *Generals in Politics: Pakistan 1958–1982* (New Delhi: Vikas Publishing House, 1983).

Khan, Muazzam Hussain, 'Fakir–Sannyasi Resistance', in: Islam and Miah (eds.) (2003), 4:39–41.

Khan, Muhammad Ayub, *Friends Not Masters* (London: Oxford University Press, 1967).

Khan, Naveeda, 'Living Paradox in Riverine Bangladesh: Whiteheadian Perspectives on Ganga Devi and Khwaja Khijir', *Anthropologica*, 58:2 (2016), 179–92.

Khan, Roedad (ed.), *The American Papers: Secret and Confidential India–Pakistan–Bangladesh Documents 1965–1973* (Dhaka: University Press Limited, 1999).

(ed.), *The British Papers: Secret and Confidential India–Pakistan–Bangladesh Documents 1958–1969* (Oxford: Oxford University Press, 2002).

Khan, Saad Adnan, 'Dhee: Unknowability and Queering Realities in Bangladesh', *E-International Relations* (2016). www.e-ir.info/2016/02/09/dhee-unknowability-and-queering-realities-in-bangladesh

Khan, Shahedul Anam, and Shaheen Afroze (eds.), *Chandabaji versus Entrepreneurship: Economic Liberalisation and Youth Force in Bangladesh* (Dhaka: Academic Press and Publishers, 1999).

Khan, Shamsuzzaman (ed.), *Folklore of Bangladesh* (Dhaka: Bangla Academy, 1987), 2 vols.

Khan, Taufiq M., and A. Bergan, 'Measurement of Structural Change in the Pakistan Economy: A Review of the National Income Estimates, 1949/50 to 1963/64', *Pakistan Development Review*, 6:2 (1966), 168–75.

Khan, Zarina Rahman, and Helaluddin Khan Arefeen, *Potita Nari: A Study of Prostitution in Bangladesh* (Dhaka: Centre for Social Studies, 1989).

Khan, Zillur R., *Leadership Crisis in Bangladesh: Martial Law to Martial Law* (Dhaka: University Press Limited, 1984).

Khanom, Shahida, and Ralph Buckley, 'Tiger Tourism in the Bangladesh Sundarbans', *Annals of Tourism Research*, 55 (2015), 171–83.

Khasru, Syed Munir, and Md. Tahmid Zami, 'Student Politics in Bangladesh: An Historical Overview', in: Imtiaz Ahmed and Iqbal (eds.) (2016), 49–69.

Kirkpatrick, Joanna, *Transports of Delight: The Ricksha Art of Bangladesh* (Bloomington: University of Indiana Press, 2003).

Klein, Ira, 'Development and Death: Reinterpreting Malaria, Economics and Ecology in British India', *Indian Economic and Social History Review*, 38:2 (2001), 147–79.

Kling, Blair B., *The Blue Mutiny: The Indigo Disturbances in Bengal, 1859–1862* (Philadelphia: University of Pennsylvania Press, 1966).

Knight, Lisa I., *Contradictory Lives: Baul Women in India and Bangladesh* (New York: Oxford University Press, 2011).

Knights, Melanie, 'Bangladeshi Immigrants in Italy: From Geopolitics to Micropolitics', *Transactions of the Institute of British Geographers* (NS), 21:1 (1996), 105–23.

Knutson, Jesse Ross, 'History Beyond the Reality Principle: Literary and Political Territories in Sena Period Bengal', *Comparative Studies of South Asia, Africa and the Middle East*, 32:3 (2012), 633–43.

Kochanek, Stanley A., 'Governance, Patronage Politics, and Democratic Transition in Bangladesh', *Asian Survey*, 40:3 (2000), 530–50.

Kuttig, Julian, 'Urban Political Machines and Student Politics in "Middle" Bangladesh: Violent Party Labor in Rajshahi City', *Critical Asian Studies*, 51:3 (2019), 403–18.

Lambert, Richard D., 'Factors in Bengali Regionalism in Pakistan', *Far Eastern Survey*, 28:4 (1959), 49–58.

Landell Mills, Samuel, 'The Hardware of Sanctity: Anthropomorphic Objects in Bangladeshi Sufism', in: Pnina Werbner and Helene Basu (eds.), *Embodying Charisma: Modernity, Locality and the Performance of Emotion in Sufi Cults* (London: Routledge, 1998), 31–54.

Laushey, David M., *Bengal Terrorism and the Marxist Left: Aspects of Regional Nationalism in India, 1905–1942* (Kolkata: Firma K. L. Mukhopadhyay, 1975).

Leach, E. R., 'The Frontiers of "Burma"', *Comparative Studies in Society and History*, 3:1 (1960), 49–68.

Lees, James, '"A Character to Lose": Richard Goodlad, the Rangpur *Dhing*, and the Priorities of the East India Company's Early Colonial Administrators', *Journal of the Royal Asiatic Society* (Series 3), 25:2 (2015), 301–15.

Leider, Jacques P., 'Competing Identities and the Hybridized History of the Rohingyas', in: Renaud Egreteau and François Robinne (eds.), *Metamorphosis: Studies in Social and Political Change in Myanmar* (Singapore: NUS Press, 2016a), 151–78.

'Der Zeitgenössische Theravāda-Buddhismus in Bangladesh' [Contemporary Theravada Buddhism in Bangladesh], in: Manfred Hutter, Günter Mayer and Heinz Bechert (eds.), *Der Buddhismus II, Theravada-Buddhismus und Tibetischer Buddhismus* (Stuttgart: Verlag W. Kohlhammer, 2016b), 99–121.

Lerski, George J., 'The American-Pakistan Alliance: A Reevaluation of the Past Decade', *Asian Survey*, 8:5 (1968), 400–15.

Lewin, T. H., *The Hill Tracts of Chittagong and the Dwellers Therein, with Comparative Vocabularies of the Hill Dialects* (Kolkata: Bengal Printing Company, 1869).

Lewis, David, 'NGOs, Organizational Culture, and Institutional Sustainability', *Annals of the American Academy of Political and Social Science*, 590 (2003), 212–26.

Bangladesh: Politics, Economy and Civil Society (Cambridge: Cambridge University Press, 2011).

Li, Yu-chun, Hua-Wei Wang, Jiao-Yang Tian et al., 'Cultural Diffusion of Indo-Aryan Languages into Bangladesh: A Perspective from Mitochondrial DNA', *Mitochondrion*, 38 (2018), 23–30.

'Life Is Not Ours': Land and Human Rights in the Chittagong Hill Tracts, Bangladesh – Update 3 (Amsterdam: Chittagong Hill Tracts Commission, 1997).

'Life Is Not Ours': *Land and Human Rights in the Chittagong Hill Tracts, Bangladesh – Update 4* (Amsterdam: Chittagong Hill Tracts Commission, 2000).

Lifschultz, Lawrence, *Bangladesh: The Unfinished Revolution* (London: Zed Books, 1979).

Lintner, Bertil, 'Bangladesh: Breeding Ground for Muslim Terror', *Asia Times* (21 September 2002).

Liu, Peng, and Priyanka Pandit, 'Building Ports with China's Assistance: Perspectives from Littoral Countries', *Maritime Affairs*, 14:1 (2018), 99–107.

Long, J., *Adam's Reports on Vernacular Education in Bengal and Behar, Submitted to Government in 1835, 1836, and 1838, with a Brief View of Its Past and Present Condition* (Kolkata: Home Secretariat Press, 1868).

Lorea, Carola Erika, 'Bengali Settlers in the Andaman Islands', *Newsletter – International Institute of Asian Studies*, 77 (2017), 4–5.

'Pregnant Males, Barren Mothers, and Religious Transvestism: Transcending Gender in the Songs and Practices of "Heterodox" Bengali Lineages', *Asian Ethnology*, 77:1–2 (2018a), 169–213.

'Snake Charmers on Parade: A Performance-Centered Study of the Crisis of the Ojhā Healers', *Asian Medicine*, 13 (2018b), 247–75.

Low, D. A. (ed.), *The Political Inheritance of Pakistan* (Cambridge: Cambridge University Press, 1991).

Ludden, David, 'Investing in Nature around Sylhet: An Excursion into Geographical History', *Economic and Political Weekly*, 38:48 (2003a), 5080–8.

'The First Boundary of Bangladesh on Sylhet's Northern Frontiers', *Journal of the Asiatic Society of Bangladesh (Humanities)*, 48:1 (2003b), 1–54.

'Country Politics and Agrarian Systems: Land Grab on Bengal Frontiers, 1750–1800', *Modern Asian Studies*, 51:2 (2017), 319–49.

'Cowry Country: Mobile Space and Imperial Territory', in: Eric Tagliacozzo, Helen F. Siu and Peter C. Perdue (eds.), *Asia Inside Out: Itinerant People* (Cambridge, MA: Harvard University Press, 2019), 75–100.

Luthfa, Samina, 'Transnational Ties and Reciprocal Tenacity: Resisting Mining in Bangladesh with Transnational Coalition', *Sociology*, 51:1 (2017), 127–45.

Mackintosh-Smith, Tim (ed.), *The Travels of Ibn Battutah* (London: Picador, 2002).

Magon de Clos-Doré, A., *Souvenirs d'un voyageur en Asie, depuis 1802 jusqu'en 1815 inclusivement* [Memories of a traveller in Asia, from 1802 to 1815] (Paris: Nepveu, 1822).

Mamoon, Muntassir, *Dhaka: Smriti Bismritir Nogori* [Dhaka: Recalling the forgotten city] (Dhaka: Bangla Academy, 1993).

Unish Shotoker Bangladesher Songbad-Shamoyikpotro, 1847–1905 [Nineteenth-century newspapers and periodicals of Bangladesh, 1847-1905] (Dhaka: Bangla Academy, 1985–2000), 9 vols.

'Bengal Partition (1905): Reaction in Eastern Bengal', *Journal of Social Studies*, 114 (2007), 1–32.

Mamoon, Muntassir, and Jayanta Kumar Ray, *Civil Society in Bangladesh: Resilience and Retreat* (Dhaka: Subarna, 1998).

Mandal, Akhtaruzzaman, and Nayanika Mookherjee, '"Research" on Bangladesh War', *Economic and Political Weekly*, 42:50 (2007), 118–21.

Mani, Muthukumara, Sushenjit Bandyopadhay, Shun Chonabayashi et al., *South Asia's Hotspots: The Impact of Temperature and Precipitation Changes on Living Standards* (Washington, DC: World Bank, 2018).

Maniruzzaman, Talukder, 'National Integration and Political Development in Pakistan', *Asian Survey*, 7:12 (1967), 876–85.

'Bangladesh in 1974: Economic Crisis and Political Polarization', *Asian Survey*, 15:2 (1975), 117–28.

'Bangladesh in 1975: The Fall of the Mujib Regime and Its Aftermath', *Asian Survey*, 16:2 (1976), 119–29.

The Bangladesh Revolution and Its Aftermath (Dhaka: Bangladesh Books International, 1980).

Mannan, Xulhaz, 'Confronting the Comfortable Closet in Bangladesh', *Pink Pages: India's National LGBT Magazine*, n.d. https://pink-pages.co.in

Mapping Bangladesh's Political Crisis (Brussels: International Crisis Group, 2015).

Mapril, Jose, 'A Shahid Minar in Lisbon: Long Distance Nationalism, Politics of Memory and Community among Luso-Bangladeshis', *Samaj: South Asia Multidisciplinary Academic Journal*, 9 (2014), 1–20.

'Martial Law to Save Nation: Democracy Will Be Restored: Ershad', *Bangladesh Observer* (25 March 1982), 1.

Maswani, A. M. K., *Subversion in East Pakistan* (Lahore: Amir Publications, 1979).

Mazumdar, Shudha, *A Pattern of Life: The Memoirs of an Indian Woman*, edited by Geraldine Forbes (New Delhi: Manohar Book Publications, 1977).

Mazumder, Rajashree, 'Illegal Border Crossers and Unruly Citizens: Burma-Pakistan-Indian Borderlands from the Nineteenth to the Mid-Twentieth Centuries', *Modern Asian Studies*, 53:4 (2019), 1144–82.

'Medical Education: Bibliographical Record', *Indian Annals of Medical Science*, 2 (1855), 723, quoted in Christian Hochmuth, 'Patterns of Medical Culture in Colonial Bengal, 1835–1880', *Bulletin of the History of Medicine*, 80:1 (2006), 39–72.

Memon, Muhammad Umar, 'Urdu Creative Writing on National Disintegration: The Case of Bangladesh', *Journal of Asian Studies*, 43:1 (1983), 105–27.

Mevissen, Gerd J. R., 'Stone Image of Jina Rsabhanatha with Astadikpalas in Dinajpur Museum', *Journal of the Asiatic Society of Bangladesh (Humanities)*, 50:1–2 (2005), 83–96.

Mey, Wolfgang (ed.), *They Are Now Burning Village after Village: Genocide in the Chittagong Hill Tracts, Bangladesh* (Copenhagen: International Work Group for Indigenous Affairs, 1984).

Mirza, M. Monirul Qader, 'Three Recent Extreme Floods in Bangladesh: A Hydro-Metereological Analysis', *Natural Hazards*, 28 (2003), 35–64.

Misbahuzzaman, Khaled, 'Traditional Farming in the Mountainous Region of Bangladesh and Its Modifications', *Journal of Mountain Science*, 13:8 (2016), 1489–1502.

Mishra, Raghavendra, 'The "Grey Area" in the Northern Bay of Bengal: A Note on a Functional Cooperative Solution', *Ocean Development and International Law*, 47:1 (2016), 29–39.

Misra, K. P., 'Intra-State Imperialism: The Case of Pakistan', *Journal of Peace Research*, 9:1 (1972), 27–39.

Misra, Sanghamitra, 'The Sovereignty of Political Economy: The Garos in a Pre-Conquest and Early Conquest Era', *Indian Economic and Social History Review*, 55:3 (2018), 1–43.

Mitri, Marco, and Dhiraj Neog, 'Preliminary Report on the Excavations of Neolithic Sites from Khasi Hills, Meghalaya', *Ancient Asia*, 7:7 (2016), 1–17.

Mizan, Mizanur Rahman, *Muktijuddhe Ohidur Bahini* [The Ohidur Bahini in the Liberation War] (Khulna: Gonohotta-Nirjaton O Muktijuddho Bishoyok Gobeshona Kendro, 2018).

Mohaiemen, Naeem, 'Flying Blind: Waiting for a Real Reckoning on 1971', *Economic and Political Weekly*, 46:36 (2011a), 40–52.

'Another Reckoning', *Economic and Political Weekly*, 46:53 (2011b), 79–80.

'Simulation at Wars' End: A "Documentary" in the Field of Evidence Quest', *BioScope: South Asian Screen Studies* 7:1 (2016), 31–57.

Mohsin, Amena, *The Politics of Nationalism: The Case of the Chittagong Hill Tracts, Bangladesh* (Dhaka: University Press Limited, 1997).

Mookherjee, Nayanika, '"Remembering to Forget": Public Secrecy and Memory of Sexual Violence in the Bangladesh War of 1971', *Journal of the Royal Anthropological Institute* (NS), 12 (2006), 433–50.

'The "Dead and Their Double Duties": Mourning, Melancholia, and the Martyred Intellectual Memorials in Bangladesh', *Space and Culture*, 10 (2007), 271–91.

'Culinary Boundaries and the Making of Place in Bangladesh', *South Asia: Journal of South Asian Studies*, 31:1 (2008), 56–75.

The Spectral Wound: Sexual Violence, Public Memories, and the Bangladesh War of 1971 (Durham, NC: Duke University Press, 2015).

'Pakistan's Past and Knowing What Not to Narrate', *Comparative Studies of South Asia, Africa and the Middle East*, 39:1 (2019), 212–22.

Mookherjee, Nayanika, and Najmunnahar Keya, *Birangonas: Towards Ethical Testimonies of Sexual Violence during Conflict* (Durham, UK: University of Durham, 2019). www.ethical-testimonies-svc.org.uk

Mooney, Turloch, 'Geopolitics Hamper Modernization of Bangladesh Ports', *JOC.com* (19 October 2016). www.joc.com

Moudud, Hasna Jasimuddin, *A Thousand Year Old Bengali Mystic Poetry* (Dhaka: University Press Limited, 1992).

Muhammad, Anu, 'Globalisation and Economic Transformation in a Peripheral Economy: The Bangladesh Experience', *Economic and Political Weekly*, 41:15 (2006), 1459–64.

Muhammed, Yunus (ed.), *Album: Gono Andolon (1982–1990)* [Album: People's movement (1982–1990)], vol. 1 (Chittagong: Tolpar, 1993).

Mujahid, Sharif al, 'Pakistan: First General Elections', *Asian Survey*, 11:2 (1971), 159–71.

Mukharji, Projit, 'Lokman, Chholeman and Manik Pir: Multiple Frames of Institutionalising Islamic Medicine in Modern Bengal', *Social History of Medicine*, 24:3 (2011), 720–38.

Mukherjee, Sipra, 'In Opposition and Allegiance to Hinduism: Exploring the Bengali Matua Hagiography of Harichand Thakur', *South Asia: Journal of South Asian Studies*, 41:2 (2018), 435–51.

Mukul, Sharif Ahmed, A. Z. M. Manzoor Rashid and Mohammad Belal Uddin, 'The Role of Spiritual Beliefs in Conserving Wildlife Species in Religious Shrines of Bangladesh', *Biodiversity*, 13:2 (2012), 108–14.

Murshid, Navine, 'Bangladesh Copes with the Rohingya Crisis by Itself', *Current History*, 117:798 (2018), 129–34.

Murshid, Tazeen M., *The Sacred and the Secular: Bengal Muslim Discourses, 1871–1977* (New York: Oxford University Press, 1995).

'The Rise of the Religious Right in Bangladesh: Taslima Nasrin and the Media', in: A. Imam et al. (2004), 99–105.

'Muslim League Debacle in E. Bengal Elections: Habibullah Proposes Top-Level Inquiry', *Pakistan Times* (25 September 1954), 1, 3.

Nandi, Rajib, 'Spectacles of Ethnographic and Historical Imaginations: Kamatapur Movement and the Rajbanshi Quest to Rediscover Their Past and Selves', *History and Anthropology*, 25:5 (2014), 571–91.

Nandy, Ashis, 'A Report on the Present State of Health of the Gods and Goddesses in South Asia', *Postcolonial Studies*, 4:2 (2001), 125–41.

Nargis, Deena and Faustina Pereira, 'Taking Cognizance of Illegal Fatwa', *Interventions: International Journal of Postcolonial Studies*, 4:2 (2002), 215–19.

Nasrin, Taslima, *Behula Eka Bhasiyechila Bhela* [Behula floated the raft alone] (Dhaka: Shikha Prakashani, 1993).

Shame: A Novel (Guilford, CT: Prometheus, 1997).

'Bhongo Bongo Desh'. English translation: 'Broken Bengal' by Subhoranjan Dasgupta, published in 'Porous Borders, Divided Selves: A Symposium on Partition', *Seminar, The Monthly Symposium*, 510 (2002), 38.

Nathan, Mīrzā, *Bahāristan-i-Ghaybī: A History of the Mughal Wars in Assam, Cooch Behar, Bengal, Bihar and Orissa during the Reign of Jahangir and Shahjahan* (translated from the original Persian by M. I. Borah) (Gauhati: Narayani Handiqui Historical Institute, Department of Historical and Antiquarian Studies, Government of Assam, 1936), 2 vols.

Naved, Ruchira Tabassum, and Lars Ake Persson, 'Dowry and Spousal Physical Violence Against Women in Bangladesh', *Journal of Family Issues*, 31:6 (2010), 830–56.

Niazi, A. A. K., *The Betrayal of East Pakistan* (Dhaka: University Press Limited, 1999).

Nicholas, Ralph W., 'The Goddess Sitala and Epidemic Smallpox in Bengal', *Journal of Asian Studies*, 41:1 (1981), 21–44.

'Islam and Vaishnavism in the Environment of Rural Bengal', in: Rafiuddin Ahmed (ed.), *Understanding the Bengal Muslims: Interpretative Essays* (New Delhi: Oxford University Press, 2001), 52–70.

Fruits of Worship: Practical Religion in Bengal (New Delhi: Chronicle Books, 2003).

Nicholls, Robert J., Craig W. Hutton, W. Neil Adger et al. (eds.), *Ecosystem Services for Well-Being in Deltas: Integrated Assessment for Policy Analysis* (Cham: Palgrave Macmillan, 2018).

Nuremowla, Sadid, 'Land, Place and Resistance to Displacement in Phulbari', *Samaj: South Asia Multidisciplinary Academic Journal*, 13 (2016), 1–17.

Nuruzzaman, Mohammed, 'Labor Resistance to Pro-market Economic Reforms in Bangladesh', *Journal of Asian and African Studies*, 41:4 (2006), 341–57.

Oldenburg, Philip, '"A Place Insufficiently Imagined": Language, Belief and the Pakistan Crisis of 1971', *Journal of Asian Studies*, 44:4 (1985), 711–33.

Oliver, Thomas W., *The United Nations in Bangladesh* (Princeton, NJ: Princeton University Press, 1978).

Openshaw, Jeanne, *Seeking Bauls of Bengal* (Cambridge: Cambridge University Press, 2002).

Orgeret, Kristin Skare, and Hillol Sobhan, 'The BDR Mutiny in Bangladeshi Media: From a "Proletarian Revolution" to a "Brutal Massacre"', *Conflict and Communication Online*, 11:1 (2012), 1–16.

Panday, Pranab, and Linda Che-lan Li, 'Women's Political Participation in Bangladesh: Role of Women's Organizations', *International Journal of Public Administration*, 37:11 (2014), 724–36.

Panja, Sheena, 'Monuments in a Flood Zone: "Builders" and "Recipients" in Ancient Varendri (Eastern India and Bangladesh)', *Antiquity*, 77:297 (2003), 497–504.

Paprocki, Kasia, 'Threatening Dystopias: Development and Adaptation Regimes in Bangladesh', *Annals of the American Association of Geographers*, 108:4 (2018), 955–73.

Paprocki, Kasia, and Jason Cons, 'Life in a Shrimp Zone: Aqua- and Other Cultures of Bangladesh's Coastal Landscape', *Journal of Peasant Studies*, 41:6 (2014), 1109–30.

Park, Richard L., and Richard S. Wheeler, 'East Bengal under Governor's Rule', *Far Eastern Survey*, 23:9 (1954), 129–34.

Parvez, Mahbub, and Md. Jahid Bin Kashem, 'Young Tourists' Attitude towards Domestic Tourism: A Study on Bangladesh', *Problems and Perspectives in Management*, 16:3 (2018), 117–29.

Permanent Court of Arbitration, *Bay of Bengal Maritime Boundary Arbitration between Bangladesh and India* (2014). https://pca-cpa.org/en/cases/18/

Peterson, David A., 'Bangladesh Khumi', in: Alice Vittrant and Justin Watkins (eds.), *The Mainland Southeast Asia Linguistic Area* (Berlin: De Gruyter Mouton, 2019), 12–55.

Philip, Sjoukje, Sarah Sparrow, Sarah F. Kew et al., 'Attributing the 2017 Bangladesh Floods from Meteorological and Hydrological Perspectives', *Hydrology and Earth System Sciences*, 23 (2019), 1409–29.

Pokrant, Bob, Peter Reeves and John McGuire, 'Bengal Fishers and Fisheries: A Historiographical Essay', in: S. Bandyopadhyay (ed.) (2001), 93–117.

'Political Activities Banned: Awami League is Outlawed – Defiance of Law Act of Treason – A. L. Insulted National Flag and Quaid – Transfer of Power Pledge Reiterated – President's Address to Nation', *Pakistan Times* (27 March 1971).

Prakash, Om, *The Dutch East India Company and the Economy of Bengal, 1630–1720* (Princeton, NJ: Princeton University Press, 1985).

'The Indian Maritime Merchant, 1500–1800', *Journal of the Economic and Social History of the Orient*, 47:3 (2004), 435–57.

Prasad, Srirupa, 'Sanitizing the Domestic: Hygiene and Gender in Late Colonial Bengal', *Journal of Women's History*, 27:3 (2015), 132–53.

Prasse-Freeman, Elliott, and Kirt Mausert, 'Two Sides of the Same Arakanese Coin: "Rakhine", "Rohingya", and Ethnogenesis as Schismogenesis', in: Pavin Chachavalpongpun, Elliott Prasse-Freeman and Patrick Strefford (eds.), *Unravelling Myanmar's Transition: Progress, Retrenchment, and Ambiguity Amidst Liberalization* (Kyoto: Kyoto University Press, 2020).

'Presidential Address of M. A. Jinnah – Lahore, March 1940', in: Mushirul Hasan (ed.), *India's Partition: Process, Strategy and Mobilization* (Delhi: Oxford University Press, 1993), 44–58.

Quaderi, Fazlul Quader (comp. and ed.), *Bangladesh Genocide and World Press* (Dhaka: Begum Dilafroz Quaderi, 1972).

Quadir, Muhammad Nurul, *Dusho Chheshotti Dine Swadhinota* [Independence in 266 days] (Dhaka: Mukto Publishers, 1997).

Quayum, Mohammad A., 'Gender and Education: The Vision and Activism of Rokeya Sakhawat Hossain', *Journal of Human Values*, 22:2 (2016), 139–50.

Quibria, M. G. (ed.), *The Bangladesh Economy in Transition* (Delhi: Oxford University Press, 1997).

Qureshi, Mahmud Shah (ed.), *Tribal Cultures in Bangladesh* (Rajshahi: Institute of Bangladesh Studies, 1984).

Raghavan, Srinath, *1971: A Global History of the Creation of Bangladesh* (Cambridge, MA: Harvard University Press, 2013).

Rahman, Hafizur, 'Can the Bengalis Forgive Us?' in: Salim (ed.) (2012), 17–19.

Rahman, Mahbubur (ed.), *Dhaka: An Urban Reader* (Dhaka: University Press Limited, 2016).

Rahman, Matiur, and Naeem Hasan, *Iron Bars of Freedom* (London: News and Media, 1980).

Rahman, Md. Ashiqur, 'Governance Matters: Climate Change, Corruption, and Livelihoods in Bangladesh', *Climatic Change*, 147 (2018), 313–26.

Rahman, Md. Mahbubar, *Bangladesher Itihash, 1947–71* [History of Bangladesh, 1947–71] (Dhaka: Shomoy Prokashon, 1999).

Ekattore Gaibandha [Gaibandha District in 1971] (Dhaka: Bangladesh Chorcha, 2005).

(ed.), *Purbo Banglar Gramin Orthoniti, Shomaj O Shongskriti (1923–43): Md. Bosharot Alir Dinponji* [The village economy, society and culture of East Bengal (1923–43): Md. Bosharot Ali's diary] (Dhaka: Asiatic Society of Bangladesh, 2011).

Rahman, Md. Mahbubar, and Willem van Schendel, 'Gender and the Inheritance of Land: Living Law in Bangladesh', in: Jan Breman, Peter Kloos and Ashwani Saith (eds.), *The Village in Asia Revisited* (Delhi: Oxford University Press, 1997), 237–76.

'"I Am Not a Refugee": Rethinking Partition Migration', *Modern Asian Studies*, 37:3 (2003), 551–84.

Rahman, Mohammed, and Sharif Imon, 'Conservation of Historic Waterfront to Improve the Quality of Life in Old Dhaka', *International Journal of Architectural Research*, 11:2 (2017), 83–100.

Rahman, Mohammad Ataur, and Sowmen Rahman, 'Natural and Traditional Defense Mechanisms to Reduce Climate Risks in Coastal Zones of Bangladesh', *Weather and Climate Extremes*, 7 (2015), 84–95.

Rahman, Momin, *Homosexualities, Muslim Cultures and Modernity* (Basingstoke: Palgrave Macmillan, 2014).

Rahman, Pk. Md. Motiur, *Poverty Issues in Rural Bangladesh* (Dhaka: University Press Limited, 1994).

Rahman, S. M. Mizanur, 'Shipbreaking in Bangladesh: Perspective from Industrial Ecology, Political Ecology and Environmental Policy' (PhD thesis, Michigan Technological University, 2016).

Rahman, Sanzidur, Mohammad Mizanul Haque Kazal, Ismat Ara Begum, and Mohammad Jahangir Alam, 'Exploring the Future Potential of Jute in Bangladesh', *Agriculture*, 7:96 (2017), 1–16.

Rahman, Shadlee, 'A Critical Examination of Inter-temporal Spatial Poverty Trends in Bangladesh: The Case of the East–West Divide', *South Asia Economic Journal*, 19:1 (2018), 108–23.

Rahman, Sufi Mostafizur, Muhammad Habibulla Pathan and Md. Mahabub-ul Alam, 'Wari-Bateshwar', in: A. M. Chowdhury and Chakravarti (eds.) (2018), 1:467–96.

Rajamohan, P. G., *Harkat-ul-Jihad-al-Islami Bangladesh (HuJI-BD)* (New Delhi: Institute of Conflict Management, 2002).

Raju, Zakir Hossain, 'Bangladesh: Native Resistance and Nationalist Discourse', in: Anne Tereska Ciecko (ed.), *Contemporary Asian Cinema: Popular Culture in a Global Frame* (Oxford: Berg, 2006), 120–32.

'Indigenization of Cinema in (Post)Colonial South Asia: From Transnational to Vernacular Public Spheres', *Comparative Studies of South Asia, Africa and the Middle East*, 32:3 (2012), 611–21.

Ramachandran, Sujata, 'Of Boundaries and Border Crossings: Undocumented Bangladeshi "Infiltrators" and the Hegemony of Hindu Nationalism in India', *Interventions: International Journal of Postcolonial Studies*, 1:2 (1999), 235–53.

Raper, Arthur F., *Rural Development in Action: The Comprehensive Experiment at Comilla, East Pakistan* (Ithaca, NY: Cornell University Press, 1970).

Rashid, Haroun er, *Economic Geography of Bangladesh* (Dhaka: University Press Limited, 2005).

Rashid, Md. Shahinur, 'Agricultural Technology', in: A. M. Chowdhury and Chakravarti (eds.) (2018), 2:197–232.

Rashid, Towhida, *Holocene Sea-level Scenarios in Bangladesh* (Singapore: Springer, 2014).

Rashiduzzaman, M., *Politics and Administration in the Local Councils: A Study of Union and District Councils in East Pakistan* (Karachi: Oxford University Press, 1968).

    'The Awami League in the Political Development of Pakistan', *Asian Survey*, 10:7 (1970), 574–87.

    'The Liberals and the Religious Right in Bangladesh', *Asian Survey*, 34:11 (1994), 974–9.

Ray, Aniruddha, 'The Portuguese', in: Islam and Miah (eds.) (2003), 8:142–6.

Ray, Himangshu Prabha, *The Archaeology of Seafaring in Ancient South Asia* (Cambridge: Cambridge University Press, 2003).

    'The Archaeology of Bengal: Trading Networks, Cultural Identities', *Journal of the Economic and Social History of the Orient*, 49:1 (2006), 68–95.

Ray, Manas, 'Growing Up Refugee: On Memory and Locality', *History Workshop Journal*, 53 (2002), 149–79.

Raychaudhuri, Tapan, *Bengal under Akbar and Jahangir: An Introductory Study in Social History* (Delhi: Munshiram Manoharlal, 1969 [1953]).

Rayhan, Morshed, 'Prospects of Public Archaeology in Heritage Management in Bangladesh: Perspective of Wari-Bateshwar', *Archaeologies*, 8:2 (2012), 169–87.

Redclift, Victoria, *Statelessness and Citizenship: Camps and the Creation of Political Space* (London: Routledge, 2013).

    'Displacement, Integration and Identity in the Postcolonial World', *Identities*, 23:2 (2016), 117–35.

Reza, C. M. Tarek, *Ekush: A Photographic History of the Language Movement (1947–1956)* (Dhaka: Standard Chartered Bank, 2004).

Riaz, Ali, *State, Class and Military Rule: Political Economy of Martial Law in Bangladesh* (Dhaka: Nadi New Press, 1994).

    Islamist Militancy in Bangladesh: A Complex Web (Oxford: Routledge, 2008).

    'Bangladesh's Failed Election', *Journal of Democracy*, 25:2 (2014), 119–30.

    Bangladesh: A Political History Since Independence (London: I. B. Tauris, 2016).

Riaz, Ali, and C. Christine Fair (eds.), *Political Islam and Governance in Bangladesh* (London: Routledge, 2011).

Richards, John F., and Elizabeth P. Flint, 'Long-Term Transformations in the Sundarbans Wetlands Forests of Bengal', *Agriculture and Human Values*, 7:2 (1990), 17–33.

Ridley, Glynis, *Clara's Grand Tour: Travels with an Eighteenth-Century Rhinoceros* (London: Atlantic Books, 2004).

Rogaly, Ben, Barbara Harriss-White and Sugata Bose (eds.), *Sonar Bangla? Agricultural Growth and Agrarian Change in West Bengal and Bangladesh* (Delhi: Sage Publications, 1999).

Roy, Asim, 'Being and Becoming a Muslim: A Historiographic Perspective on the Search for Muslim Identity in Bengal', in: S. Bandyopadhyay (ed.) (2001), 167–229.

Roy, Beth, *Some Trouble with Cows: Making Sense of Social Conflict* (Berkeley: University of California Press, 1994).

Roy, Haimanti, *Partitioned Lives: Migrants, Refugees, Citizens in India and Pakistan, 1947–1965* (Delhi: Oxford University Press, 2012).

Roy, Pinaki, '2,500-year-old Crop Seeds Discovered: New Clue to Ancient Farming Practices in Bangladesh', *Daily Star* (2 March 2019).

Roy, Raja Devasish, Amena Mohsin, Meghna Guhathakurta, Prashanta Tripura and Philip Gain, *The Chittagong Hill Tracts: Life and Nature at Risk* (Dhaka: Society for Environment and Human Development, 2000).

Roy, Raja Tridiv, *The Departed Melody (Memoirs)* (Islamabad: PPA Publications, 2003).

Roy, Samaren, *The Roots of Bengali Culture* (Kolkata: Firma K. L. Mukhopadhyay, 1981).

Roy, Suprakash, *Bharoter Krishok-Bidroho o Gonotontrik Songgram* (Kolkata: DBNA Brothers, 1980). English translation: *Peasant Revolts and Democratic Struggles in India*, translated by Rita Banerjee (Kolkata: Naya Udyog, for International Centre for Bengal Studies, 1999).

Rozario, Santi, 'The New Burqa in Bangladesh: Empowerment or Violation of Women's Rights?' *Women's Studies International Forum*, 29 (2006), 368–80.

'Outside the Moral Economy? Single Female Migrants and the Changing Bangladeshi Family', *Australian Journal of Anthropology*, 18:2 (2007), 154–71.

Rummel, Rudolph J., *Statistics of Democide: Genocide and Mass Murder since 1900* (Münster: LIT Verlag, 1998).

Rural Life in Bengal Illustrative of Anglo-Indian Suburban Life; More Particularly in Connection with the Planter and Peasantry, the Varied Produce of the Soil and Seasons; With Copious Details of the Culture and Manufacture of Indigo – Letters from an Artist in India to His Sisters in England. . . (London: W. Thacker, 1860).

Ruud, Arild Engelsen, 'The Political Bully in Bangladesh', in: Anastasia Piliavsky (ed.), *Patronage as Politics in South Asia* (Cambridge: Cambridge University Press, 2014), 303–25.

Ruud, Arild Engelsen, 'The Osman Dynasty: The Making and Unmaking of a Political Family', *Studies in Indian Politics*, 6:2 (2018), 209–24.

Ruud, Arild Engelsen, and Mohammad Mozahidul Islam, 'Political Dynasty Formation in Bangladesh', *South Asia: Journal of South Asian Studies*, 39:2 (2016), 401–14.

Saaz, Sadaf, 'Dying to Tell a Story: The List of What Bangladeshi Writers Cannot Talk about Is Getting Longer, But That Isn't Stopping Some from Writing', *Index on Censorship*, 46:1 (2017), 34–6.

Sabur, Seuty, 'Mobility through Affinal Relations: Bangladeshi "Middle Class", Transmigrants and Networks' (PhD thesis, National University of Singapore, 2010).

'Post Card from Shahabag', *isa e-Forum for Sociology* (2013), 1–18.

'Marital Mobility in the Bangladeshi Middle Class: Matchmaking Strategies and Transnational Networks', *South Asia: Journal of South Asian Studies*, 37:4 (2014), 586–604.

Saikia, Arupjyoti, 'Borders, Commodities and Citizens across Mud and River: Assam, 1947–50s', *Studies in History*, 32:1 (2016), 72–96.

Saikia, Yasmin, 'History on the Line: Beyond the Archive of Silence: Narratives of Violence of the 1971 Liberation War of Bangladesh', *History Workshop Journal*, 58 (2004), 275–87.

Women, War, and the Making of Bangladesh: Remembering 1971 (Durham, NC: Duke University Press, 2011).

Saleem, Ahmad (comp. and ed.), *It Is My Mother's Face: Selected Readings on Bengali Language Movement* (Lahore: Sanjh Publications, n.d. [2006]).

Salik, Siddiq, *The Wounded Pride: Reminiscences of a Pakistani Prisoner of War in India (1971–1973)* (Lahore: Wajidalis, 1984a).

'Witness to Surrender: 26th April–2nd May, 1971', in: *Bangladesher Swadhinota Juddho: Dolilpottro/History of Bangladesh War of Independence: Documents* (Dhaka: Ministry of Information, Government of the People's Republic of Bangladesh, 1984b), 7:4–8.

Witness to Surrender (Karachi: Oxford University Press, 1998 [1977]).

Salim, Ahmad (comp. and ed.), *Ten Days That Dismembered Pakistan: March 15–March 25, 1971: The Real Story of the Yahya–Mujib–Bhutto Talks* (Islamabad: Dost Publications, 2001).

(ed.), *We Owe an Apology to Bangladesh* (Dhaka: Sahitya Prakash, 2012).

Salles, Jean-François, 'Mahasthan', in: A. M. Chowdhury and Chakravarti (eds.) (2018), 1:224–62.

Sarkar, Jadunath (ed.), *The History of Bengal. Volume II: Muslim Period, 1200–1757* (Dhaka: University of Dhaka, 1976 [1948]).

Sarkar, Mahua, 'Changing Together, Changing Apart: Urban Muslim and Hindu Women in Pre-Partition Bengal', *History and Memory*, 27:1 (2015), 5–42.

Sarker, Masud, and Shahidul Islam, 'Impacts of International Migration on Socio-economic Development in Bangladesh', *European Review of Applied Sociology*, 11:16 (2018), 27–35.

Sarkar, Nikhil, *A Matter of Conscience: Artists Bear Witness to the Great Bengal Famine of 1943*, translated by Satyabrata Dutta (Kolkata: Punascha, 1998).

Sarkar, Sumit, *The Swadeshi Movement in Bengal, 1903–1908* (New Delhi: People's Publishing House, 1973).

Sarkar, Tanika (ed.), *Words to Win: The Making of Amar Jiban: A Modern Autobiography* (New Delhi: Kali for Women, 1999).

Sartori, Andrew, *Bengal in Global Concept History: Culturalism in the Age of Capital* (Chicago: University of Chicago Press, 2008).

'A Liberal Discourse of Custom in Colonial Bengal', *Past and Present*, 212 (2011), 163–97.

Schoff, Wilfred H. (trans. and ed.), *The Periplus of the Erythraean Sea: Travel and Trade in the Indian Ocean by a Merchant of the First Century* (New York: Longmans Green, 1912).

Schouten, Wouter, *Reistogt naar en door Oostindien* [Journey to and across the East Indies], 4th ed. (Utrecht, 1775 [1676]).

Schuler, Sidney Ruth, Rachel Lenzi, Shamsul Huda Badal and Sohela Nazneen, 'Men's Perspectives on Women's Empowerment and Intimate Partner Violence in Rural Bangladesh', *Culture, Health and Sexuality*, 20:1 (2018), 113–27.

Seabrook, Jeremy, *Freedom Unfinished: Fundamentalism and Popular Resistance in Bangladesh Today* (London: Zed Books, 2001).

Seddiky, Md. Assraf, 'Poverty and Social Vulnerability of Stone Quarry Workers in Bangladesh: An Ethnographic Study', *Journal of Emerging Trends in Educational Research and Policy Studies (JETERAPS)*, 5:6 (2014), 684–94.

Selim, Lala Rukh, 'Art of Bangladesh: The Changing Role of Tradition, Search for Identity and Globalization', *Samaj: South Asia Multidisciplinary Academic Journal*, 9 (2014), 1–21.

Sen, Amartya, *Poverty and Famines: An Essay on Entitlement and Deprivation* (Oxford: Clarendon Press, 1981).

Sen, Dwaipayan, '"No Matter How, Jogendranath Had to Be Defeated": The Scheduled Castes Federation and the Making of Partition in Bengal, 1945–1947', *Indian Economic and Social History Review*, 49:3 (2012), 321–64.

Sen, Krishna, 'Lessons in Self-Fashioning: "Bamabodhini Patrika" and the Education of Women in Colonial Bengal', *Victorian Periodicals Review*, 37:2 (2004), 176–91.

Sen, Sudipta, 'Betwixt Hindus and Muslims: The Many Lives of Zafar Khan, Ghazi of Tribeni', *Asian Ethnology*, 76:2 (2017), 213–34.

Sen, Sukumar, *History of Bengali Literature* (New Delhi: Sahitya Akademi, 1960).

Sen, Swadhin, 'Community Boundary, Secularized Religion and Imagined Past in Bangladesh: Archaeology and Historiography of Unequal Encounter', *World Archaeology*, 34:2 (2002), 346–62.

'The Transformative Context of a Temple in Early Medieval Varendri: Report of the Excavation at Tileshwarir Aara in Dinajpur District, Bangladesh', *South Asian Studies*, 31:1 (2015), 71–110.

'Landscape Contexts of the Early Mediaeval Settlements in Varendri/Gauda: An Outline on the Basis of Total Surveying and Excavations in Dinajpur-Joypurhat Districts, Bangladesh', *Pratna Samiksha: A Journal of Archaeology* (NS), 8 (2017), 59–109.

Sen, Swadhin, A. K. M. Syfur Rahman and S. M. K. Ahsan, 'Crossing the Boundaries of the Archaeology of Somapura Mahavihara: Alternative Approaches and Propositions', *Pratnatattva, Journal of the Dept. of Archaeology Jahangirnagar University*, 20 (2014), 49–79.

Sen, Uditi, 'The Myths Refugees Live By: Memory and History in the Making of Bengali Refugee Identity', *Modern Asian Studies*, 48:1 (2014), 37–76.

Sengupta, Anwesha, *'They Must Have to Go Therefore, Elsewhere': Mapping the Many Displacements of Bengali Hindu Refugees from East Pakistan, 1947 to 1960s* (Patna: Tata Institute of Social Sciences, 2017).

'Unthreading Partition: The Politics of Jute Sharing between Two Bengals', *Economic and Political Weekly*, 53:4 (2018), 43–9.

Sengupta, Ashis (ed.), *Mapping South Asia through Contemporary Theatre: Essays on the Theatres of India, Pakistan, Bangladesh, Nepal and Sri Lanka* (Basingstoke: Palgrave Macmillan, 2014).

Sengupta, Gautam, Sima Roy Chowdhury and Sharmi Chakraborty, *Eloquent Earth: Early Terracottas in the State Archaeological Museum, West Bengal* (Kolkata: Directorate of Archaeology and Museums, West Bengal, 2007).

Sengupta, Jyoti, *Bangladesh in Blood and Tears* (Kolkata: Naya Prakash, 1981).

Shurjo Sen Smriti [Surya Sen memento] (Kolkata: Biplobtirtho Chottogram Smritishongstha Prokashon, 2003 [1971]).

Sengupta, Tania, 'Between Country and City: Fluid Spaces of Provincial Administrative Towns in Nineteenth-Century Bengal', *Urban History*, 39:1 (2012), 56–82.

'Living in the Periphery: Provinciality and Domestic Space in Colonial Bengal', *Journal of Architecture*, 18:6 (2013), 905–43.

Shahaduzzaman, *Kracher Kornel* [The colonel on crutches] (Dhaka: Mowla Brothers, 2010).

Shahed, Syed Mohammad, 'Bengali Folk Rhymes: An Introduction', *Asian Folklore Studies*, 52:1 (1993), 143–60.

'Caryāpada', in: A. M. Chowdhury and Chakravarti (eds.) (2018), 2:591–606.

Shamshad, Rizwana, 'Bengaliness, Hindu Nationalism and Bangladeshi Migrants in West Bengal, India', *Asian Ethnicity*, 18:4 (2017), 433–51.

Shamsuddin, Dara, *Bangladesher Sthannam Itihasher Podocinho* [Traces of history in Bangladeshi place names] (Dhaka: Shahityo Prokash, 2015).

'Shara Deshe Shamorik Ain Jari' [The entire country under martial law], *Doinik Ittefaq* (24 March 1982), 1.

'A Shattering First-Person Account of Just How Dangerous It Is to Be Queer in Bangladesh' (2016). www.youthkiawaaz.com/2016/06/being-queer-in-bangladesh

Shehabuddin, Elora, 'Jamaat-i-Islami in Bangladesh: Women, Democracy and the Transformation of Islamist Politics', *Modern Asian Studies*, 42:2–3 (2008), 577–603.

'Bangladeshi Civil Society and Islamist Politics', in: Riaz and Fair (eds.) (2011), 91–114.

'Feminism and Nationalism in Cold War East Pakistan', *Südasien-Chronik – South Asia Chronicle*, 4 (2014), 49–68.

Shewly, Hosna J., 'Life in De Facto Statelessness in Enclaves in India and Bangladesh', *Singapore Journal of Tropical Geography*, 38 (2017), 108–22.

Shoesmith, Brian, Jude William Genilo and Md. Asiuzzaman (eds.), *Bangladesh's Changing Mediascape: From State Control to Market Forces* (Bristol: Intellect, 2013).

Siddiki, Ishrak Ahmed, 'The Rooppur Nuclear Power Plant: Is Bangladesh Really Ready for Nuclear Power?' *Journal of World Energy Law and Business*, 8:1 (2015), 20–5.

Siddiki, Mamun, *Kumilla Pulish Lains Gonohotta* [Genocide in the police lines of Comilla] (Khulna: Gonohotta-Nirjaton O Muktijuddho Bishoyok Gobeshona Kendro, 2018).

Siddiqi, Abdul Rahman, *East Pakistan – The End Game: An Onlooker's Journal 1969–1971* (Karachi: Oxford University Press, 2004).

Siddiqi, Bulbul, *Becoming 'Good Muslim': The Tablighi Jamaat in the UK and Bangladesh* (Singapore: Springer Nature, 2018).

Siddiqi, Dina M., 'Islam, Gender and the Nation: The Social Life of Bangladeshi Fatwas', in: Deana Heath and Chandana Mathur (eds.), *Communalism and Globalization in South Asia and Its Diaspora* (Abingdon: Routledge, 2011a), 181–203.

'Transnational Feminism and "Local" Realities: The Imperiled Muslim Woman and the Production of (In)Justice', *Journal of Women of the Middle East and the Islamic World*, 9 (2011b), 76–96.

'Sexuality, Rights and Personhood: Tensions in a Transnational World', *BMC International Health and Human Rights*, 11 (Suppl. 3) (2011c), S5, 1–11.

'Starving for Justice: Bangladeshi Garment Workers in a "Post-Rana Plaza" World', *International Labor and Working-Class History*, 87 (2015), 165–73.

'Secular Quests, National Others: Revisiting Bangladesh's Constituent Assembly Debates', *Asian Affairs*, 49:2 (2018), 238–58.

'Exceptional Sexuality in a Time of Terror: "Muslim" Subjects and Dissenting/ Unmournable Bodies', *Samaj: South Asia Multidisciplinary Academic Journal*, 20 (2019), 1–17.

Siddiqui, Kamal, Jamshed Ahmed, Kaniz Siddique et al., *Social Formation in Dhaka City: A Study in Third World Urban Sociology* (Dhaka: University Press Limited, 1990).

Siddiqui, Tasneem, Institutionalising *Diaspora Linkage: The Emigrant Bangladeshis in UK and USA* (Dhaka: Ministry of Expatriates' Welfare and Overseas Employment, Government of Bangladesh, and International Organization for Migration, 2004).

International Labour Migration from Bangladesh: A Decent Work Perspective (Geneva: International Organization for Migration, 2005).

Siddiqui, Zillur Rahman, *Visions and Revisions: Higher Education in Bangladesh, 1947–1992* (Dhaka: University Press Limited, 1997).

Sil, Narasingha P., 'Bande Mataram: Bankimchandra Chattopadhyay's Nationalist Thought Revisited', *South Asia: Journal of South Asian Studies*, 25:1 (2002), 121–42.

Singh, Moni, *Jibon-Shongram* (Dhaka: n.p., 1983–1992), 2 vols. English translation: *Life Is a Struggle* (New Delhi: People's Publishing House, 1988).

Singhal, D. P., 'The New Constitution of Pakistan', *Asian Survey*, 2:6 (1962), 15–23.

Sinha, Mrinalini, *Colonial Masculinity: The 'Manly Englishman' and the 'Effeminate Bengali' in the Late Nineteenth Century* (Manchester: Manchester University Press, 1995).

Sinha-Kerkhoff, Kathinka, *Tyranny of Partition: Hindus in Bangladesh and Muslims in India* (New Delhi: Gyan Publishing House, 2006).

Siraj, Nasrin, and Ellen Bal, '"Hunger Has Brought Us into This Jungle": Understanding Mobility and Immobility of Bengali Immigrants in the Chittagong Hills of Bangladesh', *Social Identities*, 23:4 (2017), 396–412.

Sisson, Richard and Leo E. Rose, *War and Secession: Pakistan, India and the Creation of Bangladesh* (Berkeley: University of California Press, 1990).

Smith, Allan H., Elena O. Lingas and Mahfuzar Rahman, 'Contamination of Drinking-Water by Arsenic in Bangladesh: A Public Health Emergency', *Bulletin of the World Health Organization*, 78:9 (2000), 1093–103.

Smith, William L., 'The *Pati-Nindā* in Medieval Bengali Literature', *Journal of the American Oriental Society*, 99:1 (1979), 105–9.

   The One-Eyed Goddess: A Study of the Manasa Mangal (Stockholm: Almqvist and Wiksell, 1980).

Sobhan, Rehman, *Basic Democracies, Works Programme and Rural Development in East Pakistan* (Dhaka: Oxford University Press, 1968).

   'Who Pays for Development?' *Pakistan Forum*, 1:4 (1971), 6–7.

   The Crisis of External Dependence: The Political Economy of Foreign Aid to Bangladesh (Dhaka: University Press Limited, 1982).

   (ed.), *Bangladesh–India Relations: Perspectives from Civil Society Dialogues* (Dhaka: Centre for Policy Dialogue and University Press Limited, 2002).

Solomon, Carol, Keith Cantú and Saymon Zakaria, *City of Mirrors: Songs of Lālan Sāĩ* (New York: Oxford University Press, 2017).

Solvyns, François Balthazar, *The Costume of Hindostan, Elucidated by Sixty Coloured Engravings: With Descriptions in English and French* (London: Edward Orme, 1804).

Sommer, Alfred, and W. Henry Mosley, 'The Cyclone: Medical Assessment and Determination of Relief and Rehabilitation Needs', in: Lincoln C. Chen (ed.), *Disaster in Bangladesh* (New York: Oxford University Press, 1973), 119–32.

Sopher, David E., 'The Swidden/Wet-Rice Transition Zone in the Chittagong Hills', *Annals of the Association of American Geographers*, 54:1 (1964), 107–26.

Southard, Barbara, *The Women's Movement and Colonial Politics in Bengal, 1921–1936* (Dhaka: University Press Limited, 1996).

The State of Governance in Bangladesh 2006: Knowledge, Perceptions, Reality (Dhaka: Centre for Governance Studies, BRAC University, 2006).

Statistical Pocket-Book of Pakistan 1970 (Karachi: Manager of Publications, 1970).

Statistical Digest of Bangladesh No. 9: 1973 (Dhaka: Bangladesh Bureau of Statistics, 1973).

Statistical Pocket Book of Bangladesh 1987 (Dhaka: Bangladesh Bureau of Statistics, 1988).

Stewart, Tony K., 'In Search of Equivalence: Conceiving Muslim-Hindu Encounter through Translation Theory', *History of Religions*, 40:3 (2001), 261–88.

Fabulous Females and Peerless Pirs: Tales of Mad Adventure in Old Bengal (New York: Oxford University Press, 2004).

'Foreword', in: S. Zakaria (2013a), ix–xii.

'Religion in the Subjunctive: Vaiṣṇava Narrative, Sufi Counter-Narrative in Early Modern Bengal', *Journal of Hindu Studies*, 6 (2013b), 52–72.

Stojanov, Robert, Ingrid Boas, Ilan Kelman and Barbora Duží, 'Local Expert Experiences and Perceptions of Environmentally Induced Migration from Bangladesh to India', *Asia Pacific Viewpoint*, 58:3 (2017), 347–61.

Straume, E. O., C. Gaina, S. Medvedev et al., 'GlobSed: Updated Total Sediment Thickness in the World's Oceans', *Geochemistry, Geophysics, Geosystems*, 20:4 (2019), 1756–72.

Sultana, Gazi Nurun Nahar, Mohd Istiaq Sharif, Md. Asaduzzaman and Gyaneshwar Chaubey, 'Evaluating the Genetic Impact of South and Southeast Asia on the Peopling of Bangladesh', *Legal Medicine*, 17 (2015), 446–50.

Sultana, Habiba, 'Sex Worker Activism, Feminist Discourse and HIV in Bangladesh', *Culture, Health and Sexuality*, 17:6 (2015), 777–88.

Sultana, Razia, 'Women's Occupation in Medieval Bengal', in: Firdous Azim and Niaz Zaman (eds.), *Infinite Variety: Women in Society and Literature* (Dhaka: University Press Limited, 1994), 55–82.

Sultana, Umme Busra Fateha, 'Gender, Sexuality and Contraceptive Advertisements in Bangladesh: Representation and Lived Experience across Social Classes and Generations' (DPhil thesis, University of Sussex, 2015).

Sunderason, Sanjukta, 'Shadow-Lines: Zainul Abedin and the Afterlives of the Bengal Famine of 1943', *Third Text*, 31:2–3 (2017), 239–59.

Sur, Malini, 'Through Metal Fences: Material Mobility and the Politics of Transnationality at Borders', *Mobilities*, 8:1 (2013), 70–89.

'Battles for the Golden Grain: Paddy Soldiers and the Making of the Northeast India–East Pakistan Border, 1930–1970', *Comparative Studies in Society and History*, 58:3 (2016), 804–32.

Sur, Malini, and Masja van Meeteren, 'The Borders of Integration: Paperwork between Bangladesh and Belgium', in: Reece Jones and Md. Azmeary Ferdoush (eds.), *Borders and Mobility in South Asia and Beyond* (Amsterdam: Amsterdam University Press, 2018), 207–27.

Suykens, Bert, 'The Bangladesh Party-State: A Diachronic Comparative Analysis of Party-Political Regimes', *Commonwealth and Comparative Politics*, 55:2 (2017), 187–213.

'"A Hundred Per Cent Good Man Cannot Do Politics": Violent Self-Sacrifice, Student Authority, and Party-State Integration in Bangladesh', *Modern Asian Studies*, 52:3 (2018), 883–916.

Swain, Ashok, *The Environmental Trap: The Ganges River Diversion, Bangladeshi Migration and Conflicts in India* (Department of Peace and Conflict Research, Uppsala University, 1996).

Swinnerton, A. R., 'The Colombo Plan and Pakistan', *Pakistan Horizon*, 6:3 (1953), 117–23.

Tagore, Rabindranath, *The Home and the World* (London: Macmillan, 1919).

Talbot, Ian, *Pakistan: A Modern History* (London: Hurst, 1998).

Tan, Tai Yong, *The Garrison State: The Military, Government and Society in Colonial* Punjab, *1849–1947* (New Delhi: Sage, 2005).

Taniguchi, Sinkichi, Masahiko Togawa and Tetsuya Nakatani (eds.), *Grambangla: Itihash, Shomaj O Orthoniti* [Rural Bengal: History, society and economy] (Kolkata: K. P. Bagchi, for International Centre for Bengal Studies, Delhi Branch, 2007).

Tarafdar, Momtazur Rahman, *Husain Shahi Bengal, 1494–1538 A.D.: A Socio-Political Study* (Dhaka: Asiatic Society of Pakistan, 1965).

Tetens, I., Ole Hels, Nazrul I. Khan, Shakuntala H. Thilsted, and Nazmul Hassan, 'Rice-Based Diets in Rural Bangladesh: How Do Different Age and Sex Groups Adapt to Seasonal Changes in Energy Intake?' *American Journal of Clinical Nutrition*, 78 (2003), 406–13.

Thompson, Paul M., and Md. Anwarul Islam (eds.), *Environmental Profile of St. Martin's Island* (Dhaka: United Nations Development Programme, 2010).

Timsina, J., J. Wolf, N. Guilpart et al., 'Can Bangladesh Produce Enough Cereals to Meet Future Demand?' *Agricultural Systems*, 163 (2018), 36–44.

Togawa, Masahiko, 'Syncretism Revisited: Hindus and Muslims over a Saintly Cult in Bengal', *Numen*, 55 (2008), 27–43.

Toor, Saadia, 'Containing East Bengal: Language, Nation, and State Formation in Pakistan, 1947–1952', *Cultural Dynamics*, 21:2 (2009), 185–210.

Travis, Anthony J., Gareth J. Norton, Sutapa Datta et al., 'Assessing the Genetic Diversity of Rice Originating from Bangladesh, Assam and West Bengal', *Rice*, 8:35 (2015), 1–9.

Trotter, Lewis, Ashraf Dewan and T. P. Robinson, 'Effects of Rapid Urbanisation on the Urban Thermal Environment Between 1990 and 2011 in Dhaka Megacity, Bangladesh', *AIMS Environmental Science*, 4:1 (2017), 145–67.

Tun, Than, 'Rakhaing Thungran in Cox's Bazar: Celebrating Buddhist New Year in Southern Bangladesh' (PhD thesis, University of Western Australia, 2015).

Uddin, Moyeen, Shah Ali Akbar Ashrafi, Abul Kalam Azad et al., 'Improving Coverage of Civil Registration and Vital Statistics, Bangladesh', *Bulletin of the World Health Organization*, 97:9 (2019), 637–41.

Uddin, Nasir, 'In Search of Self: Identity, Indigeneity, and Cultural Politics in Bangladesh', in: Gerharz et al. (eds.) (2018), 119–39.

Uddin, Nasir, and Eva Gerharz, 'The Many Faces of the State: Living in Peace and Conflict in the Chittagong Hill Tracts, Bangladesh', *Conflict and Society: Advances in Research* 3 (2017), 208–26.

Uddin, Shahzad, 'Privatization in Bangladesh: The Emergence of "Family Capitalism"', *Development and Change*, 36:1 (2005), 157–82.

Uddin, Sufia M., *Constructing Bangladesh: Religion, Ethnicity, and Language in an Islamic Nation* (Chapel Hill: University of North Carolina Press, 2006).

Umar, Badruddin, *The Emergence of Bangladesh: Class Struggles in East Pakistan (1947–1958)* (Karachi: Oxford University Press, 2004).

Van der Heijden, Frans Jansz, *Relation du Naufrage d'un Vaisseau Hollandois nomme Ter Schelling vers la Cote de Bengala...* [Account of a Dutch ship named Ter Schelling shipwrecked off the Bengal coast] (Amsterdam: La veuve de Jacob van Meurs, 1681).

Van Driem, George, 'The Eastern Himalayan Corridor in Prehistory', in: Elena Nikolaevna Kolpačkova (ed.), Проблемы китайского и общего языкознания [Problems in Chinese and general linguistics] (St. Petersburg: Izdatel'stvo Studija NP-Print, 2016), 2:467–524.

'The Domestications and the Domesticators of Asian Rice', in: Martine Robbeets and Alexander Savelyev (eds.), *Language Dispersal Beyond Farming* (Amsterdam: John Benjamins, 2017), 183–214.

Van Schendel, Willem, *Peasant Mobility: The Odds of Life in Rural Bangladesh* (Assen: Van Gorcum, 1981 and Delhi: Manohar, 1982).

'Madmen of Mymensingh: Peasant Resistance and the Colonial Process in Eastern India, 1824–1833', *Indian Economic and Social History Review*, 22:2 (1985), 139–73.

'Self-Rescue and Survival: The Rural Poor in Bangladesh', *South Asia, Journal of South Asian Studies*, 9:1 (1986), 41–60.

Three Deltas: Accumulation and Poverty in Rural Burma, Bengal and South India (Delhi: Sage Publications, 1991).

'The Invention of the "Jummas": State Formation and Ethnicity in Southeastern Bangladesh', *Modern Asian Studies*, 26:1 (1992a), 95–128.

(ed.), *Francis Buchanan in Southeast Bengal (1798): His Journey to Chittagong, the Chittagong Hill Tracts, Noakhali and Comilla* (Dhaka: University Press Limited, 1992b); Bengali translation: *Dokkhinpurbo Banglay Francis Buchanan (1798): Kumilla, Noakhali, Chottogram, Parbotyo Chottograme Tanr Bhromon* (Dhaka: International Centre for Bengal Studies, 1994).

Reviving a Rural Industry: Silk Producers and Officials in India and Bangladesh, 1880s to 1980s (Dhaka: University Press Limited, 1995).

'Modern Times in Bangladesh', in: van Schendel and Schulte Nordholt (eds.) (2001a), 37–55.

'Working Through Partition: Making a Living in the Bengal Borderlands', *International Review of Social History*, 46 (2001b), 393–421.

'Stateless in South Asia: The Making of the India-Bangladesh Enclaves', *Journal of Asian Studies*, 61:1 (2002), 115–47.

The Bengal Borderland: Beyond State and Nation in South Asia (London: Anthem Press, 2005).

'Green Plants into Blue Cakes: Working for Wages in Colonial Bengal's Indigo Industry', in: Marcel van der Linden and Leo Lucassen (eds.), *Working on Labor: Essays in Honor of Jan Lucassen* (Leiden: Brill, 2012), 47–73.

'From Dhaka with Love: The Nepal Nag Papers and the Sino-Soviet Split', in: Aad Blok, Jan Lucassen and Huub Sanders (eds.), *A Usable Collection: Essays in Honour of Jaap Kloosterman on Collecting Social History* (Amsterdam: Amsterdam University Press, 2014), 426–33.

'Spatial Moments: Chittagong in Four Scenes', in: Eric Tagliacozzo, Helen F. Siu and Peter C. Perdue (eds.), *Asia Inside Out: Connected Places* (Cambridge, MA: Harvard University Press, 2015a), 98–127.

'What Is Agrarian Labour? Contrasting Indigo Production in Colonial India and Indonesia', *International Review of Social History*, 60:1 (2015b), 1–23.

'A War Within a War: Mizo Rebels and the Bangladesh Liberation Struggle', *Modern Asian Studies*, 50:1 (2016), 75–117.

'Staying Embedded: The Rocky Existence of an Indigo Maker in Bengal', in: Willem van Schendel (ed.), *Embedding Agricultural Commodities: Using Historical Evidence, 1840s–1940s* (London: Routledge, 2017), 11–29.

Van Schendel, Willem, and Aminul Haque Faraizi, *Rural Labourers in Bengal, 1880–1980* (Rotterdam: Comparative Asian Studies Programme, Erasmus University Rotterdam, 1984).

Van Schendel, Willem, and Henk Schulte Nordholt (eds.), *Time Matters: Global and Local Time in Asian Societies* (Amsterdam: VU University Press, 2001).

Van Schendel, Willem, Wolfgang Mey and Aditya Kumar Dewan, *The Chittagong Hill Tracts: Living in a Borderland* (Bangkok: White Lotus, 2000).

Vanita, Ruth, 'Born of Two Vaginas: Love and Reproduction between Co-Wives in Some Medieval Indian Texts', *GLQ: A Journal of Lesbian and Gay Studies*, 11:4 (2005), 547–77.

Wahed, Mohammad Shakil, and Mizan Rahman, 'China's Outward Foreign Direct Investment to Bangladesh: Perspectives of the Host Country Stakeholders', *Strategic Change*, 27 (2018), 455–67.

Wahid, Zeenat Huda, 'Emergence of Satellite Television and Enigmatic Geo-Political Strategy of Bangladesh Government', *Bangladesh e-Journal of Sociology*, 4:1 (2007), 1–15.

Weinraub, Bernard, 'Bangladesh, at Age 3, Is Still a Disaster Area; A Worrisome Portent Key Enterprises Taken Over, Premier's Nephew Accused, Sluggish Bureaucracy, U.S. Leads the Donors', *New York Times* (13 September 1974).

Whitcombe, Elizabeth, 'Indo-Gangetic River Systems, Monsoon and Malaria', *Philosophical Transactions of the Royal Society A*, 370:1966 (2012), 2216–39.

White, Sarah C., 'Patriarchal Investments: Marriage, Dowry and the Political Economy of Development in Bangladesh', *Journal of Contemporary Asia*, 47:2 (2017), 247–72.

Who Gets What and Why? Resource Allocation in a Bangladesh Village (Dhaka: Bangladesh Rural Advancement Committee, n.d. [1979]).

Wilce, James M., Jr, 'The Kalimah in the Kaleidophone: Ranges of Multivocality in Bangladeshi Muslim's Discourses', *Ethos*, 26:2 (1998), 229–57.

Wilcox, Wayne, 'Pakistan: A Decade of Ayub', *Asian Survey*, 9:2 (1969), 87–93.

Wood, Geoffrey D., *Bangladesh: Whose Ideas, Whose Interests* (Dhaka: University Press Limited, 1994).

World Bank, 'Net ODA received per capita (current US$)' (2017). https://data .worldbank.org

    Promising Progress: A Diagnostic of Water Supply, Sanitation, Hygiene, and Poverty in Bangladesh (Washington, DC: WASH Poverty Diagnostic, World Bank, 2018).

Yang, Bin, 'Horses, Silver, and Cowries: Yunnan in Global Perspective', *Journal of World History*, 15:3 (2004), 281–322.

Yarrington, Matthew D., 'Lived Islam in Bangladesh: Contemporary Religious Discourse between Ahl-i-Hadith, "Hanafis" and Authoritative Texts, with Special Reference to *al-barzakh*' (PhD thesis, Edinburgh University, 2010).

Yasmin, T., M. A. Farrelly and B. C. Rogers, 'Evolution of Water Governance in Bangladesh: An Urban Perspective', *World Development*, 109 (2018), 386–400.

Yount, Kathryn M., Stephanie Miedema, Chris Martin, Aliceann Crandall and Ruchira Naved, 'Men's Coercive Control, Partner Violence Perpetration, and Life Satisfaction in Bangladesh', *Sex Roles*, 74 (2016), 450–63.

Yousuf, Mostafa, 'Stone Mining in Hills: 200 Streams in Peril', *Daily Star* (24 May 2018).

Zafar, Manmay, 'Under the Gaze of the State: Policing Literature and the Case of Taslima Nasrin', *Inter-Asia Cultural Studies*, 6:3 (2005), 410–21.

Zaheer, Hasan, *The Separation of East Pakistan: The Rise and Realization of Bengali Muslim Nationalism* (Dhaka: University Press Limited, 1994).

Zaidi, Z. H. (ed.), *Jinnah Papers: Pakistan – Struggling for Survival, 1 January–30 September 1948*, vol. 7, Quaid-i-Azam Papers Project, Government of Pakistan (Karachi: Oxford University Press, 2003).

Zakaria, Muhammad, 'A Grammar of Hyow' (PhD thesis, Nanyang Technological University, 2017).

Zakaria, Saymon, *Pronomohi Bongomata: Indigenous Cultural Forms of Bangladesh*, 2nd ed. (Dhaka: Nymphea Publication, 2013).

Zaman, Niaz, *A Divided Legacy: The Partition in Selected Novels of India, Pakistan, and Bangladesh* (Dhaka: University Press Limited, 1999).

    (ed.), *1971 and After: Selected Stories* (Dhaka: University Press Limited, 2001).

    (ed.), *Under the Krishnachura: Fifty Years of Bangladeshi Writing* (Dhaka: University Press Limited, 2003).

Zaman, Rashed Uz, and Niloy Ranjan Biswas, 'The Contribution of Commonwealth Armed Forces in UN Peacekeeping: The Case of Bangladesh', *Round Table*, 106:4 (2017), 437–52.

Zaman, Shahaduz, *Broken Limbs, Broken Lives: Ethnography of a Hospital Ward in Bangladesh* (Amsterdam: Het Spinhuis, 2005).

Zami, Tahmidal, and Carola Erika Lorea, 'Interreligious Encounter and Proselytism in Pre-Mughal Bengal: An Analysis of the Report by the Jesuit Father Nicolas Pimenta', *Indian Historical Review*, 43:2 (2016), 234–69.

Zeitlyn, Benjamin, 'Watching the International Crimes Tribunal from London', *Samaj: South Asia Multidisciplinary Academic Journal*, 9 (2014), 1–19.

FILMS

Asian Century: The Rise and Fall of Mujib, directed by Shehzad Hameed Ahmad (2017).

Deshantori [The Migrant], directed by Sujan Mahmud and Mridul Chowdhury (2006).

Eclipse, directed by Shaheen Akhter and Shameem Akhtar (1994).

Every Good Marriage Begins With Tears, directed by Simon Chambers (2006).

Ghare-Baire [Home and the World], directed by Satyajit Ray (1984).

Hazaribagh: Toxic Leather, directed by Eric de la Varène and Elise Darblay (2013).

Iron Crows, directed by Bong-Nam Park (2009).

Licu's Holidays/Le Ferie di Licu, directed by Vittorio Moroni (2007).

A Life Suspended, directed by Kazuyo Minamide (2013).

Lohakhor [Iron Eaters], directed by Shaheen Dil-Riaz (2007).

Muktir Gan [Song of Freedom] (1995) and *Muktir Kotha* [Words of Freedom] (1998), directed by Tareque and Catherine Masud.

Okul Nodi [Endless River], directed by Tuni Chatterji (2012).

The Young Man Was (four parts), directed by Naeem Mohaiemen (2011–2016).

Index